Rick Steves'

ROME

2011

Vatican Museum

Villa Borghese

Spanish Steps

Termini Train Station

Piazza Venezia

Trevi Fountain

St. Peter's

Pantheon

TIBER

Ghetto

Trajan's Column

Forum

Trastevere

Colosseum

San Giovanni in Laterano

Appian Way

DCH

CONTENTS

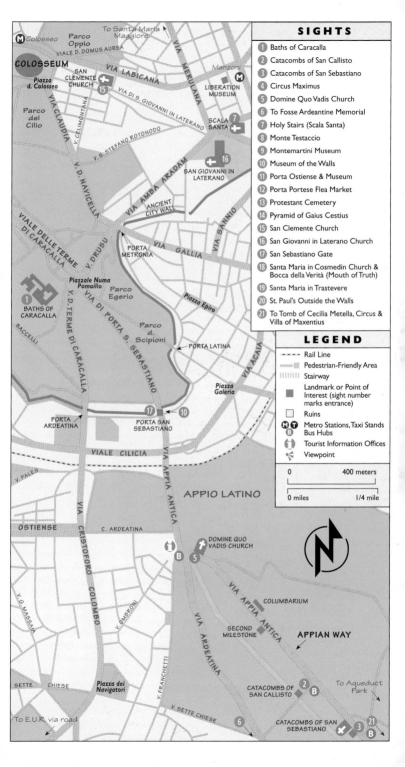

SIGHTS

1. Baths of Caracalla
2. Catacombs of San Callisto
3. Catacombs of San Sebastiano
4. Circus Maximus
5. Domine Quo Vadis Church
6. To Fosse Ardeantine Memorial
7. Holy Stairs (Scala Santa)
8. Monte Testaccio
9. Montemartini Museum
10. Museum of the Walls
11. Porta Ostiense & Museum
12. Porta Portese Flea Market
13. Protestant Cemetery
14. Pyramid of Gaius Cestius
15. San Clemente Church
16. San Giovanni in Laterano Church
17. San Sebastiano Gate
18. Santa Maria in Cosmedin Church & Bocca della Verità (Mouth of Truth)
19. Santa Maria in Trastevere
20. St. Paul's Outside the Walls
21. To Tomb of Cecilia Metella, Circus & Villa of Maxentius

LEGEND

- - - - - Rail Line
▬▬▬■▬▬▬ Pedestrian-Friendly Area
|||||||| Stairway
■ Landmark or Point of Interest (sight number marks entrance)
□ Ruins
Ⓜ Ⓣ Ⓑ Metro Stations, Taxi Stands Bus Hubs
ℹ Tourist Information Offices
⚐ Viewpoint

0 ————— 400 meters
0 miles ————— 1/4 mile

Overview of Maps

INTRODUCTION

Rome is magnificent and brutal at the same time. It's a showcase of Western civilization, with astonishingly ancient sights and a modern vibrancy. But if you're careless, you'll be run down or pick-pocketed. And with the wrong attitude, you'll be frustrated by the kind of chaos that only an Italian can understand. On my last visit, a cabbie struggling with the traffic said, *"Roma chaos."* I responded, *"Bella chaos."* He agreed.

While Paris is an urban garden, Rome is a magnificent tangled forest. If your hotel provides a comfortable refuge; if you pace yourself; if you accept—and even partake in—the siesta plan; if you're well-organized for sightseeing; and if you protect yourself and your valuables with extra caution and discretion, you'll love it. (And Rome is much easier to live with if you avoid the midsummer heat.)

For me, Rome is in a three-way tie with Paris and London as Europe's greatest city. Two thousand years ago, the word "Rome" meant civilization itself. Everything was either civilized (part of the Roman Empire, Latin- or Greek-speaking) or barbarian. Today, Rome is Italy's political capital, the capital of Catholicism, and the center of the ancient world, littered with evocative remains. As you peel through its fascinating and jumbled layers, you'll find Rome's buildings, cats, laundry, traffic, and 2.6 million people endlessly entertaining. And then, of course, there are its stupendous sights.

Visit St. Peter's, the greatest church on earth, and scale Michelangelo's 448-foot-tall dome, the world's tallest. Learn something about eternity by touring the huge Vatican Museum. You'll find the story of creation—bright as the day it was painted—in the restored Sistine Chapel. Do the "Caesar Shuffle" through ancient Rome's Forum and Colosseum. Savor Europe's most sumptuous building, the Borghese Gallery, and take an early evening "Dolce

INTRODUCTION

Vita Stroll" down Via del Corso with Rome's beautiful people. Enjoy an after-dark walk from Campo de' Fiori to the Spanish Steps, lacing together Rome's Baroque and bubbly nightspots. Dine well at least once.

About This Book

Rick Steves' Rome 2011 is a personal tour guide in your pocket. Better yet, it's actually two tour guides in your pocket: The co-author of this book is Gene Openshaw. Since our first "Europe through the gutter" trip together as high school buddies in the 1970s, Gene and I have been exploring the wonders of the Old World. An inquisitive historian and lover of European culture, Gene wrote most of this book's self-guided museum tours and neighborhood walks. Together, Gene and I keep this book current (though for simplicity, from this point "we" will shed our respective egos and become "I").

In this book, you'll find the following chapters:

Orientation includes specifics on public transportation, helpful hints, local tour options, easy-to-read maps, and tourist information. The "Planning Your Time" section offers a suggested schedule for how to best use your limited time.

Sights describes the top attractions and includes cost, hours, location, and contact information.

The **Self-Guided Tours** lead you through ancient Rome, with tours of the Colosseum, Roman Forum, Palatine Hill, Trajan's Column, Pantheon, and Baths of Diocletian. You'll also tour the pilgrimage churches, including the grandest of all—St. Peter's. You'll see the great museums: Vatican Museum, National Museum of Rome, Capitoline Museums, and the exciting Borghese Gallery. And you'll take a spin on the ancient Appian Way.

The **Self-Guided Walks** take you through Rome at night, connecting the great monuments and atmospheric squares; guide you through Trastevere, the heart of the crusty, colorful neighborhood across the river; and give meaning to the Jewish Ghetto, the city's medieval Jewish quarter.

Sleeping describes my favorite hotels, from good-value deals to cushy splurges, mainly in several convenient (and for Rome, relatively quiet) neighborhoods near the sights.

Eating serves up a range of options, from inexpensive eateries to fancy restaurants.

Rome with Children, Shopping, and **Nightlife** offer my best suggestions on those topics.

Connections lays the groundwork for your smooth arrival and departure, covering transportation by train, bus, car, plane, and cruise ship, with detailed information on Rome's two airports

Key to This Book

Updates

This book is updated every year—but once you pin down Italy, it wiggles. For the latest, visit www.ricksteves.com /update. For a valuable list of reports and experiences—good and bad—from fellow travelers, check www.ricksteves.com /feedback.

Abbreviations and Times

I use the following symbols and abbreviations in this book: Sights are rated:

▲▲▲	Don't miss
▲▲	Try hard to see
▲	Worthwhile if you can make it
No rating	Worth knowing about

When you see a ☉ in a sight listing, it means that the sight is covered in much more detail in one of the tour chapters.

Tourist information offices are abbreviated as **TI**s, and bathrooms are **WC**s. To categorize accommodations, I use a **Sleep Code** (described on page 316).

Like Europe, this book uses the **24-hour clock.** It's the same through 12:00 noon, then keep going: 13:00, 14:00, and so on. For anything over 12, subtract 12 and add p.m. (14:00 is 2:00 p.m.).

When giving **opening times,** I include both peak season and off-season hours if they differ. So, if a museum is listed as "May–Oct daily 9:00–16:00," it should be open from 9 a.m. until 4 p.m. from the first day of May until the last day of October (but expect exceptions).

For **transit** or **tour departures,** I first list the frequency, then the duration. So, a train connection listed as "2/hour, 1.5 hours" departs twice each hour and the journey lasts an hour and a half.

(Fiumicino and Ciampino) and its two train stations (the main Termini Station and smaller Tiburtina).

Day Trips cover nearby sights: Ostia Antica (includes self-guided tour), Tivoli, Naples, and Pompeii.

Roman History takes you on a whirlwind tour through the ages, covering three millennia from ancient Rome to the city today.

The **appendix** is a traveler's tool kit, with telephone tips, useful phone numbers, the basics on transportation in Italy, recommended books and films, a festival list, a climate chart, a handy packing checklist, hotel reservation form, and Italian survival phrases.

Browse through this book and choose your favorite sights. Then have a great trip! Traveling like a temporary local, you'll get the absolute most out of every mile, minute, and euro. As you visit places I know and love, I'm happy you'll be meeting my favorite Romans.

Planning

This section will help you get started planning your trip—with notes on trip costs, when to go, and things to know before you take off.

Travel Smart

Many people visit Rome and think it's a chaotic mess. Rome, which seems as orderly as spilled spaghetti, actually functions well. Only those who understand this and travel smart can enjoy Rome on a budget.

This book can save you lots of time and money. But to have an "A" trip, you need to be an "A" student. Read it all before your trip, noting holidays, specific advice on sights, and days when sights are closed. For instance, to see the Borghese Gallery, you must reserve ahead. If you go to the Vatican Museum on a Sunday, you'll run smack into closed doors, or—if it's the last Sunday of the month—huge crowds. You can wait an hour to buy a ticket at the Colosseum, or save time by ordering your ticket online or at the nearby Palatine Hill. Day-tripping to Ostia Antica on Monday is bad news. A smart trip is a puzzle—a fun, doable, and worthwhile challenge.

Be sure to mix intense and relaxed periods in your itinerary. Every trip—and every traveler—needs at least a few slack days (for picnics, laundry, people-watching, and so on). Pace yourself. Assume you will return.

As you travel, take advantage of the Internet and phones to make your trip go smoothly. Get online at cafés or your hotel, and use the phone (buy a phone card or carry a mobile phone). You can get tourist information (check websites), learn the latest on sights (special events, English tour schedule, etc.), book tickets and tours, make reservations, reconfirm hotels, research transportation connections, and keep in touch with your loved ones.

Enjoy the friendliness of the Romans. Connect with the culture. Slow down and be open to unexpected experiences. Ask questions— most locals are eager to point you in their idea of the right direction. Keep a notepad in your pocket for organizing your thoughts. Wear your money belt, learn the currency, and figure out how to estimate prices in dollars. Those who expect to travel smart, do.

Trip Costs

Six components make up your trip costs: airfare, surface trans-portation, room and board, sightseeing/entertainment, shopping/miscellany, and gelato.

Airfare: A basic round-trip US-to-Rome (or even cheaper, to Milan) flight should cost $950–1,600, depending on where you fly from and when. If your trip covers a wide area, consider saving time and money in Europe by flying "open jaw" (into one city and out of another—e.g., into Rome and out of Paris).

Surface Transportation: For a typical one-week visit, allow $60 to $100 for taxis (which can be shared by up to four people); if you opt for buses and the Metro, figure about $25 per person. The cost of round-trip transportation to day-trip destinations ranges from minimal (a few dollars to get to Tivoli or Ostia Antica) to affordable ($60 for second-class train tickets for a day trip to Naples and Pompeii). For a one-way trip between Rome's main airport and the city center, allow $21 per person by train or about $60 by taxi (can be shared by up to 4 people). For information on train travel and car rental, see the appendix.

Room and Board: You can enjoy Rome on $140 a day per person for room and board. This allows $15 for lunch, $25 for din-ner, and $100 for lodging (based on two people splitting the cost of a $200 double room that includes breakfast). If you've got more money, I've listed great ways to spend it. Students and tightwads can enjoy Rome for as little as $65 a day ($35 for a hostel bed, $30 for meals and snacks).

Sightseeing and Entertainment: Figure about $10–17 per major sight (Colosseum, museums), $2 for minor ones (church treasuries), and $30 for splurge experiences (such as concerts). An overall average of $20 per day works for most people. Don't skimp here. After all, this category is the driving force behind your trip—you came to sightsee, enjoy, and experience Rome.

Shopping and Miscellany: Figure $2 per postcard and $6 per coffee, soft drink, and gelato. Shopping can vary in cost from nearly nothing to a small fortune. Good budget travelers find that this category has little to do with assembling a trip full of lifelong and wonderful memories.

When to Go

Rome's best travel months (also busiest and most expensive) are May, June, September, and October. These months combine the convenience of peak season with pleasant weather.

The most grueling thing about travel in Rome is the sum-mer heat in July and August, when temperatures can soar to the high 90s and pricier hotels discount their rooms. Fortunately air-conditioning is the norm in all but the cheapest hotels (though it's

Major Holidays and Weekends

Popular places are even busier on weekends...and inundated on three-day weekends. Plan ahead and reserve your accommodations and transportation well in advance.

In Rome, hotels get booked up on Easter weekend (in 2011, that's Friday, April 22, through Monday, April 25), April 25 (Liberation Day), May 1 (Labor Day), June 29 (Saints Peter and Paul), November 1 (All Saints' Day), and on Fridays and Saturdays year-round. Note that the Vatican Museum closes for many lesser-known Catholic holidays; confirm its schedule at http://mv.vatican.va. For more information, check "Holidays and Festivals" in the appendix. A myriad of religious and neighborhood celebrations can catch you by surprise anywhere in Italy.

generally available only from June through September).

Spring and fall can be cool, and many hotels do not turn on their heat. Rome is fine in winter—cold and crisp with temperatures in the 40s and 50s (for more information, see the climate chart in the appendix). Off-season has none of the sweat and stress of the tourist season, but sights may have shorter hours, lunchtime breaks, and fewer activities. Confirm your sightseeing plans locally, especially when traveling off-season.

Know Before You Go

Your trip is more likely to go smoothly if you plan ahead. Check this list of things to arrange while you're still at home.

You need a **passport**—but no visa or shots—to travel in Italy. You may be denied entry into certain European countries if your passport is due to expire within three to six months of your ticketed date of return. Get it renewed if you'll be cutting it close. It can take up to six weeks to get or renew a passport (for more on passports, see www.travel.state.gov). Pack a photocopy of your passport in your luggage in case the original is lost or stolen.

Book rooms in advance, particularly during peak season (May-Sept). Check to see if you'll be visiting Rome during any holidays, when rooms can cost more and get booked up quickly. (See "Major Holidays and Weekends" above.)

The **Borghese Gallery** requires advance reservations; book at least a week ahead in high season (see page 191 for instructions). At the **Vatican Museum,** lines are extremely long—skip the ticket-buying line altogether by reserving an entry time on their website (see page 204).

Call your **debit and credit card companies** to let them know the countries you'll be visiting, and be sure you understand how your cards will work in Europe (for more details—including some questions you might want to ask—see page 10).

Do your homework if you want to buy **travel insurance.** Compare the cost of the insurance to the likelihood of your using it and your potential loss if something goes wrong. For more information, see www.ricksteves.com/plan/tips/insurance.htm.

If you're bringing an MP3 player, you can download free information from **Rick Steves Audio Europe,** featuring hours of travel interviews on Italy, audio tours of major sights, and more (at www.ricksteves.com and in iTunes; for details, see page 457).

Bring your driver's license if you're planning on **renting a car** in Italy, and consider getting an International Driving Permit from AAA (see page 452). Driving is prohibited in some city centers; obey the signage or risk getting a huge fine (see page 455).

If you're taking an **overnight train** (especially between Rome and Paris), and you need a couchette *(cuccetta)* or sleeper—and you *must* leave on a certain day—consider booking it in advance through a US agent (such as www.raileurope.com), even though it may cost more than buying it in Italy. Other Italian trains, like the high-speed ES trains, require a seat reservation, but it's usually possible to make arrangements in Italy just a few days ahead. (For more on train travel, see the Connections chapter and www .ricksteves.com/rail.)

Because **airline carry-on restrictions** are always changing, visit the Transportation Security Administration's website (www .tsa.gov/travelers) for an up-to-date list of what you can bring on the plane with you...and what you have to check.

Practicalities

Emergency and Medical Help: In Italy, dial 113 for English-speaking police help. To summon an ambulance, call 118.

If you get sick, do as the Romans do and go to a pharmacist. They can help you with almost any ailment. Or ask at your hotel for help. They'll know the nearest medical services.

Time Zones: Italy, like most of continental Europe, is generally six/nine hours ahead of the East/West Coasts of the US. The exceptions are the beginning and end of Daylight Saving Time: Europe "springs forward" the last Sunday in March (two weeks after most of North America), and "falls back" the last Sunday in October (one week before North America). For a handy online converter, try www.timeanddate.com/worldclock.

Business Hours: Traditionally, Italy uses the siesta plan, though many businesses have adopted the government's recommended 8:00 to 14:00 workday. In tourist areas, shops are open longer. People usually work from about 9:00 to 13:00 and from

Rome vs. Milan: A Classic Squabble

In Italy, the North and South bicker about each other, hurling barbs, quips, and generalizations. All the classic North/South traits can be applied to Rome (the government capital) and Milan (the business capital). Although the differences have become less pronounced lately, the sniping continues.

The Milanese say the Romans are lazy. Roman government jobs come with short hours—cut even shorter by too many coffee breaks, three-hour lunches, chats with colleagues, and phone calls to friends and relatives. Milanese contend that *Roma ladrona* (Rome the big thief) is a parasite that lives off the taxes of people up North. Until recently, there was a strong Milan-based movement seriously promoting secession from the South.

Romans, meanwhile, dismiss the Milanese as uptight workaholics with nothing else to live for—gray like their foggy city. Romans do admit that in Milan, job opportunities are better and based on merit. And the Milanese grudgingly concede that the Romans have a gift for enjoying life.

While Rome is more of a family city, Milan is the place for high-powered singles on the career fast track. Milanese yuppies

15:30 to 19:00. Stores are usually closed on Sunday, and often on Monday. Banking hours are generally Monday through Friday 8:30 to 13:30 and 15:30 to 16:30, but they can vary wildly.

Saturdays are virtually weekdays, with earlier closing hours. Sundays have the same pros and cons as they do in the US: Sightseeing attractions are generally open, while shops and banks are closed. City traffic is light. Rowdy evenings are rare on Sundays.

Watt's Up? Europe's electrical system is different from North America's in two ways: the shape of the plug (two round prongs) and the voltage of the current (220 volts instead of 110 volts). For your North American plug to work in Europe, you'll need an adapter, sold inexpensively at travel stores in the US. As for the voltage, most newer electronics or travel appliances (such as hair dryers, laptops, and battery chargers) automatically convert the voltage—if you see a range of voltages printed on the item or its plug (such as "110–220"), it'll work in Europe. Otherwise, you can buy a converter separately in the US (about $20).

mix with each other...not the city's long-time residents. Milan is seen as inward-looking and wary of foreigners, and Rome as fun-loving, tolerant, and friendly. In Milan, bureaucracy (like social services) works logically and efficiently, while in Rome, accomplishing even small chores can be exasperating. In Rome, everything—from finding a babysitter to buying a car—is done through friends. In Milan, while people are not as willing to discuss their personal matters, they are generous and active in charity work.

Milanese find Romans vulgar. The Roman dialect is considered one of the coarsest in the country. Much as they try, Milanese just can't say, "Damn your dead relatives" quite as effectively as the Romans. Still, they enjoy Roman comedians and love to imitate the accent.

The Milanese feel that Rome is dirty and Roman driving nerve-wracking. But despite the craziness, Rome maintains a genuine village feel. People share family news with their neighborhood grocer. Milan lacks people-friendly piazzas, and entertainment comes at a high price. But in Rome, *la dolce vita* is as close as the nearest square, and a full moon is enjoyed by all.

Discounts: Discounts are not listed in this book. However, children (under 18), students (with International Student Identity Cards, www.isic.org), and seniors can sometimes get discounts at sights—but only by asking.

News: Americans keep in touch via the *International Herald Tribune* (published almost daily throughout Europe and online at www.iht.com). Other newsy sites are http://news.bbc.co.uk and www.europeantimes.com. Every Tuesday, the European editions of *Time* and *Newsweek* hit the stands with articles of particular interest to travelers in Europe. Sports addicts can get their daily fix online or from *USA Today*. Many hotels have CNN and BBC News television channels.

Money

This section offers advice on how to pay for purchases on your trip (including getting cash from ATMs and paying with plastic), dealing with lost or stolen cards, VAT (sales tax) refunds, and tipping.

What to Bring

Bring both a credit card and a debit card. You'll use the debit card at cash machines (ATMs) to withdraw local cash for most purchases, and the credit card to pay for larger items. Some travelers carry a third card as a backup, in case one gets demagnetized or eaten by a temperamental machine.

I also carry a few hundred dollars in hard cash as an emergency backup (in $20 bills rather than hard-to-exchange $100 bills). Don't bother changing cash before you leave home—European ATMs are easy to find and easy to use. And skip traveler's checks—they're a waste of time (long waits at slow banks) and a waste of money in fees.

Cash

Cash is just as desirable in Europe as it is at home. Small European businesses (hotels, restaurants, shops, etc.) prefer that you pay your bills with cash. Some vendors will charge you extra for using a credit card, and some won't take credit cards at all.

Throughout Europe, ATMs offer the best and simplest way to get local currency. To use an ATM (called a *bancomat*) to withdraw money from your account, you'll need a debit card—ideally with a Visa or MasterCard logo for maximum usability—plus a PIN code. Know your PIN code in numbers; there are only numbers—no letters—on European keypads. You could use a credit card for ATM transactions, but it's generally more expensive (because it's considered a "cash advance" rather than a "withdrawal").

When using an ATM, taking out large sums of money can reduce your per-transaction bank fees. If the machine refuses your request, try again and select a smaller amount (some cash machines limit the amount you can withdraw—don't take it personally). If that doesn't work, try a different machine. It's easier to pay for purchases with smaller bills; if the ATM gives you big bills, try to break them at a bank or larger store.

To keep your cash safe, use a money belt—a pouch with a strap that you buckle around your waist like a belt, and wear under your clothes. Pickpockets target tourists. A money belt provides peace of mind, allowing you to carry lots of cash safely. Don't waste time every few days tracking down a cash machine—withdraw a week's worth of money, stuff it in your money belt, and travel!

Credit and Debit Cards

For purchases, Visa and MasterCard are more commonly accepted than American Express. While you can use either a credit card or a debit card for most transactions, credit cards offer a greater degree of fraud protection (since debit cards draw funds directly from your account).

Exchange Rate

1 euro (€) = about $1.25

To convert prices in euros to dollars, add about 25 percent: €20 = about $25, €50 = about $65. (Check www.oanda.com for the latest exchange rates.) Just like the dollar, one euro is broken down into 100 cents. You'll find coins ranging from €0.01 to €2, and bills ranging from €5 to €500.

Look carefully at any €2 coin you get in change. Some unscrupulous merchants give out similar-looking gold-rimmed old 500-lire coins (worth $0) instead of €2 coins (worth $2.50). You have been warned!

Just like at home, credit or debit cards work easily at larger hotels, restaurants, and shops. I typically use my credit card only in a few specific situations: to book hotel reservations by phone, to make major purchases (such as car rentals, plane tickets, and long hotel stays), and to pay for things near the end of my trip (to avoid another visit to the ATM).

Ask Your Credit- or Debit-Card Company: Before your trip, contact the company that issued your debit or credit cards.

• Confirm your card will work overseas, and alert them that you'll be using it in Europe; otherwise, they may deny transactions if they perceive unusual spending patterns.

• Ask for the specifics on transaction **fees**. When you use your credit or debit card—either for purchases or ATM withdrawals—you'll often be charged additional "international transaction" fees of up to 3 percent plus $5 per transaction. If your card's fees are too high, consider getting a card just for your trip: Capital One (www .capitalone.com) and most credit unions have low-to-no international fees.

• If you plan to withdraw cash from ATMs, confirm your daily **withdrawal limit.** Some travelers prefer a high limit that allows them to take out more cash at each ATM stop, while others prefer to set a lower limit in case their card is stolen.

• Ask for your credit card's **PIN** in case you encounter Europe's "chip-and-PIN" system.

Chip and PIN: If your card is declined for a purchase in Europe, it may be because of chip and PIN, which requires cardholders to punch in a PIN instead of signing a receipt. While chip and PIN is not yet common in Italy, much of Europe is adopting it. Chip and PIN is used by some merchants, and also at automated payment machines—such as those at train and subway stations, toll roads, parking garages, luggage lockers, bike-rental kiosks, and self-serve pumps at gas stations. If you're prompted to enter your PIN (but don't know it), ask if the cashier can print a receipt for you to sign instead, or just pay cash. If you're dealing with an automated machine that won't take your card, look for a cashier nearby who can make your card work. But if the place is unstaffed and you don't have cash, you might simply be out of luck.

Dynamic Currency Conversion: If merchants offer to convert your purchase price into dollars (called dynamic currency conversion, or DCC), refuse this "service." You'll pay even more in fees for the expensive convenience of seeing your charge in dollars.

Damage Control for Lost Cards

If you lose your credit, debit, or ATM card, you can stop people from using your card by reporting the loss immediately to the respective global customer-assistance centers. Call these 24-hour US numbers collect: Visa (410/581-9994), MasterCard (636/722-7111), and American Express (623/492-8427).

At a minimum, you'll need to know the name of the financial institution that issued you the card, along with the type of card (classic, platinum, or whatever). Providing the following information allows for a quicker cancellation of your missing card: full card number, whether you are the primary or secondary cardholder, the cardholder's name exactly as printed on the card, billing address, home phone number, circumstances of the loss or theft, and identification verification (your birth date, your mother's maiden name, or your Social Security number—memorize this, don't carry a copy). If you are the secondary cardholder, you'll also need to provide the primary cardholder's identification-verification details. You can generally receive a temporary card within two or three business days in Europe (see www.ricksteves.com/help for more).

If you promptly report your card lost or stolen, you typically won't be responsible for any unauthorized transactions on your account, although many banks charge a liability fee of $50.

Tipping

Tipping in Italy isn't as automatic and generous as it is in the US, but for special service, tips are appreciated, if not expected. As in the US, the proper amount depends on your resources, tipping philosophy, and the circumstances, but some general guidelines apply.

Restaurants: The "service" charge (*servizio*) is generally already included in your bill. If you're pleased with the service, you can round up the bill by a euro or two (though Italians rarely add this additional tip). For more on tipping in restaurants, see page 334.

Taxis: To tip the cabbie, round up. For a typical ride, round up to the next euro on the fare (to pay a €4.50 fare, give €5). If the cabbie hauls your bags and zips you to the airport to help you catch your flight, you might want to toss in a little more. But if you feel like you're being driven in circles or otherwise ripped off, skip the tip.

Special Services: Tour guides at sights sometimes hold out their hands for tips after they give their spiel. If I've already paid for the tour, I don't tip extra, unless they've really impressed me. At hotels, if you let the porter carry your luggage, it's polite to give them a euro for each bag. I don't tip the maid, but if you do, you can leave a euro per overnight at the end of your stay. In general, if someone in the service industry does a super job for you, a small tip (the equivalent of a euro or two) is appropriate...but not required.

When in doubt, ask. If you're not sure whether (or how much) to tip for a service, ask your hotelier or the tourist information office; they'll fill you in on how it's done on their turf.

Getting a VAT Refund

Wrapped into the purchase price of your Italian souvenirs is a Value-Added Tax (VAT) of about 20 percent. You're entitled to get most of that tax back if you purchase more than €155 (about $190) worth of goods at a store that participates in the VAT-refund scheme. Getting your refund is usually straightforward and, if you buy a substantial amount of souvenirs, well worth the hassle. If you're lucky, the merchant will subtract the tax when you make your purchase. (This is more likely to occur if the store ships the goods to your home.) Otherwise, you'll need to:

Get the paperwork. Have the merchant completely fill out the necessary refund document, called a "cheque." You'll have to present your passport.

Get your stamp at the border or airport. Process your cheque(s) at your last stop in the EU with the customs agent who deals with VAT refunds. It's best to keep your purchases in your carry-on for viewing, but if they're too large or dangerous (such as knives) to carry on, track down the proper customs agent to inspect them before you check your bag. You're not supposed to use your purchased goods before you leave. If you show up at customs wearing your new leather shoes, officials might look the other way—or deny you a refund.

Collect your refund. You'll need to return your stamped document to the retailer or its representative. Many merchants work with a service, such as Global Refund (www.globalrefund.com) or Premier Tax Free (www.premiertaxfree.com), which have offices at major airports, ports, or border crossings. These services, which extract a 4 percent fee, can refund your money immediately in your currency of choice or credit your card (within two billing cycles). If the retailer handles VAT refunds directly, it's up to you to contact the merchant for your refund. You can mail the documents from home, or quicker, from your point of departure (using a stamped, addressed envelope you've prepared or one that's been provided by the merchant). You'll then have to wait—it can take months.

Customs for American Shoppers

You are allowed to take home $800 worth of items per person duty-free, once every 30 days. The next $1,000 is taxed at a flat 3 percent. After that, you pay the individual item's duty rate. You can also bring in duty-free a liter of alcohol (slightly more than a bottle of wine; you must be at least 21), 200 cigarettes, and up to 100 non-Cuban cigars.

As for food, you can take home vacuum-packed cheeses; dried herbs, spices, or mushrooms; and canned fruits or vegetables, including jams and vegetable spreads. Baked goods, candy, chocolate, oil, vinegar, mustard, and honey are OK. Fresh fruits and vegetables (even that banana from your airplane breakfast) are not permitted. Meats are generally not allowed, though canned pâtés from some countries are usually permitted if made from geese, duck, or pork. Just because a duty-free shop in an airport sells a food product, that doesn't mean it will automatically pass US customs. Be prepared to lose your investment.

Note that you'll need to carefully pack any bottles of wine, jam, honey, oil, and other liquid-containing items in your checked luggage, due to the three-ounce limit on liquids in carry-on baggage. To check customs rules and duty rates before you go, visit www.cbp.gov, and click on "Travel," then "Know Before You Go."

Sightseeing

Sightseeing can be hard work. Use these tips to make your visits to Rome's finest sights meaningful, fun, efficient, and painless.

Plan Ahead

Set up an itinerary that allows you to fit in all your must-see sights. For a one-stop look at opening hours, see "Rome at a Glance" (page 52; also see "Daily Reminder" on page 24). Most sights keep stable hours, but you can easily confirm the latest by checking their websites or asking at the local TI.

If you'll be visiting during a holiday, find out if a particular sight will be open by phoning ahead or checking its website. And don't put off visiting a must-see sight—you never know when a place will close unexpectedly for a holiday, strike, or restoration. If you want to see the Borghese Gallery, make reservations in advance (see page 191). It's smart to reserve for the Vatican Museum as well.

When possible, visit key museums in the morning (when your energy is best) and save other activities for the afternoon. Hit the highlights first, then go back to other things if you have the stamina and time.

Depending on the sight, there are ways to avoid crowds. This book offers tips on specific sights. Try visiting the sight very early, at lunch, or very late. Evening visits are usually peaceful with fewer crowds.

Study up. To get the most out of the self-guided tours and sight descriptions in this book, read them before you visit.

At Sights

Here's what you can typically expect:

Some important sights such as the Colosseum have metal detectors or conduct bag searches that will slow your entry, while others require you to check daypacks and coats. They'll be kept safely. If you have something you can't bear to part with, stash it in a pocket or purse. To avoid checking a small backpack, carry it under your arm like a purse as you enter. From a guard's point of view, a backpack is generally a problem while a purse is not.

Photography is normally allowed, but flashes or tripods usually are not. Look for signs or ask. Flashes damage oil paintings and distract others in the room. Even without a flash, a handheld camera will take a decent picture (or you can buy postcards or posters at the museum bookstore). If photos are permitted, video cameras generally are, too.

You'll likely have to pay cash for the admission fee; few sights take credit cards. Museums may have special exhibits in addition to their permanent collections. Some exhibits are included in the entry price, while others come at an extra cost (which you may have to pay even if you don't want to see the exhibit).

Expect changes—artwork can be on tour, on loan, out sick, or shifted at the whim of the curator. To adapt, pick up any available free floor plans as you enter, and ask the museum staff if you can't find a particular item. Say the title or artist's name, or point to the photograph in this book and ask, *"Dov'è?"* (doh-VEH, meaning "Where is?").

Many sights rent audioguides, which generally offer excellent recorded descriptions in English (about $4). If you bring along your own pair of headphones and a Y-jack, you can sometimes share an audioguide with your travel partner and save money. I have produced free audio tours for the major sights in this book (see page 457).

INTRODUCTION

How Was Your Trip?

Were your travels fun, smooth, and meaningful? If you'd like to share your tips, concerns, and discoveries, please fill out the survey at www.ricksteves.com/feedback. I value your feedback. Thanks in advance—it helps a lot.

Guided tours are most likely to occur during peak season (usually €4–10 and widely ranging in quality). Some sights also run short films about the attraction. These are generally well worth your time. I make it standard operating procedure to ask when I arrive at a sight if there is a film in English.

In museums, art is dated with *sec* for *secolo* (century, often indicated with Roman numerals), A.C. (for *Avanti Cristo*, i.e., before Christ) and D.C. (for *Dopo Cristo*, a.k.a. A.D.). OK?

Some important sights have an on-site café or cafeteria (usually a good place to rest and have a snack or light meal). The WCs at many sights are free and generally clean.

Many sights sell postcards and guidebooks that highlight their attractions. Before you leave, scan the postcards and thumb through the biggest guidebook (or skim its index) to be sure you haven't overlooked something that you'd like to see.

Most sights stop admitting people 30–60 minutes before closing time, and some rooms close early (generally about 45 minutes before the actual closing time). Guards usher people out, so don't save the best for last.

Every sight or museum offers more than what is covered in this book. Use the information in this book as an introduction—not the final word.

Find Religion

Churches offer some amazing art (usually free), a cool respite from heat, and a welcome seat.

A modest dress code (no bare shoulders or shorts for anyone, even kids) is enforced at larger churches, such as St. Peter's Basilica and St. Paul's Outside the Walls, but is often overlooked elsewhere. If you are caught by surprise, you can improvise, using maps to cover your shoulders and a jacket for your knees. (I wear a super-lightweight pair of long pants rather than shorts for my hot and muggy big-city Italian sightseeing.)

Some churches have coin-operated audioboxes that describe the art and history; just set the dial on English, put in your coins, and listen. Coin boxes near a piece of art illuminate the art (and present a better photo opportunity). I pop in a coin whenever I can. It improves my experience, is a favor to other visitors trying to appreciate a great piece of art in the dark, and is a little contribution to that church and its work. Whenever possible, let there be light.

Traveling as a Temporary Local

We travel all the way to Italy to enjoy differences—to become temporary locals. You'll experience frustrations. Certain truths that we find "God-given" or "self-evident," such as cold beer, ice in drinks, bottomless cups of coffee, hot showers, and bigger being better, are suddenly not so true. One of the benefits of travel is the eye-opening realization that there are logical, civil, and even better alternatives. A willingness to go local ensures that you'll enjoy a full dose of Italian hospitality.

Europeans generally like Americans. But if there is a negative aspect to Italians' image of Americans (apart from our foreign policy), it's that we are big, loud, aggressive, impolite, rich, and a bit naive. Think about the rationale behind "crazy" Italian decisions. For instance, many hoteliers turn off the heat in early April and can't turn on air-conditioning until June. The point is to conserve energy, and it's mandated by the Italian government. You could complain about being cold or hot...or bring a sweater in winter, and in summer, be prepared to sweat a little like everyone else.

While Italians, flabbergasted by our Yankee excesses, say in disbelief, *"Mi sono cadute le braccia!"* ("I throw my arms down!"), they nearly always afford us individual travelers all the warmth we deserve. Judging from all the happy feedback I receive from travelers who have used this book, it's safe to assume you'll enjoy a great, affordable vacation—with the finesse of an independent, experienced traveler.

Thanks, and *buon viaggio!*

Back Door Travel Philosophy
From *Rick Steves' Europe Through the Back Door*

Travel is intensified living—maximum thrills per minute and one of the last great sources of legal adventure. Travel is freedom. It's recess, and we need it.

Experiencing the real Europe requires catching it by surprise, going casual..."Through the Back Door."

Affording travel is a matter of priorities. (Make do with the old car.) You can eat and sleep—simply, safely, and enjoyably—anywhere in Europe for $120 a day plus transportation costs. In many ways, spending more money only builds a thicker wall between you and what you traveled so far to see. Europe is a cultural carnival, and time after time, you'll find that its best acts are free and the best seats are the cheap ones.

A tight budget forces you to travel close to the ground, meeting and communicating with the people. Never sacrifice sleep, nutrition, safety, or cleanliness to save money. Simply enjoy the local-style alternatives to expensive hotels and restaurants.

Connecting with people carbonates your experience. Extroverts have more fun. If your trip is low on magic moments, kick yourself and make things happen. If you don't enjoy a place, maybe you don't know enough about it. Seek the truth. Recognize tourist traps. Give a culture the benefit of your open mind. See things as different, but not better or worse. Any culture has plenty to share.

Of course, travel, like the world, is a series of hills and valleys. Be fanatically positive and militantly optimistic. If something's not to your liking, change your liking.

Travel can make you a happier American, as well as a citizen of the world. Our Earth is home to six and a half billion equally precious people. It's humbling to travel and find that other people don't have the "American Dream"—they have their own dreams. Europeans like us, but with all due respect, they wouldn't trade passports.

Thoughtful travel engages us with the world. In tough economic times, it reminds us what is truly important. By broadening perspectives, travel teaches new ways to measure quality of life.

Globetrotting destroys ethnocentricity, helping us understand and appreciate other cultures. Rather than fear the diversity on this planet, celebrate it. Among your most prized souvenirs will be the strands of different cultures you choose to knit into your own character. The world is a cultural yarn shop, and Back Door travelers are weaving the ultimate tapestry. Join in!

ORIENTATION

Sprawling Rome actually feels manageable once you get to know it. The old core, with most of the tourist sights, sits in a diamond formed by Termini train station (in the east), the Vatican (west), Villa Borghese Gardens (north), and the Colosseum (south). The Tiber River runs through the diamond from north to south. In the center of the diamond sits Piazza Venezia, a busy square and traffic hub. It takes about an hour to walk from Termini train station to the Vatican.

Think of Rome as a series of neighborhoods, huddling around major landmarks.

Ancient Rome: In ancient times, this was home for the grandest buildings of a city of a million people. Today, the best of the classical sights stand in a line from the Colosseum to the Forum to the Pantheon.

Pantheon Neighborhood: The Pantheon anchors the neighborhood I like to call the heart of Rome. It stretches eastward from the Tiber River through Campo de' Fiori and Piazza Navona, past the Pantheon to the Trevi Fountain.

North Rome: With the Spanish Steps, Villa Borghese Gardens, and trendy shopping streets (Via Veneto and the "shopping triangle"), this is a more modern, classy area.

Vatican City: Located west of the Tiber, it's a compact world of its own, with two great, huge sights: St. Peter's Basilica and the Vatican Museum.

Trastevere: This seedy, colorful wrong-side-of-the-river neighborhood is village Rome. It's the city at its crustiest—and perhaps most "Roman."

Termini: Though light on sightseeing highlights, the train-station neighborhood has many recommended hotels and public-transportation connections.

Pilgrim's Rome: Several prominent churches dot the area south of Termini train station.

South Rome: South of the city center, you'll find the gritty/colorful Testaccio neighborhood, the 1930s suburb of E.U.R., and the Appian Way, home of the catacombs.

Within each of these neighborhoods, you'll find elements from the many layers of Rome's 2,000-year history: the marble ruins of ancient times; tangled streets of the medieval world; early Christian churches; grand Renaissance buildings and statues; Baroque fountains and church facades; 19th-century apartments; and 20th-century boulevards choked with traffic.

Since no one is allowed to build taller than St. Peter's dome, and virtually no buildings have been constructed in the city center since Mussolini got distracted in 1938, Rome has no modern skyline. The Tiber River is basically ignored—after the last floods (1870), the banks were built up very high, and Rome turned its back on its naughty river.

Planning Your Time

After considering Rome's major tourist sights, I've covered just my favorites. You won't be able to see all of these, so don't try—you'll keep coming back to Rome. After several dozen visits, I still have a healthy list of excuses to return.

Rome in a Day

Some people actually try to "do" Rome in a day. Crazy as that sounds, if all you have is a day, it's one of the most exciting days Europe has to offer. Start at 8:30 at the Colosseum. Then explore the Forum, hike over Capitol Hill, and cap your "Caesar Shuffle" with a visit to the Pantheon. After a quick lunch, taxi to the Vatican Museum (the lines usually die down mid-afternoon). See the Vatican Museum and take a short-cut from the Sistine Chapel directly into St. Peter's Basilica (open until 19:00 April–Sept). Taxi back to Campo de' Fiori to find dinner. Finish your day lacing together all the famous floodlit spots (see the Night Walk Across Rome chapter).

Rome in Two to Three Days

On the first day, do the "Caesar Shuffle" from the Colosseum to the Forum, then over Capitol Hill to the Pantheon. After a siesta, join the locals strolling from Piazza del Popolo to the Spanish Steps (see the "Dolce Vita Stroll" in the Nightlife chapter). On the second day, see Vatican City (St. Peter's, climb the dome, tour the Vatican Museum). Have dinner on the atmospheric Campo de' Fiori, then walk to the Trevi Fountain and Spanish Steps (following the Night Walk Across Rome chapter). With a third day,

Rome's Neighborhoods

add the Borghese Gallery (reservations required) and the National Museum of Rome.

Rome in Seven Days

Rome is a great one-week getaway. Its sights can keep even the most fidgety traveler well-entertained for a week.

Day 1: Do the "Caesar Shuffle" from the Colosseum to the Forum, Trajan's Column, Capitol Hill, and Pantheon.

Day 2: Morning—National Museum of Rome and the nearby Baths of Diocletian. Afternoon—"Dolce Vita Stroll" and shopping.

Day 3: Vatican City—St. Peter's Basilica, dome climb, and Vatican Museum (see "Avoiding Lines," page 204).

Day 4: Side-trip to Ostia Antica (closed Mon). Take the recommended Night Walk Across Rome from Campo de' Fiori to the Spanish Steps.

Day 5: Borghese Gallery (reservation required) and Pilgrims' Rome: the churches of San Giovanni in Laterano, Santa Maria Maggiore, and San Clemente (see Pilgrim's Rome Tour chapter).

ORIENTATION

Greater Rome

Day 6: Side-trip to Naples and Pompeii.

Day 7: You choose—Hadrian's Villa, Appian Way with Catacombs, E.U.R., Castel Sant'Angelo, Testaccio sights, Baths of Caracalla, Cappuccin Crypt, shopping, or more time at the Vatican.

Overview

Tourist Information

Rome has two tourist information offices and numerous kiosks (abbreviated TI in this book, generally open daily 9:30–19:00). The TI offices are at the airport (terminal 3) and Termini train station (open until 20:30, way down track 24, look for signs). Little kiosks are near the Forum (on Piazza del Tempio della Pace), in

Trastevere (on Piazza Sonnino), on Via Nazionale (at Palazzo delle Esposizioni), near Castel Sant'Angelo (at Piazza Pia), at the Church of Santa Maria Maggiore (on Via dell'Olmata), near Piazza Navona (at Piazza delle Cinque Lune), and near the Trevi Fountain (at Via del Corso and Via Minghetti). The TI's website is http://en.turismoroma.it.

At any TI, ask for a city map, a listing of sights and hours (in the free *Museums of Rome* booklet), and the free *Evento* booklet, with English-language pages listing the month's cultural events. The TIs don't offer room-booking services. If a commercial info-center offers to book you a room, just say no—you'll save money by booking direct.

If all you need is a **map,** skip the TI and pick up a freebie map at your hotel. The best map I found is published by Rough Guide (€8 in bookstores).

Rome's single best source of up-to-date tourist information is its **call center,** with English-speakers on staff. Dial 06-0608 (answered daily 9:00–21:00, press 2 for English). You can call to buy museum tickets, sightseeing passes (see page 46), and theater tickets using your credit card. There's usually only a €1.50 fee.

Several English-oriented **websites** provide insight into events and daily life in the city: www.inromenow.com (light tourist info on lots of topics), www.wantedinrome.com (events and accommodation rentals), and http://rome.angloinfo.com (on living in and moving to Rome).

Arrival in Rome

For a rundown of Rome's train stations and airports, see the Connections chapter.

Helpful Hints

Sightseeing Tips: Avid sightseers can save money by buying the Roma Pass (see page 46), available at TIs and participating sights—buy one before visiting the Colosseum or Forum, and you can skip the long lines there. If you want to see the Borghese Gallery, remember to reserve ahead (see page 191). To bypass the long Vatican Museum line, reserve an entry time online (see page 204 for details).

Internet Access: If your hotel doesn't offer free or cheap Internet access, your hotelier can point you to the nearest Internet café. Remember to bring your passport, which you may be asked to show before going online.

Bookstores: These stores (all open daily except Anglo American and Open Door) sell travel guidebooks, including mine. The first two are chains, while the others have a more personal touch. **Borri Books** is at Termini train station, and **Feltrinelli**

ORIENTATION

Daily Reminder

Sunday: These sights are closed—the Vatican Museum (except for the last Sunday of the month, when it's free and even more crowded), Villa Farnesina, Santa Susanna Church, and the Catacombs of San Sebastiano. In the morning, the Porta Portese flea market hops, and the old center is delightfully quiet.

Monday: Many sights are closed, including the National Museum of Rome, Borghese Gallery, Capitoline Museums, Catacombs of Priscilla, Museum of the Bath (at the Baths of Diocletian), Museum of the Imperial Forums (includes Trajan's Market and Trajan's Forum), Castel Sant'Angelo, Ara Pacis, Montemartini Museum, E.U.R.'s Museum of Roman Civilization, Etruscan Museum, Museum of the Liberation of Rome, some Appian Way sights (Tomb of Cecilia Metella; Circus and Villa of Maxentius; and the San Sebastiano Gate and Museum of the Walls), Ostia Antica, and Villa d'Este (at Tivoli). Many of the ancient sights (e.g., Colosseum and Forum) and the Vatican Museum, among others, are open. Churches are open as usual. The Baths of Caracalla closes early in the afternoon.

Tuesday: All sights are open in Rome. This isn't a good day to side-trip to Naples because its Archaeological Museum is closed.

Wednesday: All sights are open, except for the Catacombs of San Callisto. St. Peter's Basilica may be closed in the morning for a papal audience.

Thursday: All sights are open (though the Cappuccin Crypt occasionally closes).

Friday: All sights are open in Rome.

Saturday: Most sights are open in Rome, except for the Synagogue, Jewish Museum, and Santa Susanna Church.

International has two branches (at Largo Argentina, and just off Piazza della Repubblica at Via Vittorio Emanuele Orlando 84, tel. 06-482-7878). **Anglo American Bookshop** has great art and history sections (closed Sun and Mon morning, a few blocks south of Spanish Steps at Via della Vite 102, tel. 06-679-5222). **Libreria Fanucci** is centrally located (a block toward the Pantheon from Piazza Navona at Piazza Madama 8, tel. 06-686-1141). In Trastevere, Irishman Dermot at the **Almost Corner Bookshop** stocks an Italian-interest section (Via del Moro 45, tel. 06-583-6942), and the **Open Door Bookshop** carries the only used books in English in town (closed Sun, Via della Lungaretta 23, tel. 06-589-6478).

Laundry: Your hotelier can direct you to the nearest launderette. The **ondablu** chain usually comes with Internet access; one of their more central locations is near Termini train station (€2/ hour, about €8 to wash and dry a 15-pound load, usually open daily 8:00–22:00, Via Principe Amedeo 70b, tel. 06-474-4647).

Travel Agencies: You can get train tickets and railpass-related reservations and supplements at travel agencies (at little or no additional cost), avoiding a trip to a train station. Your hotelier will know of a convenient agency nearby. The **American Express** office near the Spanish Steps sells train tickets and makes reservations for no extra fee (Mon–Fri 9:00–17:30, Sat 9:00–12:30, closed Sun, Piazza di Spagna 38, tel. 06-67641).

Dealing with (and Avoiding) Problems

Theft Alert: While violent crime is rare in the city center, petty theft is rampant. With sweet-talking con artists meeting you at the station, well-dressed pickpockets on buses, and thieving gangs of children at the ancient sites, Rome is a gauntlet of rip-offs. While it's not as bad as it was a few years ago, and pickpockets don't want to hurt you—they usually just want your money—green or sloppy tourists will be scammed. Thieves strike when you're distracted. Don't trust kind strangers. Keep nothing important in your pockets. Be most on guard while boarding and leaving buses and subways. Thieves crowd the door, then stop and turn while others crowd and push from behind. You'll find less crowding and commotion—and less risk—waiting for the end cars of a subway rather than the middle cars. The sneakiest thieves pretend to be well-dressed businessmen (generally with something in their hands), or tourists wearing fanny packs and toting cameras and even Rick Steves guidebooks.

Scams abound: Don't give your wallet to self-proclaimed "police" who stop you on the street, warn you about counterfeit (or drug) money, and ask to see your cash. If a bank machine eats your ATM card, see if there's a thin plastic insert with a tongue hanging out that thieves use to extract it.

If you know what to look out for, fast-fingered moms with babies and gangs of children picking the pockets and handbags of naive tourists are not a threat, but an interesting, albeit sad, spectacle. Pickpockets troll through the tourist crowds around the Colosseum, Forum, Piazza della Repubblica, and train and Metro stations. Watch them target tourists who are overloaded with bags or distracted with a video camera. The kids look like beggars and hold up newspapers or cardboard signs to confuse their victims. They scram like stray cats if you're on to them.

Reporting Losses: To report lost or stolen passports and documents, or to make an insurance claim, you must file a police report (at Termini train station, with *polizia* at track 11 or with Carabinieri at track 20; offices are also at Piazza Venezia). To replace a passport, file the police report, then call your embassy to make an appointment (US embassy: tel. 06-46741, Via Vittorio Veneto 121, www.usembassy.it). To report lost or stolen credit cards, see page 12.

Emergency Numbers: Police—tel. 113. Ambulance—tel. 118.

Pedestrian Safety: Your main safety concern in Rome is crossing streets safely, using extreme caution. Scooters don't need to stop at red lights, and even cars exercise what drivers call the "logical option" of not stopping if they see no oncoming traffic. As noisy gasoline-powered scooters are replaced by electric ones, they'll be quieter (hooray) but more dangerous for pedestrians. Follow locals like a shadow when you cross a street (or spend a good part of your visit stranded on curbs). When you do cross alone, don't be a deer in the headlights. Find a gap in the traffic and walk with confidence while making eye contact with approaching drivers—they won't hit you if they can tell where you intend to go.

Staying/Getting Healthy: The siesta is a key to survival in summertime Rome. Lie down and contemplate the extraordinary power of gravity in the Eternal City. I drink lots of cold, refreshing water from Rome's many drinking fountains (the Forum has three).

There's a pharmacy (marked by a green cross) in every neighborhood. Several pharmacies stay open late in Termini train station (daily 7:30–22:00) and at Piazza dei Cinquecento 51 (open 24 hours daily, next to Termini train station on the corner of Via Cavour, tel. 06-488-0019).

Embassies can recommend English-speaking doctors. Consider MEDline, a 24-hour home-medical service; doctors speak English and make calls at hotels for €150–180 (tel. 06-808-0995). Anyone is entitled to free emergency treatment at public hospitals. The hospital closest to Termini train station is Policlinico Umberto 1 (entrance for emergency treatment on Via Lancisi, translators available, Metro: Policlinico). The American Hospital, a private hospital on the edge of town, is accustomed to helping Yankees (Via Emilio Longoni 69, tel. 06-22-551).

Getting Around Rome

Sightsee on foot, by city bus, by Metro, or by taxi. I've grouped your sightseeing into walkable neighborhoods. Make it a point to visit sights in a logical order. Needless backtracking wastes precious time.

The public transportation system, which is cheap and efficient, consists primarily of buses, a few trams, and the two underground subway (Metro) lines. Consider it part of your Roman experience.

Buying Tickets

All public transportation uses the same ticket (€1, valid for one Metro ride—including transfers underground—plus unlimited city buses and *elettrico* buses during a 75-minute period). Passes good on buses and the Metro are sold in increments of one day (€4, good until midnight), three days (€11), and one week (€16, about the cost of two taxi rides).

You can purchase tickets and passes at some newsstands, tobacco shops (*tabacchi*, marked by a black-and-white *T* sign), and major Metro stations and bus stops, but not onboard. It's smart to stock up on tickets early, or to buy a pass or a Roma Pass (which includes a three-day transit pass—see page 46). That way, you don't have to run around searching for an open *tabacchi* when you spot your bus approaching. Metro stations rarely have human ticket-sellers, and the machines are often either broken or require exact change (it helps to insert your smallest coin first).

Validate your ticket by sticking it in the Metro turnstile (magnetic strip-side up, arrow-side first) or in the machine when you board the bus (magnetic strip-side down, arrow-side first)—watch others and imitate. To get through a Metro turnstile with a transit pass or Roma Pass, use it just like a ticket (on buses, however, you only need to validate your pass if that's your first time using it). If the validation machine won't work, you can ride with your ticket unstamped, but you must write the date, time, and bus number on it, or risk getting fined. For more information, visit www.atac .roma.it (which has a useful route planner in English), or call 800-431-784 or 06-57-003.

By Metro

The Roman subway system (Metropolitana, or "Metro") is sim-

ple, with two clean, cheap, fast lines—A and B—that intersect at Termini train station. The Metro runs from 5:30 to 23:30 (Fri–Sat until 1:30 in the morning). The subway's first and last compartments are generally the least crowded (and the least likely to harbor pickpockets).

You'll notice lots of big holes in the city as a new line is built.

ORIENTATION

ORIENTATION

Rome's Metro

NOT TO SCALE

Cipro · Ottaviano · Lepanto · Flaminio · Spagna
Valle Aurelia
Barberini
Cornelia · Baldo d. Ubaldi
Repubblica
Battistini
Cavour
Colosseo
Circo Massimo
TO FIUMICINO (DA VINCI) AIRPORT
Piramide
Porta San Paolo Train Stn.
Garbatella
San Paolo Basilica
TO OSTIA ANTICA
Marconi
EUR Magliana
EUR Palasport
EUR Fermi
Laurentina

— LINE A
— LINE B
+++ RAIL
---- BUS

Line C, from the Colosseum to Largo Argentina, will likely be done in 2020.

While much of Rome is not served by its skimpy subway, the following stops are helpful:

Termini (intersection of lines A and B): Termini train station, shuttle train to airport, National Museum of Rome, and recommended hotels

ORIENTATION

Rebibbia
Ponte Mammolo
TO TIVOLI
S.M. Soccorso
Pietralata
Monti Tiburtini
Quintiliani
Tiburtina (LONG DISTANCE BUS & TRAIN STATION)
Bologna
Policlinico
Castro Pretorio
Termini (MAIN TRAIN STATION)
Vittorio Emanuele
Manzoni
San Giovanni
Re di Roma
Ponte Lungo
Tuscolana
Furio Camillo
Colli Albani
Arco di Travertino
Porta Furba
Numidio Quadrato
Lucio Sesto
Giulio Agricola
Subaugusta
Cinecittà
Anagnina
TO CIAMPINO AIRPORT

DCH

Repubblica (line A): Baths of Diocletian/Octagonal Hall, Via Nazionale, and recommended hotels

Barberini (line A): Cappuccin Crypt, Trevi Fountain, and Villa Borghese

Spagna (line A): Spanish Steps and classy shopping area

Flaminio (line A): Piazza del Popolo, start of recommended "Dolce Vita Stroll" down Via del Corso

Ottaviano (line A): St. Peter's and Vatican City

Cipro (line A): Vatican Museum and recommended hotels

Tiburtina (line B): Tiburtina train and bus station

Colosseo (line B): Colosseum, Roman Forum, bike rental, and recommended hotels

Piramide (line B): Protestant Cemetery and trains to Ostia Antica

E.U.R. (line B): Mussolini's futuristic suburb

By Bus

The Metro is handy, but it won't get you everywhere—take the bus. Bus routes are clearly listed at the stops. TIs usually don't have bus maps, but with some knowledge of major stops, you won't necessarily need one (though if you do want a route map, buy it from *tabacchi* shops; bus info: www .atac.roma.it with good route planner in English, or tel. 06-57003, usually not in English).

Buses (especially the touristy #40 and #64) are havens for thieves and pickpockets. Assume any commotion is a thief-created distraction. If one bus is packed, there's likely a second one on its tail with far fewer crowds and thieves. Once you know the bus system, you'll find it's easier than searching for a cab.

Tickets have a barcode and must be stamped on the bus in the yellow box with the digital readout (be sure to retrieve your ticket). Validate your ticket as you board (magnetic-strip side down, arrow-side first), or you are cheating. While relatively safe, riding without a stamped ticket on the bus is stressful. Inspectors fine even innocent-looking tourists €50. Remember that there's no need to validate a transit pass or Roma Pass on the bus, unless your pass is new and hasn't yet been stamped elsewhere in the transit system. Bus etiquette (not always followed) is to board at the front or rear doors and exit out the middle.

Regular bus lines start running at about 5:30, and during the day they run every 5–10 minutes. After 23:30, and sometimes earlier (such as on Sundays), buses are less frequent but dependable. Night buses are also reliable, and are marked with an *N* and an owl symbol on the bus-stop signs.

These are the major bus routes:

Bus #64: This bus cuts across the city, linking Termini train station with the Vatican, stopping at Piazza della Repubblica (sights), Via Nazionale (recommended hotels), Piazza Venezia (near Forum), Largo Argentina (near Pantheon), and St. Peter's Basilica

Bus Bravado

Zip around Rome by bus like a local by using the following tips to read bus signs.

The sign in the photo shows the three buses (#40, #60, and #64) that stop at the "Nazionale" stop. Bus #64, for example, starts its journey at "Pza Stz San Pietro" (Piazza Stazione San Pietro), goes to Fornaci, then Cavalleggeri, makes a few more stops, and then arrives at Nazionale—this stop. From here it continues to Terme Diocleziano and ends its journey at Termini. Easy.

❶ **Where am I?** You're at Nazionale. Your current stop (or *fermata*) appears at the top of the sign. It's also on the list of bus stops, with a box drawn around it.

❷ **When will my bus come?** If the bus number has an X or a U, the bus runs during normal waking hours. If it has an owl symbol and an N, it's a night bus. If the number is red within a rounded square, ignore it—that bus doesn't run often. The bottom of the sign lists the first and last departure times from the beginning of the route. *Feriale* means weekdays and *festiva* means only Sundays or holidays.

❸ **Where do I catch the bus?** Figure out if you're standing on the right side of the street. See the arrow? The bus is heading in that direction—if your destination is listed *above* your current bus stop, you need to cross the street to catch the bus going in the right direction.

❹ **Where am I going?** Scan the list to see if any of these buses stops at your destination. If you don't see a particular street or piazza, look for a major landmark where you can transfer. Keep in mind that the major bus transfer points are Largo Argentina, Piazza Venezia, and Termini train station.

Will pickpockets take my wallet? Probably, if you read this entire sidebar at the bus stop without paying attention to your surroundings.

(get off just past the tunnel). Ride it for a city overview and to watch pickpockets in action. The #64 can get horribly crowded, awkward for female travelers uncomfortably close to male strangers.

Bus #40: This express bus following the #64 route is especially helpful—fewer stops and crowds.

The following three routes conveniently connect Trastevere with other parts of Rome:

Bus #H: This express bus, linking Termini Station and Trastevere, makes a few stops on Via Nazionale (for Trastevere, get off at Piazza Belli, just after crossing the Tiber River).

Bus #8: This tram connects Largo Argentina with Trastevere (get off at Piazza Belli).

Buses #23 and #280: These link the Vatican with Trastevere and Testaccio, stopping at the Vatican Museum (nearest stop is Via Leone IV), Castel Sant'Angelo, Trastevere (Piazza Belli), Porta Portese (Sunday flea market), and Piramide (Metro and gateway to Testaccio).

Here are other useful routes:

Bus #62: Largo Argentina to St. Peter's Square.

Bus #81: San Giovanni in Laterano, Largo Argentina, and Piazza Risorgimento (Vatican).

Buses #85 and #87: Piazza Venezia, Colosseum, San Clemente, and San Giovanni in Laterano.

Bus #492: Travels east–west across the city, connecting Tiburtina (train and bus stations), Piazza Barberini, Piazza Venezia, Piazza Cavour (Castel Sant'Angelo), and Piazza Risorgimento (Vatican).

Bus #714: Termini train station, Santa Maria Maggiore, San Giovanni in Laterano, Terme di Caracalla (Baths of Caracalla), and on to E.U.R.

Elettrico Minibuses: Two cute *elettrico* minibuses wind through the narrow streets of old and interesting neighborhoods, and are great for transport or simple joyriding:

Elettrico **#116:** Through the medieval core of Rome: Ponte Vittorio Emanuele II (near Castel Sant'Angelo) to Campo de' Fiori, Pantheon, Piazza Barberini, and the southern edge of the scenic Villa Borghese Gardens.

Elettrico **#117:** San Giovanni in Laterano, Colosseo, Via dei Serpenti, Trevi Fountain, Piazza di Spagna, and Piazza del Popolo.

By Taxi

I use taxis in Rome more often than in other cities. They're reasonable and useful for efficient sightseeing in this big, hot metropolis. Taxis start at €2.80, then charge about €1.30 per kilometer (surcharges: €1 on Sun, €3 for nighttime hours of 22:00–7:00, one regular suitcase or bag rides free, tip by rounding up to the nearest euro). Sample fares: Termini train station to Vatican-€10; Termini train station to Colosseum-€6; Colosseum to Trastevere-€7 (or look up your route at www.worldtaximeter.com). Three or four companions with more money than time should taxi almost everywhere.

It's tough to wave down a taxi in Rome, especially at night. Find the nearest taxi stand by asking a passerby or a clerk in a shop, *"Dov'è una fermata dei taxi?"* (doh-VEH OO-nah fehr-MAH-tah DEHee TAHK-see). Some taxi stands are listed on my maps. To save time and energy, have your hotel or restaurant call a taxi for you; the meter starts when the call is received (generally adding a euro or two to the bill). To call a cab on your own, dial 06-4994 or 06-6645. It's routine for Romans to ask the waiter in a restaurant to call a taxi when they ask for the bill. The waiter will tell you how many minutes you have to enjoy your coffee.

Beware of corrupt taxis. A common cabbie scam is to take your €20 note, drop it, and pick up a €5 note (similar color), claiming that's what you gave him. To avoid this scam, pay in small bills; if you only have a large bill, show it to the cabbie as you state its face value.

If hailing a cab on the street, be sure the meter is restarted when you get in (should be around €2.80, or around €5 if you or your hotelier phoned for the taxi). Many meters show both the fare and the time elapsed during the ride—and some tourists pay €10 for an eight-and-a-half-minute trip (more than the fair meter rate).

When you arrive at the train station or airport, beware of hustlers conning naive visitors into unmarked, rip-off "express taxis." Only use official taxis, with a *taxi* sign and phone number marked on the door. By law, they must display a multilingual official price chart. If you have any problems with a taxi, point to the chart and ask the cabbie to explain it to you. Making a show of writing down the taxi number (to file a complaint) can motivate a driver to quickly settle the matter.

If you take a Rome city cab from the airport to anywhere in central Rome within the old city walls, the cost should be €45 (covering up to four people and their bags); however, every year some readers report being ripped off. The catch is that cabbies not based in Rome can charge €60. At the airport, look specifically for a Rome city cab, with the "SPQR" shield on the door. By law, they can charge only €45 for the ride.

Tired travelers arriving at the airport will likely find it less stressful to take the airport shuttle van to their hotel, or catch the train to Termini train station and take the Metro or a cheaper taxi from there (see page 373 for details on getting from the airport to downtown Rome via taxi, shuttle, or train).

ORIENTATION

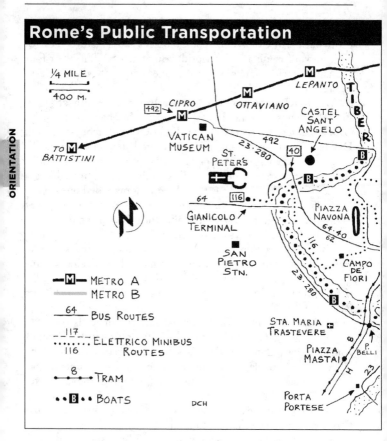

Rome's Public Transportation

¼ MILE
400 M.

TO M BATTISTINI

492 CIPRO M

LEPANTO

TIBER

OTTAVIANO

CASTEL SANT ANGELO

VATICAN MUSEUM

23·280 492

ST. PETER'S

40

B

B

64 116

GIANICOLO TERMINAL

PIAZZA NAVONA

64·40
62

SAN PIETRO STN.

116

CAMPO DE' FIORI

23·280

B

STA. MARIA TRASTEVERE

PIAZZA MASTAI

P. BELLI

PORTA PORTESE

DCH

—M— METRO A
▬▬▬ METRO B
—64— BUS ROUTES
– 117 –
······· ELETTRICO MINIBUS
116   ROUTES
•—8—• TRAM
••B•• BOATS

By Bike

Biking in the big city of Rome can speed up sightseeing or simply be an enjoyable way to explore. Though Roman traffic can be stressful, Roman drivers are respectful of cyclists. The best rides are on small streets in the city center. A bike path along the banks of the Tiber River makes a good 20-minute ride (easily accessed from the ramps at Porta Portese and Ponte Regina Margherita near Piazza del Popolo). Get a bike with a well-padded seat—the little stones that pave Roman streets are unforgiving.

Top Bike Rental and Tours is professionally run by Roman bike enthusiasts who want to show off their city. Your rental comes with a handy map that suggests a route and indicates less-trafficked streets. Ciro and Marta also offer four-hour-long English-only guided tours around the city and the Ancient Appian Way; check their website for days and times (rental: €8/ half-day, €13/day, 10 percent discount with this book, best to reserve in advance via email; bike tours: start at €29, reservations required; daily 9:30–19:00, leave ID for deposit, from Santa Maria Maggiore TI kiosk take Via dell'Olmata and turn left one block down, Via dei Quattro Cantoni 40, tel. 06-488-2893, www.topbikerental.com, info@topbikerental.com).

Cool Rent, near the Colosseo Metro stop, is cheaper but less helpful (€3/hour, €10/day, 3-person bike cart €10/hour, daily 9:30–20:00, driver's license or other ID for deposit, 10 yards to the right as you exit the Metro). A second outlet is just off Via del Corso (on Largo di Lombardi, near corner of Via del Corso and Via della Croce). You can also rent a bike at the Appian Way (see Ancient Appian Way Tour chapter).

By Car with Driver

You can hire your own private car with driver through **Autoservizi Monti Concezio,** run by gentle, capable, and English-speaking Ezio (car-€35/hour, minibus-€40/hour, 3-hour minimum for city sightseeing, long rides outside Rome are more expensive, mobile 335-636-5907 or 349-674-5643, www.montitours.com, concezio monti@gmail.com).

Tours

Walking Tours

Finding the best guided tours in Rome is challenging. Local guides are good but pricey. Tour companies are cheaper, but quality and organization are unreliable. To help, I've produced a series of free audio tours that illuminate the major sights and neighborhoods, covered the way my readers appreciate.

You have several main tour options: Download my audio tours to your iPod or other MP3 player (easy, perfectly reliable, and free—see next page for details); hire a private Italian guide (around €150–180 for a half-day tour—those listed here are excellent and worth every euro, if you can afford it); organize a group of 4–6 people from your hotel to split the cost of hiring a private guide (this ends up costing about the same as joining a tour from one of the companies listed here); or go on a scheduled walking tour with one of the companies listed below (about €25, generally expat guides).

Local Guides—Consider hiring your own personal tour guide. I've worked with each of these licensed independent local guides. They speak excellent English, and enjoy tailoring tours to your interests. Their prices (roughly €50/hour, €180/half-day) flex with the day, season, and demand. Arrange your date and price by email.

Francesca Caruso loves to teach and share her appreciation of her city, and has contributed generously to this book (francesca inroma@gmail.com). Popular with my readers, Francesca understandably books up quickly; if she's busy, she'll recommend one of her colleagues. **Carla Zaia** is an engaging expert on all things Roman (mobile 349-759-0723, carlaromeguide@gmail.com). **Cristina Giannicchi** has an archaeology background (mobile 338-111-4573, www.crisacross.com, crisgiannicchi@gmail.com). **Sara Magister** is a Roman with a doctorate in art history, who wrote a book on Renaissance Rome (tel. 06-583-6783, mobile 339-379-3813, a.magister@iol.it). **Giovanna Terzulli** is a personable, knowledgeable art historian (terzulli@tiscali.it).

Walking-Tour Companies—Rome has many highly competitive tour companies, each offering a series of themed walks through various slices of Rome. Three-hour guided walks generally cost €25–30 per person. Guides are usually native English speakers, often American expats. Tours are limited to small groups, geared to American tourists, and given in English only. I've listed some

Is the Pope Catholic?

Rome's tour guides, who introduce tourists to the city's great art and Christian history, field a lot of interesting questions and comments from their groups. Here are a few of their favorites:

- Oh, to be here in Rome...where our Lord Jesus walked.
- Is this where Christ fought the lions?
- Who's the guy on the cross?
- This guy who made so many nice things, Rene Sance, who is he? (Say it fast, and you'll get the gist.)
- Was John Paul II the son of John Paul I?
- What's the Sistine Chapel worth in US dollars?
- How did Michelangelo get Moses to pose for him?
- What's Michelangelo doing now?
- (Upon seeing the arrow-pierced St. Sebastian) Oh, you Italians had problems with the Indians, too.

here, but without a lot of details on their offerings. Before your trip, spend some time on these companies' websites to get to know your options, as each company has a particular teaching and guiding personality. Some are highbrow, and others are less scholarly. It's sometimes required, and always smart, to book a spot in advance (easy online). I must add that we get a lot of negative feedback on some of these tour companies. Readers report that their advertising can be misleading, and that scheduling mishaps are not uncommon.

Context Rome's walking tours are more intellectual than most, designed for travelers with longer-than-average attention spans. They are more expensive than others, and are led by "docents" rather than guides (tel. 06-9762-5204, US tel. 800-691-6036, www.contextrome.com). **Enjoy Rome** offers five different walks and a website filled with helpful information (Via Marghera 8a, tel. 06-445-1843, www.enjoyrome.com, info@enjoyrome.com). **Rome Walks** has put together several particularly creative itineraries (mobile 347-795-5175, www.romewalks.com, info@romewalks.com, Annie). **Roman Odyssey** gives readers of this book a 10 percent discount on their walks and private tours (tel. 06-580-9902, mobile 328-912-3720, www.romanodyssey.com, Rahul). **Through Eternity** offers travelers with this book a 10 percent discount on most tours and a 20 percent discount on its Underground

ORIENTATION

Rome and Secret Rome tours; book through their website for the best discount (tel. 06-700-9336, mobile 347-336-5298, www.througheternity.com, info@thro.eternity.com, Rob).

Free Rick Steves Audio Tours—Given the costliness of guided tours, budget travelers should consider simply using this book's self-guided tours. For your convenience, I've produced free audio versions of the major tours, allowing you to wander without having to read along. With an iPod (or other MP3 player) or a smartphone, you can tour the Colosseum, Roman Forum, Pantheon, St. Peter's Basilica, Sistine Chapel, Trastevere, Jewish Ghetto, Ostia Antica, and Pompeii (download them from www.ricksteves.com or iTunes—search for "Rick Steves Audio Tours" in the iTunes Store). If you don't mind me in your ear, these audio tours are hard to beat: Nobody will stand you up, the quality is reliable (if not live), you can take the tour exactly when you like, and they're free.

Hop-on, Hop-off Bus Tours

Several different agencies, including the ATAC public bus company, run hop-on, hop-off tours around Rome. These tours are constantly evolving and offer varying combinations of sights. You can grab one (and pay as you board) at any stop; Termini train station and Piazza Venezia are handy hubs. Although the city is perfectly walkable and traffic jams can make the bus dreadfully slow, these open-top bus tours remain popular.

Trambus 110 seems to be the best. It's operated by the ATAC city-bus lines, and offers an orientation tour on big red double-decker buses with an open-air upper deck. In less than two hours, you'll have 80 sights pointed out to you (with a next-to-worthless recorded narration). While you can hop on and off, the service can be erratic (mobbed midday, not ideal in bad weather) and it can be very slow in heavy traffic.

It's best to think of this as a two-hour quickie orientation with scant information and lots of images. The 11 stops include Via Veneto, Via Tritone, Ara Pacis, Piazza Cavour, St. Peter's Square, Corso Vittorio Emanuele (for Piazza Navona), Piazza Venezia, Colosseum, and Via Nazionale. Bus #110 departs every 20 minutes (runs daily 8:30–20:30, tel. 06-684-0901, www.trambusopen.com). Buy the €20 ticket as you board.

Archeobus is an open-top bus, also operated by ATAC, that runs twice hourly from Termini train station out to the Appian Way (with stops at the Colosseum, Baths of Caracalla, San

Callisto, San Sebastiano, and the Tomb of Cecilia Metella). This is a handy way to see the sights down this ancient Roman road, but it can be frustrating for various reasons—sparse narration, sporadic service, and not ideal for hopping on and off (€15, €30 combo-ticket with Trambus 110, ticket valid 24 hours, 1.5-hour loop, daily 8:30–16:30, from Termini train station and Piazza Venezia, tel. 06-684-0901, www.trambusopen.com). A similar bus laces together all the Christian sights.

ORIENTATION

SIGHTS

I've clustered Rome's sights into walkable neighborhoods, some quite close together (see the "Rome's Neighborhoods" map on page 21). For example, the Colosseum and the Forum are a few minutes' walk from Capitol Hill; a 10-minute walk beyond that is the Pantheon. I like to group these sights into one great day, starting at the Colosseum and ending at the Pantheon.

Don't let the length of my descriptions determine your sightseeing priorities. In this chapter, Rome's most important sights have the shortest listings and are marked with a ✪. These sights are covered in much more detail in one of the tours included in this book.

To connect some of the sights by night, try my Night Walk Across Rome (see the chapter of the same name), which takes you from the Campo de' Fiori to the Trevi Fountain and Spanish Steps. To join the parade of people strolling down Via del Corso every evening, take my "Dolce Vita Stroll" (see the end of the Nightlife chapter).

Price Hike Alert: Some of Rome's sights have found a clever way to squeeze more money out of visitors. They host a special exhibit that few tourists really care to see, and require you to pay for extra for your ticket, even if all you want to see is the permanent collection. This means already steep admission fees jump by about €3. A prime example: The Colosseum/Palatine Hill/Roman Forum combo-ticket is technically only €9. But for most of the year, temporary exhibits raise the price to a mandatory €12. Expect this practice at the Capitoline Museums, National Museum of Rome, and others as well.

The prices I've listed here include obligatory temporary exhibits. Come expecting this higher price...and consider yourself lucky if you happen to visit on the rare occasion when you can get in for less.

Ancient Rome

The core of the ancient city, where the grandest monuments were built, is between the Colosseum and Capitol Hill. To the north, this ancient area flows into the Renaissance at Capitol Hill, then into the modern era at Piazza Venezia.

The Colosseum and Nearby

▲▲▲Colosseum (Colosseo)—This 2,000-year-old building is the classic example of Roman engineering. Used as a venue for entertaining the masses, this colossal, functional stadium is one

of Europe's most recognizable landmarks. Whether you're playing gladiator or simply marveling at the remarkable ancient design and construction, the Colosseum gets a unanimous thumbs-up (€12 combo-ticket includes Roman Forum and Palatine Hill—see page 46, audioguide and tours available; open daily 8:30 until one hour before sunset: April–Sept until 19:15, Oct until 18:30, off-season closes as early as 16:30; last entry one hour before closing, Metro: Colosseo).

○ See the Colosseum Tour chapter.

▲Arch of Constantine—This well-preserved arch, which stands between the Colosseum and the Forum, commemorates a military coup and, more importantly, the acceptance of Christianity by the

Roman Empire. When the ambitious Emperor Constantine (who had a vision that he'd win under the sign of the cross) defeated his rival Maxentius in A.D. 312, Constantine became sole emperor of the Roman Empire and legalized Christianity. The arch is free to see—always open and viewable.

○ See the Colosseum Tour chapter.

▲St. Peter-in-Chains Church (San Pietro in Vincoli)—Built in the fifth century to house the chains that held St. Peter, this church is most famous for its Michelangelo statue. Check out the much-venerated chains under the high altar, then focus on mighty Moses (free, April–Sept 8:00–12:30 & 15:30–19:00, Oct–March 8:00–12:30 & 15:00–18:00, modest dress required; the church is a 15-minute uphill, zigzag walk from the Colosseum, or a shorter,

Rome

VIA MILIZIE
VIA ANDREA DORIA
VIA OTTAVIANO
CESARE GIULIO
M LEPANTO
M OTTAVIANO
VIA CANDIA
PIAZZA RISORGIMENTO
VIA COLA DI RIENZO
PIAZZA CAVOUR
CIPRO M
VIA CRESCENZIO
P. CAVOUR
VIA VASPINTI
VIALE VATICANO
VAT. MUSEUM
CASTEL SANT' ANGELO
VATICAN CITY
ST. PETER'S
VIA CONC.
VIA CORONARI
P. UMB.
VIALE
TUNNEL
AOSTA
PIAZZA NAVONA
CORSO VITTORIO
CAVALLEGGERI
VIA AURELIA
VIA AURELIA
P. RIT
P. ANG
LUNGO-TEVERE
P. MAZZ
CAMPO DE' FIORI
PAL. FARNESE
LUNGOTEVERE
G I A N I C O L O
VIA AURELIE
VIA MURA
S. MARIA
VIA LUNG.

N

400 YARDS
400 METERS

M METRO STATION

DCH

T R A S T E V E R E
PORTA PORTESE MKT.

TIBER

simpler walk from the Cavour Metro stop). Note that this isn't the famous St. Peter's Basilica, which is at Vatican City.

☼ See the St. Peter-in-Chains Tour chapter.

Nero's Golden House (Domus Aurea)—The sparse underground remains of Emperor Nero's "Golden House" are a faint shadow of their ancient grandeur. In its heyday, the gold leaf–encrusted residence was huge, with its original entrance all the way over at the Arch of Titus in the Forum. Nero's massive estate once sprawled across the valley (where the Colosseum now stands) and up the hill—the part that's been open on-and-off to the public. While it's exciting to think that Nero's house survives, it's in a sad state of ruin, and has been closed to the public indefinitely.

The Roman Forum and Nearby

▲▲▲Roman Forum (Foro Romano)—This is ancient Rome's birthplace and civic center, and the common ground between

Rome's famous seven hills. As just about anything important that happened in ancient Rome happened here, it's arguably the

most important piece of real estate in Western civilization. While only a few fragments of that glorious past remain, history-seekers find plenty to ignite their imaginations amid the half-broken columns and arches (€12 combo-ticket includes Colosseum and Palatine Hill—see page 46, audioguide available; open daily 8:30 until one hour before sunset: April–Sept until 19:15, Oct until 18:30, off-season closes as early as 16:30; last entry one hour before closing, Metro: Colosseo, tel. 06-3996-7700).

✪ See the Roman Forum Tour chapter.

▲▲Palatine Hill (Monte Palatino)—The hill overlooking the Forum was the home of the emperors and now contains a museum, scant (but impressive when understood) remains of imperial palaces, and a view of the Circus Maximus (€12 combo-ticket includes Roman Forum and Colosseum—see page 46, audioguide and tours available; open same hours as Roman Forum and Colosseum, Metro: Colosseo).

○ See the Palatine Hill Tour chapter.

▲Mamertine Prison—This 2,500-year-old cistern-like prison, which once held the bodies of Saints Peter and Paul, is worth a look—unless it's still closed for renovation when you visit. When you step into the room, ignore the modern floor and look up at the hole in the ceiling, through which prisoners were lowered. Then take the stairs down to the level of the actual prison floor. Downstairs, you'll see the column to which Peter was chained. It's said that a miraculous fountain sprang up in this room so that Peter could convert and baptize his jailers, who were also subsequently martyred. The upside-down cross commemorates Peter's upside-down crucifixion (donation requested, daily 9:00–19:00 if renovation completed, at the foot of Capitol Hill, near Forum's Arch of Septimius Severus).

Imagine humans, amid fat rats and rotting corpses, awaiting slow deaths. On the walls near the entry are lists of notable prisoners (Christian and non-Christian) and the ways they were executed: *strangolati, decapitato, morto per fame* (died of hunger). The sign by the Christian names reads, "Here suffered, victorious for the triumph of Christ, these martyr saints."

▲Trajan's Column, Market, and Imperial Forums—This grand column is the best example of "continuous narration" that we have from antiquity (free, always open and viewable, on Piazza Venezia across street from Victor Emmanuel Monument). The market ruins are viewable for free from Via dei Fori Imperiali. Paying the admission fee gets you inside Trajan's Market, Trajan's Forum, and the Museum of the Imperial Forums. The museum takes you through discoveries from the forums of emperors Julius Caesar, Augustus, Nerva, and Trajan, with fragments of statues and a slideshow that reconstructs how the forum looked in each emperor's time (€6.50, Tue–Sun 9:00–19:00, closed Mon, last entry 30 minutes before closing, entrance is uphill from the column on Via IV Novembre 94, tel. 06-0608, www.mercatiditraiano.it).

Ancient Rome

STAIRS
ENTRANCES TO SIGHTS
M METRO STATION
F FOOD
WATER FOUNTAIN
WC RESTROOM

TO TIME ELEVATOR ROMA

CORSO

VICTOR EMMANUEL MONUMENT

TRAJAN'S COLUMN + FORUM

TO PANTHEON

BATT.

PLEB.

PIAZZA VENEZIA

VIA D'ARA COELI

4 NOV.

MUSEUM OF IMPERIAL FORUMS

+ TRAJAN'S MARKET

TO TERMINI STATION

CAVOUR

VIA LEONINA M

CAVOUR

ST. PETER-IN-CHAINS

CAPITOL HILL

MAMERTINE PRISON

EXIT

CAPITOLINE MUSEUMS
F + WC

VIA TEATRO MARCELLO

ROMAN
WC FORUM

VIA SAN TEODORO

VIA

FORI DI ROMA VISITORS CENTER

F + WC

VIA DEI FORI IMPERIALI

VIA ANNIBALDI

F

COLOS-SEO

M

NERO'S GOLDEN HOUSE (CLOSED)

VIA DELLE TERME

ARCH OF TITUS

EXIT

WC

F

COLOSSEUM

TIBER

WC

WC

PALATINE
HILL

ARCH OF CONSTANTINE

VIA DI SAN GREGORIO

VIA CLAUDIA

S. MARIA COSMEDIN + BOCCA DELLA VERITÀ

CIRCUS

MAXIMUS

VIA CERCHI

WC

200 YARDS
200 METERS

TO BATHS OF CARACALLA

SIGHTS

○ See the Trajan's Column, Market, and Imperial Forums Tour chapter.

Bocca della Verità—The legendary "Mouth of Truth" at the Church of Santa Maria in Cosmedin draws a playful crowd. Stick your hand in the mouth of the gaping stone face in the porch wall. As the legend goes (and was popularized by the 1953 film *Roman Holiday*, starring Gregory Peck and Audrey Hepburn), if you're a liar, your hand will be gobbled up. The mouth is only accessible when the church gate is open (€0.50, daily 9:30–17:50, closes earlier off-season, Piazza Bocca della Verità, near the north end of Circus Maximus).

Capitol Hill

Of Rome's famous seven hills, this is the smallest, tallest, and most famous—home of the ancient Temple of Jupiter and the center

Tips on Sightseeing in Rome

These tips will help you use your time and money efficiently, making the Eternal City seem less eternal and more entertaining. For general advice on sightseeing, see page 14.

Roma Pass: Rome offers several sightseeing passes to help you save money. For most visitors, the Roma Pass (www.roma pass.it) is the clear winner. The Roma Pass costs €25 and is valid for three days, covering public transportation and free or discounted entry to Roman sights. You get free admission to your first two sights (where you also get to skip the ticket line), and then a discount on the rest within the three-day window. Sights covered (or discounted) by the pass include

the following: Colosseum/Palatine Hill/Roman Forum, Borghese Gallery (though you still must make a reservation and pay the €2-3 booking fee), Capitoline Museums, Castel Sant'Angelo, Montemartini Museum, Ara Pacis, Museum of Roman Civilization, Etruscan Museum, Baths of Caracalla, Trajan's Market, and some of the Appian Way sights. The pass also covers all four branches of the National Museum of Rome, considered as a single "sight": Palazzo Massimo (clearly the most important of the lot), Museum of the Bath at the Baths of Diocletian (Roman inscriptions), Crypta Balbi (medieval art), and Palazzo Altemps (sculpture collection).

If you'll be visiting any two of the major sights in a three-day period, get the pass. It's sold at participating sights, TIs, and even the Colosseum *tabacchi* shop. Try to buy it at a less crowded TI or sight. Don't bother to order it online because you have to physically pick up the pass in Rome, negating any time-saving advantage.

Validate your Roma Pass by writing your name and validation date on the card. Then insert it directly into the turnstile at your first two (free) sights. At other sights, show it at the ticket office to get your reduced *(ridotto)* price—about 30 percent off.

To get the most of your pass, visit the two most expensive sights first—for example, the Colosseum (€12) and the National Museum (€10). Definitely use it to bypass the long ticket line at the Colosseum. For sights that normally sell a combined ticket (such as the Colosseum/Palatine Hill/Roman Forum or the four National Museum branches), visiting the combined sight counts as a single entry.

The Roma Pass comes with a three-day transit pass. Write your name and birth date on the transit pass, validate it on your first bus or Metro ride by passing it over a sensor at a turnstile or validation machine (look for a yellow circle), and you can take unlimited rides within Rome's city limits until midnight of the third day.

The TI's other passes—Roma and Pui Pass ("Rome and More") and the Archeologia Card—are generally not worth the trouble for most tourists.

Combo-Ticket for Colosseum, Forum, and Palatine Hill: A €12 combo-ticket covers these three adjacent sights (no individual tickets are sold per sight). The combo-ticket allows one entry per sight, and is valid for two days. Note that these sights are also covered by the Roma Pass. To avoid ticket-buying lines at the Colosseum and Forum, purchase your combo-ticket or Roma Pass at the lesser-visited Palatine Hill. If you're deciding between the combo-ticket or Roma Pass, the pass is the better deal, unless you're planning on seeing only the sights covered by the combo-ticket.

Museum Reservations: The marvelous Borghese Gallery requires reservations well in advance (for specifics, see page 191). You can reserve online to avoid long lines at the Vatican Museum (see page 203).

Opening Hours: Rome's sights have notoriously variable hours from season to season. Get a current listing of opening times from one of Rome's TIs—ask for the free booklet *Museums of Rome*. Or check online at www.060608.it (click on "Culture and Leisure"; although the pages are in English, search by using the Italian names of sights). On holidays, expect shorter hours or closures.

Churches: Many churches, which have divine art and free entry, open early (around 7:00–7:30), close for lunch (roughly 12:00–15:00), and close late (about 19:00). Kamikaze tourists maximize their sightseeing hours by visiting churches before 9:00 or late in the day, and during the siesta seeing major sights that stay open all day (St. Peter's, Colosseum, Forum, Capitoline Museums, and National Museum of Rome). Dress modestly for church visits.

Picnic Discreetly: Public drinking and eating is no longer allowed at major sights, though the ban is proving difficult to enforce. To avoid the risk of being fined, choose an empty piazza for your picnic, or keep a low profile.

Miscellaneous Tips: I carry a plastic water bottle and refill it at Rome's many public drinking spouts. Because public restrooms are scarce, use toilets at museums, restaurants, and bars.

of city government for 2,500 years. There are several ways to get to the top of Capitol Hill. (While I call it "Capitol Hill" for simplicity, it's correctly called "Capitoline Hill.") If you're coming from the north (from Piazza Venezia), take Michelangelo's impressive stairway to the right of the big, white Victor Emmanuel Monument. Coming from the southeast (the Forum), take the steep staircase near the Arch of Septimius Severus. From near Trajan's Forum along Via dei Fori Imperiali, take the winding road. All three converge at the top, in the square called Campidoglio (kahm-pee-DOHL-yoh).

Shortcut: A clever little "back door" gives you access from the top of Capitol Hill directly to the top of the Victor Emmanuel Monument and the Santa Maria in Aracoeli church, saving lots of uphill stair-climbing. To find the back door, locate the She-Wolf statue (to the left of the mayoral palace). Climb the wide set of stairs near the statue (the highest set of stairs you see). To reach the church, turn left at the column in the middle of the staircase, following signs to *Aracoeli*. To reach the Victor Emmanuel Monument, continue up to the top of the steps, pass through the iron gate, and enter the small unmarked door at #13 on the right. You'll soon emerge on a café terrace midway up the monument with vast views. The Rome from the Sky elevator to the top is just around the corner (see page 54).

▲**Capitol Hill Square (Campidoglio)**—This square atop the hill, once the religious and political center of ancient Rome, is still the home of the city's government. In the 1530s, the pope called on Michelangelo to re-establish this square as a grand center. Michelangelo placed the ancient equestrian statue of Marcus Aurelius as the square's focal point. Effective. (The original statue is now in the adjacent museum.) The twin buildings on either side are the Capitoline Museums. Behind the replica of the statue is the mayoral palace (Palazzo Senatorio).

Michelangelo intended that people approach the square from his grand stairway off Piazza Venezia. From the top of the stairway, you see the new Renaissance face of Rome, with its back to the Forum. Michelangelo gave the buildings the "giant order"—huge pilasters make the existing two-story buildings feel one-storied and more harmonious with the new square. Notice how the statues atop these buildings welcome you and then draw you in.

The terraces just downhill (past either side of the mayor's palace) offer grand views of the Forum. To the left of the mayor's

Capitol Hill & Piazza Venezia

■ CAPITOLINE MUSEUMS

→ ENTRY POINT TO SIGHTS

Ⓜ METRO STATION

Ⓣ TAXI STAND

Ⓑ BUS STOP

S. APOST.
CORSO
TIME ELEVATOR ROMA
VIA BATTISTI
Ⓑ #64, 40
VIA PLEBISCITO
❽
Ⓣ
PALAZZO VENEZIA
Ⓑ
PIAZZA
VENEZIA
S. MARCO
TRAJAN'S COLUMN
TRAJAN'S
Ⓑ #64
TO GESÙ & PANTHEON
VICTOR EMMANUEL MONUMENT
CAFÉ
❶❶
FORUM
VIA D'ARACOELI
#110
Ⓑ
Ⓣ
VIA DEI FORI IMPERIALI
GRAND STAIRCASE
STA. MARIA ARACOELI
❻
PALAZZO NUOVO
❼
TO COLOSSEUM & Ⓜ
❾
❶
STATUE
❸
❹
MAMERTINE PRISON
TO
❿
VIA TEATRO MARCELLO
PIAZZA CAFFARELLI
❷
❺
EXIT
ARCH OF SEPTIMIUS SEVERUS
PUBLIC CAFÉ ENTRANCE
TABULARIUM
CAFÉ→
❺
PALAZZO SENATORIO
ROMAN
PALAZZO DEI CONSERVATORI
✝
SAN TEODORO
FORUM
DCH

100 YARDS
100 METERS

❶ Capitol Hill Square
❷ Capitoline Museums Entrance
❸ Copy of She-Wolf Statue
❹ "Il Nasone" Water Fountain
❺ Views of Forum
❻ Shortcut to Santa Maria in Aracoeli Church
❼ Shortcut to Victor Emmanuel Monument
❽ Mussolini's Balcony
❾ Michelangelo's Grand Staircase
❿ To Teatro di Marcello Ruins
⓫ Rome from the Sky

SIGHTS

palace is a copy of the famous She-Wolf statue on a column. Farther down is *il nasone* ("the big nose"), a refreshing water fountain (see photo on the right). Block the spout with your fingers, and water spurts up for drinking. Romans joke that a cheap Roman boy takes his date out for a drink at *il nasone*. Near the She-Wolf statue is the staircase leading to a shortcut to the Victor Emmanuel Monument (for details, see "Shortcut" near the beginning of this section).

▲▲Capitoline Museums (Musei Capitolini)— Some of ancient Rome's most famous statues and art are housed in the two palaces that flank the equestrian statue in the Campidoglio. You'll see the Dying Gaul, the original She-Wolf, and the original version of the equestrian statue of Marcus Aurelius. Admission includes access to the underground vacant Tabularium, with its panoramic overlook of the Forum (€8–11 depending on cost of temporary exhibit, €8.50–13 combo-ticket with Montemartini Museum, Tue–Sun 9:00–20:00, closed Mon, last entry one hour before closing; good €5 audioguide, €6.20/2 people; tel. 06-8205-9127, www.museicapitolini.org).

۞ See the Capitoline Museums Tour chapter.

Santa Maria in Aracoeli—This church is built on the site where Emperor Augustus (supposedly) had a premonition of the com-

ing of Mary and Christ standing on an "altar in the sky" *(ara coeli)*. The church is Rome in a nutshell, where you can time-travel across 2,000 years by standing in one spot (daily 9:00–12:30 & 15:00–18:30). It's atop Capitol Hill, squeezed between the Victor Emmanuel Monument and the square called Campidoglio. While dedicated pilgrims climb up the long, steep staircase from street level (the right side of Victor Emmanuel Monument, as you face it), savvy sightseers prefer to enter through the "back door" atop Capitol Hill (see "Shortcut" earlier in this section).

The building itself dates from Byzantine times (sixth century) and was expanded in the 1200s. Napoleon's occupying troops used the building as a horse stable. But like Rome itself, it survived and retained its splendor. Inside, the mismatched columns and marble floor are ancient, plundered from many different monuments. The early Renaissance is featured in beautiful frescoes by Pinturicchio (first chapel on the right if you entered through the main entrance and didn't take the shortcut). The coffered ceiling celebrates the Christian victory over the Ottoman Turks (Battle of Lepanto, 1571), and the side chapels are a compressed history of architecture, from Gothic to Baroque. A famous wooden statue of the baby Jesus (Santo Bambino) was stolen in 1994, but the copy is still venerated at Christmastime, a Roman tradition. The daunting 125-step staircase up Capitol Hill to the entrance was once climbed—on their knees—by Roman women who wished for a child. Today, they don't...and Italy has Europe's lowest birthrate.

Piazza Venezia

This vast square, dominated by the big, white Victor Emmanuel Monument, is a major transportation hub and the focal point of modern Rome. (The square will be dug up for years—Metro line C is under construction, and when anything of archaeological importance is uncovered, progress is interrupted.) Stand with your back to the monument and look down Via del Corso, the city's axis, surrounded by Rome's classiest shopping district. In the 1930s, Benito Mussolini whipped up Italy's nationalistic fervor from a balcony above the square (with your back to Victor Emmanuel Monument, it's the less-grand balcony on the left). Fascist masses filled the square screaming, "Four more years!"—or something like that. Mussolini created boulevard Via dei Fori Imperiali (to your right) to open up views of the Colosseum in the distance to impress his visiting friend Adolf Hitler. Mussolini lied to his people, mixing fear and patriotism to push his country to the right and embroil the Italians in expensive and regrettable wars. In 1945, they shot and hung Mussolini from a meat hook in Milan.

Circling around the right side of the Victor Emmanuel Monument, look down into the ditch on your left to see the ruins of an ancient apartment building from the first century A.D.; part of it was transformed into a tiny church (faded frescoes and bell tower). Rome was built in layers—almost everywhere you go, there's an earlier version beneath your feet. (The hop-on, hop-off Trambus 110 stops just across the busy intersection from here.)

Continuing on, you reach two staircases leading up Capitol Hill. One is Michelangelo's grand staircase up to the Campidoglio. The longer of the two leads to the Santa Maria in Aracoeli church, a good example of the earliest style of Christian churches (described earlier). The contrast between this climb-on-your-knees ramp to God's house and Michelangelo's elegant stairs illustrates the changes Renaissance humanism brought civilization.

From the bottom of Michelangelo's stairs, look right several blocks down the street to see a condominium actually built upon the surviving ancient pillars and arches of Teatro di Marcello.

SIGHTS

Rome at a Glance

▲▲▲**Colosseum** Huge stadium where gladiators fought. **Hours:** Daily 8:30 until one hour before sunset: April–Sept until 19:15, Oct until 18:30, off-season closes as early as 16:30. See page 41.

▲▲▲**Roman Forum** Ancient Rome's main square, with ruins and grand arches. **Hours:** Same hours as Colosseum. See page 42.

▲▲▲**Pantheon** The defining domed temple. **Hours:** Mon–Sat 8:30-19:30, Sun 9:00-18:00, holidays 9:00-13:00, closed for Mass Sat at 17:00 and Sun at 10:30. See page 55.

▲▲▲**National Museum of Rome** Greatest collection of Roman sculpture anywhere. **Hours:** Tue–Sun 9:00-19:45, closed Mon. See page 57.

▲▲▲**Borghese Gallery** Bernini sculptures and paintings by Caravaggio, Raphael, and Titian in a Baroque palazzo. Reservations mandatory. **Hours:** Tue–Sun 9:00-19:00, closed Mon. See page 61.

▲▲▲**Vatican Museum** Four miles of the finest art of Western civilization, culminating in Michelangelo's glorious Sistine Chapel. **Hours:** Mon–Sat 9:00-18:00, last entry at 16:00 and they start ushering you out at 17:30. Closed on religious holidays and Sun, except last Sun of the month (when it's open 9:00-14:00, last entry at 12:30). May be open some Fri nights April-Oct 19:00-23:00 (last entry at 21:30) by reservation only. Hours are notoriously subject to constant change. See page 69.

▲▲▲**St. Peter's Basilica** Most impressive church on earth, with Michelangelo's *Pietà* and dome. **Hours:** Church—daily April–Sept 7:00-19:00, Oct–March 7:00-18:00, often closed Wed mornings; dome—daily April–Sept 8:00-18:00, Oct–March 8:00-17:00. See page 71.

▲▲**Palatine Hill** Ruins of emperors' palaces, Circus Maximus view, and museum. **Hours:** Same as Colosseum. See page 44.

▲▲**Capitoline Museums** Ancient statues, mosaics, and expansive view of Forum. **Hours:** Tue–Sun 9:00-20:00, closed Mon. See page 50.

▲▲**Ara Pacis** Shrine marking the beginning of Rome's Golden Age. **Hours:** Tue–Sun 9:00-19:00, closed Mon. See page 66.

▲▲**Catacombs** Underground tombs, mainly Christian, outside the city. **Hours:** Generally open 9:00–12:00 & 14:00–17:00. See pages 68 and 88.

▲**Arch of Constantine** Honors the emperor who legalized Christianity. **Hours:** Always viewable. See page 41.

▲**St. Peter-in-Chains** Church with Michelangelo's *Moses*. **Hours:** Daily 8:00–12:30 & 15:30–19:00, until 18:00 in winter. See page 41.

▲**Trajan's Column** Tall column with narrative relief, on Piazza Venezia. **Hours:** Always viewable. See page 44.

▲**Museum of the Imperial Forums** Includes entry to Trajan's Market. **Hours:** Tue–Sun 9:00–19:00, closed Mon. See page 44.

▲**Capitol Hill Square** Hilltop piazza designed by Michelangelo, with a museum, grand stairway, and Forum overlooks. **Hours:** Always open. See page 48.

▲**Trevi Fountain** Baroque hot spot into which tourists throw coins to ensure a return trip to Rome. **Hours:** Always flowing. See page 57.

▲**Baths of Diocletian** Once ancient Rome's immense public baths, now a Michelangelo church. **Hours:** Mon–Sat 7:00–18:30, Sun 7:00–19:30. See page 58.

▲**Santa Maria della Vittoria** Church with Bernini's swooning *St. Teresa in Ecstasy*. **Hours:** Mon–Sat 8:30–12:00 & 15:30–18:00, Sun 15:30–18:00. See page 58.

▲**Rome from the Sky** Elevator to the top of the Victor Emmanuel Monument for a 360-degree city view. **Hours:** Mon–Thu 9:30–18:30, Fri–Sun 9:30–19:30. See page 54.

▲**Cappuccin Crypt** Decorated with the bones of 4,000 Franciscan friars. **Hours:** Daily 9:00–12:00 & 15:00–18:00, sometimes closed Thu. See page 62.

▲**Castel Sant'Angelo** Hadrian's Tomb turned castle, prison, papal refuge, now museum. **Hours:** Tue–Sun 9:00–19:30, closed Mon. See page 71.

Victor Emmanuel Monument—This oversize monument to Italy's first king, built to celebrate the 50th anniversary of the country's unification in 1870, was part of Italy's push to overcome the new country's strong regionalism and create a national identity. The scale of the monument is over-the-top. The 43-foot-long statue of the king on the horse is the biggest equestrian statue in the world.

The king's moustache is over five feet wide, and a person could fit into the horse's hoof. Open to the public, the structure offers a grand view of the Eternal City.

Locals love to hate the "Altar of the Nation." Romans think of the 200-foot-high, 500-foot-wide monument not as an altar of the fatherland, but as "the wedding cake," "the typewriter," or "the dentures." (For short, they call it "the Vittoriano.") It wouldn't be so bad if it weren't sitting on a priceless acre of ancient Rome and if they had chosen better marble (the in-your-face white picks up the pollution horribly, requiring frequent cleaning). Soldiers guard Italy's Tomb of the Unknown Soldier as the eternal flame flickers.

The monument is filled with symbolism connecting the modern city and nation with its grand ancient past. The Tomb of the Unknown Soldier (flanked by Italian flags and armed guards) is overlooked by the goddess Roma (with the gold mosaic background). The eternal flames are reminiscent of the Vestal Virgins and the ancient flame of Rome. And it's crowned by glorious chariots like those that topped the ancient Arch of Constantine (free, 242 punishing steps to the highest viewpoint accessible on foot—unless you take the shortcut from Capitol Hill described on page 48).

The Victor Emmanuel Monument also houses a little-visited **Museum of the Risorgimento,** which explains the movement and war that led to the unification of Italy in 1870 (free, daily 9:30–18:30, tel. 06-679-3598, café).

▲**Rome from the Sky**—This elevator, located near the top of the

Victor Emmanuel Monument next to the outdoor café, zips you to the rooftop for the grandest, 360-degree view of the center of Rome (even better than from the top of St. Peter's dome). Helpful panoramic diagrams describe the skyline, with powerful binoculars available for zooming in on particular sights. Go in late afternoon, when it's beginning to cool off and Rome glows (€7; Mon–Thu 9:30–18:30, Fri–Sun 9:30–19:30, ticket office closes 45 minutes earlier, tel. 06-6920-2049, follow signs inside the Victor Emmanuel Monument to *ascensori panoramici* or take the shortcut from Capitol Hill).

Pantheon Neighborhood

The area around the Pantheon is the heart of Rome. This neighborhood stretches eastward from the Tiber River through Campo de' Fiori and Piazza Navona, past the Pantheon to the Trevi Fountain. Besides being home to ancient sights and historic churches, it's also the place that gives Rome its urban-village feel. Wander narrow streets, sample the many shops and eateries, and gather with the locals in squares marked by a bubbling fountain. Exploring is especially good in the evening, when the restaurants bustle and streets are jammed with foot traffic. For more on nocturnal sightseeing, ✪ see the Night Walk Across Rome chapter.

▲▲▲**Pantheon**—For the greatest look at the splendor of Rome, antiquity's best-preserved interior is a must. Built two millennia ago, this influential domed temple served as the model for Michelangelo's dome of St. Peter's and many others (free, Mon–Sat 8:30–19:30, Sun 9:00–18:00, holidays 9:00–13:00, closed for Mass Sat at 17:00 and Sun at 10:30, tel. 06-6830-0230).

✪ See the Pantheon Tour chapter.

▲▲**Churches near the Pantheon**—For more information on the following churches, see the latter half of the Pantheon Tour chapter. Modest dress is recommended at all churches.

The **Church of San Luigi dei Francesi** has a magnificent chapel painted by Caravaggio (free, daily 10:00–12:30 & 16:00–19:00). The only Gothic church in Rome is **Santa Maria sopra Minerva,** with a little-known Michelangelo statue, *Christ Bearing the Cross* (free, Mon–Fri 7:00–19:00, Sat–Sun 8:00–13:00 & 15:30–19:00, on a little square behind Pantheon, to the east). The **Church of San Ignazio,** several blocks east of the Pantheon, is a riot of Baroque illusions with a false dome (free, daily 7:30–12:30 & 15:00–19:15). A few blocks away, across Corso Vittorio Emanuele, is the rich and Baroque **Gesù Church,** headquarters of the Jesuits in Rome (free, daily 7:00–12:30 & 16:00–19:45).

Leaving the Gesù Church, head two blocks down Corso Vittorio Emanuele, and you'll hit Sacred Area (Largo Argentina), an excavated square facing the boulevard, about four blocks south of the Pantheon. Stroll around this square and look into the excavated pit at some of the oldest ruins in Rome. Julius Caesar was assassinated near here. The far (west) side of the square is a refuge

SIGHTS

Pantheon Neighborhood

TO PIAZZA
DEL POPOLO

TO
SPANISH
STEPS

TO [M]
BARB.

PONTE
UMBERTO

T I B E R

LUNGOTEVERE MARZIO

SAN LUIGI
(CARAVAGGIO)

ANCIENT
STADIUM
ENTRANCE

CORONARI

TRE
SCALINI

PIAZZA
NAVONA

PIAZZA
PASQUINO

CITY
MUSEUM

CORSO VITTORIO

CAMPO
DE'
FIORI

PALAZZO
FARNESE

LUNGOTEVERE

PONTE
SISTO

TO
TRASTEVERE

VIA

PIAZZA
COLONNA

VIA TRITONE

PARL.

TREVI

UFF. VICARIO

P. MONT.

COPPELLE

SABINA

MURATTE

DATAR.

AQUIRO

PIAZZA DI
PIETRA

SALV.

GIUST.

PIAZZA
ROTUNDA

PASTI

SEMINARIO

S. EUST.

PANTHEON

VITTORIO EMAN.

STA. MARIA
SOPRA
MINERVA

SAN
IGNAZIO

GALLERIA
DORIA
PAMPHILJ

IV NOV.

GESÙ

PIAZZA
VENEZIA

FORI IMP.

VIA PLEBISCITO

VIA BOTT. OSC.

VICTOR
EM. MON.

LARGO
ARGENTINA RUINS
(& CAT HOSPICE)

CAPITOL
HILL
& CAP.
MUSEUMS

TO
COLOSSEUM
[M]

F O R U M

→ ENTRY POINT
TO SIGHTS

[T] TAXI STAND

[M] METRO STATION

[B] BUS STOP

200 YARDS

200 METERS

DCH

for cats—volunteers care for some 250 of them.

▲**Galleria Doria Pamphilj**—This underappreciated gallery, tucked away in the heart of the old city, fills a palace on Piazza del Collegio Romano. It offers a rare chance to wander through a noble family's lavish rooms with the prince who calls this downtown mansion home. Well, almost. Through an audioguide, the prince lovingly narrates his family's story, including how the Doria Pamphilj (pahm-FEEL-yee) family's cozy relationship with the pope inspired the word "nepotism." Highlights include paintings by Caravaggio, Titian, and Raphael, and portraits of Pope Innocent X by Diego Velázquez (on canvas) and Gian Lorenzo Bernini (in marble). The fancy rooms of the palace are interesting, with a mini-Versailles-like hall of mirrors and paintings lining the walls to the ceiling in the style typical of 18th-century galleries (€9.50, includes worthwhile audioguide, daily 10:00–17:00, last entry 45 minutes before closing, café, from Piazza Venezia walk 2 blocks up Via del Corso to #305, tel. 06-679-7323, www.dopart.it/roma).

Time Elevator Roma—This cheesy, overpriced show is really just for kids. The 45-minute multiscreen show jolts you through the centuries. Equipped with headphones, you get nauseous in a comfortable, air-conditioned theater as the history of Rome unfolds before you—from the founding of the city, through its rise and fall, to its Renaissance rebound, and up to the present (€12, children 5-12-€9, daily 10:30–19:30, shows at the bottom of each hour, last showing at 19:30, no kids under 39 inches, just off Via del Corso, a 3-minute walk from Piazza Venezia, across from Galleria Doria Pamphilj at Via dei S.S. Apostoli 20, tel. 06-9774-6243, www.timeelevator.it).

Piazza di Pietra (Piazza of Stone)—The square was actually a quarry set up to chew away at the abandoned Roman building. You can still see the holes that hungry medieval scavengers chipped into the columns to steal the metal pins that held the slabs together (two blocks toward Via del Corso from Pantheon).

▲**Trevi Fountain**—The bubbly Baroque fountain, worth ▲▲ by night, is a minor sight to art scholars...but a major nighttime gathering spot for teens on the make and tourists tossing coins. The coins tourists deposit daily are collected to feed Rome's poor.

○ See the Night Walk Across Rome chapter.

Near Termini Train Station

These sights are within a 10-minute walk of the train station. By Metro, use the Termini stop for the National Museum and the Repubblica stop for the rest.

▲▲▲**National Museum of Rome (Museo Nazionale Romano Palazzo Massimo alle Terme)**—The National Museum's main branch, at Palazzo Massimo, houses the greatest collection of ancient Roman art anywhere, including busts of emperors and a Roman copy of the Greek *Discus Thrower* (€10 combo-ticket covers nearby Museum of the Bath and other forgettable branches, audioguide-€4, Tue–Sun 9:00–19:45, closed Mon, last entry 45 minutes before closing, Metro: Termini, tel. 06-3996-7700). The museum is about 100 yards from the train station—as you leave the station, it's the sandstone-brick building on your left. Enter at the far end, at Largo di Villa Peretti.

Near Termini Train Station

○ See the National Museum of Rome Tour chapter.

▲**Baths of Diocletian (Terme di Diocleziano)**—Around A.D. 300, Emperor Diocletian built the largest baths in Rome. This sprawling meeting place—with baths and schmoozing spaces to accommodate 3,000 bathers at a time—was a big deal in ancient times. While much of it is still closed, three sections are open: the Church of Santa Maria degli Angeli, once the great central hall of the baths (free, Mon–Sat 7:00–18:30, Sun 7:00–19:30, closed to sightseers during Mass, faces Piazza della Repubblica); the Octagonal Hall, once a gymnasium, now a gallery of Roman bronze and marble statues (free, open sporadically Sun 9:00–13:00 only, faces Piazza della Repubblica); and the skippable Museum of the Bath, which, despite its name, has nothing on the baths (€10 combo-ticket covers National Museum of Rome and more, Tue–Sun 9:00–19:45, closed Mon, last entry 45 minutes before closing, audioguide-€4, Viale Enrico de Nicola 79, entrance faces Termini train station, tel. 06-3996-7700).

○ See the Baths of Diocletian Tour chapter.

▲**Santa Maria della Vittoria**—This church houses Bernini's statue, the swooning *St. Teresa in Ecstasy* (free, pay €0.50 for light,

Mon–Sat 8:30–12:00 & 15:30–18:00, Sun 15:30–18:00, about 5 blocks northwest of Termini train station on Largo Susanna, Metro: Repubblica).

Once inside the church, you'll find St. Teresa to the left of the altar. Teresa has just been stabbed with God's arrow of fire. Now, the angel pulls it out and watches her reaction. Teresa swoons, her eyes roll up, her hand goes limp, she parts her lips...and moans. The smiling, cherubic angel understands just how she feels. Teresa, a 16th-century Spanish nun, later talked of the "sweetness" of "this intense pain," describing her oneness with God in ecstatic, even erotic, terms.

Bernini, the master of multimedia, pulls out all the stops to make this mystical vision real. Actual sunlight pours through the alabaster windows, bronze sunbeams shine on a marble angel holding a golden arrow. Teresa leans back on a cloud and her robe ripples from within, charged with her spiritual arousal. Bernini has created a little stage-setting of heaven. And watching from the "theater boxes" on either side are members of the family that commissioned the work.

Santa Susanna Church—The home of the American Catholic Church in Rome, Santa Susanna holds Mass in English daily at 18:00 and on Sunday at 9:00 and 10:30. They arrange papal audiences (see page 238), and their excellent website contains tips for travelers and a list of convents that rent out rooms (Mon–Fri 9:00–12:00 & 16:00–18:00, closed Sat–Sun, Via XX Settembre 15, near recommended Via Firenze hotels, Metro: Repubblica, tel. 06-4201-4554, www.santasusanna.org).

Pilgrim's Rome

East of the Colosseum (and south of Termini train station) are several venerable churches that Catholic pilgrims make a point of visiting. Near one of the churches is a small WWII museum. For more on the churches, ✪ see the Pilgrim's Rome Tour chapter.

Church of San Giovanni in Laterano—Built by Constantine, the first Christian emperor, this was Rome's most important church through medieval times. A building alongside the church houses the Holy Stairs said to have been walked up by Jesus, which today are ascended by pilgrims on their knees (free, church—daily 7:00–18:30, Holy Stairs—daily April–Sept 6:15–12:00 & 15:30–18:30, Oct–March 6:15–12:00 & 15:00–18:00, audioguide-€5;

Pilgrim's Rome

TERMINI · TERMINI TRAIN STATION

SANTA MARIA MAGGIORE

CAVOUR

STA. PRASSEDE

VIA G. LANZA

PIAZZA VITTORIO EM.

VITTORIO EMANUELE

ST. PETER-IN-CHAINS

COLOSSEO

SAN CLEMENTE

MUSEUM OF THE LIBERATION OF ROME

MANZONI

COLOSSEUM

VIA LABICANA

S. GIOVANNI LAT.

HOLY STAIRS

→ ENTRY POINT TO SIGHTS

M METRO STATION

≋ STAIRS

1/4 MILE

400 METERS

SAN GIOVANNI IN LATERANO

CITY WALLS

VIA SANNIO

S. GIO.

DCH

SIGHTS

Piazza San Giovanni in Laterano, Metro: San Giovanni, or bus #85 or #87; tel. 06-6988-6409).

Museum of the Liberation of Rome (Museo Storico della Liberazione di Roma)—This small memorial museum, near the Church of San Giovanni in Laterano, is housed in the prison wing of the former Nazi police headquarters of occupied Rome. Other than a single printed sheet to help, there's little in English. Still, for those interested in resistance movements and the Nazi occupation, it's a stirring visit. You'll see a few artifacts, many photos of heroes, and a couple of cells preserved as they were found on June 4, 1944, when the city was liberated (free, Tue–Sun 9:30–12:30; Tue and Thu–Fri also 15:30–19:00; closed Mon and Aug; just behind the Holy Stairs at Via Tasso 145; tel. 06-700-3866).

Church of Santa Maria Maggiore—Some of Rome's best-surviving mosaics line the nave of this church built as Rome was falling. The nearby Church of Santa Prassede has still more early mosaics (free, daily 8:30–18:00, Piazza Santa Maria Maggiore, Metro: Termini or Vittorio Emanuele, tel. 06-6988-6802).

▲**Church of San Clemente**—Besides visiting the church itself, with frescoes by Masolino, you can also descend into the ruins of an earlier church. Descend yet one more level and enter the eerie remains of a pagan temple to Mithras (upper church—free, lower church—€5, both open Mon–Sat 9:00–12:30 & 15:00–18:00, Sun 12:00–18:00, last entry for lower church 20 minutes earlier; Via di San Giovanni in Laterano, Metro: Colosseo, or bus #85 or #87; tel. 06-774-0021, www.basilicasanclemente.com).

North Rome

Borghese Gardens and Via Veneto

▲**Villa Borghese Gardens**—Rome's scruffy three-square-mile "Central Park" is great for its shade and people-watching (plenty

of modern-day Romeos and Juliets). The best entrance is at the head of Via Veneto (Metro: Barberini, then 10-minute walk up Via Veneto and through the old Roman wall at Porta Pinciana). There you'll find a cluster of buildings with a café, a kiddie arcade, and bike rental (€4/hour). Rent a bike (or, for romantics, a pedaled rickshaw—*riscio*) and follow signs to discover the park's cafés, fountains, statues, lake, great viewpoint over Piazza del Popolo, and prime picnic spots.

▲▲▲**Borghese Gallery (Galleria Borghese)**—This plush museum, filling a cardinal's mansion in the park, was recently restored and offers one of Europe's most sumptuous art experiences. You'll enjoy a collection of world-class Baroque sculpture, including Bernini's *David* and his excited statue of Apollo chasing Daphne, as well as paintings by Caravaggio, Raphael, Titian, and Rubens. The museum's slick, mandatory reservation system keeps crowds to a manageable size.

Cost, Hours, Reservations: €8.50, €12.50 during special exhibits, both prices include basic €2 reservation fee, credit cards accepted, Tue–Sun 9:00–19:00, ticket office closes one hour earlier, closed Mon. Reservations are mandatory and easy to get in English online (www.ticketeria.it, €1 extra booking fee, user-friendly website) or by calling 06-32810 (if you get an Italian recording, wait for the English translation to get the most up-to-date information, or press 2 for their standard information in English; office hours

Mon–Fri 9:00–18:00, Sat 9:00–13:00, office closed Sat in Aug and Sun year-round, www.galleriaborghese.it). Reserve a minimum of several days in advance for a weekday visit, at least a week ahead for weekends. For more on reservations, as well as a self-guided tour, ✪ see the Borghese Gallery Tour chapter.

Etruscan Museum (Villa Giulia Museo Nazionale Etrusco)—

The fascinating Etruscan civilization thrived in this part of Italy around 600 B.C., when Rome was an Etruscan town. The Villa Giulia (a fine Renaissance palace) hosts a museum that tells the story. Aficionados of all things Etruscan come here for the famous "husband and wife sarcophagus"—a dead couple seeming to enjoy an everlasting banquet from atop their tomb (sixth century B.C. from Cerveteri); the *Apollo from Veii* statue (of textbook fame); and an impressive room filled with gold sheets of Etruscan printing and temple statuary from the Sanctuary of Pyrgi (€4, Tue–Sun 8:30–19:30, closed Mon, last entry one hour before closing, scant English information, 20-minute walk from Borghese Gallery, Piazzale di Villa Giulia 9, tel. 06-322-6571).

Via Veneto—In the 1960s, movie stars from around the world paraded down curvy Via Veneto, one of Rome's glitziest nightspots. Today it's still lined with the city's poshest hotels and the American Embassy, but any hint of local color has faded to bland.

▲Cappuccin Crypt—If you want to see artistically arranged bones, this is the place. The crypt is below the church of Santa Maria della Immacolata Concezione on Via Veneto, just up from Piazza Barberini.

Cost and Hours: €1 donation, daily 9:00–12:00 & 15:00–18:00, sometimes closed Thu, modest dress required, no photos, turn off mobile phones, Metro: Barberini, tel. 06-487-1185.

➋ **Self-Guided Tour:** The bones of more than 4,000 friars who died between 1528 and 1870 are in the basement, all lined up in a series of six crypts for the delight—or disgust—of the always-wide-eyed visitor. As you enter, you'll see a monastic message on the wall reminding you that this is more than just a macabre exercise: "We were what you are...you will become what we are now."

North Rome

SIGHTS

The Crypt of the Resurrection (#1), with a painting of Jesus bringing Lazarus back to life, sets the theme of your visit: the Christian faith in resurrection.

In the Crypt of the Skulls (#2), the central scene is an hourglass with wings. Yes, time on Earth flies. Between crypts #3 and #4, look up to see the jaunty skull with a shoulder-blade bowtie.

The Crypt of the Hips (#4) is named for the canopy of hipbones with vertebrae bangles over its central altar.

In the Crypt of the Tibia and Fibia (#5), niches are inhabited by Capuchin friars, whose robes gave the name to the brown coffee with the frothy white cowl. (Unlike monks, who live apart from society, the Capuchins are friars, who depend on charity and live among the people, and are part of the Franciscan order.) In this chapel we see the Franciscan symbol: the bare arm of Christ and the robed arm of a Franciscan friar embracing the faithful. Above that is a bony crown. And below, in dirt brought from Jerusalem 400 years ago, are 18 graves with simple crosses.

Finally, in the Crypt of the Three Skeletons (#6), the ceiling is decorated by a skeleton with a grim-reaper scythe, and scales weighing the "good deeds and the bad deeds so God can judge the soul"—illustrating the Catholic doctrine of earning salvation through good works. The clock with no hands, on the ceiling above the aisle, is a symbol: It means that life goes on forever, once led into the afterlife by "Sister Death." The chapel's bony chandelier and the stars and floral motifs made by ribs and vertebrae are particularly inspired.

As you leave, pick up a few of Rome's most interesting postcards (proceeds support Capuchin mission work) and head back outside, where it's not just the bright light that provides contrast with the crypt. Within a few steps are the American Embassy, Hard Rock Cafe, and fancy Via Veneto cafés, filled with the poor and envious keeping an eye out for the rich and famous.

Piazza del Popolo—This vast oval square marks the traditional north entrance to Rome (its oval shape dates from the early 19th century). Today the square, known for its symmetrical design and its art-filled churches, is the starting point for the city's evening *passeggiata* (see the "Dolce Vita Stroll" at the end of the Nightlife chapter). Since ancient times, visitors arriving along the main highway

from northern Europe have entered Rome at this point. In 1480, Pope Sixtus IV recognized that the ramshackle medieval city was making a miserable first impression on pilgrims who walked here from all over Europe (similar to the Muslim pilgrimage to Mecca). He authorized city planners to appropriate property (establishing "eminent domain"), demolish old buildings, and create straight streets to accommodate traffic. This was the first of several papal campaigns to spruce up the square and make it a suitable entrance for the grand city.

From the Flaminio Metro stop, pass through the third-century Aurelian Wall via the Porta del Popolo, and look south. The 10-story obelisk in the center of the square once graced the temple of Ramses II in Egypt and the Roman Circus Maximus racetrack. The obelisk was brought here in 1589 as one of the square's beautification projects. At the south side of the square, twin domed churches mark the spot where three main boulevards exit the square and form a trident. The central boulevard (running between the churches) is Via del Corso, which since ancient times has been the main north–south drag through town, running to Capitol Hill (the governing center) and the Forum. Along the north side of the square (flanking the Porta del Popolo) are two more buildings, which give the square a pleasant symmetry: the Carabinieri station and the church of Santa Maria del Popolo.

From the square, the *Tridente* of roads takes people south to the city center (along Via del Corso), to the Spanish Steps (Via Babuino), and to the Tiber River (Via Ripetta). Two large fountains grace the sides of the square—Neptune to the west and Roma to the east (marking the base of Pincio Hill). Though the name Piazza del Popolo means "Square of the People" (and it is a popular hangout), the word was probably derived from the Latin *populus*, after the poplar trees along the square's northeast side.

Santa Maria del Popolo—One of Rome's most overlooked churches, this features two chapels with top-notch art and a facade built of travertine scavenged from the Colosseum. The church is brought to you by the Rovere family, which produced two popes, and you'll see their symbol—the oak tree and acorns—throughout (free, Mon–Sat 7:00–12:00 & 16:00–19:00, Sun 8:00–13:30 & 16:30– 19:30; on north side of Piazza del Popolo; as you face gate in old wall from the square, church entrance is to your right).

Go inside. The Chigi Chapel (second on the left) was designed by Raphael and inspired (as Raphael was) by the Pantheon. Notice the Pantheon-like dome, pilasters, and capitals. Above in the oculus, God looks in, aided by angels who power the eight known planets. Raphael built the chapel for his wealthy banker friend Agostino Chigi, buried in the pyramid-shaped tomb in the wall to the right of the altar. Later, Chigi's great-grandson hired Bernini to make two of the four statues, and Bernini delivered a theatrical episode. In one corner, Daniel straddles a lion and raises his praying hands to God for help. Kitty-corner across the chapel, an angel grabs Habbakuk's hair and tells him to go take some food to poor Daniel.

In the Cerasi Chapel (left of altar), Caravaggio's *The Conversion on the Way to Damascus* shows Paul sprawled on his back

beside his horse while his servant looks on. The startled future saint is blinded by the harsh light as Jesus' voice asks him, "Why do you persecute me?" In the style of the Counter-Reformation, Paul receives his new faith with open arms.

In the same chapel, Caravaggio's *Crucifixion of St. Peter* is shown as a banal chore; the workers toil like faceless animals. The light and dark are in high contrast. Caravaggio liked to say, "Where light falls, I will paint it."

SIGHTS

▲▲**Catacombs of Priscilla (Catacombe di Priscilla)**—Of the countless catacombs honeycombing the ground just outside the ancient city walls, only five are open to the public. While most tourists and nearly all tour groups go out to the ancient Appian Way to see the famous catacombs of San Sebastiano and San Callisto, the Catacombs of Priscilla (on the other side of town) are less commercialized and crowded, and just feel more intimate, as catacombs should.

The Catacombs of Priscilla likely originated as underground tombs for Christians, who'd meet to worship in the wealthy Christian's home that was on this spot. As poor people couldn't generally afford a nice plot in a cemetery, they would dig graves at a generous person's home...and dig and dig.

At the Catacombs of Priscilla, you enter from a convent and explore the result of 250 years of tunneling that occurred from the second to the fifth centuries. Visits are by 30-minute guided tour

only (English-language tours go whenever a small group gathers—generally every 20 minutes or so). You'll see a few thousand of the 40,000 niches carved here, along with some beautiful frescoes, including what is considered the first depiction of Mary nursing the baby Jesus.

As in other catacombs, some of the tunnels date from an earlier quarry. Volcanic tuff, the stone ancient Rome was built with, works great for burial niches—it's easy to dig, and dries hard when exposed to air.

Cost and Hours: €8, Tue–Sun 8:30–12:00 & 14:30–17:00, closed Mon, last entry 30 minutes before closing, closed one random month a year—check website or call first, tel. 06-8620-6272, www.catacombepriscilla.com.

Location: The catacombs are northeast of Termini Station (at Via Salaria 430), far from the center but well-served by buses (20-30 minutes). From Termini, take bus #92 or #86 from Piazza Cinquecento; from Piazza Venezia and along Via del Corso take bus #63. Tell the driver "kah-tah-KOHM-bay" and he'll let you off near Piazza Crati, which is close to the catacombs.

For more information on catacombs, ❂ see the Ancient Appian Way Tour chapter.

From the Spanish Steps to Ara Pacis

▲**Spanish Steps**—The wide, curving staircase, culminating with an obelisk between two Baroque church towers, makes for one of Rome's iconic sights. Beyond that, it's a people-gathering place. By day, the area hosts shoppers looking for high-end fashions; on warm evenings, it attracts young people in love with the city. For more, ❂ see the Night Walk Across Rome chapter.

"Shopping Triangle"—The triangular-shaped area between the Spanish Steps, Piazza Venezia, and Piazza del Popolo (along Via del Corso) contains Rome's highest concentration of upscale boutiques and fashion stores (see triangle at bottom of map on page 63).

▲▲**Ara Pacis (Altar of Peace)**—On January 30, 9 B.C., soon-to-be-emperor Augustus led a procession of priests up the steps and into this newly built "Altar of Peace." They sacrificed an ani-

mal on the altar and poured an offering of wine, thanking the gods for helping Augustus pacify barbarians abroad and rivals at home. This marked the dawn of the Pax Romana (c. A.D. 1–200), a Golden Age of good living, stability, dominance, and peace *(pax)*. The Ara Pacis (AH-rah PAH-chees) hosted annual sacrifices by the emperor until the area was flooded by the Tiber River. Buried under silt, it was abandoned and forgotten until the 16th century, when various parts were discovered and excavated. Mussolini gathered the altar's scattered parts and reconstructed them here in 1938. In 2006, the Altar of Peace reopened to the public in a striking modern building. As the first new building allowed to be built in the old center since 1938, it's been controversial, but its quiet, air-conditioned interior may signal the dawn of another new age in Rome.

Cost, Hours, Location: €9, tightwads can look in through huge windows for free; Tue–Sun 9:00–19:00, closed Mon, last entry one hour before closing; €3.50 audioguide also available as free podcast at www.arapacis.it, good WC downstairs. The Ara Pacis is a long block west of Via del Corso on Via di Ara Pacis, on the east bank of the Tiber near Ponte Cavour, Metro: Spagna; a 10-minute walk down Via dei Condotti. Tel. 06-0608.

➋ Self-Guided Tour: Start with the model in the museum's lobby. The Altar of Peace was originally located east of here, along today's Via del Corso. The model shows where it stood in relation to the Mausoleum of Augustus (now next door) and the Pantheon. (The Ara Pacis originally faced west; now it faces east. The compass directions given here match the altar's current orientation, but be aware that some art-history books and even the Ara Pacis website may describe it using the original—and opposite—orientation.)

Entrance (East) Side: Approach the Ara Pacis and look through the doorway to see the raised altar. This simple structure has just the basics of a Roman temple: an altar for sacrifices surrounded by cubicle-like walls that enclose a consecrated space. Its well-preserved reliefs celebrate Rome's success. After a sacrifice, the altar was washed, and the blood flowed out drain holes still visible at the base of the walls. Flanking the doorway are (badly damaged) reliefs of Rome's legendary founders—Romulus and Remus—being suckled by the she-wolf (left), and bearded Aeneas (right), who's pouring a wine offering and preparing to sacrifice a sow.

North Side: This relief probably depicts the parade of dignitaries who consecrated the altar. Near the head is Augustus (his body sliced in two vertically by missing stone), honored with a crown of laurel leaves, having just conquered parts of Spain and Gaul. Augustus is followed by a half-dozen bigwigs and priests (with spiked hats) and the man shouldering the sacrificial axe. Next comes Agrippa (wearing the hood of a priest), Augustus' right-hand man in battles against Mark Antony and Cleopatra. Agrippa married Augustus' daughter, Julia—their little son, Gaius, tugs on his dad's toga while turning to look at Livia, Augustus' wife. When Agrippa died, Gaius was adopted and named as successor by Augustus. Gaius also died young, making the next in line Tiberius, Livia's son by a first marriage, shown standing next to his mother. Confused? Find these names and other descendants of Julius Caesar on the genealogical chart in the museum lobby.

Before proceeding farther around the altar, look out the window to see the overgrown Mausoleum of Augustus and his family, once capped with a dome of earth, elegant spruces, and statues of the emperor. To the left is an example of Mussolini's fascist architecture—intended to remind Italians of their imperial

Roman roots. Note the travertine, brick, low-relief propaganda, stony inscriptions, Roman numerals, and cold rationality. (Locals don't like it.) This area was the Field of Mars, Rome's only neighborhood continuously inhabited since ancient times.

West Side: The altar's back door is flanked with reliefs celebrating the two things Augustus brought to Rome: peace (goddess Roma as a conquering Amazon, right side) and prosperity (fertility goddess surrounded by children, plants, and animals). For a closer look at details from the various reliefs, see the model downstairs.

South Side: Leading the parade of senators is a *lictor*—a ceremonial bodyguard—carrying the *fasces.* This bundle of sticks symbolized how unity brings strength, and it gave us the modern word "fascism." The reliefs feature the first official portrayal of women and children in a public monument.

Beneath the parade, notice the elaborate floral relief that runs all the way around the Ara Pacis. Acanthus tendrils spiral out forming decorative garlands, intertwining with ivy, laurel, and more. Swans with outstretched wings hide among the patterns. Some 50 plants are blooming in this display of abundance. Imagine the altar as it once was, standing in an open field, painted in bright colors—a mingling of myth, man, and nature.

Vatican City

Vatican City, a tiny independent country, contains the Vatican Museum (with Michelangelo's Sistine Chapel) and St. Peter's Basilica

(with Michelangelo's exquisite *Pietà*). A helpful **TI** is just to the left of St. Peter's Basilica as you're facing it (Mon–Sat 8:30–19:00, closed Sun, tel. 06-6988-1662, Vatican switchboard tel. 06-6982, www.vatican.va). The entrances to St. Peter's and to the Vatican Museum are a 15-minute walk apart (follow the outside of the Vatican wall, which links the two sights). The nearest Metro stops still involve a 10-minute walk to either sight: For St. Peter's, the closest stop is Ottaviano; for the Vatican Museum, it's Cipro. For information on Vatican tours, post offices, and the pope's schedule, see page 238.

▲▲▲**Vatican Museum (Musei Vaticani)**—The four miles of displays in this immense museum—from ancient statues to Christian frescoes to modern paintings—culminate in the Raphael Rooms and Michelangelo's glorious Sistine Chapel. Modest dress is required.

Vatican City

T Taxi Stand
M Metro Station
B Bus Stop

❶ Entrance to
Vatican Museum

❷ Tourist Info,
Post Office & WC

DCH

Cost and Hours: €15 plus optional €4 reservation fee, Mon–Sat 9:00–18:00, last entry at 16:00 (though the official closing time is 18:00, the staff starts ushering you out at 17:30), closed on religious holidays and Sun except last Sun of the month (when it's free, more crowded, and open 9:00–14:00, last entry at 12:30). Hours are subject to constant change and frequent holidays; check http://mv.vatican.va for current times. Lines are extremely long in the morning—go in the afternoon, or skip the ticket-buying line altogether by reserving an entry time on their website for €19 (€15 ticket plus €4 booking fee, pay with credit card). Guided tours and audioguides are available.

○ See the Vatican Museum Tour chapter.

▲▲▲**St. Peter's Basilica (Basilica San Pietro)**—There is no doubt: This is the richest and grandest church on earth. To call it vast is like calling Einstein smart. The church strictly enforces its dress code. Dress modestly—a not-too-short dress or long pants, with shoulders covered (men, women, and children).

Cost and Hours: Free, daily April–Sept 7:00–19:00, Oct–March 7:00–18:00. The church often closes on Wednesday mornings during papal audiences. Free guided tours (Mon–Fri) and €5 audioguides are available. Masses occur daily throughout the day. The view from the dome is worth the climb (€7 for elevator to roof, then take stairs; €5 to climb stairs all the way; allow an hour to go up and down, daily April–Sept 8:00–18:00, Oct–March 8:00–17:00, www.saintpetersbasilica.org).

○ See the St. Peter's Basilica Tour chapter.

▲**Castel Sant'Angelo**—Built as a tomb for the emperor, used through the Middle Ages as a castle, prison, and place of last ref-

uge for popes under attack, and today a museum, this giant pile of ancient bricks is packed with history.

Ancient Rome allowed no tombs—not even the emperor's—within its walls. So Emperor Hadrian grabbed the most commanding position just outside the walls and across the river and built a towering tomb (c. A.D. 139) well within view of the city. His mausoleum was a huge cylinder (210 by 70 feet) topped by a cypress grove and crowned by a huge statue of Hadrian himself riding a chariot. For nearly a hundred years, Roman emperors (from Hadrian to Caracalla, in A.D. 217) were buried here.

In the year 590, the archangel Michael appeared above the mausoleum to Pope Gregory the Great. Sheathing his sword, the angel signaled the end of a plague. The fortress that was Hadrian's mausoleum eventually became a fortified palace, renamed for the "holy angel."

Castel Sant'Angelo spent centuries of the Dark Ages as a fortress and prison, but was eventually connected to the Vatican via an elevated corridor at the pope's request (1277). Since Rome was repeatedly plundered by invaders, Castel Sant'Angelo was a handy place of last refuge for threatened popes. In anticipation of long sieges, rooms were decorated with papal splendor (you'll see paintings by Carlo Crivelli, Luca Signorelli, and Andrea Mantegna). In 1527, during a sack of Rome by troops of Charles V of Spain, the pope lived inside the castle for months with his entourage of hundreds (an unimaginable ordeal, considering the food service at the top-floor bar).

Touring the place is a stair-stepping workout. After you walk around the entire base of the castle, take the small staircase down to the original Roman floor (following the route of Hadrian's funeral procession). In the atrium, study the model of the mausoleum as it was in Roman times. Imagine being surrounded by a veneer of marble, and the niche in the wall filled with a towering "welcome to my tomb" statue of Hadrian. From here, a ramp leads to the right, spiraling 400 feet. While some of the fine original brickwork and bits of mosaic survive, the marble veneer is long gone (notice the holes in the wall that held it in place). At the end of the ramp, a bridge crosses over the room where the ashes of the emperors were kept. From here, the stairs continue out of the ancient section and into the medieval structure (built atop the mausoleum) that housed the papal apartments. Don't miss the Sala del Tesoro (Treasury), where the wealth of the Vatican was locked up in a huge chest. (*Do* miss the 58 rooms of the military museum.) From the pope's piggy bank, a narrow flight of stairs leads to the rooftop and perhaps the finest view of Rome anywhere (pick out landmarks as you stroll around). From the safety of this dramatic vantage point, the pope surveyed the city in times of siege. Look down at the bend of the Tiber, which for 2,700 years has cradled the Eternal City.

Cost, Hours, Location: €5, more for special exhibits, Tue–Sun 9:00–19:30, closed Mon, last entry one hour before closing, near Vatican City, Metro: Lepanto or bus #64, tel. 06-681-9111.

Ponte Sant'Angelo—The bridge leading to Castel Sant'Angelo was built by Hadrian for quick and regal access from downtown

to his tomb. The three middle arches are actually Roman originals, and a fine example of the empire's engineering expertise. The statues of angels (each bearing a symbol of the passion of Christ—nail, sponge, shroud, and so on) are Bernini-designed and textbook Baroque. In the Middle Ages, this was the only bridge in the area that connected St. Peter's and the Vatican with downtown Rome. Nearly all pilgrims passed this bridge to and from the church. Its shoulder-high banisters recall a tragedy: During a Jubilee Year festival in 1450, the crowd got so huge that the mob pushed out the original banisters, causing nearly 200 to fall to their deaths.

Today, as through the ages, pilgrims cross the bridge, turn left, and set their sights on the Vatican dome. Around the year 1600, they would have also set their sights on a bunch of heads hanging from the crenellations of the castle. Ponte Sant'Angelo was infamous as a place for beheadings (banditry in the countryside was

rife). Locals said, "There are more heads at Castel Sant'Angelo than there are melons in the market."

Trastevere

Trastevere is the colorful neighborhood across *(tras)* the Tiber *(Tevere)* River. Trastevere (trahs-TAY-veh-ray) offers the best look

at medieval-village Rome. The action unwinds to the chime of the church bells. Go there and wander. Wonder. Be a poet. This is Rome's Left Bank. For a self-guided tour, ❏ see the Trastevere Walk chapter.

This proud neighborhood was long a working-class area. Now that it's becoming trendy, high rents are driving out the source of so much color. Still, it's a great people scene, especially at night. Stroll the back streets (for restaurant recommendations, see the Eating chapter).

To reach Trastevere by foot from Capitol Hill, cross the Tiber on Ponte Cestio (over Isola Tiberina). You can also take tram #8 from Largo Argentina, or bus #H from Termini and Via Nazionale (get off at Piazza Belli). From the Vatican (Piazza Risorgimento), it's bus #23 or #271.

Linking Trastevere with the Night Walk Across Rome: You can walk from Trastevere to Campo de' Fiori to link up with the beginning of the Night Walk Across Rome (see chapter of same name): From Trastevere's church square (Piazza di Santa Maria), take Via del Moro to the river and cross at Ponte Sisto, a pedestrian bridge that has a good view of St. Peter's dome. Continue straight ahead for one block. Take the first left, which leads down Via di Capo di Ferro through the scary and narrow darkness to Piazza Farnese, with the imposing Palazzo Farnese. Michelangelo contributed to the facade of this palace, now the French Embassy. The fountains on the square feature huge one-piece granite hot tubs from the ancient Roman Baths of Caracalla. One block from there (opposite the palace) is the atmospheric square, Campo de' Fiori.

▲**Santa Maria in Trastevere Church**—One of Rome's oldest churches, this was made a basilica in the fourth century, when

Christianity was legalized (free, daily 7:30–21:00). It was the first church dedicated to the Virgin Mary. Its portico (covered area just outside the door) is decorated with fascinating fragments of stone—many of them lids from catacomb burial niches—and filled with early Christian symbolism. The church is on Piazza di Santa Maria. While today's fountain is from the 17th century, there has been a fountain here since Roman times.

▲**Villa Farnesina**—Here's a unique opportunity to see a sumptuous Renaissance villa in Rome decorated with Raphael paintings.

It was built in the early 1500s for the richest man in Renaissance Europe, Siennese banker Agostino Chigi. Architect Baldassare Peruzzi's design—a U-shaped building with wings enfolding what used to be a vast garden—successfully blended architecture and nature in a way that both ancient and Renaissance

Romans loved. Orchards and flower beds flowed down in terraces from the palace to the riverbanks. Later construction of modern embankments and avenues robbed the garden of its grandeur, leaving it with a more melancholy charm.

Kings and popes of the day depended on generous loans from Agostino Chigi, whose bank had more than 100 branches in places as far-flung as London and Cairo. This villa was the meeting place of aristocrats, artists, beautiful women, and philosophers.

Cost, Hours, Location: €5; April–June and mid-Sept–Oct Mon–Sat 9:00–16:00, closed Sun; July–mid-Sept and Nov–March Mon–Sat 9:00–13:00, closed Sun; across the river from Campo de' Fiori, a short walk from Ponte Sisto on Via della Lungara, tel. 06-6802-7268.

⊙ **Self-Guided Tour:** Enjoy the best bits of the villa with this commentary.

• *Begin in Room 1.*

Loggia of Galatea: Note the ceiling painted by Peruzzi,

showing the position of the signs of the horoscope at the exact moment of Agostino's birth (21:30, November 29, 1466). The room's claim to fame is Raphael's painting of the nymph Galatea (on the wall by the entrance door). She shuns the doting atten- tion of the ungainly one-eyed giant Polyphemus (in the niche to the left, painted by another artist) and speeds away in the company of her rambunc- tious entourage on a chariot led by dolphins. She turns back and looks

up, amused by the cyclops' crude love song (which, I believe, was "I Only Have Eye for You"). The trigger-happy cupids and lusty, entwined fauns and nymphs announce the pagan spirit revived in Renaissance Rome. All the painting's lines of sight (especially the cupids' arrows) point to the center of the work, Galatea's radiant face. Galatea is considered Raphael's vision of female perfection— not a portrait of an individual woman, but a composite of his many lovers in an idealized vision.

• *Continue into Room 2.*

Loggia of Psyche: This room was painted by Raphael and his assistants. Imagine it without the glass windows, as a continua-

tion of the garden outside, where plays were performed to entertain Agostino's guests. Raphael's two ceiling frescoes were painted to look like tapestries (complete with ruffled edges), suspended from the ceiling by garlands, making the room appear to be an open bower. View the frescoes from the top, with your back to the garden.

The ceiling shows episodes in the myth of a lovely mortal woman, Psyche, who caught the eye of the winged boy-god Cupid (Eros). See the loving couple at the far left end, at the base of the ceil- ing. The big ceiling fresco on the left depicts the gods of Olympus gathered to plan a series of ordeals to test whether Psyche is wor- thy to marry a god. (Find Hercules with white beard and club, and Dionysius pouring the wine.) The other shows the happy ending, as Cupid (boy with wings) and Psyche (to his left, in topless robe) stand before Zeus to celebrate their wedding feast attended by the pantheon of gods.

The whole setting—the room by the gardens, the subject of the frescoes, the fleshy bodies—has an erotic subtext. At the

SIGHTS

time, Raphael was having a passionate affair with the celebrated Fornarina (the "baker's daughter," who lived down the street). Agostino, noticing that his painter was constantly interrupting his workday to be with her, had the girl kidnapped so that Raphael would finally concentrate. But production slowed even more, as Raphael was depressed. Agostino gave up and had the Fornarina move in with Raphael to keep him company as he happily resumed work in this cheery room. The room's imagery abounds with images both phallic and yonic (the female counterpart of phallic). Next to the ripe and split-open cantaloupe (right end, base of ceiling), find the gourd wearing a condom.

• Upstairs, accessed from the stairway near the entrance, is the...

Room of the Perspectives: Peruzzi, another trendsetter, painted this room. Walls seem to open onto views and perspectives that actually correspond with what lies outside. The insulting-to-Catholics graffiti (for example, on the wall at the far end) date from 1527, when Protestant mercenaries sent by Charles V sacked the city.

Agostino had his wedding banquet in this room. His parties were the talk of the town. On one occasion, he invited his guests in the (now lost) dining loggia overlooking the Tiber to toss the gold and silver dishes they had just used into the river. (The banker had nets conveniently placed just below the river's surface.)

The small chamber at the end of the Room of the Perspectives was the **bedroom.** The painting on the wall depicts the wedding of Alexander the Great and Roxanne. Roxanne has the features of Agostino's bride, and the bed is the jewel-encrusted ebony bed that received Agostino and his bride here in this room. On the entrance wall, find the three-arched ruins of the Basilica of Constantine in the Forum.

The room was painted by Il Sodoma, a devoted fan of Michelangelo and one of the artists who was canned when Raphael took over the decoration of the papal apartments at the Vatican. Had that not happened, the Raphael Rooms at the Vatican might have looked like this.

Agostino had famous affairs with the most beautiful courtesans of his day. He eventually settled down, but his wild-living descendants didn't, and—in the space of a couple of generations—the Chigi family lost its fabulous fortune.

Gianicolo Hill Viewpoint—From this park atop a hill, the city views are superb, and the walk to the top holds a treat for architecture buffs. Start at Trastevere's Piazza di San Cosimato, and follow

Via Luciano Manara to Via Garibaldi, at the base of the hill. Via Garibaldi winds its way up the side of the hill to the church of San Pietro in Montorio. To the right of the church, in a small court-yard, is the Tempietto by Donato Bramante. This tiny church, built to commemorate the martyrdom of St. Peter, is considered a jewel of Italian Renaissance architecture.

Continuing up the hill, Via Garibaldi connects to Passeggiata del Gianicolo. From here, you'll find a pleasant park with pan-oramic city views. Ponder the many Victorian-era statues, includ-ing that of baby-carrying, gun-wielding, horse-riding Anita Garibaldi. She was the Brazilian wife of the revolutionary General Giuseppe Garibaldi, who helped forge a united Italy in the late 19th century.

Near Trastevere: Jewish Quarter

From the 16th through the 19th centuries, Rome's Jewish popula-tion was forced to live in a cramped ghetto at an often-flooded bend of the Tiber River. While the medieval Jewish ghetto is long gone, this area—just across the river and toward Capitol Hill from Trastevere—is still home to Rome's synagogue and fragments of its Jewish heritage.

 ✪ See the Jewish Ghetto Walk chapter.

Synagogue (Sinagoga) and Jewish Museum (Museo Ebraico)—Rome's modern synagogue stands proudly on the spot where the medieval Jewish community lived in squalor for more than 300 years. The site of a historic visit by Pope John Paul II, this synagogue features a fine interior and a museum filled with artifacts of Rome's Jewish community. Modest dress is required. The only way to visit the synagogue—un-less you're here for daily prayer service—is with a tour (€7.50 ticket includes museum and guided hourly tour of synagogue; June–Sept Sun–Thu 10:00–19:00, Fri 10:00–16:00, closed Sat; Oct–May Sun–Thu 10:00–17:00, Fri 9:00–14:00, closed Sat; last entry 45 minutes before closing, English tours usu-ally at :15 past the hour, 30 minutes, check schedule at ticket counter; on Lungotevere dei Cenci, tel. 06-6840-0661, www .museoebraico.roma.it). Walking tours of the Jewish Ghetto are conducted at least once a day except Saturday (€8, usually at 13:15, sign up at museum 30 minutes before departure, mini-mum of 3 required).

South Rome

The area south of the center contains some interesting but widely scattered areas. See the color map of South Rome at the beginning of this book.

Testaccio

In the gritty Testaccio neighborhood, several fascinating but lesser sights cluster at the Piramide Metro stop between the Colosseum and E.U.R. (This is a quick and easy stop as you return from E.U.R., or when changing trains en route to Ostia Antica.)

Working-class since ancient times, the Testaccio neighborhood has recently gone trendy-bohemian. Visitors wander through an awkward mix of yuppie and proletarian worlds, not noticing—but perhaps sensing—the "Keep Testaccio for the Testaccians" graffiti.

Pyramid of Gaius Cestius—An Egyptian-style pyramid from ancient Rome stands next to the Piramide Metro stop. The Mark Antony/Cleopatra scandal (c. 30 B.C.) brought exotic Egyptian styles into vogue. A rich Roman magistrate, Gaius Cestius, had this pyramid built as his tomb, complete with a burial chamber inside. Made of brick covered in marble, the 90-foot structure was completed in just 330 days (as stated in its Latin inscription). While smaller than actual Egyptian pyramids, its proportions are correct. It was later incorporated into the Aurelian Wall, and it now stands as a marker to the entrance of Testaccio.

Porta Ostiense and Museo della Via Ostiense—This formidable gate (also next to the Piramide Metro stop) is from the Aurelian Wall, begun in the third century under Emperor Aurelian. The wall, which encircled the city, was 12 miles long and averaged about 26 feet high, with 14 main gates and 380 72-foot-tall towers. Most of what you'll see today is circa A.D. 400, but the barbarians reconstructed the gate later, in the sixth century.

Inside the gate is a tiny free museum (find entrance near pyramid; open Tue–Sat and first Sun of month 9:00–13:30, closed Mon and most Sun). The museum offers a free ramble along the ramparts, plus exhibits on Ostia Antica, Rome's ancient port (for more information, see the Ostia Antica Day Trip chapter). You'll see models of the ancient city and its famed hexagonal harbor, and of the Ostian Way—the straight Roman road that paralleled the curvy Tiber for 15 miles from Rome to the sea.

For more on the Aurelian Wall, visit the San Sebastiano Gate and Museum of the Walls (described in the Ancient Appian Way Tour chapter).

Protestant Cemetery—The Cemetery for the Burial of Non-Catholic Foreigners (Cimitero Acattolico per gli Stranieri al Testaccio) is a tomb-filled park, running along the wall just beyond

Testaccio

the pyramid. The cemetery is also the only English-style landscape (rolling hills, calculated vistas) in Rome, and a favorite spot for

quiet picnics and strolls. From the Piramide Metro stop, walk between the pyramid and the Roman gate on Via Persichetti, then go left on Caio Cestio to the gate of the cemetery. If locked, ring the bell to get inside (€2 suggested donation—leave in box by entrance, Mon–Sat 9:00–17:00, Sun 9:00–13:00, last entry 30 minutes before closing, staff at info office can help you find specific graves, www.protestantcemetery.it).

Originally, none of the Protestant epitaphs were allowed to make any mention of heaven. Signs direct visitors to the graves of notable non-Catholics who died in Rome since 1738. Many of the buried were diplomats. And many, such as the poets Percy Shelley (1792–1822) and John Keats (1795–1821), were from the Romantic Age. They came on the Grand Tour and—"captivated by the fatal charms of Rome," as Shelley wrote—never left.

SIGHTS

Keats and Shelley on Mortality

Ponder mortality along with Keats and Shelley, with these quotes from their poetry:

From Keats' "Ode to a Nightingale"
Adieu! adieu! thy plaintive anthem fades
Past the near meadows, over the still stream,
Up the hill-side; and now 'tis buried deep
In the next valley-glades:
Was it a vision, or a waking dream?
Fled is that music:—Do I wake or sleep?

From Shelley's "Adonais: An Elegy on the Death of John Keats"
I weep for Adonais—he is dead!
Oh, weep for Adonais! though our tears
Thaw not the frost which binds so dear a head!
...I am borne darkly, fearfully, afar;
Whilst, burning through the inmost veil of Heaven,
The soul of Adonais, like a star,
Beacons from the abode where the Eternal are.

Head 90 degrees left to find Keats' tomb, in the far corner. Keats died in his twenties, unrecognized. He wanted to be unnamed on a tomb that read, "Young English Poet, 1821. Here lies one whose name was writ in water." (To see Keats' tomb if the cemetery is closed, look through the tiny peephole on Via Caio Cestio, 10 yards off Via Marmarata.) Shelley's tomb is straight ahead from the entrance, up the hill, at the base of the stubby tower.

There are cats everywhere. At the pyramid, look down and to the right to find Matilde Talli's cat hospice. Volunteers use donations to care for these "Guardians of the Departed" who "provide loyal companionship to these dead," and who even have their own website (as posters nearby explain).

Across the big street from the cemetery, notice the beige travertine post office from 1932. This is textbook Mussolini-era fascist architecture. The huge X design on the stairwells celebrates the 10th anniversary of the dictator's reign.

Monte Testaccio—This small hill is a popular nightlife spot near the Protestant Cemetery (as you leave the cemetery, turn left and continue two blocks down Caio Cestio). The hill, actually a 115-foot-tall ancient trash pile, is made of broken *testae*—earthenware jars mostly used to haul oil 2,000 years ago, when this was a gritty port warehouse district. For 500 years, rancid oil vessels were discarded here. Slowly, Rome's lowly eighth hill was built. Because the caves dug into the hill stay cool, trendy bars, clubs, and restaurants compete with gritty car-repair places for a spot. The neighborhood was once known for a huge slaughterhouse and a Roma (Gypsy) camp that squatted inside an old military base. Now it's home to the Testaccio Village, a site for concerts and techno raves. To do the full monty, arrive after 21:00, when the restaurant-and-club scene is youthful and lively (Metro: Piramide).

Testaccio Market and Neighborhood—The covered Mercato di Testaccio (on Piazza Testaccio, two blocks west of Via Marmarata) dominates the center of the neighborhood. This is hands-down the best, most authentic food market in Rome (Mon–Sat until 13:00). It's where Romans shop while tourists flock to Campo de' Fiori. High-end shoe and clothing boutiques have moved into the market and the neighborhood nearby, and this is now one of the best areas in Rome to have shoes custom-made. Testaccio has long been the neighborhood of slaughterhouses, and its restaurants are renowned for their ability to cook up the least palatable part of the animals...the "fifth quarter."

South of Testaccio

▲Montemartini Museum (Musei Capitolini Centrale Montemartini)—This museum houses a dreamy collection of 400 ancient statues, set evocatively in a classic 1932 electric power plant, among generators and *Metropolis*-type cast-iron machinery. While the art is not as famous as the collections you'll see downtown, the effect is fun and memorable—and you'll encounter absolutely no tourists (€4.50, often €6.50–9 with special exhibits, €8.50–13 combo-ticket with Capitoline Museums, Tue–Sun 9:00–19:00, closed Mon, last entry 30 minutes before closing, Via Ostiense 106, a short walk from Metro: Garbatella, tel. 06-574-8042, www.centralemontemartini.org). If you're tackling Rome with kids, this museum is ideal: it's uncrowded and cool, immersed in an old power plant, with art placed at kid-level.

▲St. Paul's Outside the Walls (Basilica San Paolo Fuori le Mura)—This was the last major construction project of Imperial Rome (c. A.D. 380) and the largest church in Christendom until St. Peter's.

Cost, Hours, Location: Free, daily 7:00–18:30, modest dress code enforced, dry audioguide €5 plus ID, Via Ostiense 186, Metro: San Paolo, exit the Metro station and look for the church's round tower, www.basilicasanpaolo.org.

⊃ Self-Guided Tour: After a tragic 19th-century fire, St. Paul's was rebuilt in the same general style and size as the original. The column-lined courtyard leading up to the church is typical of early Christian churches—the first version of St. Peter's Basilica also had this kind of welcoming zone.

Step inside and feel as close as you'll get in the 21st century to experiencing a monumental Roman basilica. Marvel at the ceiling, and imagine building it with those massive wood beams in A.D. 380.

Alabaster windows light the vast interior. It feels sterile, but in a good way—like you're already in heaven. Along with St. Peter's Basilica, San Giovanni in Laterano, and Santa Maria Maggiore, this church is part of the Vatican rather than Italy. The triumphal arch leading to the altar has a fifth-century mosaic of Christ raising his hand in blessing. He's flanked by the four evangelists (in symbolic animal guise) and, in white, the mysterious 24 elders of the Apocalypse. At the bottom of the arch are the two early followers of Jesus who, according to tradition, came to Rome to spread the Gospel, and ended up dying for it: St. Peter (right) carries the keys to the kingdom of heaven, and St. Paul holds a sword symbolizing the piercing truth. Over the altar is a multicolored marble canopy (13th century). A 20-foot-tall Easter candlestick (c. 1170) stands to the right.

The church is built upon the supposed grave of St. Paul. According to tradition, Paul was decapitated two miles from this spot. His head was preserved at San Giovanni in Laterano, and his body was buried here under the altar. In 2006, archaeologists unearthed a sarcophagus which had early inscriptions identifying it as Paul's. Today, you can descend a few steps in front of the altar to see the exposed end of Paul's supposed stone coffin, and look down through the glass floor to see the remains of the earlier basilica.

Ringing the upper part of the church are round mosaic portraits of 265 popes, from St. Peter (the first one in the right transept) to the present. Find the recent popes to the right of the altar—not in the nave, but farther to the right, under the arches of the dim

SIGHTS

South of Testaccio

TO CIRCUS MAXIMUS & BATHS OF CARACALLA

SEE TESTACCIO Detail

TIBER

PORTA OSTIENSE & MUSEUM

ANCIENT CITY WALL

PYRAMID

MONTE TESTACCIO

PROT. CEM.

M PIRAMIDE

PORTA SAN PAOLO TRAIN STN. (TRAINS TO OSTIA ANTICA)

OSTIENSE STATION

TO TERMINI STATION

MERCATO CENTRALE

M GARBATELLA

MONTEMARTINI MUSEUM

VIA OSTIENSE

N

400 YARDS

400 METERS

St. PAUL'S OUTSIDE THE WALLS

VIALE F. BALDELLI

M SAN PAOLO

M ━━━━ METRO

━━ OTHER TRAIN LINES

TO OSTIA ANTICA BY ROAD

TO E.U.R. BY METRO

DCH

SIGHTS

right aisle. You'll see globetrotting John Paul II *(Jo Paulus II)* and progressive John XXIII, who oversaw the Vatican II changes of the 1960s. A portrait of Pope #265—Benedict XVI—was recently installed, alongside blank medallions for future popes.

The peaceful 13th-century cloister (€3) has elegant Romanesque columns and arches, and fragments of early Christian/Roman sarcophagi.

E.U.R.

In the late 1930s, Italy's dictator, Benito Mussolini, planned an international exhibition to show off the wonders of his fascist society. But these wonders brought us World War II, and Il Duce's celebration never happened. The unfinished mega-project was completed in the 1950s, and today it houses government offices and big, obscure museums filled with important, rarely visited relics.

If Hitler and Mussolini had won the war, our world might look like E.U.R. (AY-oor). Hike down E.U.R.'s wide, pedestrian-mean boulevards. Patriotic murals, aren't-you-proud-to-be-an-extreme-right-winger pillars, and stern squares decorate the soulless planned grid and stark office blocks. Boulevards named for Astronomy, Electronics, Social Security, and Beethoven are more exhausting than inspirational. Today, E.U.R. is worth a trip for its Museum of Roman Civilization (described below). And because a few landmark buildings of Italian modernism are located here and there, E.U.R. has become an important destination for architecture buffs.

The Metro skirts E.U.R. with three stops (10 minutes from the Colosseum). Use E.U.R. Magliana for the "Square Colosseum" and E.U.R. Fermi for the Museum of Roman Civilization. Consider walking 30 minutes from the palace to the museum through the center of E.U.R.

Palace of the Civilization of Labor (Palazzo della Civiltà del Lavoro)—From the Magliana Metro stop, stairs lead uphill to this epitome of fascist architecture. With its giant no-questions-asked patriotic statues and its black-and-white simplicity, this is E.U.R.'s tallest building and key landmark. It's understandably nicknamed the "Square Colosseum." Around the corner, Caffè Palombini is still decorated in a 1930s style and is quite popular with young Romans (daily 7:00–22:00; good gelato, pastries, and snacks; Piazzale Adenauer 12, tel. 06-591-1700).

▲**Museum of Roman Civilization (Museo della Civiltà Romana)**—With 59 rooms of plaster casts and models illustrating the greatness of classical Rome, this vast and heavy museum gives a strangely lifeless, close-up look at Rome. Each room has a theme, from military tricks to musical instruments. One long hall is filled with casts of the reliefs of Trajan's Column. The highlight is the 1:250-scale model of Constantine's Rome, circa A.D. 300. The Planetarium and

Astrological Museum are mostly of interest to children—so don't bother with the €8.50 combo-ticket unless you have kids (€6.50, sometimes €9 with special exhibits, Tue–Sat 9:00–14:00, Sun 9:00–13:30, closed Mon, last entry one hour before closing, Piazza G. Agnelli; leave the E.U.R. Fermi Metro station on Via America, head toward McDonald's, and at T-intersection, turn left and go uphill three blocks to Via dell'Arte—you'll see its colonnade on the right; to return to the city center, access the Metro entrance across the street, tel. 06-5422-0919, www.museociviltaromana.it).

Ancient Appian Way and Southeast Rome

Most of these sights are covered in greater detail in the ✪ Ancient Appian Way Tour chapter.

Baths of Caracalla (Terme di Caracalla)—Inaugurated by Emperor Caracalla in A.D. 216, this massive bath complex could accommodate 1,600 visitors at a time. Today it's just a shell—a

Mussolini and Imperial Rome

Benito Mussolini incorporated much from ancient Rome during his dictatorship. His military was organized according to Roman terminology (divided into legions and run by centurions and consuls). The salute with the right arm raised, flat palm down (later used by the Nazis), was also Roman. More hygienic and quicker than a handshake, it fit the dynamic character of fascism.

While the classical values of power and discipline were stressed in the rhythmic march of military parades, convincing the Italians of the need for order was a challenge even to Mussolini. He claimed it wasn't impossible to govern the Italian people...just useless.

Mussolini's title, Il Duce, was from the Latin *dux*—a generic term for leader. When chanted by crowds and carved onto monuments, it likely fueled Mussolini's belief that he was carrying out extraordinary historical missions like Caesar and Augustus before him.

For his fascist symbol, rather than the she-wolf or eagle, Mussolini used the *lictor's fasces*—an ax belonging to a Roman officer, with rods tied around the handle, carried in front of magistrates as a sign of authority. This was aimed at destroying the popular image of Italy as a joyous, carefree country and for promoting a new image of austerity and order. In ancient times, the ax stood for decapitation, the rods for flogging.

Fascist architecture, like ancient architecture, used a monumental scale, with arches, bold statues, and rhetorical inscriptions—resulting in an austere and impersonal feel that's generally disliked by Romans today.

In spite of his supposed passion for ancient Rome, Mussolini had a dreadful approach to archaeology. He would isolate a major monument and destroy everything around it. Sections of the Imperial Forums were sacrificed to build the wide street, Via dei Fori Imperiali, from Piazza Venezia to the Colosseum. A famous fountain by the Colosseum that had survived almost 2,000 years was torn down without another thought.

huge shell—with all of its sculptures and most of its mosaics moved to museums. You'll see a two-story roofless brick building surrounded by a garden, bordered by ruined walls. The two large rooms at either end of the building were used for exercise. In between the exercise rooms was a pool flanked by two small mosaic-floored dressing rooms. Niches in the walls once held statues.

In its day, this was a remarkable place to hang out. For ancient Romans, bathing was a social experience. The Baths of Caracalla functioned until Goths severed the aqueducts in the sixth century. In modern times, grand operas are performed here (€6; Tue–Sun 9:00 until one hour before sunset: 19:00 in summer, 16:30 in winter; Mon 9:00–14:00, last entry one hour before closing, audioguide-€4, free downloadable audio tour at www .pierreci.it—choose English and search for "terme di caracalla," good €8 guidebook can be read in shaded garden while sitting on a chunk of column; Metro: Circus Maximus, plus a 5-minute walk south along Via delle Terme di Caracalla; bus #714 from Termini Station or bus #118 from the Appian Way—see the end of the Ancient Appian Way Tour; tel. 06-3996-7700). The baths' statues are displayed elsewhere: for example, the immense *Toro Farnese* (a marble sculpture of a bull surrounded by people) snorts in Naples' Archaeological Museum.

▲**Appian Way**—For a taste of the countryside around Rome and more wonders of Roman engineering, take the four-mile trip from

the Colosseum out past the wall to a stretch of the ancient Appian Way, where the original pavement stones are lined by several interesting sights. Ancient Rome's first and greatest highway, the Appian Way once ran from Rome to the Adriatic port of Brindisi, the gateway to Greece. Today you can walk (or bike) some stretches of the road, rattling over original paving stones, past crumbling monuments that once lined the sides. The Tomb of Cecilia Metella and the Circus of Maxentius are the two most impressive pagan sights. Just a few hundred yards away are two major Christian catacombs (briefly described below); of the two catacombs, which is the best to visit? All in all, they're both quite similar, and either one will fit the bill.

For more on all of these sights, ✪ see the Ancient Appian Way Tour chapter.

▲▲**Catacombs of San Sebastiano**—A guide leads you underground through the tunnels where early Christians were buried. You'll see faded frescoes and graffiti by early-Christian tag artists. Besides the catacombs themselves, there's a historic fourth-century basilica with holy relics (€8, includes 25-minute tour, 2/hour, Mon–Sat 9:00–12:00 & 14:00–17:00, last tour leaves at 17:00, closed Sun and mid-Nov–mid-Dec, Via Appia Antica 136, tel. 06-785-0350, www.catacombe.org).

▲▲**Catacombs of San Callisto**—The larger of the two sets of catacombs, San Callisto also is the more prestigious, having been the burial site for several early popes (€8, includes 30-minute tour, at least 2/hour, Thu–Tue 9:00–12:00 & 14:00–17:00, closed Wed and Feb, Via Appia Antica 110, tel. 06-5130-1580 or 06-513-0151, www.catacombe.roma.it).

COLOSSEUM TOUR

Colosseo

Rome has many layers—modern, Baroque, Renaissance, Christian. But let's face it: "Rome" is Caesars, gladiators, chariots, centurions, *"Et tu, Brute,"* trumpet fanfares, and thumbs-up or thumbs-down. That's the Rome we'll look at. Our "Caesar Shuffle" begins with the downtown core of ancient Rome, the Colosseum. A logical next stop is the Roman Forum, just next door (and the next chapter).

Orientation

Cost: €12 combo-ticket also includes Roman Forum and Palatine Hill; ticket valid two consecutive days—one entry per sight; also covered by the Roma Pass.

Hours: The Colosseum, Roman Forum, and Palatine Hill are all open daily 8:30 until one hour before sunset: April–Sept until 19:15, Oct until 18:30, off-season closes as early as 16:30; last entry one hour before closing.

Getting There: The Colosseo Metro stop on line B is just across the street from the monument. Bus #60 is handy for hotels near Via Firenze and Via Nazionale. Bus #87 links Largo Argentina with the Colosseum.

Avoiding Lines: The lines in front of the Colosseum are for buying tickets and for security checks, not for actually entering the sight. Everyone has to wait in the security line to go through the metal detectors first, but once you're through that—if you have your ticket or pass already—stay to the left and muscle your way past the ticket-buying crowd to go directly to the turnstile, which never has a line. Enter by inserting your ticket in the turnstile or flashing your pass. You'll likely save lots of time if you get your ticket or pass in advance using one of these alternatives:

1. If you're planning on getting a €25 Roma Pass, buy it at a less-crowded place to bypass the ticket-buying line at the Colosseum. You can purchase the pass at the *tabacchi* shop in the Colosseo Metro station, or at the entrance to Palatine Hill on Via di San Gregorio (facing the Forum, with Colosseum at your back, go left down the street). Avoid buying it at the Forum, which also tends to have lines.

2. If you're buying a combo-ticket, get it at the less-crowded Palatine Hill entrance. Or buy and print it online in advance at www.ticketclic.it (€1.50 booking fee, good for two consecutive days, not changeable). Note that the "free tickets" you'll see listed are valid only for EU citizens with ID.

3. Pay to join an official guided tour (€4 plus €12 combo-ticket, see "Tours," later). Once past the security check, tell one of the guards that you want to purchase a guided tour and he will usher you toward the ticket booth marked *Visite Guidate* (you'll also pay for your ticket here).

Private walking-tour guides (or their American assistants) linger outside the Colosseum, offering tours that include the admission fee and allow you to skip the line. This will cost you a few extra euros (€22 for two-hour tours of the Colosseum, Palatine Hill, and Forum, including the €12 ticket), but can save time; however, see the warning below.

Warnings: It can be hard to judge the length of the ticket line because it's tucked into the Colosseum arcade. Unscrupulous private guides tell tourists that there's a long line, when there really might be no line at all. If you do sign up with a private guide, confirm that your tour will start right away, and look at your ticket to make sure that it includes admission to Palatine Hill and Forum (some guides, claiming to cover all three sights, will purchase a group Colosseum-only ticket, then say "ciao" after the Colosseum tour).

Also beware of the **greedy gladiators.** For a fee, the incredibly crude modern-day gladiators snuff out their cigarettes and pose for photos. They take easy-to-swindle tourists for too much money. Watch out if you tangle with these guys (they're accustomed to getting as much as €100 from naive tourists). If you go for it, €4–5 for one photo usually keeps them appeased.

And finally, look out for **pickpockets.** The Colosseum's exterior is traditionally a happy hunting ground for pickpockets and con artists.

Information: Tel. 06-3996-7700.

Tours: A dry but fact-filled **audioguide** is available just past the turnstiles (€4.50 for 2 hours of use). A handheld **videoguide** senses where you are in the site and plays related video clips (€5.50, pick up after turnstiles). Guided **tours** in English (which let you skip the ticket line) depart nearly hourly between 10:00 and 17:00, and last 45 minutes to one hour (€4 plus your €12 ticket, purchase inside the Colosseum near the ticket booth marked *Visite Guidate*). My self-guided Colosseum **audio tour** is free to download to an iPod or other MP3 player (at www.ricksteves.com or search for "Rick Steves Audio Tours" in iTunes).

Length of This Tour: Allow an hour.

Services: For tips on where to eat, drink, and find a WC in the area, see the sidebar on the next page.

The Tour Begins

Exterior

• *View the Colosseum from the Forum fence, across the street from the Colosseo Metro station.*

Built when the Roman Empire was at its peak in A.D. 80, the Colosseum represents Rome at its grandest. The Flavian Amphitheater (the Colosseum's real name) was an arena for gladiator contests and public spectacles. When killing became a spectator sport, the Romans wanted to share the fun with as many people as possible, so they stuck two semicircular theaters together to create a freestanding amphitheater. The outside (where slender cypress trees stand today) was decorated with a 100-foot-tall bronze statue of Nero that gleamed in the sunlight. In a later age, the colossal structure was nicknamed a "coloss-eum," the wonder of its age. It could accommodate 50,000 roaring fans (100,000 thumbs).

The Romans pioneered the use of concrete and the rounded arch, which enabled them to build on this tremendous scale. The exterior is a skeleton of 3.5 million cubic feet of travertine stone. (Each of the pillars flanking the ground-level arches weighs five tons.) It took 200 ox-drawn wagons shuttling back and forth every day for four years just to bring the stone here from Tivoli. They stacked stone blocks (without mortar) into the shape of an arch, supported temporarily by wooden scaffolding. Finally, they wedged a keystone into the top of the arch—it not only kept the arch from falling, it could bear even more weight above. Iron pegs held the larger stones together—notice the small holes that pockmark the sides.

The exterior says a lot about the Romans. They were great engineers, not artists, and the building is more functional than beautiful. (If ancient Romans visited the US today as tourists, they might send home postcards of our greatest works of "art"—freeways.) While the essential structure of the Colosseum is Roman, the four-story facade is decorated with mostly Greek columns—Doric-like Tuscan columns on the ground level, Ionic on the second story, Corinthian on the next level, and at the top, half-columns with a mix of all three. Originally, copies of Greek statues stood in the arches of the middle two stories, giving a veneer of sophistication to this arena of death.

Only a third of the original Colosseum remains. Earthquakes destroyed some of it, but most was carted off as easy pre-cut stones for other buildings during the Middle Ages and Renaissance (see page 100).

• *To enter, first go through the security line. Once past security, queue up. If you need to buy a ticket, line up along the right. If you already have a ticket or a Roma Pass, get in the fast lane to the left of the ticket line and go directly to the turnstile. To pay for an official tour, bypass the ticket line and head directly to the ticket booth marked* Visite Guidate. *Once past the turnstiles, there may be signs directing you on a specific visitors' route.*

Interior
Entrances and Exits

As you walk through passageways and up staircases, admire the ergonomics. Fans could pour in through ground-floor entrances; there were eight total, including the emperor's private entrance on the north side. Your ticket was a piece of broken pottery marked with entrance, section, row, and seat number. You'd pass by concession stands selling fast food and souvenirs, such as wine glasses with the names of famous gladiators. The hallways leading to the seats were called by the Latin word *vomitorium*. At exit time, the Colosseum would "vomit" out its contents, giving us the English word. It's estimated that all 50,000 fans could enter and exit in 15 minutes.

• *Soon you'll spill out into the arena. Wherever you end up—upstairs or downstairs, at one side of the arena or the other—just take it all in and get oriented. The tallest side of the Colosseum (with the large Christian cross) is the north side. You might notice that the arena is currently undergoing renovation. It's being cleaned from top to bottom and given permanent lighting. This ambitious project may open up new areas previously closed to visitors, including the underground corridors.*

Colosseum

Arena

The games took place in this oval-shaped arena, 280 feet long by 165 feet wide. The ratio of length to width is 5:3, often called the golden ratio. Since the days of the Greek mathematician Pythagoras, artists considered that proportion to be ideal, with almost mystical properties. The Colosseum's architects apparently wanted their structure to embody the perfect 3-by-5 mathematical order they thought existed in nature.

When you look down into the arena, you're seeing the underground passages beneath the playing surface (there are plans to open these up for tours). The arena was originally covered with a wooden floor, then sprinkled with sand (*arena* in Latin). The new bit of reconstructed floor gives you an accurate sense of the original arena level, and the subterranean warren where animals and prisoners were held. As in modern stadiums, the spectators ringed the playing area in bleacher seats that slanted up from the arena floor. Around you are the big brick masses that supported the tiers of seats.

A variety of materials were used to build the stadium. Look around. Big white travertine blocks stacked on top of each other formed the skeleton. The brick pillars for the bleachers were made with a shell of brick, filled in with concrete. Originally the bare brick was covered with marble columns or ornamental facing, so the interior was a brilliant white (they used white plaster for the upper-floor cheap seats).

COLOSSEUM

The Colosseum's seating was strictly segregated. At ringside,

the emperor, senators, Vestal Virgins, and VIPs occupied marble seats with their names carved on them (a few marble seats have been restored, at the east end). The next level up held those of noble birth. The level tourists now occupy was for ordinary free Roman citizens, called plebeians. Up at the very top (a hundred yards from the action), there were once wooden bleachers for the poorest people—foreigners, slaves, and women.

The top story of the Colosseum is mostly ruined—only the north side still retains its high wall. This was not part of the original three-story structure, but was added around A.D. 230 after a fire necessitated repairs. Picture the awning that could be stretched across the top of the stadium by armies of sailors. Strung along horizontal beams that pointed inward to the center, the awning only covered about a third of the arena—so those at the top always enjoyed shade, while many nobles down below roasted in the sun.

Looking into the complex web of passageways beneath the arena, you can imagine how busy the backstage action was. Gladiators strolled down the central passageway, from their warm-up yard on the east end to the arena entrance on the west. Some workers tended wild animals. Others prepared stage sets of trees or fake buildings, allowing the arena to be quickly transformed from an African jungle to a Greek temple. Props and sets were hauled up to arena level on 80 different elevator shafts via a system of ropes and pulleys. (You might be able to make out some small rectangular shafts, especially near the center of the arena.) That means there were 80 different spots from which animals, warriors, and stage sets could pop up and magically appear.

The games began with a few warm-up acts—dogs bloodying themselves attacking porcupines, female gladiators fighting each other, or a dwarf battling a one-legged man. Then came the main event—the gladiators.

"Hail, Caesar! *(Ave, Cesare!)* We who are about to die salute you!" The gladiators would enter the arena from the west end, parade around to the sound of trumpets, acknowledge the Vestal Virgins (on the south side), then stop at the emperor's box (supposedly marked today by the cross that stands at the "50-yard line" on the north side—although no one knows for sure where it was). They would then raise their weapons, shout, and salute—and begin fighting. The fights pitted men against men, men against beasts, and beasts against beasts. Picture 50,000 screaming people around you (did gladiators get stage fright?), and imagine that they want to see you die.

Some gladiators wielded swords, protected only with a shield and a heavy helmet. Others represented fighting fishermen, with a net to snare opponents and a trident to spear them. The gladiators were usually slaves, criminals, or poor people who got their chance for freedom, wealth, and fame in the ring. They learned to

Modern Amenities in the Ancient World

The area around the Colosseum, Forum, and Palatine Hill is rich in history, but pretty barren when it comes to food, shelter, and WCs. Here are a few options:

The Colosseum has a few crowded **WCs** inside, but don't count on them being available. A nice big WC is behind (east of) the structure (facing ticket entrance, go counter clockwise; WC is under stairway). If you can wait, the best WCs in the area are at Palatine Hill—at the Via di San Gregorio entrance, in the museum, or in the Farnese Gardens. The Forum also has one WC at the entrance and another near the Temple of Vesta (#8 on map on page 105).

Because there are limited **eateries** in the area, consider assembling a small picnic. The Colosseo Metro stop has €5 hot sandwiches. Snack stands on street corners sell drinks, sandwiches, fruit, and candy. If you prefer to dine in, you'll find a few restaurants behind the Colosseum (with expansive views of the structure), a few recommended places a block away (no views but better value—see page 354), and a cluster of places near the Forum's main entrance (where Via Cavour spills into Via dei Fori Imperiali).

To refill your **water** bottle, stop at one of the water fountains in the area. You'll find them along a few city streets, as well as inside the Forum and Palatine Hill.

A nice oasis is the free tourist center, **I Fori di Roma,** located near the Forum entrance. It's across Via dei Fori Imperiali and a bit east, toward the Colosseum. It has a small café, a WC, and a few exhibits.

If your sightseeing takes you as far as **Capitol Hill,** you'll find services at the Capitoline Museums, including a nice view café (see page 182).

fight in training schools, then battled their way up the ranks. The best were rewarded like our modern sports stars, with fan clubs, great wealth, and, yes, product endorsements.

The animals came from all over the world: lions, tigers, and bears (oh my!), crocodiles, elephants, and hippos (not to mention exotic human "animals" from the "barbarian" lands). They were kept in cages beneath the arena floor, then lifted up in the elevators. Released at floor level, animals would pop out from behind blinds into the arena—the gladiator didn't know where, when, or by what he'd be attacked. Many a hapless warrior met his death here, and never knew what hit him. (This brought howls of laughter from the hardened fans in the cheap upper seats who had a better view of the action.)

TO TIME ELEVATOR ROMA
VICTOR EMMANUEL MONUMENT
TRAJAN'S COLUMN + FORUM
MUSEUM OF IMPERIAL FORUMS
+ TRAJAN'S MARKET

|||| STAIRS
↓ ENTRANCES TO SIGHTS
M METRO STATION
F FOOD
• WATER FOUNTAIN
WC RESTROOM

CORSO
TO PANTHEON
PLEB.
VIA D'ARA COELI
PIAZZA VENEZIA
BATT.
4 NOV.
CAPITOL HILL
TEATRO MARCELLO
CAPITOLINE MUSEUMS F + WC
MAMERTINE PRISON
EXIT
ROMAN FORUM WC
VIA SAN TEODORO
TIBER
VIA LEONINA
CAVOUR
CAVOUR
TO TERMINI STATION
M
ST. PETER-IN-CHAINS
VIA ANNIBALDI
VIA DEI FORI IMPERIALI
COLOS-SEO
NERO'S GOLDEN HOUSE. (CLOSED)
VIA TERME DI TITO
ARCH OF TITUS
EXIT ❶
M
❶ COLOSSEUM
WC F
ARCH OF CONSTANTINE
PALATINE HILL
WC •
WC
VIA DI SAN GREGORIO
VIA CLAUDIA
S. MARIA COSMEDIN + BOCCA DELLA VERITÀ
CIRCUS
VIA CERCHI
MAXIMUS
WC ❷
TO BATHS OF CARACALLA

200 YARDS
200 METERS

❶ Colosseum Entrance ❸ Forum Entrance
❷ Palatine Hill Entrance ❹ I Fori di Roma Visitors Center

COLOSSEUM

Nets ringed the arena to protect the crowd. The stadium was inaugurated with a 100-day festival in which 2,000 men and 9,000 animals were killed. Colosseum employees squirted perfumes around the stadium to mask the stench of blood.

If a gladiator fell helpless to the ground, his opponent would approach the emperor's box and ask: Should he live or die? Sometimes the emperor left the decision to the crowd, who would judge based on how valiantly the man had fought. They would make their decision—thumbs-up or thumbs-down. Consider the value of these games in placating and controlling the huge Roman populace. Seeing the king of beasts—a lion—slain by a gladiator reminded the masses of man's triumph over nature. Seeing exotic animals from Africa heralded their conquest of distant lands. And having the thumbs-up or thumbs-down authority over another person's life gave them a real sense of power. Imagine the psychological boost the otherwise downtrodden masses felt when the emperor granted them this thrilling decision.

Did they throw Christians to the lions like in the movies? Christians were definitely thrown to the lions, made to fight gladiators, crucified, and burned alive...but probably not here in this particular stadium. Maybe, but probably not.

Rome was a nation of warriors that built an empire by conquest. The battles fought against Germans and other barbarians, Egyptians, and strange animals were played out daily here in the Colosseum for the benefit of city-slicker bureaucrats, who got vicarious thrills by watching brutes battle to the death. The contests were always free, sponsored by the government to bribe the people's favor or to keep Rome's growing masses of unemployed rabble off the streets.

• *With these scenes in mind, wander around, then check out the upper level. There are stairs on both the east and the west sides, as well as an elevator at the east end. The upper deck offers more colossal views of the arena, plus a bookstore and temporary exhibits. Wherever you may Rome, find a spot at the west end of the upper deck, where you can look out over some of the sights nearby. Start with the big, white, triumphal Arch of Constantine.*

Views from the Upper Level
Arch of Constantine

If you are a Christian, were raised a Christian, or simply belong to a so-called "Christian nation," ponder this arch. It marks one

of the great turning points in history—the military coup that made Christianity mainstream. In A.D. 312, Emperor Constantine defeated his rival Maxentius in the crucial Battle of the Milvian Bridge. The night before, he had seen a vision of a cross in the sky. Constantine—whose

mother and sister were Christians—became sole emperor and legalized Christianity. With this one battle, a once-obscure Jewish sect with a handful of followers was now the state religion of the entire Western world. In A.D. 300, you could be killed for being a Christian; a century later, you could be killed for not being one. Church enrollment boomed.

The restored arch is like an ancient museum. It's decorated entirely with recycled carvings originally made for other buildings. By covering it with exquisite carvings of high Roman art—works that glorified previous emperors—Constantine put himself in their league. Hadrian is featured in the round reliefs, with Marcus Aurelius in the square reliefs higher up. The big statues on top are of Trajan and Augustus. Originally, Augustus drove a chariot similar to the one topping the modern Victor Emmanuel II Monument. Fourth-century Rome may have been in decline, but Constantine clung to its glorious past.

Surrounding Hills

Looking southwest, beyond the Arch of Constantine, you see Palatine Hill, dotted with umbrella pines. Next to the Arch of Constantine is the road called the Via Sacra, or Sacred Way, once Rome's main street. It heads west up an incline toward the Arch of Titus (you can just make out its white top from here). That marks the head of the Forum, the religious, political, and commercial heart of ancient Rome (covered in the next chapter).

The Colosseum was built between three of Rome's legendary seven hills—the Palatine (to the southwest), the Esquiline (to the north), and the Caelian (to the south). The Colosseum stands on land where the notorious Emperor Nero once had his sumptuous Golden House, which stretched from the Arch of Titus, across the valley, and up onto Esquiline Hill. After the house was replaced by the Colosseum, Nero's statue (or colossus) became the Colosseum's 100-foot-tall doorman.

• *Looking west, in the direction of the Forum, you'll see some ruins sitting atop a raised, rectangular-shaped hill. (You can recognize the hill by some door-like openings cut into the hill's support wall.) The ruins—consisting of an arched alcove made of brick and backed by a church bell tower—are all that remain of the once great Temple of Venus and Rome.*

The Temple of Venus and Rome

At 100 feet tall, this temple atop a pedestal was one of the most prominent temples in Rome—and also its biggest. The size of a football field, it once covered the entire hill. The style of the temple was Greek—surrounded by white columns and topped with a triangular pediment above the entrance. Today, the perimeter of the complex is still visible, marked by a few massive white columns, six feet thick.

The main ruin in the center—the tall brick arch with a cross-hatched ceiling—was once the *cella*, or sacred chamber of the temple. Here sat two monumental statues, back to back. Venus, the goddess of love, faced the Colosseum. The goddess called Roma Aeterna faced the Forum. Paired together, they symbolized the birth and eternal destiny of the race of people meant to endure forever. The goddesses' Latin names were written in the twin *cella*s. On one side it read "Roma," and on the other "Amor." Roma and Amor—a perfectly symmetrical palindrome, showing how Rome and Love were meant to go together. In ancient times, newlyweds ascended the staircase from the Colosseum (some parts are still visible) to the temple, to ask Venus and Roma Aeterna to bring them good luck. These days, Roman couples get married at the church with the bell tower to ensure themselves love and happiness for eternity.

The temple was designed by Hadrian, the second-century emperor and amateur architect who also designed the Pantheon. Hadrian's design was critiqued by Rome's best-known architect, who complained that the huge statues would be so cramped they'd bump their heads if they stood up. Hadrian listened patiently to the criticism...then had the architect killed.

The Colosseum's Legacy: A.D. 500 to the Present

With the coming of Christianity to Rome, the Colosseum and its deadly games slowly became politically incorrect. However, some gladiator contests continued here sporadically until they were completely banned in A.D. 435. Animal hunts continued a few decades longer. As the Roman Empire dwindled and the infrastructure crumbled, the stadium itself was neglected. Finally, around A.D. 523—after nearly 500 years of games—the last animal was slaughtered, and the Colosseum shut its doors.

For the next thousand years, the structure was inhabited by various squatters. It was used for makeshift apartments or shops, as a church, a cemetery, and as a refuge during invasions and riots. Over time, the Colosseum was eroded by wind, rain, and the strain of gravity. Earthquakes weakened it, and a powerful quake in 1349 toppled the south side.

More than anything, the Colosseum was dismantled by the Roman citizens themselves, who carted off pre-cut stones to be re-used for palaces and churches, including St. Peter's. The marble facing was pulverized into mortar, and 300 tons of iron brackets were pried out and melted down, resulting in the pock-marking you see today.

After centuries of neglect, a series of 16th-century popes took pity on the pagan structure. In memory of the Christians who may (or may not) have been martyred here, they shored up the south and west sides with bricks and placed the big cross on the north side of the arena.

Today, the Colosseum links Rome's glorious past with its vital present. Major political demonstrations begin or end here, providing protestors with an iconic backdrop for the TV cameras. On Good Friday, the pope comes here to lead pilgrims as they follow the Stations of the Cross.

The legend goes that so long as the Colosseum shall stand, the city of Rome shall also stand. For nearly 2,000 years, the Colosseum has been the enduring symbol of Rome, the Eternal City.

• *The Roman Forum is 100 yards to the right of the arch. You can enter it through the Forum entrance on Via dei Fori Imperiali or from the Palatine Hill entrance along Via di San Gregorio—see the map on page 105. (Note that what looks like an entrance gate up Via Sacra is currently exit-only.) If you're ready for a visit, turn to the next chapter.*

COLOSSEUM

ROMAN FORUM TOUR

Foro Romano

The Forum was the political, religious, and commercial center of the city. Rome's most important temples and halls of justice were here. This was the place for religious processions, political demonstrations, elections, important speeches, and parades by conquering generals. As Rome's empire expanded, these few acres of land became the center of the civilized world.

Orientation

Cost: €12 combo-ticket also includes Colosseum and Palatine Hill; ticket valid two consecutive days—one entry per sight; also covered by Roma Pass. To avoid standing in a long ticket-buying line, see tips on "Avoiding Lines" on page 89 of the Colosseum Tour.

Hours: The Roman Forum, Colosseum, and Palatine Hill are all open daily 8:30 until one hour before sunset: April–Sept until 19:15, Oct until 18:30, off-season closes as early as 16:30; last entry one hour before closing.

Tips: The ancient paving at the Forum is uneven; wear sturdy shoes. I carry a water bottle and refill it at the Forum's public drinking fountains.

Getting There: The closest Metro stop is Colosseo. The Forum has two entrances. The main entrance is on Via dei Fori Imperiali ("Road of the Imperial Forums"). From the Colosseum Metro stop, walk away from the Colosseum on Via dei Fori Imperiali to find the low-profile Forum ticket office, located where Via Cavour spills into Via dei Fori Imperiali.

The other entrance is at the Palatine Hill ticket office on Via di San Gregorio—after buying your ticket, take the path to the right (not up the hill), and wind around to enter the

Forum at the Arch of Titus.

Information: A free visitors center (called I Fori di Roma), located across Via dei Fori Imperiali from the Forum's main entrance, has a TI, bookshop, small café, WCs, and a film (daily 9:30–18:30). A bookstore is at the Forum entrance. Vendors at the Forum sell small *Rome: Past and Present* books with plastic overlays that restore the ruins (includes DVD, smaller book marked €15, prices soft, so offer €10). Info office tel. 06-3996-7700.

Tours: An unexciting yet informative **audioguide** helps decipher the rubble (€4, €6 version includes Palatine Hill, must leave ID), but you'll have to return it to one of the Forum entrances instead of being able to exit directly to Capitol Hill or the Colosseum. Official **guided tours** in English run Monday through Friday at around 13:00 (€4, 45 minutes, confirm time at ticket office). You can also download my free self-guided Roman Forum **audio tour** from www.ricksteves.com (or search for "Rick Steves Audio Tours" in iTunes).

Length of This Tour: Allow 1.5 hours.

Services: There's a WC at the main entrance and another in the middle of the Forum, near #8 on the map. For information on food and other WCs in the area, see the sidebar on page 96.

The Tour Begins

• *Start at the Arch of Titus (Arco di Tito). It's the white triumphal arch that rises above the rubble on the east end of the Forum (closest to the Colosseum). Stand at the viewpoint alongside the arch and gaze over the valley known as the Forum.*

Overview

The Forum is a rectangular valley running roughly east (the Colosseum end) to west (Capitol Hill, with its bell tower). The

rocky path at your feet is the Via Sacra. It leads from the Arch of Titus, through the trees, past the large brick Senate building, through the triumphal arch at the far end, and up Capitol Hill. The hill to your left (with all the trees) is Palatine Hill.

Picture being here when a conquering general returned to Rome with crates of booty. The valley was full of gleaming white buildings topped with bronze roofs. The Via Sacra—Main Street of the Forum—would be lined with citizens waving branches and carrying torches. The trumpets would sound as the parade began. First came porters, carrying chests full of gold and jewels. Then a parade of exotic animals from the conquered lands—elephants, giraffes, hippopotamuses—for the crowd to "ooh" and "ahh" at. Next came the prisoners in chains, with the captive king on a

wheeled platform so the people could jeer and spit at him. Finally, the conquering hero himself would drive down in his four-horse chariot, with rose petals strewn in his path. The whole procession would run the length of the Forum and up the face of Capitol Hill to the Temple of Saturn (the eight big columns midway up the hill—#13 on the map in this chapter), where they'd place the booty in Rome's coffers. Then they'd continue up to the summit to the Temple of Jupiter (only ruins of its foundation remain today) to dedicate the victory to the King of the Gods.

❶ Arch of Titus (Arco di Tito)

The Arch of Titus commemorated the Roman victory over the province of Judaea (Israel) in A.D. 70. The Romans had a reputation

as benevolent conquerors who tolerated the local customs and rulers. All they required was allegiance to the empire, shown by worshipping the emperor as a god. No problem for most conquered people, who already had half a dozen gods on their prayer lists anyway. But Israelites believed in only one god, and it wasn't the emperor. Israel revolted. After a short but bitter war, the Romans defeated the rebels, took Jerusalem, destroyed their temple (leaving only the foundation wall—today's revered "Wailing Wall"), and brought home 50,000 Jewish slaves...who were forced to build this arch (and the Colosseum).

Roman propaganda decorates the inside of the arch, where a relief shows the emperor Titus in a chariot being crowned by the goddess Victory. (Thanks to modern pollution, they both look like they've been through

Roman Forum

1. Arch of Titus
2. Basilica of Constantine
3. The Forum's Main Square
4. Temple of Julius Caesar
5. Temple of Antoninus Pius & Faustina
6. Basilica Aemilia
7. Caligula's Palace
8. Temple of Vesta
9. House of the Vestal Virgins
10. The Curia
11. Rostrum
12. Arch of Septimius Severus
13. Temple of Saturn
14. Column of Phocas

ROMAN FORUM

Rome: Republic and Empire
(500 B.C.–A.D. 500)

Ancient Rome spanned about a thousand years, from 500 B.C. to A.D. 500. During that time, Rome expanded from a small tribe of barbarians to a vast empire, then dwindled slowly to city size again. For the first 500 years, when Rome's armies made her ruler of the Italian peninsula and beyond, Rome was a republic governed by elected senators. Over the next 500 years, a time of world conquest and eventual decline, Rome was an empire ruled by a military-backed dictator.

Julius Caesar bridged the gap between republic and empire. This ambitious general and politician, popular with the people because of his military victories and charisma, suspended the Roman constitution and assumed dictatorial powers in about 50 B.C. A few years later, he was assassinated by a conspiracy of senators. His adopted son, Augustus, succeeded him, and soon "Caesar" was not just a name but a title.

Emperor Augustus ushered in the Pax Romana, or Roman peace (A.D. 1–200), a time when Rome reached her peak and controlled an empire that stretched even beyond Eurail—from England to Egypt, Turkey to Morocco.

the wars.) The other side shows booty from the sacking of the temple in Jerusalem—soldiers carrying a Jewish menorah and other plunder. The two (unfinished) plaques on poles were to have listed the conquered cities. Look at the top of the ceiling. Constructed after Titus' death, the relief shows him riding an eagle to heaven, where he'll become one of the gods.

The brutal crushing of the A.D. 70 rebellion (and another one 60 years later) devastated the nation of Israel. With no temple as a center for their faith, the Jews scattered throughout the world (the Diaspora). There would be no Jewish political entity again for almost two thousand years, until modern Israel was created after World War II.

• Walk down the Via Sacra into the Forum. After about 50 yards, turn right and follow a path uphill to the three huge arches of the...

❷ Basilica of Constantine (a.k.a. Basilica Maxentius)

Yes, these are big arches. But they represent only one-third of the original Basilica of Constantine, a mammoth hall of justice. The arches were matched by a similar set along the Via Sacra side (only a few squat brick piers remain). Between them ran the central hall, which was spanned by a roof 130 feet high—about 55 feet higher than the side arches you see. (The stub of brick you see sticking

THE
ROMAN EMPIRE
AT ITS PEAK:
PAX ROMANA A.D. 120

up began an arch that once spanned the central hall.) The hall itself was as long as a football field, lavishly furnished with colorful inlaid marble, a gilded bronze ceiling, and statues, and filled with strolling Romans. At the far (west) end was an enormous marble statue of Emperor Constantine on a throne. (Pieces of this statue, including a hand the size of a man, are on display in Rome's Capitoline Museums.)

The basilica was begun by the emperor Maxentius, but after he was trounced in battle (see page 98), the victor Constantine completed the massive building. No doubt about it, the Romans built monuments on a more epic scale than any previous Europeans, wowing their "barbarian" neighbors.

ROMAN FORUM

• *Now stroll deeper into the Forum, downhill along Via Sacra, through the trees. Many of the large basalt stones under your feet were walked on by Caesar Augustus 2,000 years ago. Pass by the only original bronze door still swinging on its ancient hinges (the green door at the Tempio di Romolo, on the right) and continue between ruined buildings until the Via Sacra opens up to a flat, grassy area.*

❸ The Forum's Main Square

The original Forum, or main square, was this flat patch about the size of a football field, stretching to the foot of Capitol Hill. Surrounding it were temples, law courts, government buildings, and triumphal arches.

Rome was born right here. According to legend, twin brothers Romulus (Rome) and Remus were orphaned in infancy and raised by a she-wolf on top of Palatine Hill. Growing up, they found it hard to get dates. So they and their cohorts attacked the nearby Sabine tribe and kidnapped their women. After they made peace, this marshy valley became the meeting place and then the trading center for the scattered tribes on the surrounding hillsides.

The square was the busiest and most crowded—and often the seediest—section of town. Besides the senators, politicians, and currency exchangers, there were even sleazier types—souvenir hawkers, pickpockets, fortune-tellers, gamblers, slave marketers, drunks, hookers, lawyers, and tour guides.

The Forum is now rubble, but imagine it in its prime: blinding white marble buildings with 40-foot-high columns and shining bronze roofs; rows of statues painted in realistic colors; processional chariots rattling down Via Sacra. Mentally replace tourists in T-shirts with tribunes in togas. Imagine the buildings towering and the people buzzing around you while an orator gives a rabble-rousing speech from the Rostrum. If things still look like just a pile of rocks, at least tell yourself, "But Julius Caesar once leaned against these rocks."

• *At the near (east) end of the main square (the Colosseum is to the east) are the foundations of a temple now capped with a peaked wood-and-metal roof.*

❹ Temple of Julius Caesar
(Tempio del Divo Giulio, or Ara di Cesare)

Julius Caesar's body was burned on this spot (under the metal roof) after his assassination. Peek behind the wall into the small

apse area, where a mound of dirt usually has fresh flowers—given to remember the man who, more than any other, personified the greatness of Rome.

Caesar (100–44 B.C.) changed Rome—and the Forum—dramatically. He cleared out many of the wooden market stalls and began to ring the square with even grander buildings. Caesar's house was located behind the temple, near that clump of trees. He walked right by here on the day he was assassinated ("Beware the Ides of March!" warned a street-corner Etruscan preacher).

Though he was popular with the masses, not everyone liked Caesar's urban design or his politics. When he assumed dictatorial powers, he was ambushed and stabbed to death by a conspiracy of senators, including his adopted son, Brutus *("Et tu, Brute?")*.

The funeral was held here, facing the main square. The citizens gathered, and speeches were made. Mark Antony stood up to say (in Shakespeare's words), "Friends, Romans, countrymen, lend me your ears. I come to bury Caesar, not to praise him." When Caesar's body was burned, the citizens who still loved him threw anything at hand on the fire, requiring the fire department to come put it out. Later, Emperor Augustus dedicated this temple in his name, making Caesar the first Roman to become a god.

• *Behind and to the left of the Temple of Julius Caesar are the 10 tall columns of the...*

❺ Temple of Antoninus
Pius and Faustina

The Senate built this temple to honor Emperor Antoninus Pius (A.D. 138–161) and his deified wife, Faustina. The 50-foot-tall Corinthian (leafy) columns must have been awe-inspiring to out-of-towners who grew up in thatched huts. Although the temple has been inhabited by a church, you can still see

ROMAN FORUM

Religion in Ancient Rome

Religion in ancient Rome was all about the *pax deorum* (peace, or pact, with the gods) that guaranteed the prosperity of the incredibly superstitious Romans. To appease the fickle gods, they performed elaborate rituals at lavish temples and shrines. Romans had a god for every moment of their days and each important event in their lives. While the Romans adopted the Greek pantheon, they also embraced the gods from many of the people they came into contact with, sometimes using elaborate ceremonies to persuade these new gods to "move" to Rome. Scholars estimate Romans had about 30,000 gods to keep happy. In this high-maintenance religion, there was Cunina, the goddess who protected cradles; Statulinus, to help children stand up; and Fabulina, for their first words. Fornax was the oven god, Pomona the fruit-tree goddess, Sterculinus the manure god, and Venus Cloacina the sewer goddess.

Priests interpreted the will of the gods by studying the internal organs of sacrificed animals, the flight of birds, and prophetic books. A clap of thunder was enough to postpone a battle.

Astrology, magic rites, the cult of deified emperors, house gods, and the near-deification of ancestors permeated Roman life. But all these gods didn't quite do it for the Romans—they were gradually replaced by the rise of monotheistic religions from the East. In A.D. 312, Emperor Constantine legalized and embraced Christianity. By 390, the Christian God was the only legal god in Rome.

the basic layout—a staircase led to a shaded porch (the columns), which admitted you to the main building (now a church), where the statue of the god sat. Originally, these columns supported a triangular pediment decorated with sculptures.

Picture these columns, with gilded capitals, supporting brightly painted statues in the pediment, and the whole building capped with a gleaming bronze roof. The stately gray rubble of today's Forum is a faded black-and-white photograph of a 3-D Technicolor era.

The building is a microcosm of many of the changes that occurred after Rome fell. In medieval times, the temple was pillaged. Note the diagonal cuts high on the marble columns—a failed attempt by scavengers to cut through the pillars to pull them down for their precious stone. (They used vinegar and rope to cut the marble...but because vinegar also eats through rope, they abandoned the attempt.) In 1550, a church was housed inside the ancient temple. The door shows the street level at the time of Michelangelo. The long staircase was underground until excavated in the 1800s.

• *There's a ramp next to the Temple of A. and F. Walk halfway up it and look to the left to view the...*

❻ Basilica Aemilia

A basilica was a covered public forum, often serving as a Roman hall of justice. In a society that was as legal-minded as America

is today, you needed a lot of lawyers—and a big place to put them. Citizens came here to work out matters such as inheritances and building permits, or to sue somebody.

Notice the layout. It was a long, rectangular building. The stubby columns all in a row form one long, central hall flanked by two side aisles. Medieval Christians required a larger meeting hall for their worship services than Roman temples provided, so they used the spacious Roman basilica as the model for their churches. Cathedrals from France to Spain to England, from Romanesque to Gothic to Renaissance, all have the same basic floor plan as a Roman basilica.

• *Return again to the Temple of Julius Caesar. To the right of the temple are the three tall Corinthian columns of the Temple of Castor and Pollux. Beyond that is Palatine Hill—the corner of which may have been...*

❼ Caligula's Palace (a.k.a. the Palace of Tiberius)

Emperor Caligula (ruled A.D. 37–41) had a huge palace on Palatine Hill overlooking the Forum. It actually sprawled down the hill into the Forum (some supporting arches remain in the hillside).

Caligula was not a nice person.

ROMAN FORUM

He tortured enemies, stole senators' wives, and parked his chariot in handicap spaces. But Rome's luxury-loving emperors only added to the glory of the Forum, with each one trying to make his mark on history.

• *To the left of the Temple of Castor and Pollux, find the remains of a small white circular temple.*

❽ Temple of Vesta

This is perhaps Rome's most sacred spot. Rome considered itself one big family, and this temple represented a circular hut, like the kind that Rome's first families lived in. Inside, a fire burned, just as in a Roman home. And back in the days before lighters and butane, you never wanted your fire to go out. As long as the sacred flame burned, Rome would stand. The flame was tended by priestesses known as Vestal Virgins.

• *Around the back of the Temple of Vesta, you'll find two rectangular brick pools. These stood in the courtyard of the...*

❾ House of the Vestal Virgins

The Vestal Virgins lived in a two-story building surrounding a long central courtyard with these two pools at one end. Rows of

statues depicting leading Vestal Virgins flanked the courtyard. This place was the model—both architecturally and sexually—for medieval convents and monasteries.

Chosen from noble families before they reached the age of 10, the six Vestal Virgins served a 30-year term. Honored and revered by the Romans, the Vestals even had their own box opposite the emperor in the Colosseum.

As the name implies, a Vestal took a vow of chastity. If she served her term faithfully—abstaining for 30 years—she was given a huge dowry, and allowed to marry. But if they found any Virgin who wasn't, she was strapped to a funeral car, paraded through the streets of the Forum, taken to a crypt, given a loaf of bread and a lamp...and buried alive. Many women suffered the latter fate.

• *Return to the Temple of Julius Caesar and head to the Forum's west end (opposite from the Colosseum). As you pass alongside the big open space of the Forum's main square, consider how the piazza is still a standard part of any Italian town. It has reflected and accommodated the gregarious and outgoing nature of the Italian people since Roman times.*

Stop at the big, well-preserved brick building (on right) with the triangular roof. Look in at...

❿ The Curia (Senate House)

The Curia was the most important political building in the Forum. While the present building dates from A.D. 283, this was the site of Rome's official center of government since the birth

of the republic. (Note that ongoing archaeological work may restrict access to the Curia, as well as the Arch of Septimius Severus—described later—and the exit to Capitol Hill.) Three hundred senators, elected by the citizens of Rome, met here to debate and create the laws of the land. Their wooden seats once circled the building in three tiers; the Senate president's podium sat at the far end. The marble floor is from ancient times. Listen to the echoes in this vast room—the acoustics are great.

Rome prided itself on being a republic. Early in the city's history, its people threw out the king and established rule by elected representatives. Each Roman citizen was free to speak his mind and have a say in public policy. Even when emperors became the supreme authority, the Senate was a power to be reckoned with. The Curia building is well-preserved, having been used as a church since early Christian times. In the 1930s, it was restored and opened to the public as a historic site. (Note: Although Julius Caesar was assassinated in "the Senate," it wasn't here—the Senate was temporarily meeting across town.)

A statue and two reliefs inside the Curia help build our mental image of the Forum. The statue, made of porphyry marble in about A.D. 100 (with its head, arms, and feet now missing), was a tribute to an emperor, probably Hadrian or Trajan. The two relief panels may have decorated the Rostrum. Those on the left show people (with big stone tablets) standing in line to burn their debt records following a government amnesty. The other shows the

Rome Falls

Remember that Rome lasted 1,000 years—500 years of growth, 200 years of peak power, and 300 years of gradual decay. The fall had many causes, among them the barbarians who pecked away at Rome's borders. Christians blamed the fall on moral decay. Pagans blamed it on Christians. Socialists blamed it on a shallow economy based on the spoils of war. (Republicans blamed it on Democrats.) Whatever the reasons, the far-flung empire could no longer keep its grip on conquered lands, and it pulled back. Barbarian tribes from Germany and Asia attacked the Italian peninsula and even looted Rome itself in A.D. 410, leveling many of the buildings in the Forum. In 476, when the last emperor checked out and switched off the lights, Europe plunged into centuries of ignorance, poverty, and weak government—the Dark Ages.

But Rome lived on in the Catholic Church. Christianity was the state religion of Rome's last generations. Emperors became popes (both called themselves "Pontifex Maximus"), senators became bishops, orators became priests, and basilicas became churches. The glory of Rome remains eternal.

ROMAN FORUM

distribution of grain (Rome's welfare system), some buildings in the background, and the latest fashion in togas.

• Go back down the Senate steps and find the 10-foot-high wall just to the left of the big arch, marked...

⑪ Rostrum (Rostri)

Nowhere was Roman freedom more apparent than at this "Speaker's Corner." The Rostrum was a raised platform, 10 feet high and 80 feet long, decorated with statues, columns, and the prows of ships (rostra).

On a stage like this, Rome's orators, great and small, tried to draw a crowd and sway public opinion. Mark Antony rose to offer Caesar the laurel-leaf crown of kingship, which Caesar publicly (and hypocritically) refused while privately becoming a dictator. Men such as Cicero railed against the corruption and decadence that came with the city's newfound wealth. In later years, daring citizens even spoke out against the emperors, reminding them that Rome was once free. Picture the backdrop these speakers would have had—a mountain of marble buildings piling up on Capitol Hill.

In front of the Rostrum are trees bearing fruits that were sacred to the ancient Romans: olives (provided food, light, and preservatives), figs (tasty), and wine grapes (made a popular export product).

• *The big arch to the right of the Rostrum is the...*

⓬ Arch of Septimius Severus

In imperial times, the Rostrum's voices of democracy would have been dwarfed by images of the empire, such as the huge six-story-

high Arch of Septimius Severus (A.D. 203). The reliefs commemorate the African-born emperor's battles in Mesopotamia. Near ground level, see soldiers marching captured barbarians back to Rome for the victory parade. Despite Severus' efficient rule, Rome's empire was crumbling under the weight of its own corruption, dis-

ease, decaying infrastructure, and the constant attacks by foreign "barbarians."

• *Pass underneath the Arch of Septimius Severus and turn left. On the slope of Capitol Hill are the eight remaining columns of the...*

⓭ Temple of Saturn

These columns framed the entrance to the Forum's oldest temple (497 B.C.). Inside was a humble, very old wooden statue of the god Saturn. But the statue's pedestal held the gold bars, coins, and jewels of Rome's state treasury, the booty collected by conquering generals.

• *Standing here, at one of the Forum's first buildings, look east at the lone, tall...*

⓮ Column of Phocas—Rome's Fall

This is the Forum's last monument (A.D. 608), a gift from the powerful Byzantine Empire to a fallen empire—Rome. Given to commemorate the pagan Pantheon's becoming a Christian church, it's like a symbolic last nail in ancient Rome's coffin. After Rome's 1,000-year reign, the city was looted by Vandals, the population of a million-plus shrank to about 10,000, and the once-grand city center—the Forum—was abandoned, slowly covered up by centuries of silt and dirt. In the 1700s, an English historian named Edward Gibbon overlooked this spot from Capitol Hill. Hearing Christian monks singing at these pagan ruins, he looked out at the few columns poking up from the ground, pondered the "Decline and Fall of the Roman Empire," and thought, "Hmm, that's a catchy title...."

• *There are several ways to exit the Forum:*

1. Exiting past the Arch of Titus lands you at the Colosseum.

2. Exiting near the Arch of Septimius Severus leads you to the stairs up to Capitol Hill.

3. The Forum's main entrance spills you back out onto Via dei Fori Imperiali.

4. From the Arch of Titus, you can climb Palatine Hill to the top and start the Palatine Hill Tour—see the next chapter.

PALATINE HILL TOUR

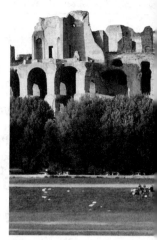

Monte Palatino

While many tourists consider the Palatine Hill just extra credit after the Forum, it offers an insight into the greatness of Rome that's well worth the effort. (And, if you're visiting the Colosseum or Forum, you've got a ticket whether you like it or not.) Palatine Hill is jam-packed with history—"the huts of Romulus," the huge Imperial Palace, a view of the Circus Maximus—but there's only the barest skeleton of rubble left to tell the story. This tour will enable the thoughtful sightseer to bring those remains to life. Palatine Hill is ideal for those who want to get away from the crowds and discover the romantic, melancholy essence of ruins. Become a 19th-century poet or a painter on the Grand Tour, meditating on the destiny of once-great civilizations, and wander through the remains of the palaces that Nature seems to have reclaimed for herself.

Orientation

Cost: €12 combo-ticket also includes Roman Forum and Colosseum; ticket valid two consecutive days—one entry per sight; also covered by Roma Pass.

Hours: The Palatine Hill, Roman Forum, and Colosseum are all open daily 8:30 until one hour before sunset: April–Sept until 19:15, Oct until 18:30, off-season closes as early as 16:30; last entry one hour before closing.

Getting There: The closest Metro stop is Colosseo. The entrance is on Via di San Gregorio (facing the Forum with the Colosseum at your back, it's down the street to your left). You can also enter the Palatine from within the Roman Forum—just climb the hill from the Arch of Titus.

Tours: Audioguides cost €4 (€6 version includes Roman Forum, must leave ID). Guided tours in English are offered once daily at 11:30 (€4, 45 minutes, not always available off-season); ask for information at the ticket booth.

Length of This Tour: Allow 1.5 hours.

Services: You'll find WCs at the museum in the center of the site. These are usually the least-crowded WCs in the whole Colosseum-Forum-Palatine area—use them. WCs are also at the ticket office when you enter, and hiding among the orange trees in the Farnese Gardens. For information on restaurants in the area, see the sidebar on page 96.

The Tour Begins

• *Start on top of the hill at the Palatine Museum (Museo Palatino, see photo; the museum is #6 on the map).*
To get there from the entrance, take the stairs on the left and follow the path up. Walk past the stadium and some more ruins to the one modern building on the crest of the hill. It's the big, gray, 1930s-style building that houses the museum. We'll visit the museum later. For now, grab a

stone and sit with your back to the museum to orient yourself, facing in the direction of the Forum (roughly north).

The Imperial Palace

You're sitting at the center of what was once a huge palace, the residence of emperors for three centuries. Orgies, royal weddings, assassinations, concerts, intrigues, births, funerals, banquets, and the occasional Tupperware party took place within these walls. What walls? The row of umbrella pines about 200 yards to the east (to your right) now marks one edge of the palace. The reconstructed brick tower (at about 11 o'clock) was the northwest corner. The palace also stretched behind you (the area behind the museum) and beneath you, since some parts of the palace had a lower floor. (Right now, you're standing not on the original palace's ground level, but several floors up.)

The area in front was the official wing of the palace; behind were the private quarters. All in all, it made for a cozy little 150,000-square-foot pad.

The palace was built by Emperor Domitian in about A.D. 81. A poet of the day described it as so grand that it "made Jupiter jealous."

Palatine Hill

- — EXISTING WALLS
- -- ANCIENT OUTLINE
- ⇗ VIEW

DCH

100 YARDS

100 METERS

❶	Main Courtyard	❻	Museum
❷	Stadium	❼	Throne Room
❸	Private Wing of the Palace	❽	Banquet Hall
❹	Domus Augustana – Lower Courtyard	❾	House of Augustus
❺	Circus Maximus	❿	Huts of Romulus
		⓫	View of Forum

• *Now proceed, following the map for this 11-stop tour. As you walk, you'll see colorful marble scraps all over Palatine Hill. Flashy building stone was used to boast of the power and vastness of the empire. Citizens knew that the Numidian yellow marble was from Tunisia, the veined Cipollino marble (with swirling designs like an onion) was from the island of Euboea in Greece, and the pink granite was from Aswan in Egypt. This was all sliced and laid out in fine pavement and wall designs, enjoyed by those who could only be thankful they were on the winning team.*

With your back to the museum, head left to a big rectangular field with an octagonal brick design in the center—the main courtyard of the palace.

❶ Main Courtyard (Peristilio)

The brick octagon was a sunken fountain in the middle of an open-air courtyard. Like many fine Roman homes, this palace was built

around an oasis of peace where you could enjoy the sun, catch the precious rain, and listen to the babble of moving water. The courtyard was lined with columns (notice the fragments) supporting an arcade for shade. Originally, the floor and walls of the courtyard were faced with colorful marble.

• *The palace's stadium is 100 yards behind you (to the east), near the long row of pine trees. Belly up to the railing and look down on the elliptical track.*

❷ Stadium (Stadio)

This cigar-shaped, sunken stadium (500 feet long) was the palace's rec room. It looks like a racetrack, but it just held gardens

with strolling paths. The oval running track at the south end was added later. The emperor had a raised box on the 50-yard line, in the curved apse across from you. At the north end were changing rooms, and the marble fragments that litter the ground once held up an arcade.

• *Now, walk through the arch in the wall and imagine the...*

❸ Private Wing of the Palace (Domus Augustana)

The area between the stadium and the museum held the private

rooms of the emperor and his extended family. Today, a lone umbrella pine on a mound marks the courtyard of this wing. To the left are the brick ruins of the Domus.

Wander southward under the arches and through the maze of brick rooms (many of them reconstructed), noticing...

* The typical Roman building method: Build a rectangular shell of brick, fill it with concrete, then finish it with either plaster (you'll see an occasional faded fresco) or slabs of marble. The small, round pockmarks on many walls show where the marble was fastened.
* The square holes in the walls that held wooden beams, used for scaffolding during construction and maintenance, for shelves, and for wooden floors.
* Over the doorways, the bricks in the walls that form the pattern of an arch. These "blind arches" were structural elements that allowed the walls to be built higher. The iron bar clamps are recent additions and hold the crumbling walls together.
* Niches and apses that once held statues. Every family had their own household gods and displayed small images of these guardian spirits, as well as busts of honored ancestors.
* The fragments of columns, reliefs, and sculpture scattered about that suggest the wealth of this great palace.

Finally, notice the floor plan—a complex fantasyland maze of small, private, sometimes even curved rooms.

* In the south part of the Domus Augustana, you can look down on the ruins of the lower story.

❹ Domus Augustana—Lower Courtyard

This open-air courtyard has the concave-convex remains of a large fountain that must have been a marvel. Try to mentally reconstruct the palace that surrounded this fountain. The emperors could look down on it

PALATINE HILL

from the upper story (where you're standing) or view it from the rooms around it on the lower story, where the emperor and his family ate their meals in private.

The lower story was built into the slope of the hill. The southern part of the palace was an extension of the hillside, supported beneath your feet by big arches.

• *Continue to the southern edge of the hill (directly behind the museum), overlooking a long, wide grassy field—what once was the Circus Maximus. Lean over the railing and you might be able to make out the concave shape of the palace's southern facade.*

❺ Circus Maximus

If the gladiator show at the Colosseum was sold out, you could always get a seat at the Circus Max. In an early version of today's demolition derby, Ben-Hur and his fellow charioteers once raced recklessly around this oblong course.

The chariots circled around the cigar-shaped mound in the center (notice the lone cypress tree that now marks one end of the mound). Bleachers (now grassy banks) originally surrounded the track (see artist's reconstruction, below).

The track was 1,300 feet long, while the whole stadium measured 2,130 feet by 720 feet and seated—get this—250,000 people.

The wooden bleachers once collapsed during a race, killing thousands.

The horses began at a starting gate at the west end (to your right), while the public entered at the other end. Races consisted of seven laps (about 3.5 miles total). In such a small space, collisions and overturned chariots were common. The charioteers were usually poor, lowborn people who used this dangerous sport to get rich and famous. Some succeeded. Most died.

The public was crazy about the races. There were 12 per day, 240 days a year. Four teams dominated the competition—Reds, Whites, Blues, and Greens—and every citizen was fanatically devoted to one of them. Obviously, the emperors had the best seats in the house; built into the palace's curved facade was a box overlooking the track. For their pleasure, emperors occasionally had the circus floor carpeted with designs in colored powders.

Picture the scene: intact palace; emperor watching; a quarter of a million Romans cheering, jeering, and furiously betting. Horses raced here for more than a thousand years. The track dates from 300 B.C., and the spectacles continued into the Christian era, until A.D. 549, despite Church disapproval.

PALATINE HILL

From this viewpoint, looking to the left, you can see the ruins of the Baths of Caracalla (not worth touring if you've seen the Palatine) rising above the trees a half-mile away. About a mile beyond that, the Appian Way led from a grand gate in the ancient wall, past the catacombs, to Brindisi.

• *Turn around and head back toward the museum.*

❻ Museum (Museo Palatino)

The museum contains statues and frescoes that help you imagine the luxury of the imperial Palatine. To the left after you enter, pause at the statue of "Magna Mater" on her throne. This Great Mother brought life and fertility to the Roman people, who worshipped her at the nearby Temple of Cybele. Her arms and foot were destroyed by time, but there was always a cavity where her head should be—this was a standard Roman device in which interchangeable heads could be inserted. In this case, the Magna Mater's "head" was actually a sacred black cone-shaped meteorite that caused astonishment when it fell from the sky.

Also on this floor, Room V holds frescoes and statues from the time of Augustus and fine decorative terra-cotta panels. Room VII has a bust of the notorious Emperor Nero ("Nerone") and exquisite marble-inlay work. In Room VIII is a statue fragment of a river god's stomach. And finally, back near the entrance is a large headless statue of a Muse that once decorated the Hippodrome.

There's more in the basement (go back outside, down the stairs, and into the doorway directly below the staircase). Room II holds a model of the eighth-century B.C. Iron Age huts of Romulus that we'll see later in the tour. (There's also a 21st-century WC nearby.)

• *From the museum, begin circling the main courtyard (with its octagonal fountain) counterclockwise. When the path turns left, keep walking another 40 feet or so to the squat brick pillar with a stubby column on top. Step into the...*

❼ Throne Room

The nerve center of an empire that controlled some 50 million people from England to Africa, this was the official seat of power. The curved apse of the largest brick stump (there's now a plaque on it) marks the spot where the emperor sat on his throne for official business.

Imagine being a Roman citizen summoned by the emperor. You'd enter the palace through the main doorway (now a gap) at the far (Forum) end of the room, having climbed up three

flights of a monumental staircase. The floor and walls dazzled with green, purple, red, white, and yellow marble. Along the walls were 12 colossal statues of Roman gods. The ceiling towered seven stories overhead. On either side were doorways leading to a basilica and the emperor's private temple.

You'd approach the emperor, who sat on a raised throne in the apse, dressed in royal purple, with a crown of laurel leaves on his head and a scepter cradled in his arm. Big braziers burned on either side, throwing off a flickering light. As you approached, you'd raise your arm to greet him, saying, *"Ave, Cesare!"* The words would echo through the great hall.

Now imagine yourself as emperor. Stand on the small white stone marking the location of the throne (a few feet in front of the plaque) and look out over your palace. (The ceiling was a barrel vault sitting upon towers as high as the brick tower in the distance to the left.)

• *Continue circling the main courtyard counterclockwise until it dead-ends at the...*

❽ Banquet Hall (Triclinium)

The floor of the banquet room had a hollow space beneath it (you can see the two-foot gap between the two original floors). Slaves

stoked fires from underground stoves to heat the floor with forced air. At the far end of the room, the platform and curved apse mark the spot where the emperor ate while looking down on his subjects. Guests could look into the adjoining room, where an elliptical-shaped fountain (see the brick remains) spurted for their amusement.

Here, the wealthiest Romans enjoyed the spoils that poured into Rome from its vast empire. Reclining on a couch, waited on by slaves, you'd order bowls of larks' tongues or a roast pig stuffed with live birds, then wash it down with wine. If you were full but tempted by yet another delicacy, you could call for a feather, vomit, and start all over. Dancing dark-skinned slave girls from Egypt or flute players from Greece entertained. If you fancied one, he or she was yours—the bedrooms were just down the hall.

Or so went the stories. In fact, many emperors were just and simple men, continuing the old Roman traditions of hard work and moderate tastes. But just as many were power-mad scoundrels who used their authority to indulge their every desire.

• From the Banquet Hall, work your way west through openings in the low brick wall. You'll run into a railing overlooking some ruins (the Casa di Livia). Circle clockwise around the ruins and down the ramp, following signs to the nearby Casa di Augusto. Find the queue to get inside (the wait is usually about 15 to 30 minutes). Only five visitors at a time are allowed to enter the actual dwelling of Augustus—and then for just five minutes.

❾ House of Augustus (Casa di Augusto)

Augustus, a.k.a. Octavian, the first emperor, lived in this house (and the neighboring Casa di Livia) with his wife, Livia. This relatively modest dwelling, dating from before Octavian became emperor, is a far cry from the later Imperial Palace that was built on top. The three humble rooms with their finely restored frescoes (opened in 2008) are well worth the wait. See rooms vibrantly painted with fake columns and arches, and with fake windows that once looked out on illusionary landscapes. Climb the steps outside to see a fourth room. You'll see that Livia and Augustus had little of the lavish marble found in most homes of the wealthy.

Augustus was a modest man who believed in traditional Roman values. His wife and daughter wove the clothes he wore. He slept in the same small bedroom for 40 years. He burned the midnight oil in his study, where he read and wrote his memoirs. Augustus set a standard for emperors' conduct that would last... until his death.

Augustus wanted to be the new Romulus, building his house adjacent to the home of the mythological founder of Rome.

• After exiting the Casa di Augusto, make your way to the nearby section of ruins, protected by a metal roof. Cozy up to the railing to see ruined walls and foundations.

❿ The Huts of Romulus ("Romulean Huts")

Looking down into this pit filled with big blocks of stone, you can make out some elliptical and rectangular shapes carved into

the stony ground. These are the partial outlines of huts from about 850 B.C. Some have holes that once held the wooden posts of round thatched huts.

According to legend, Romulus and Remus (see photo of statue on page 185) were children of the first

Vestal Virgin. For complicated family reasons, she was executed and her babies were set adrift on the flooding Tiber River, eventually to be washed ashore at the foot of Palatine Hill. In a cave just downhill from here, a shepherd discovered them being suckled by a mother wolf. He took them home—maybe right here—and raised them as his own. When Romulus grew up, he killed his brother and built a square wall (Roma Quadrata) on the hilltop, thus founding the city of Rome.

For centuries, the Romans believed this myth. They honored the wolf's cave (called the "Lupercale," where every February 15 men dressed up in animal skins and whipped women), as well as the spot where Romulus was said to have lived. Lo and behold, in the 1940s, these huts were unearthed, and the legend became history. The more they dig, the more they find to confirm the legends. A nearby cave discovered in 2007—ornamented with seashells, colored marble, and a wolf mosaic—may be that original Lupercale. (It's not open to the public, and dissenting archaeologists believe it's a temple to water nymphs.)

Here at Rome's birthplace, reflect on the rise of this great culture—from thatched huts to the modest house of Augustus to the massive Imperial Palace of Domitian, with its stadium and view over the Circus Maximus. It's no wonder that the hill's name gave us our English word "palace."

• *Climb a few steps to the summit of the hill, and walk among the trees of the Farnese Gardens. Start making your way toward the Forum.*

⓫ View of Forum Fit for an Emperor

Finish your tour with a stroll through the Renaissance gardens of the Farnese family. Admire the exotic plants, fountains, underground grotto, and pavilions. When you see the incredible view of the Forum from the end of the gardens, you'll know why the Palatine Hill was Rome's best address.

• *To exit, wind down Palatine Hill to the Forum, ending up at the Arch of Titus.*

TRAJAN'S COLUMN, MARKET, AND IMPERIAL FORUMS TOUR

Colonna, Mercati de Traiano, e Fori Imperiali

Rome peaked under Emperor Trajan (ruled A.D. 98–117)—the empire stretched from England to the Sahara, from Spain to the Fertile Crescent. A triumphant Trajan returned to Rome with his booty and shook it all over the city. He extended the Forum by building his own commercial, political, and religious center nearby, complete with temples, law courts, squares lined with shops, and a monumental column covered with detailed carvings that tell the story of one of his most famous conquests. This column, Trajan's Market, and the Museum of the Imperial Forums are the highlights of this tour. Much of Trajan's Forum (the broad expanse of really ruined ruins) can be seen quickly on your way to visit other nearby sights.

Orientation

Trajan's Column: It's free and viewable at all times.

Trajan's Market: You can view it for free from Via dei Fori Imperiali, but wandering through the market is possible only with paid admission to the Museum of the Imperial Forums.

Museum of the Imperial Forums: €6.50, includes entry to the market ruins, Tue–Sun 9:00–19:00, closed Mon, last entry 30 minutes before closing, Via IV Novembre 94 (up the staircase from Trajan's Column), tel. 06-0608, www.mercatiditraiano .it. Skip the museum's slow, dry €3.50 audioguide.

Getting There: Trajan's Column is just a few steps off Piazza Venezia (a hub for major bus routes #40, #64, and #87), on Via dei Fori Imperiali, across the street from the Victor Emmanuel Monument. Trajan's Market can be entered only through the Museum of the Imperial Forums at Via IV Novembre 94. Trajan's Forum stretches southeast of the column toward the Colosseo Metro stop and the Colosseum itself.

Length of This Tour: Allow 30 minutes if you're viewing the column and market from the street, and another hour if you pay admission to enter the museum and market ruins.

The Tour Begins

Trajan's Column

Rising 140 feet and decorated with a spiral relief of 2,500 figures trumpeting Trajan's exploits, this is the world's grandest column from antiquity. At one point, the ashes of Trajan and his wife were held in the base, and the sun glinted off a polished bronze statue of Trajan at the top. (Today, St. Peter is on top.) Built as a stack of 17 marble doughnuts, the column is hollow (note the small window slots) with a spiral staircase inside, leading up to the balcony.

The relief unfolds like a scroll, telling the story of Trajan's conquest of Dacia (modern-day Romania). It starts at the bottom with a trickle of water that becomes a river and soon picks up boats full of supplies. Then come the soldiers themselves, who spill out from the gates of the city. A river god (bottom band, south side) surfaces

to bless the journey. Along the way (second band), they build roads and forts to sustain the vast enterprise, including (third band, south side) Trajan's half-mile-long bridge over the Danube, the longest for a thousand years. (Find the three tiny crisscross rectangles representing the wooden span.) Trajan himself (fourth band, in military skirt with toga over his arm) mounts a podium to fire up the troops. They hop into a Roman galley ship (fifth band) and head off to fight the valiant Dacians in the middle of a forest (eighth band). Finally, at the very top, the Romans hold a sacrifice to give thanks for the victory, while the captured armor is displayed on the pedestal.

Originally, the entire story was painted in bright colors—and

Trajan's Column, Market & Imperial Forums

- ━━━ EXISTING PORTION
- --- ANCIENT OUTLINE
- ▨ RUINS (BELOW STREET LEVEL)
- Ⓜ METRO STATION

100 YARDS
100 METERS

MUSEUM OF IMPERIAL FORUMS

TRAJAN'S COLUMN

TRAJAN'S MARKET

BASILICA ULPIA

PIAZZA VENEZIA

TRAJAN'S FORUM

VIA ALESSANDRINA

AUGUSTUS FORUM

VIA S. EUF

VIA

IV NOV

TO TERMINI

VICTOR EMMANUEL MONUMENT

VIA DEI FORI IMPERIALI

CAESAR'S FORUM

TO COLOSSEO Ⓜ

TO COLOSSEUM & ROMAN FORUM

DCH

plans are afoot to re-create the column's colors with bright lights on weekend nights. If you were to unwind the scroll, it would stretch over two football fields—it's far longer than the frieze around the Greek Parthenon. (An unscrolled copy is in E.U.R.'s Museum of Roman Civilization; see page 84.)

Trajan's conquest of the Dacians was Rome's last and greatest foreign conquest. It produced Trajan's Forum, which stood for centuries as a symbol of a truly cosmopolitan civilization.

• *You can view Trajan's Market for free from Via dei Fori Imperiali. To walk around inside the market, you must pay admission and enter through the Museum of the Imperial Forums (described on the next page).*

Trajan's Market (Mercati di Traiano)

Nestled into the cutaway curve of Quirinal Hill is the semicircular brick complex of Trajan's Market. It was likely part shopping mall, part warehouse, and part administration building. Or, as some archaeologists have recently suggested, it may have contained mostly government offices.

For now the conventional wisdom holds that at ground

level, the 13 tall (shallow) arches housed shops selling fresh fruit, vegetables, and flowers to people who passed by on the street. The 26 arched windows (above) lit a covered walkway lined with shops that sold wine and olive oil. On the roof (now lined with a metal railing) ran a street that likely held still more shops, making about 150 in all. Shoppers could browse through goods from every corner of Rome's vast empire—exotic fruits from Africa, spices from Asia, and fish-and-chips from Londinium.

Above the semicircle, the upper floors of the complex housed bureaucrats in charge of a crucial element of city life: doling out free grain to unemployed citizens, who lived off the wealth plundered from distant lands. Better to pacify them than risk a riot. Above the offices, at the very top, rises a tower added in the Middle Ages.

The market was beautiful and functional, filling the space of the curved hill perfectly and echoing the curved side of the Forum's main courtyard. (The wall of rough volcanic stones on the ground once extended into a semicircle.) Unlike most Roman buildings, the brick facade wasn't covered with plaster or marble. The architect liked the simple contrast between the warm brick and the white stone lining the arches and windows.

• *If you want to actually walk around the market—worth it only for those with a good imagination, stamina for stairs, or a Masters in Food Distribution—you'll have to pay to enter the museum, which also has exhibits about the entire site.*

Museum of the Imperial Forums (Museo dei Fori Imperiali)

The museum, housed in buildings from Trajan's Market, features discoveries from forums built by several different emperors. Though its collection of statues is not impressive compared to Rome's other museums, it's well-displayed, and it's your only chance to get up close to Trajan's Market and Forum. Skip the detail-oriented audioguide and focus on the big picture to mentally resurrect the fabulous forums.

Each emperor commissioned a series of public piazzas—surrounded by temples, civic buildings, businesses, and markets—that stood in a line from the Colosseum to Trajan's Column. Julius Caesar built the first one (46 B.C.), figuring that the old Roman Forum was not a big enough public space for the expanding city. Over the next 150 years, it was added onto by Augustus (2 B.C.),

Vespasian (A.D. 75), Nerva (A.D. 97), and Trajan (A.D. 112).

Start with the introductory slideshow that virtually reconstructs the forums and Vespasian's Temple of Peace. Next, see the statues and broken columns that once decorated the sites. A caryatid (a female statue serving as a column) from the Forum of Augustus stands in the museum's entryway, alongside a bearded mask of Giove. Nearby, a bronze foot in a glass case is all that's left of a larger-than-life Winged Victory that adorned Augustus' Temple of Mars the Avenger.

Upstairs, a section on Julius Caesar's Forum displays baby Cupids (the son of Venus and Mars) carved from the pure white stone that would eventually adorn all of Rome—Carrara marble.

The rest of the upstairs is dedicated to the Forum of Augustus. A model of the Temple of Mars and some large column fragments give a sense of the enormous scale. You'll see a reconstruction of the hand of the 40-foot statue of Augustus that once stood in his forum.

From here, you can descend to the ground level for a close-up look at Trajan's Market (described earlier). As you walk by the shops in the welcome shade of the arcade, you'll get a better sense of how inviting the market must have been in its heyday. Walking along the curved top of Trajan's Market, you'll enjoy expansive views of Trajan's Forum, other forums in the distance, and the modern Victor Emmanuel Monument.

• *Look down into the ruins of Trajan's Forum, either from atop Trajan's Market or from a viewpoint along Via dei Fori Imperiali.*

The Rest of Trajan's Forum (Foro di Traiano)

Trajan's Forum starts at Trajan's Column and runs about 120 yards southeast toward the Colosseum. It's mostly rubble today, except for Trajan's Market rising up the flank of Quirinal Hill.

In Roman times, you would have entered at the Colosseum end through a triumphal arch and been greeted in the main square by a large statue of the soldier-king on a horse. Continuing on, you'd enter the Basilica Ulpia (the gray granite columns near Trajan's Column), the largest law court of its day. Finally, at the far end, you would have found Trajan's Column, flanked by two libraries that contained the world's knowledge in Greek and Latin. Balconies on the libraries gave close-up looks at the upper reliefs of the column, in case anyone doubted the outcome of Trajan's war.

Trajan's Forum was a crucial expansion of the old Roman Forum, which was too small and ceremonial to fill the commercial needs of a booming city of more than a million people. It trumped the forums of previous Romans (the adjacent forums of Julius Caesar, Augustus, and Vespasian). Built with the staggering haul of gold plundered from Dacia, this was the largest forum ever—its opulence astounded even the jaded Romans.

To build his forum, Trajan literally moved mountains. He cut away a ridge that once connected the Quirinal and Capitol hills, creating this valley. Trajan's Column marks the hill's original height—140 feet.

• *The tour is over. You are just a toga's toss from many other sights of ancient Rome. From here, you can cross over to the other side of the busy Via dei Fori Imperiali and visit the Capitol Hill sights, the Roman Forum, or the Colosseum that looms in the distance.*

PANTHEON TOUR

*The Roman Temple
and Nearby Churches*

If your imagination is fried from trying to reconstruct ancient buildings out of today's rubble, visit the Pantheon, Rome's best-preserved monument. Engineers still admire how the Romans built such a mathematically precise structure without computers, fossil fuel–run machinery, or electricity. (Having unlimited slave power didn't hurt.) Stand under the Pantheon's solemn dome to gain a new appreciation for the sophistication of these ancient people.

Several interesting churches are clustered nearby, easy to visit after you tour the Pantheon.

Orientation

Pantheon: Free, Mon–Sat 8:30–19:30, Sun 9:00–18:00, holidays 9:00–13:00, closed for Mass Sat at 17:00 and Sun at 10:30. Audioguide-€5, €8.50/2 people, 25 minutes. You can download my free Pantheon **audio tour** at www.ricksteves.com (or search for "Rick Steves Audio Tours" in iTunes). Tel. 06-6830-0230.

Church of San Luigi dei Francesi: Free, daily 10:00–12:30 & 16:00–19:00, good €3 booklet, www.saintlouis-rome.net. Bring coins to light the Caravaggios.

Gesù Church: Free, daily 7:00–12:30 & 16:00–19:45, www.chiesadelgesu.org.

Church of Santa Maria sopra Minerva: Free, Mon–Fri 7:00–19:00, Sat–Sun 8:00–13:00 & 15:30–19:00.

Church of San Ignazio: Free, daily 7:30–12:30 & 15:00–19:15.

Dress Code: Modest dress is recommended for the churches near the Pantheon.

Getting There: To reach the Pantheon neighborhood, you can walk (it's a 20-minute walk from Capitol Hill), take a taxi, or catch a bus. Buses #64 and #40 carry tourists and pickpockets frequently between Termini train station and Vatican City, stopping at a chaotic square called Largo Argentina, located a few blocks south of the Pantheon. (Take either Via dei Cestari or Via di Torre Argentina north to the Pantheon.) The *elettrico* minibus #116 runs between Campo de' Fiori and Piazza Barberini via the Pantheon. The most dramatic approach is on foot coming from Piazza Navona along Via Giustiniani, which spills directly into Piazza della Rotunda, offering the classic Pantheon view. ✪ See the Night Walk Across Rome chapter.

Length of This Tour: Allow a half-hour to see the Pantheon, and at least another hour to visit all the churches.

Photography: It's allowed—even with flash—in the Pantheon. No flash in churches.

WCs: The nearest WCs are at bars and downstairs in the McDonald's on the Pantheon's square.

Cuisine Art: Restaurants abound. Several reasonable eateries are a block or two north up Via del Pantheon. Some of Rome's best gelato is nearby. For recommendations, see page 351.

Drinks: A drinking fountain spurts near the obelisk in Piazza della Rotonda. For those who prefer their liquids caffeinated, two of Rome's most venerable (and busiest) coffee shops are just steps away: **Tazza d'Oro Casa del Caffè** (their icy *granita di caffè* is heaven on a hot day, Via degli Orfani 84) and **Bar Sant'Eustachio** (they add sugar to their coffee drinks unless you request otherwise, Piazza di Sant'Eustachio 82).

Overview

The Pantheon is the centerpiece of this tour, and is a must-see on any visit to Rome. The second part of this tour features several nearby churches with art by Michelangelo and Caravaggio, and connections with Galileo, St. Ignatius, and the Jesuit order.

The Tour Begins

• *Start the tour at the top of the square called Piazza della Rotunda, with cafés and restaurants around the edges and an obelisk-topped fountain in the center. You're looking at...*

The Pantheon

Exterior

The Pantheon was a Roman temple dedicated to all *(pan)* of the gods *(theos)*. The original temple was built in 27 B.C. by Augustus' son-in-law, Marcus Agrippa. In fact, the inscription below the triangular **pediment** proclaims in Latin, "Marcus Agrippa, son of Lucio, three

PANTHEON

times consul made this." But after a couple of fires, the structure we
see today was completely rebuilt by the emperor Hadrian around
A.D. 120. Some say that Hadrian,
an amateur architect (and voracious traveler), helped design it.

The Pantheon looks like a
pretty typical temple from the outside, but this is perhaps the most
influential building in art history.
Its dome was the model for the
Florence cathedral dome, which
launched the Renaissance, and for
Michelangelo's dome of St. Peter's, which capped it all off. Even
Washington, D.C.'s capitol building was inspired by this dome.

The 40-foot-high columns of the **portico** (entrance porch)
are made from single pieces of red-gray granite (not the standard
stacks of cylindrical pieces). They were taken from an Egyptian
temple. The holes in the triangular pediment once held a huge
bronze Roman eagle. Back up or step to one side to look above the
pediment to the building itself. You'll see a roofline that was abandoned mid-construction. The pediment was originally intended to
be higher, but when the support columns arrived, they were shorter
than expected. Even the most enlightened can forget to "measure
twice, cut once."

• *Pass through the portico, with its forest of enormous columns. Look up
at the porch roof, and imagine the ceiling covered in its original bronze
plating. It was removed in the 17th century by a scavenging pope from
the Barberini family, inspiring the well-known quip, "What the barbarians didn't do, the Barberini did." Melted down, some of the bronze
was used to build the huge bronze canopy over the altar at St. Peter's.
Now pass through the giant* **bronze door**—*a copy of the original. Take
a seat and take it all in.*

Interior

The dome, which was the largest made until the Renaissance, is set
on a circular base. The mathematical perfection of this dome-on-
a-base design is a testament to Roman engineering. The dome is as
high as it is wide—142 feet from floor to rooftop and from side to
side. To picture it, imagine a basketball set inside a wastebasket so
that it just touches bottom.

The dome—recently cleaned and feeling loftier than ever—is
made from concrete (a Roman invention) that gets lighter and thin-
ner as it reaches the top. The base of the dome is 23 feet thick and
made from heavy concrete mixed with travertine, while near the
top, it's less than five feet thick and made with a lighter volcanic
rock (pumice) mixed in. Note the square indentations in the sur-

Pantheon Cross-Section

100 FEET

GRAY CIRCLE INDICATES HOW A
142' DIAMETER BALL FITS PERFECTLY INSIDE

1 Pediment   **4** Thinnest Part of Dome
2 Portico   **5** Coffered Ceiling
3 Thickest Part of Dome   **6** Oculus

face of the dome. This **coffered ceiling** reduces the weight of the dome without compromising strength. The walls are strengthened by blind arches built into the wall (visible outside).

Both Brunelleschi and Michelangelo studied this dome before building their own (in Florence and the Vatican, respectively). Remember, St. Peter's Basilica is really only the dome of the Pantheon atop the Forum's Basilica of Constantine.

At the top, the **oculus,** or eye-in-the-sky, is the building's only light source and is almost 30 feet

across. The 1,800-year-old floor has holes in it and slants toward the edges to let the rainwater drain. Though some of the floor's marble has been replaced over the years, the design—alternating circles and squares—is original.

In ancient times, this was a one-stop-shopping temple where you could worship any of the gods

PANTHEON

Pantheon

❶ Portico Columns
❷ Bronze Door
❸ Oculus
❹ Main Altar
❺ Tomb of Raphael
❻ Tomb of Victor Emmanuel II
❼ Tomb of Umberto I & Margherita

100 FEET

PIAZZA DELLA ROTUNDA

whose statues decorated the niches. Entering the temple, Romans came face-to-face with a larger-than-life statue of Jupiter, the King of the Gods, where the **altar** stands today. Early in the Middle Ages, the Pantheon became a Christian church (from "all the gods" to "all the martyrs"), which saved it from architectural cannibalism and ensured its upkeep through the Dark Ages. (The year 2009 was the building's 1,400th anniversary as a church.) In the seventh century, a Byzantine emperor stripped the dome's inte-

rior of its original golden-tile ceiling. The twin, grilled windows just right of the altar (at 2 o'clock) are original and, along with the inlaid marble floor, give you a sense of the ancient decor.

Tombs

The only new things in the interior are the decorative statues and the tombs of famous people. The artist Raphael lies to the left of the main altar, which is in the lighted glass niche (pictured here). Above him is a statue of the Madonna and Child that Raphael himself commissioned for his tomb. The Latin inscription on his

The Italian Royal Family...
in Switzerland

From Italy's unification in 1870 to the end of World War II, the country had four kings, all members of the Savoy family. One of Europe's oldest royal families (from the 10th century), the Savoia had long ruled the kingdom of Piedmont (in present-day northern Italy).

In 1946, the Italians voted for a republic and sent the Savoia into exile. Until 2002, a law proclaimed that no male Savoia could set foot on Italian soil. That's why only the first two kings are buried in the Pantheon (the last two died in exile).

The Savoia lost favor with their Italian subjects for several good reasons: When Mussolini marched on Rome in 1922, King Victor Emmanuel III actually asked him to form a government. When the Mussolini government issued anti-Semitic laws, the king signed them. And in 1943, instead of standing by his people, the king abandoned Rome to the Germans and fled south to Allied protection.

Even today, the Savoia heir to Italy's throne is considered a jerk with a knack for saying stupid things. When asked to comment on the racist laws signed by his grandfather, he candidly answered that he was too young at the time so he did not need to apologize, and, he said, the laws were not really all that bad. When the Savoia were allowed back into Italy in 2002, their first mistake was to visit the pope rather than the president of the republic. And while they live in stunning wealth in Switzerland, they still complain that Italy owes them more of the family riches. In 2007 their lawyers claimed that the Italian government should pay the family at least €260 million for damages as a result of their exile.

tomb reads, "In life, Nature feared to be outdone by him. In death, she feared she too would die."

You'll also see the tombs of modern Italy's first two kings. To the right is Victor Emmanuel II (*"Padre della Patria,"* father of his country). To the left is Umberto I (son of the father). These tombs are a hit with royalists. In fact, there is often a guard standing by a guestbook, where visitors can register their support for these two kings' now-controversial family, the Savoys (see sidebar on preceding page). And finally, under Umberto lies his queen, Margherita...for whom the classic pizza Margherita (mozzarella, tomato sauce, and basil) was named in 1889.

The Pantheon is the only ancient building in Rome continuously used since its construction. When you leave, notice that the building is sunken below current street level, showing how the rest of the city has risen on 20 centuries of rubble.

The Pantheon also contains the world's greatest Roman column. There it is, spanning the entire 142 feet from heaven to earth—the pillar of light from the oculus.

Churches near the Pantheon

Many visitors just see the Pantheon and leave. But consider visiting one or more of these four unique churches, all less than 10 minutes' walk from the Pantheon (see map for locations). If you're budgeting your energy, here's a quick rundown on what each has to offer: San Luigi houses several stunning Caravaggio paintings. The Gesù is packed with ornate art and Jesuit history. Santa Maria sopra Minerva, Rome's only Gothic church, has a Michelangelo sculpture and St. Catherine's tomb. Finally, San Ignazio is full of Baroque perspective illusions that will leave your head spinning.

Church of San Luigi dei Francesi

This is the French national church in Rome. Outside, check out the salamander, symbol of François I, the French king who brought Leonardo (and the Renaissance) north to France. The stylized fleur-de-lis symbols found all over the interior are the emblem of French royalty. The one truly *magnifique* sight is the chapel in the far left corner, which was decorated by Caravaggio. This church makes a great little detour between the Pantheon and nearby Piazza Navona.

• *In the Caravaggio chapel, first look to the left wall.*

The Calling of St. Matthew

Matthew (old man with beard) and his well-dressed, tax-collecting cronies sit in a dingy bar and count the money they've extorted. Suddenly, two men in robes and bare feet enter from the right—Jesus and Peter. Jesus' "Creation-of-Adam" hand emerges from the darkness to point at Matthew. A shaft of light extends the gesture, lighting up the face of Matthew, who points to himself, *Last Supper*–style, to ask, "You talkin' to me?" Jesus came to convince Matthew to leave his sleazy job and preach Love. Matthew did.

Churches near the Pantheon

In this, his first large-scale work, 29-year-old Caravaggio (1571–1610) shocked critics and clerics by showing a holy scene

in a down-to-earth location. Lower-class people in everyday clothes were his models; his setting was a dive bar (which he knew well). Christ's teeny gold halo is the only hint of the supernatural, as Caravaggio makes a bold proclamation—that miracles are natural events experienced in a profound way.

• *Now look to the center wall.*

PANTHEON

The Inspiration of St. Matthew

Matthew followed Christ's call, traveled with him, and (supposedly) wrote Jesus' life story (the Gospel according to Matthew).

Here, Matthew is hard at work when he's interrupted by an angel with a few suggestions. This sets the scene in motion. Matthew kneels on a stool, which is just about to fall out of the painting and into our zone. Matthew's bald head, wrinkled face, and grizzled beard make him an all-too-human saint. Even the teen angel lacks a holy glow—he just hangs there. Caravaggio paints a dark background, then shines a dramatic spotlight on the few things that tell the story.

• *Finally, check out the right wall.*

The Martyrdom of St. Matthew

Matthew lies prone, while a truly scary man straddles him and brandishes a sword. The bystanders shrink away from this angry

executioner. Caravaggio shines his harsh third-degree spotlight on Matthew and the killer, who are the focus of the painting. The other figures swirl around them in a circle (with the executioner's arm as the radius). Matthew, who

thought he had given up everything to follow Christ, now gives up his life as well. He is as open as a crucifix, accepting his fate, and reaching for a palm frond—symbolic of victory over death. The bearded face in the background (to the left of the executioner's shoulder) is a self-portrait of Caravaggio, observing the violence without getting involved.

When the chapel was unveiled in 1600, Caravaggio's ultra-realism shocked Rome. Although he died only 10 years later, his uncompromising details, emotional subjects, odd compositions, and dramatic lighting set the tone for later Baroque painters.

Gesù Church

The center of the Jesuit order and the best symbol of the Catholic Counter-Reformation, the Gesù (jay-zoo) is packed with over-

Gesù Church

A P S E

TRANSEPT

NAVE

❹ ❸ ❺
❷
❶

DCH

ENTER

PIAZZA DEL GESÙ

❶ Ceiling Fresco & Stucco
❷ Nave
❸ Tomb & Altarpiece of St. Ignatius of Loyola
❹ Religion Overthrowing Heresy
❺ Tomb & Altarpiece of St. Francis Xavier

10 YARDS
10 METERS

blown art and underappreciated history. Consider seeing this church en route to Capitol Hill.

Exterior

The facade looks ho-hum, like a thousand no-name Catholic churches scattered from Europe to Southern California...until you realize that this was the first, the model for the others. Its scroll-like shoulders were revolutionary, breaking up the rigid rectangles of Renaissance architecture and signaling the coming of Baroque. The travertine stone facade was recently cleaned but—with its sponge-like properties and Rome's pollution—it will be black again soon enough.

The building to the right of the church—called Camere of St. Ignatius—is where Ignatius of Loyola, the founder of the Jesuits, lived, worked, and died (Mon–Sat 16:00–18:00, Sun 10:00–12:00).

• *Step inside the Gesù Church, grab a seat, and look up at the huge painting on the ceiling.*

Interior

❶ Ceiling Fresco and Stucco—
The Triumph of the Name of Jesus (by Il Baciccio)

The church's sunroof opens, and we can see right up to heaven. A glowing cross with the initials "I.H.S." (In Hoc Signo, adopted as the seal of the Society of Jesus) astounds the faithful and sends the infidels plunging downward. The twisted tangle of bodies—the damned—spills over the edge of the painting's frame on their way to hell. The painted bodies mingle with 3-D stucco bodies and a riot of decoration in a classic example of Baroque multimedia.

During the Counter-Reformation, when Catholics fought Protestants for the hearts and minds of the world's Christians, art became propaganda. The moral here is clear—this is the fate of Protestant heretics who dared to pervert the true teachings of Jesus.

❷ The Nave

When the church was originally built (1568), the walls were white and the decor was simple. It was designed for what the Jesuits did best—teaching. The Jesuits wanted to educate Catholics to prepare them for the onslaught of probing Protestant questions. The church's nave is like one big lecture hall, with no traditional side aisles.

In the 1500s, the best way to keep Protestants from stealing your church members was to reason with them. By the 1600s, it was easier to kill them, and so the Thirty Years' War raged across Europe. The church became crusted over with the colorful, bombastic, jingoistic Baroque we see today.

• *Now look toward the left transept.*

❸ Tomb and Altarpiece of St. Ignatius of Loyola (left transept)

A big altarpiece with towering columns and topped with statues of the Trinity marks the burial spot of the humble war veteran who founded the Jesuit order.

In the center of this altarpiece, you'll see a painting (by Andrea Pozzo) of Ignatius receiving his call. Behind the painting rests a gleaming statue of the saint, who spreads his arms wide and gazes up, receiving a vision from on high. But you won't be able to see it unless you come at 17:30. Every day at that time, church attendants turn a crank, the painting lowers, and the silver statue of Ignatius is on view.

Ignatius (1491–1556) was a Spanish soldier during the era of conquistadors. Then, at age 30, he was struck down by a cannon-ball. While convalescing, he was seized by the burning desire to change his life. He wandered Europe and traveled to Jerusalem. He meditated with monks. He lived in a cave. At 33, he enrolled in a school for boys to fill in the knowledge he'd missed. He studied in Paris and in Rome. Finally, after almost two decades of learning and seeking, he found a way to combine his military training with his spiritual aspirations.

In 1540, the pope gave approval to Ignatius and his small band of followers—the Society of Jesus (Jesuits). These monks, organized like a military company, vowed complete obedience to their "General," and placed themselves at the service of the pope. Their mission: To be intellectual warriors doing battle with heretics. They were in the right place at the right time—Ignatius and Martin Luther were almost exact contemporaries.

Ignatius' body lies in the small coffin beneath the statue (near ground level). This simple, intense man might have been embarrassed by the lavish memorial to him, with its silver, gold, green marble, and lapis lazuli columns. Above Ignatius, a statue of God stands near a lapis lazuli globe (the biggest in the world) and gestures as though to say, "Go and spread the Word to every land"... which the Jesuits tried to do.

• *Look at the marble statue group to the right of Ignatius.*

❹ Religion Overthrowing Heresy
This statue (and a similar one to the left of Ignatius) shows the Church as an angry nun hauling back with a whip and just spanking a bunch of miserable Protestants. The serpent (Luther) is being stepped upon while the angry cherub rips pages out of a heretical book. Not too subtle.

Yes, the Jesuits got a reputation for unfeeling dedication to truth above all else, but their weapons were words, ideas, and critical reasoning. They taught and defended the recently revamped doctrines of the Council of Trent (1545–1563).

• *Now view the right transept.*

❺ Tomb and Altarpiece of St. Francis Xavier
This was also the Age of Discovery, when Spain and Portugal were colonizing and Christianizing the world, using force if necessary. Francis Xavier joined a Portuguese expedition and headed out to convert the heathens. He touched down in Africa, India, Indonesia,

The Jesuit Legacy

The Jesuits produced some great, open-minded thinkers, from the poet Gerard Manley Hopkins to modern mystic Pierre Teilhard de Chardin.

The great sculptor Bernini attended this church. He honored the Jesuit Robert Bellarmine (1542–1621) with a bust, which is sometimes on display in the Gesù Church. Bellarmine, a theologian at the height of Catholic-Protestant differences, was a voice of reason in the often bitter controversy. He's best known as the man who ordered Galileo to stop teaching the Copernican theory, though he was actually a moderating influence in the debate.

Because of their spiritual fervor, the Jesuits caught flack for being closed-minded. In the 1700s, several countries expelled them, and finally the pope even banned the Society (1773). Chastened, they were brought back (1814), and today they fill the staff of many a Catholic college.

China, and Japan. Along the way, he learned new languages and customs, trying to communicate a strange, monotheistic religion to puzzled polytheists.

He had been on the road for more than a decade (1552) when he died on an island off China (see the dim painting over the altar). Thanks largely to zealous Jesuits such as Francis, Catholicism became a truly worldwide religion.

Church of Santa Maria sopra Minerva

From the outside, survey the many layers of Rome: An Egyptian obelisk sits on a Baroque elephant (by Bernini) in front of a Gothic church built over *(sopra)* a pre-Christian, pagan Temple of Minerva.

Before stepping in, notice the high-water-mark plaques *(alluvione)* on the wall to the right of the door. Inside, you'll see that the lower parts of some frescoes were lost to floods. After the last great flood, in 1870, Rome built the present embankments along the river, finally breaking the spirit of the mighty Tiber.

Nave

This is the only Gothic church you'll see in Rome. The ceiling has pointed crisscross arches in a starry, luminous blue sky, and the nave is lit by rows of round stained-glass windows. When this Dominican church was built, Gothic was the rage in northern Europe, with large windows to let in the light—though churches in sunny Italy don't require big expanses of glass. During the Middle Ages, Rome was almost a ghost town, and what little was built during this time was later gussied up in the Baroque style. The simplicity of this church is a refreshing exception.

Main Altar

The body of St. Catherine of Siena lies under the altar (her head is in Siena). In the 1300s, this Italian nun was renowned for her righ-

teousness and her visions of a mystical marriage with Jesus. Her impassioned letters convinced the pope to return from France to Rome, thus saving Italy from untold chaos. Behind her are buried two Medici popes: Leo X, the son of Lorenzo the Magnificent and the man who excommunicated Martin Luther, and his cousin Clement VII.

In 1634, a frail 70-year-old Galileo knelt at this altar on the way to his trial before the Inquisition in the church's monastery. Facing the fierce Dominican lawyers, he renounced his heretical belief that the earth moved around the sun. (Legend has it that as he walked out, he whispered, "But it *does* move.")

• *Left of the altar stands a little-known Michelangelo statue...*

Christ Bearing the Cross (1519–1520)

Note Jesus' athletic body, a striking contrast to the docile Jesus of medieval art. This sculpture shares the same bulging biceps as the Christ in Michelangelo's *The Last Judgment* in the Sistine Chapel.

Christ's pose is slightly twisted, with one leg forward in typical *contrapposto* style, leaning on a large cross along with the symbols of the Crucifixion. Originally, Christ was buck naked, but later prudish Counter-Reformation censors gave him his bronze girdle. A bronze shoe was later added to protect the right toe from the kisses of the faithful.

This statue was Michelangelo's second attempt—he was forced to abandon a first effort due to a flaw in the block of Carrara marble. In this version, he left parts—including the face—to be finished by an apprentice, who took the liberty of working on and botching the feet and hands. This ineptitude led him to be replaced by yet another sculptor who finally finished the job. Michelangelo, disturbed that anyone would mess up his work, offered to redo the sculpture, but apparently the patrons were pleased. One contemporary said, "The knees alone are worth more than all of Rome together."

The tomb of the great early Renaissance painter (and Dominican brother) Fra Angelico ("Beato Angelico 1387–1455") is farther to the left, just up the three stairs.

Over in the right (south) transept, pop in a coin for light, and enjoy a Filippino Lippi fresco showing scenes of the life of the great Dominican scholar St. Thomas Aquinas (big man in blue and white). In the central scene, Thomas presents the chapel's patron to Mary, while on the right wall, he displays a book to show everyone the true dogma, causing a heretic to slump defeated at his feet.

• *Exit the church via its rear door (behind the Michelangelo statue), walk down tiny Fra Angelico lane, turn left, and walk to the next square. On your right, you'll find the last church on our tour.*

Church of San Ignazio

This church is a riot of Baroque illusions. Find a seat in the nave and look up at the large colorful ceiling fresco. ❶ St. Ignatius, whom

we met in the Gesù Church, was the founder of the Jesuits, a disciplined Catholic teaching order charged with spreading the word of God around a world that was rapidly being "discovered." Here you see him (a small figure perched on a cloud in the center) having a ❷ vision of Christ with the Cross. Heavenly light from the vision bounces off his chest, and the rays beam to the four corners of the earth (including ❸ America, to the left, depicted as a bare-breasted Native American maiden spearing naked men). This fresco epitomizes pure Baroque drama, with perspective illusions that fool the eye into thinking the fresco is an extension of the church architecture. Note how the actual columns of the church are extended into the two-dimensional fresco. Now fix your eyes on the ❹ arch at the far end of the painting. Walk up the nave, and watch the arch grow and tower over you.

Before you reach the center of the church, stop at the small yellow disk on the floor and look up into the central (black) dome. Keeping your eye on the dome, walk under and past it. Building project runs out of money? Hire a painter to paint a fake, flat dome.

Back outside, the church faces the headquarters of the Carabinieri police force, forming Piazza San Ignazio, a square with several converging streets that has been compared to a stage set. Sit on the church steps, admire the theatrical yellow backdrop, and watch the "actors" enter one way and exit another, in the human opera that is modern Rome.

• *From here it's a short walk to the left down Via del Seminario back to the Pantheon. Or go right, cross busy Via del Corso, and follow the crowds to the Trevi Fountain.*

BATHS OF DIOCLETIAN TOUR

Terme di Diocleziano

Of all the marvelous structures built by the Romans, their public baths were arguably the grandest, and the Baths of Diocletian were the granddaddy of them all. These baths sprawled over 10 acres—roughly twice the area of the entire Forum—and could cleanse 3,000 Romans at once. Today, there are several sections you can visit.

The **Church of Santa Maria degli Angeli,** housed in the former main hall of the baths, is the single most impressive sight of the bunch. The entrance is on Piazza della Repubblica (free, Mon–Sat 7:00–18:30, Sun 7:00–19:30, closed to sightseers during Mass).

The skippable **Museum of the Bath** (Museo Nazionale Romano Terme di Diocleziano) has a shaded garden with Roman tombstones outside, and early Roman jewelry, masks, burial items, and Roman inscriptions on tombs and tablets inside. The entrance faces Termini train station (€10 combo-ticket includes entry within three days to three other National Museum branches, including nearby National Museum of Rome—see page 167, open Tue–Sun 9:00–19:45, closed Mon, last entry 45 minutes before closing, audioguide–€4, Viale Enrico de Nicola 79, tel. 06-3996-7700).

Energetic architecture wonks can even walk the perimeter of the baths: from Via Torino to Piazza dei Cinquecento to Via Volturno to Via XX Settembre.

The Tour Begins

Santa Maria degli Angeli
• *Start your tour standing outside the church.*

Exterior—The Baths' Caldarium
The curved brick facade of today's church was once part of the *caldarium,* or steam room of the ancient baths. Romans loved to

sweat out last night's indulgences. After entering the main lobby (located where Piazza della Repubblica is today), they'd strip in the locker rooms, then enter the steam room. The *caldarium* had wood furnaces under the raised floors. Stoked by slaves, these furnaces were used to heat the floors and hot tubs. The low ceiling helped keep the room steamy.

From the *caldarium,* the Romans moved into the next room, and so should you.

• *From noisy Piazza della Repubblica, step into the vast and cool church built upon the remains of a vast and steamy Roman bath complex.*

The Church's Entry Hall—The Baths' Tepidarium

This round-domed room with an oculus (open skylight, now with modern stained glass) was once the *tepidarium*—the cooling-off room of the baths, where medium, "tepid" temperatures were maintained. This is where masseuses would rub you down and scrape you off with a stick (Romans didn't use soap).

• *In ancient times, Romans would have continued on to the central area of the baths. You'll continue to the...*

The Church's Large Transept—
The Baths' Central Hall

This hall retains the grandeur of the ancient baths. It's the size of a football field and seven stories high—once even higher, since the original ancient floor was about 15 feet below its present level. The

ceiling's crisscross arches were an architectural feat unmatched for a thousand years. The eight red granite columns are original, from ancient Rome—stand next to one and feel its five-foot girth. (Only the eight in the transept proper are original.

The others are made of plastered-over brick.) In Roman times, this hall was covered with mosaics, marble, and gold, and lined with statues.

From here, Romans could continue (through what is now the apse, near the altar) into an open-air courtyard to take a dip in the vast 32,000-square-foot swimming pool (in the *frigidarium*) that paralleled this huge hall. Many other rooms, gardens, and

Baths of Diocletian

courtyards extended beyond what we see here. The huge complex was built in only 10 years (around A.D. 300)—amazing when you think of the centuries it took builders of puny medieval cathedrals, such as Paris' Notre-Dame.

Mentally undress your fellow tourists and churchgoers, and imagine hundreds of naked or toga-clad Romans wrestling, doing jumping jacks, singing in the baths, networking, or just milling about.

The baths were more than washrooms. They were health clubs with exercising areas, equipment, and swimming pools. They had gardens for socializing. Libraries, shops, bars, fast-food vendors, pedicurists, depilatories, and brothels catered to every Roman need. Most important, perhaps, the baths offered a spacious, cool-in-summer/warm-in-winter place for Romans to get out of their stuffy apartments and schmooze or simply hang out.

Admission was virtually free, requiring only the smallest coin. Baths were open to men and women—and during Nero's reign, coed bathing was popular—but generally there were either separate rooms or separate entry times. Most Romans went daily.

The church we see today was (at least partly) designed by Michelangelo (1561), who used the baths' main hall as the nave. Later, when Piazza della Repubblica became an important Roman intersection, another architect renovated the church. To allow people to enter from the grand new piazza, he spun it 90 degrees, turning Michelangelo's nave into a long transept.

• *Embedded in the floor of the right transept (roped off) is a brass rod called...*

La Meridiana (1702)

This is a meridian, pointing due north. It acts as a sundial. As the sun arcs across the southern sky, a ray of light beams into the church

through a tiny hole high in the wall and a cut in the cornice of the right transept. (To find the hole, follow the rod to the right to the wall and look up 65 feet.) The sunbeam sweeps across the church floor, crossing the meridian rod at exactly noon. (Allow for variances due to Daylight Saving Time and the approximate time zones of Greenwich Mean Time.)

This celestial clock is also a calendar. In summer, when the sun is high overhead, the sunbeam strikes the southern end of the rod. With each passing day, the sun travels up the rod (toward the apse), passing through the signs of the zodiac (the 28-day months of the moon's phases) marked alongside the rod. Many of the meridian's markings were intended for its other use, charting the movement of the stars. However, the tiny window that once let in light from the North Star (originally above the archway of the entrance to the apse) has been filled in.

Find some key dates in the Christian calendar, particularly the spring equinox and Easter (near Aries the Ram). Most Christians agree that Easter is the first Sunday after the first full moon after the vernal equinox (established with the Nicene Creed, A.D. 325). It took large meridians like this to measure the sun's movements accurately enough to predict Easter and other holidays years in advance.

La Meridiana was Rome's official city timekeeper until 1846, when it was replaced by the cannon atop Gianicolo Hill (which is still fired every day at exactly noon).

In the left transept (opposite end), you'll find a monumental organ built for the Jubilee Year of 2000. Free concerts are held regularly; check the schedule posted near the organ.

• *Step into the* Sacrestia, *the small room to the left of the main altar, which now houses...*

Exhibits

Temporary exhibits often illuminate the church's rich architectural history. Admire both the immensity and height of the ancient Roman brickwork in this room. Step outside into the courtyard (where there's a WC), and re-create the grand architecture. Notice the *exedra* (semicircular recess in a wall or building)—a motif Romans used for decoration and as a kind of stage for philosophers and orators. See the niches that once housed statues, the rectangular holes that could be used to hold wood-beam scaffolding, and the small pockmarks where iron pegs once secured the marble paneling.

Large building projects like this were political security: They provided employment and fed the masses. Diocletian (ruled A.D. 285–305) struggled with a system to rule his unwieldy empire. He broke it into zones ruled by four "tetrarchs." During Diocletian's "tetrarchs" period, architecture and art were grandiose, but almost a caricature of greatness—meant to proclaim to Romans that their city was still the power it had once been.

The baths were one of the last great structures built before Rome's 200-year fall. They functioned until A.D. 537, when barbarians cut the city's aqueducts, plunging Rome into a thousand years of poverty, darkness, and B.O.

• *Exit where you entered. If you're feeling lucky, turn right and walk 100 yards to the entrance of the rarely open...*

Octagonal Hall (Aula Ottagona)

This octagonal building, capped by a dome with a hole in the top, may have served as a cool room *(frigidarium),* with small pools of cold water for plunging into. Or, because of its many doors, it may simply have been a large intersection, connecting other parts of the baths. Originally, the floor was 25 feet lower—as you can see through the glass-covered hole in the floor. The graceful iron grid overhead supported the canopy of a 1928 planetarium.

Piazza della Repubblica

The piazza, shaped like an *exedra* (curved recess), echoes the wall of a stadium adjoining the original baths. It was called Piazza Esedra until Italian unification (and is still called that by many Romans).

The thundering Via Nazionale starts at what was an ancient door. Look down it (past the erotic nymphs of the Naiad fountain) to the Victor Emmanuel Monument. The Art Nouveau fountain of the four water nymphs created quite a stir when unveiled in 1911. The nymphs were modeled after a set of twins, who kept coming to visit as late as the 1960s to remind themselves of their nubile youth.

ANCIENT APPIAN WAY TOUR

Via Appia Antica

The wonder of its day, the Appian Way was the largest, widest, fastest road ever, called the "Queen of Roads." Built in 312 B.C. and named after Appius Claudius Caecus (a Roman official), it connected Rome with Capua (near Naples), running in a straight line for much of the way, ignoring the natural contour of the land. Eventually, this most important of Roman roads stretched 430 miles to the port of Brindisi—the gateway to the East—where boats sailed for Greece and Egypt. Twenty-nine such roads fanned out from Rome. Just as Hitler built the Autobahn system in anticipation of empire maintenance, the expansion-minded Roman government realized the military and political value of a good road system.

Hollywood created the famous image of the Appian Way lined with the crucified bodies of Spartacus and his gang of slave rebels. This image is only partially accurate—Spartacus was killed in battle after a two-year conflict. But historians do believe that after his defeat in 71 B.C., 6,000 slaves from the revolt were crucified on crosses spaced about 30 yards apart along the length of the Appian Way—a distance of over 100 miles. Their bodies were left to hang for several months as a warning to other slaves. Imagine the eerie welcome this provided visitors arriving in Rome.

When the Christian faith permeated Rome, the Appian Way became a popular underground burial place for Christians. It later entered Romantic lore (though untrue) as a place where Christians hid from persecution. Today the road and the landscape around it are preserved as a cultural park.

For the tourist, the ancient Appian Way offers three attractions: the road itself, with its ruined monuments; the two major Christian catacombs open to visitors; and the peaceful atmosphere, which provides a respite from the city. Be aware, however, that the road today is busy with traffic—and actually quite treacherous in spots. I recommend following this tour's route, which lets you avoid the worst of the traffic, making the area a pleasant place for strolling or biking.

Orientation

Tomb of Cecilia Metella: €6, includes entry to a small museum, Tue–Sun 9:00–19:30 in summer, closes earlier off-season, closed Mon, last entry one hour before closing, tel. 06-3996-7700.

Circus and Villa of Maxentius: €3, Tue–Sun 9:00–13:30, closed Mon, last entry 30 minutes before closing.

Catacombs of San Sebastiano: Guided 25-minute tours leave 2/hour, €8, Mon–Sat 9:00–12:00 & 14:00–17:00, last tour leaves at 17:00, closed Sun and mid-Nov–mid-Dec, Via Appia Antica 136, tel. 06-785-0350, www.catacombe.org.

Catacombs of San Callisto: Guided 30-minute tours leave at least 2/hour, €8, Thu–Tue 9:00–12:00 & 14:00–17:00, closed Wed and Feb, Via Appia Antica 110, tel. 06-5130-1580 or 06-5130-151. Dig this: There's a website—www.catacombe.roma.it—that focuses mainly on San Callisto, featuring photos, site info, and history.

Domine Quo Vadis Church: Free, daily 8:00–19:30 (until 18:30 off-season).

San Sebastiano Gate and Museum of the Walls: €3, Tue–Sun 9:00–14:00, closed Mon, last entry 30 minutes before closing, tel. 06-7047-5284.

Information: The **Via Appia Antica TI** near Domine Quo Vadis Church gives out maps and information on the entire park, which stretches east and south of the visit outlined here (daily April–Oct 9:30–17:30, Nov–March 9:30–16:30, also rents bikes, Via Appia Antica 58/60, tel. 06-513-5316, www.parcoappiaantica.it). The Archeobus map shows everything clearly. **Capo di Bove**—part active excavations, part relaxing garden—has a small info center with a good €4 map/guide (Mon–Sat 10:00–16:00, Sun 10:00–18:00, great place for a discreet picnic, clean WCs, 100 yards uphill from Appia Antica Caffè, tel. 06-3996-7700). Appia Antica Caffè also has good maps (see "Bike Rental," later).

When to Go: Visit in the morning or late afternoon, since many of the sights—including the catacombs—shut down from 12:00 to 14:30. All of the recommended sights are open on Tuesday, Thursday, Friday, and Saturday. On Monday, several sights are closed, including the Tomb of Cecilia Metella, the Circus and Villa of Maxentius, and the San Sebastiano Gate and

Museum of the Walls. On Wednesday, the Catacombs of San Callisto and the pedestrian path through the park are closed. On Sunday, the Catacombs of San Sebastiano are closed; however, the Appian Way is closed to car traffic, making it a great day for walking or biking.

Getting There: Bus #660 drops you off right where our tour starts, at the Tomb of Cecilia Metella. In Rome, take Metro line A to the Colli Albani stop, where you catch bus #660 (2/hour, along Via Appia Nuova) and ride 10 minutes to the last stop—Cecilia Metella/Via Appia Antica (at the intersection of Via Cecilia Metella and Via Appia Antica). As it can be frustrating to buy a bus ticket on the Appian Way, have one in hand for your return trip.

A **taxi** will get you from Rome to the Tomb of Cecilia Metella for about €20. However, to return by taxi, you'll have to phone for one, as there are no taxi stands on the Appian Way (or just take handy bus #118 back to Rome).

Bus #118 gets you to the sights on the northern part of the Appian Way, if you want to visit just a few sights without following the exact tour route outlined here. In Rome, catch #118 from either the Piramide or Circo Massimo Metro stops; going away from the city center, it stops at the San Sebastiano Gate, Domine Quo Vadis Church, Catacombs of San Callisto, and Catacombs of San Sebastiano. Although bus #118 does not stop at the Tomb of Cecilia Metella, the Tomb is only 500 yards away from the bus stop at the Catacombs of San Sebastiano. Going back to Rome, bus #118 takes a somewhat different route (skipping the Catacombs of San Sebastiano); catch this northbound bus just up the road at the Catacombs of San Callisto.

Bus #218 goes from San Giovanni in Laterano to Domine Quo Vadis Church and the west entrance of the Catacombs of San Callisto, but isn't handy for other Appian Way sights.

The handy, but much more expensive, **Archeobus** runs from Termini train station to the Appian Way sights (see "Tours," page 38). It stops at all the key attractions—you can hop off, tour the sights, and pick up a later bus (officially runs twice hourly, but service can be spotty).

Getting Back: No matter how you arrive at the Appian Way, **bus #118** is the easiest and cheapest way to return to Rome (get off at the end of the line, the Piramide Metro stop).

Bike Rental: The best day for biking is Sunday, when the Appian Way is closed to traffic. Take bus #660 to the last stop (Cecilia Metella/Via Appia Antica) and you'll find **Appia Antica Caffè**, where you can rent a bike (€3.50/hour, €12/4 hours, 10 percent discount on bikes and food with this book,

Ancient Appian Way

TO
SAN SEBASTIANO GATE,
MUSEUM OF THE WALLS
& DOWNTOWN ROME

A Bus #660 Stop
B Bus #118 Stops
C Bus #118 (Southbound Stop Only)
D Bus #218 Stop
E Archeobus Stops

DOMINE QUO VADIS CHURCH

VIA APPIA

ARDEATINA

PEDESTRIAN WALKWAY (CLOSED WED)

COLUMBARIUM

SECOND MILESTONE

VICOLO DELLA BASILICA

CATACOMBS OF SAN CALLISTO
& WC

VIA D. SETTE CHIESE

FOSSE ARDEANTINE

VILLA OF MAXENTIUS

CIRCUS OF MAXENTIUS

CATACOMBS OF SAN SEBASTIANO
& WC

VIA APPIA ANTICA

VIA DI SAN SEB.

TOMB OF CECILIA METELLA

VIA CECILIA METELLA

THIRD MILESTONE

TO AQUEDUCT PARK

APPIA ANTICA CAFFÈ
& BIKE RENTAL

ALIMENTARI

TORRE DI CAPO DI BOVE

VIA CAPO DI BOVE

SCENIC SECTION

¼ MILE
.5 KM

DCH

TO
4TH THROUGH 11TH
MILESTONES & BRINDISI

includes free info map when available, handy €1 map, daily 10:00–sunset, at corner of the Appian Way and Via Cecilia Metella, near Tomb of Cecilia Metella at Via Appia Antica 175, mobile 338-3465-440, www.appiaanticacaffe.it). You can also rent a bike from the **Via Appia Antica TI** (€3/hour, €10/day; see "Information," earlier). If you don't mind heavy traffic, you could even bike from the Colosseum or Santa Maria

Maggiore out past the wall and down the Appian Way. For bike rental in the city center, see "By Bike," on page 34.

WCs: Free WCs are at the San Sebastiano and San Callisto catacombs and at Capo di Bove, and WCs for paying customers at the Tomb of Cecilia Metella and the Appia Antica Caffè. There are several water fountains along the way to refill water bottles.

Length of This Tour: Budget five hours to get to and from the Appian Way, walk or bike the stretch of sights, and visit one of the catacombs.

Cuisine Art: Appia Antica Caffè (see "Bike Rental," earlier) makes big salads and abundant sandwiches and has a shady, restful seating area in back. Or go 50 yards uphill (south) from the café to buy food at a hole-in-the-wall *alimentari* (market), perfect for assembling a picnic (Mon–Sat 7:00–14:00 & 15:00–20:00, Sun 9:00–15:00). Great picnic spots are just a half-mile farther uphill (south) from here. Several pricey restaurants are along the stretch between the Tomb of Cecilia Metella and the Catacombs of San Sebastiano (which normally has a sandwich-and-drinks cart).

Starring: An old road, crumbling tombs, and underground Christian cemeteries.

Overview

Our tour begins near the Tomb of Cecilia Metella, at the far (southern) end of the sightseeing highlights, and works back northward—mostly downhill—to Domine Quo Vadis Church, toward the center of Rome. We'll arrive by bus #660 or taxi, walk a mile-and-a-half along the Appian Way, and return to Rome on bus #118. Or take the Archeobus, hopping on and off at key stops.

Sightseers share the road with speeding drivers talking on mobile phones (except on traffic-free Sundays), but there's really only one bad stretch—between the Catacombs of San Sebastiano and Domine Quo Vadis Church. We'll avoid that traffic by taking a pedestrian path through a quiet park that parallels the busy road (except on Wednesdays, when the path is closed).

The Tour Begins

• *From the café near the Tomb of Cecilia Metella, head downhill 100 yards, where you walk (or rattle your bike) over a stretch of the...*

Original Paved Road

Huge basalt stones formed the sturdy base of a road 14 feet across. In its heyday, a central strip accommodated animal-powered vehicles, and elevated sidewalks served pedestrians. The first section (near Rome) was perfectly straight, and lined with tombs and funerary monuments.

Nearby (to the right of the entrance to the Tomb of Cecilia Metella) is the original **mile marker III,** one of more than 400 such stones that counted the distance from Rome to Brindisi. Emperors knew that a fine network of roads was key to expanding and administering the empire. This road, from c. 312 B.C., kicks off the expansion period.

• *You can't miss (on the right side) the...*

Tomb of Cecilia Metella (Mausoleo di Cecilia Metella)

This massive cylindrical tomb, one of the best preserved of the many tombs of prominent Romans that line the road, was built

in the time of Augustus (c. 30 B.C.) for the daughter-in-law of Crassus, Rome's richest man. Faced with white travertine and situated on the crest of a hill, the tomb was an imposing sight. This grand tomb in the suburbs rivaled Augustus' own round mausoleum in the city center (near the Ara Pacis, see page 67).

Since no one was allowed to be buried inside the city walls, the Appian Way was a popular place to have a tomb where everyone could see and admire it. Later, Christians were buried here, though not in tombs (they preferred to be buried underground). Picture a funeral procession passing under the pines and cypresses, past a long line of pyramids, private mini-temples, altars, and tombs.

If you pay to go inside, you'll see the tomb's hollow interior; a few statues of deceased Romans that once adorned tombs; and a former paving-stone quarry with a preserved wagon-wheel groove.

• *About 200 yards farther downhill from the tomb (on the right) are the ruins of the...*

Circus and Villa of Maxentius (Circo e Villa di Massenzio)

This was the suburban home of the emperor who was eventually defeated by Constantine in A.D. 312. The main sight to see here is a whole lot of nothing—that is, the expansive stretch of open space contained by this huge former chariot race track. You can see essentially all of it for free from the road. If you pay the admission, you can walk between the entrance towers to the long central

---

Sebastiano vs. Callisto

Which of the two catacombs is the best? They're actually quite similar. Both include a half-hour tour, where you go underground to see the niches where early Christians were buried (but no bones). Both have some faded frescoes and graffiti with Christian symbols. Both have small chapels and a few memorial statues. Most people pick one catacomb to visit, and either will fit the bill. I lean slightly in favor of San Callisto, but only because of its historical importance, not because it's inherently more interesting.

(Note that the **Catacombs of Priscilla**—more intimate and less crowded than these two more famous ones—can be found at the other end of town, northeast of the Villa Borghese Gardens; see page 66.)

---

spine, and imagine chariots racing around it while 10,000 fans cheered. Maxentius watched from the building rising up above the bleachers, where the chariots made their hairiest turn. At the far end of the 260-yard track is the triumphal arch under which the winner rode to receive his reward.

Also, just down the Appian Way from this circus is a square wall of ruins enclosing a modern building. Behind that modern building, you can glimpse the circular mausoleum of Maxentius' son, Romulus.

• *About 300 yards farther down the road (on the left) are the...*

▲▲Catacombs of San Sebastiano

This underground cemetery is named for the Christian soldier who was tied to a column and shot through with arrows because

of his faith—a subject depicted by many artists through history. A guide takes you below ground to see burial niches, frescoes, and graffiti. It's said that the bodies of Peter and Paul were kept here for a while in the third century.

Besides the catacombs, the site also has a basilica (free) containing various relics. In the first chapel to the left are St. Sebastian's supposed remains, marked with a statue of an arrow-pierced corpse. On the opposite side of the nave, a chapel displays an arrow he was shot with, a section of the column he was tied to, and a couple of footprints from the Domine Quo Vadis legend (see below). Nearby stands a curly-haired bust of *The Savior (Il Salvatore)* by Bernini.

• *The stretch of the Appian Way past the Catacombs of San Sebastiano is the least interesting and most crowded (even dangerous). Avoid it by taking the pedestrian and bike path (open daily except Wed), which begins just past the Catacombs of San Sebastiano, at the intersection with Via delle Sette Chiese. To reach the path, go through the arch at #126. The quiet path parallels the Appian Way and takes you directly to the Catacombs of San Callisto. On Wednesdays, when the gate is closed, you'll have to stay straight on Via Appia Antica, being careful of traffic.*

▲▲Catacombs of San Callisto

These are my favorite catacombs, named for the cemetery's first caretaker, St. Callixtus. This was the official cemetery for Rome's early Christians and the burial place of nine third-century popes, other bishops of Rome, and various martyrs. The most famous martyr was Sta. Cecilia, patron saint of music, a Roman noble who was killed for converting to Christianity. Her tomb is marked with a copy of a famous Maderno statue. (For more on Cecilia and the statue, ✪ see the Trastevere Walk chapter.)

Buy your €8 ticket and wait for your language to be called. They move lots of people quickly. If one group seems ridiculously large (more than 50 people), wait for the next tour in English.

• *After you visit the catacombs, an optional detour brings you to the evocative* **Fosse Ardeantine**, *a memorial tomb to 335 Italians gunned down by Nazis during World War II to avenge a bomb attack in Rome that killed 32 German soldiers. With your back to the San Callisto ticket booth, go right, walk downhill through the gate (where you can also catch bus #218 back to San Giovanni), and follow signs to* Fosse Ardeantine—*about a five-minute walk (Mon-Fri 8:15-15:00, Sat-Sun 8:15-16:45).*

Back at the catacombs, continue north (downhill) another three-quarters of a mile, where the pedestrian path spills out at a busy three-way intersection. There you'll find the small...

Domine Quo Vadis Church

The tiny ninth-century church (redone in the 17th) was built on the spot where Peter, while fleeing the city to escape Nero's persecution, saw a vision of Christ. Peter asked Jesus, "Lord, where are you going?" (*"Domine quo vadis?"* in Latin), to which Christ replied, "I am going to Rome to be crucified again." This miraculous sign gave Peter faith and courage and caused him to return to Rome.

Catacombs

The catacombs are burial places for (mostly) Christians who died in ancient Roman times. By law, no one was allowed to be buried within the walls of Rome. While pagan Romans were into cremation, Christians preferred to be buried (so that they could be resurrected when the time came). But land was expensive, and most Christians were poor. A few wealthy, landowning Christians allowed their properties to be used as burial places.

The 40 or so known catacombs are scattered outside the ancient walls of Rome. From the first through the fifth centuries, Christians dug an estimated 375 miles of tomb-lined tunnels, with networks of galleries as many as five layers deep. The volcanic tuff that Rome sits atop—which is soft and easy to cut, but hardens when exposed to air—was perfect for the job. The Christians burrowed many layers deep for two reasons: to get more mileage out of the donated land, and to be near martyrs and saints already buried there. Bodies were wrapped in linen (like Christ's). Since they figured the Second Coming was imminent, there was no interest in embalming the body.

When Emperor Constantine legalized Christianity in A.D. 313, Christians had a new, interesting problem: There would be no more recently persecuted martyrs to bind them together and inspire them. Instead, the early martyrs and popes assumed more importance, and Christians began making pilgrimages to their burial places in the catacombs.

In the 800s, when barbarian invaders started ransacking the tombs, Christians moved the relics of saints and martyrs to the safety of churches in the city center. For a thousand years, the catacombs were forgotten. In early modern times, they were excavated and became part of the Romantic Age's Grand Tour of Europe.

Inside the nave of the church, stumble over the stone marked with the supposed footprints of Jesus. You'll see a fresco of Peter with keys on the left wall and one of Jesus on the right. A bust depicts Nobel Prize–winning Polish author Henryk Sienkiewicz, who wrote a historical novel that was the basis for the 1951 Hollywood movie *Quo Vadis*.

• *The tour is over. "Quo vadis, pilgrim?"*

To return to central Rome, it's another two miles north along a busy stretch of road, not recommended on foot or bike. Instead, catch bus #118 from the bus stop about 75 yards past Domine Quo Vadis Church (across from the TI). Bus #118 makes several interesting stops (see below) on its way to the Piramide Metro stop. (Note that there's also another bus, the #218, that goes from here to San Giovanni in Laterano.)

When abandoned plates and utensils from ritual meals were found, 18th- and 19th-century Romantics guessed that persecuted Christians hid out in these candlelit galleries. The popularity of this legend grew—even though it was untrue. By the second century, more than a million people lived in Rome, and the 10,000 early Christians didn't need to camp out in the catacombs. They hid in plain view, melting into obscurity within the city itself.

The underground tunnels, while empty of bones, are rich in early Christian symbolism, which functioned as a secret language. The dove represented the soul. You'll see it quenching its thirst (worshipping), with an olive branch (at rest), or happily perched (in paradise). Peacocks, known for their purport-

edly "incorruptible flesh," embodied immortality. The shepherd with a lamb on his shoulders was the "good shepherd," the first portrayal of Christ as a kindly leader of his flock. The fish was used because the first letters of these words—"Jesus Christ, Son of God, Savior"—spelled "fish" in Greek. And the anchor is a cross in disguise. A second-century bishop had written on his tomb, "All who understand these things, pray for me." You'll see pictures of people praying with their hands raised—the custom at the time.

For those with more energy, there's more to see, especially if you're renting a bike and want to just get away from it all.

Other Sights on or near the Appian Way

Consider these diversions if you have the time and interest.

More of the Appian Way: Heading south (away from downtown Rome), past the Tomb of Cecilia Metella, you'll find the best-preserved part of the Appian Way—quieter, less touristed, and lined with cypresses, pines, and crumbling tombs. It's all downhill after the first few hundred yards. On a bike, you'll travel over lots of rough paving stones (or dirt sidewalks) for about 30 minutes to reach a big pyramid-shaped ruin on its tiny base, and then five minutes more to the back side of the Villa di Quintilli. You can't enter the villa from here, but you can admire the semi-circular nymphaeum, or fake grotto. Enjoy a picnic, then turn around and pedal up that long hill to return your bike.

Aqueduct Park: Rome's mighty aqueducts kept water flowing into the thriving and thirsty ancient city of one million. (They also eventually provided a handy Achilles' heel for invading barbarians: Simply break an arch in the aqueduct, and life becomes very tough within the city walls.) This sprawling and evocative park—which seems miles from anywhere, but is the last stop on the Archeobus route—is a favorite these days for local joggers. Hardier cyclists not afraid of riding in traffic can also visit.

To get there from the Appia Antica Caffè near the Tomb of Cecilia Metella, go east on Via Cecilia Metella/Almone. Turn right onto busy Via Appia Nuova—there's a sidewalk on the left side—then left onto Via Torre dei Fiscale, to reach a small park with a few ruined aqueducts. To reach a larger park with more ruins, continue south down Via Appia Nuova and turn left onto Via del Quadraro. Go under the tracks, then over, then right onto Via Allesandro Viviani. It's 45 minutes from the café to this farthest point.

Sights on Bus #118 Route Back to Rome: On the way back, about a half-mile from Domine Quo Vadis Church, the bus stops alongside Rome's ancient city wall. The **San Sebastiano Gate and Museum of the Walls** offers an interesting look at Roman defense and a chance to scramble along a stretch of the ramparts. The Aurelian Walls (c. A.D. 270) was built in five years because of threat of invasions. At 12 miles around, it was the biggest building project ever undertaken within the city of Rome.

A few minutes farther on, bus #118 stops near the **Baths of Caracalla.** Next, it makes a stop at the east end of the **Circus Maximus** (the Circo Massimo Metro stop is nearby). The bus terminates at **Piramide,** which has several interesting sights clustered around the Metro station (see page 78). From Piramide, catch the Metro home.

NATIONAL MUSEUM OF ROME TOUR

*Museo Nazionale Romano
Palazzo Massimo alle Terme*

Rome lasted a thousand years...and so do most Roman history courses. But if you want a breezy overview of this fascinating society, there's no better place than the National Museum of Rome.

Rome took Greek culture and wrote it in capital letters. Thanks to this lack of originality, ancient Greek statues were preserved for our enjoyment today. But the Romans also pioneered a totally new form of art—sculpting painfully realistic portraits of emperors and important citizens.

Think of this museum as a walk back in time. As you gaze at the same statues that the Romans swooned over, the history of Rome comes alive—from Julius Caesar's murder to Caligula's incest to Vespasian's Colosseum to the coming of Christianity.

Orientation

Cost: €10 combo-ticket includes entry to three lesser National Museum branches within three days: Museum of the Bath at the nearby Baths of Diocletian (see Baths of Diocletian Tour chapter), Palazzo Altemps (lackluster sculptures), and Crypta Balbi (medieval art).

Hours: Tue–Sun 9:00–19:45, closed Mon, last entry 45 minutes before closing.

When to Go: The museum is never crowded. Since it has a convenient and free bag check (even for backpacks and suitcases), consider a visit en route from the train station.

Getting There: The museum is about 100 yards from Termini train station (Metro: Termini). As you leave the station, it's the sandstone-brick building on your left. Enter at the far end, at Largo di Villa Peretti.

Information: Tel. 06-3996-7700.

Tours: An audioguide costs €4.
Length of This Tour: Allow two hours.
Photography: Photos allowed without flash.
Starring: Roman emperor busts, the Discus Thrower, original Greek statues, and fine Roman copies.

The Tour Begins

Overview

The Palazzo Massimo is the permanent home of major Greek and Roman statues that were formerly scattered in other national museums around town.

The museum is rectangular, with rooms and hallways built around a central courtyard. The ground-floor displays follow Rome's history as it changes from a democratic republic to a dictatorial empire. The first-floor exhibits take Rome from its peak through its slow decline. The second floor houses rare frescoes and fine mosaics, and the basement displays coins and everyday objects. As you tour this museum, note that in Italian, "room" is *sala* and "hall" is *galleria*.

Ground Floor— From Senators to Caesars

• *Buy your ticket and pass through the turnstile, where you'll find...*

Minerva

It's big, it's gaudy, it's a weird goddess from a pagan cult. Welcome to the Roman world. The statue is also a good reminder that all the statues in this museum—now missing limbs, scarred by erosion, or weathered down to bare stone—were once whole, and painted to look as lifelike as possible.

• *Turning to the right, you'll find Gallery I; this hallway is lined with portrait busts.*

Gallery I—Portrait Heads from the Republic (500–1 B.C.)

Stare into the eyes of these stern, hardy, no-nonsense farmer-stock people who founded Rome. The wrinkles and crags of these original "ugly republicans" tell the story of Rome's roots as a small agricultural tribe, fighting for survival with neighboring bands.

These faces are brutally realistic, unlike more idealized Greek statues. Romans honored their ancestors and worthy citizens in the

(side margin) **NATIONAL MUSEUM**

"family" *(gens)* of Rome. They wanted lifelike statues to remember them by, and to instruct the young with their air of moral rectitude.

In its first 500 years, Rome was a republic ruled by a Senate of wealthy landowners. But as Rome expanded throughout Italy, and the economy shifted from farming to booty, changes became necessary.

• *Enter Room I (Sala I). Along the wall between the doorways, find the portrait bust that some scholars think may be Julius Caesar.*

Room I
Julius Caesar
(Rilievo con Ritratto dalla collezione Von Bergen)

Julius Caesar (c. 100–44 B.C.)—with his prominent brow, high cheekbones, and male-pattern baldness with the forward comb-over—changed Rome forever.

When this charismatic general swept onto the scene, Rome was in chaos. Rich landowners were fighting middle-class plebs, who wanted their slice of the plunder. Slaves such as Spartacus were picking up hoes and hacking up masters. And renegade generals—the new providers of wealth and security in an economy of plunder—were becoming dictators. (Notice the **life-size statue** with a shaved-off head, of an unknown but obviously once-renowned general.)

Caesar was a people's favorite. He conquered Gaul (France), then sacked Egypt, then impregnated Cleopatra. He defeated rivals and made them his allies. He gave great speeches. Chicks dug him.

With the army at his back and the people in awe, he took the reins of government, instituted sweeping changes, made himself the center of power...and antagonized the Senate.

A band of republican assassins surrounded him in a Senate meeting. He called out for help as one by one they stepped up to take turns stabbing him. The senators sat and watched in silence. One of the killers was his adopted son, Brutus, and Caesar—astonished that even he joined in—died saying, *"Et tu, Brute?"*

• *At the end of Gallery I, turn left and enter the large glassed-in Room V, with a life-size statue of Augustus.*

Room V—Augustus
Statue of Augustus as Pontifex Maximus
(Ritratto di Augusto in Vesta di Offerente)

Julius Caesar died, but his family name, his politics, and his flamboyance lived on. Julius had adopted his grandnephew, Octavian,

National Museum—Ground Floor

ROOM III

ROOM II

ROOM I ❸

STAIRS ☒ ELEV.

BAGGAGE CHECK

❻ ❼

GALLERY I ← ❷

WC

❺

VIA

ROOM IV

GALL. II

ROOM V

STEPS

OPEN-AIR COURTYARD

❶

TICKETS

DCH

❹

← ENTRY →

❽

GALLERY III ❾

VIMINALE

ROOM VI ❿ ⓫ ROOM VII

ROOM VIII

STAIRS UP TO FIRST FLOOR

← TO TERMINI TRAIN STATION

TO PIAZZA REPUBBLICA →

NATIONAL MUSEUM

❶ Minerva

❷ Portrait Heads

❸ Julius Caesar

❹ Augustus as Pontifex Maximus

❺ Livia

❻ Tiberius

❼ Caligula

❽ Alexander the Great

❾ Socrates

❿ Niobid

⓫ The Boxer at Rest & Hellenistic Prince

who united Rome's warring factions and took the title "Augustus."

Here, Emperor Augustus has taken off his armor and laurel-leaf crown, donning the simple hooded robes of a priest. He's retiring to a desk job after a lifetime of fighting to reunite Rome. He killed Brutus and eliminated his rivals, Mark Antony and Cleopatra. For the first time in almost a century of fighting, one general reigned supreme. Augustus became the first of the emperors who would rule Rome for the next 500 years.

In fact, Augustus was a down-to-earth man who lived simply, worked hard, read books, listened to underlings, and tried to restore traditional Roman values after the turbulence of Julius Caesar's time. He outwardly praised the Senate, while actually reducing it to a rubber-stamp body. Augustus' reign marked the start of 200 years of peace and prosperity, the Pax Romana.

See if the statue matches this description of Augustus by a

contemporary, the historian Suetonius: "He was unusually hand-some. His expression was calm and mild. He had clear, bright eyes, in which was a kind of divine power. His hair was slightly curly and somewhat golden." Any variations were made by sculp-tors who idealized features to make him almost godlike.

Augustus proclaimed himself a god—not arrogantly or blas-phemously, as Caligula later did, but as the honored "father" of the "family" of Rome. As the empire expanded, the vanquished had to worship statues like this one as a show of loyalty.

• *Cross the hallway into Room IV. Near the doorway, find the bust of the empress Livia.*

Room IV—The Julio-Claudian Family: Rome's First Emperors (c. 50 B.C.–A.D. 68)

Julius Caesar's descendants ruled Rome for a century after his death, turning the family surname "Caesar" into a title.

Livia

Augustus' wife, Livia, was a major power behind the throne. Her stern, thin-lipped gaze withered rivals at court. Her hairstyle—bunched up in a peak, braided down the center, and tied in back—became the rage throughout the empire, as her face appeared everywhere, from statues to coins.

Notice that by the next generation, a sim-pler bun was chic (Antonia Minore, Livia's daughter-in-law, next to Livia). And by the following generation, the trend was tight curls. Empresses dictated fashion the way that emperors dictated policy.

Livia bore Augustus no sons. She lob-bied hard for Tiberius, her own son by a first marriage, to succeed as emperor. Augustus didn't like him, but Livia was persuasive. He relented, ate some bad figs, and died—the gossip was that Livia poisoned him to seal the bargain. The pattern of succession was established—adopt a son from within the extended family—and Tiberius was proclaimed emperor. (The fine frescoed walls of Livia's Anzio villa are upstairs on the second floor.)

• *In the corner of the room, find the well-worn bust of...*

Tiberius (*Tiberio,* ruled A.D. 14–37)

Scholars speculate that acne may have soured Tiberius to the world (but this statue is pocked by erosion). Shy and sullen but diligent, he worked hard to be the easygoing leader that Augustus had been. Early on, he was wise and patient, but he suffered personal setbacks. Politics forced him to divorce his only beloved and marry a slut. His favorite brother died, then his son. Embittered, he let subordinates run things and retired to Capri, where he built a villa with underground dungeons. There he hosted orgies of sex, drugs, torture, really loud music, and execution. At his side was his young grandnephew, whom he adopted as next emperor.

• *To your right, in the glass case, is the small bust of...*

Caligula (*Caligola,* ruled A.D. 37–41)

This emperor had sex with his sisters, tortured his enemies, made off with friends' wives during dinner parties and then returned to rate their performance in bed, crucified Christians, took cuts in line at the Vatican Museum, and ordered men to kneel before him as a god. Caligula has become the archetype of a man with enough power to act out his basest fantasies.

Politically, he squandered Rome's money, then taxed and extorted from the citizens. Perhaps he was made mad by illness, perhaps he was the victim of vindictive historians, but still, no one mourned when assassins ambushed him and ran a sword through his privates. Rome was tiring of this family dynasty's dysfunction.

• *Continue down Gallery II and turn left. Busts line Gallery III. Find Alexander the Great (outside Room VI) and Socrates (farther down the hall, outside Room VIII).*

Gallery III—Rome's Greek Mentors

Rome's legions easily conquered the less-organized but more-cultured Greek civilization that had dominated the Mediterranean for centuries. Romans adopted Greek gods, art styles, and fashions, and sophisticates sprinkled their conversation with Greek phrases.

Alexander the Great (*Alessandro Magno*)

Alexander the Great (356–323 B.C.) single-handedly created a Greek-speaking empire by conquering, in just a few short years, lands from Greece to Egypt to Persia. Later, when the Romans conquered Greece (c. 200 B.C.), they inherited this pre-existing collection of cultured Greek cities ringing the Mediterranean.

Alexander's handsome statues set the standard for those of later Roman emperors. His features were chiseled and youthful, and this statue was adorned with pompous decorations, like a golden sunburst aura (fitted into the holes). The greatest man of his day, he ruled the known world by the age of 30.

Alexander's teacher was none other than the philosopher Aristotle. Aristotle's teacher was Plato, whose mentor was...

Socrates *(Socrate)*

This nonconformist critic of complacent thinking is the father of philosophy. The Greeks were an intellectual, introspective, sensitive, and artistic people. The Romans were practical, no-nonsense soldiers, salesmen, and bureaucrats. Many a Greek slave was more cultured than his master, reduced to the role of warning his boss not to wear a plaid toga with a polka-dot robe.

• *Backtrack and enter Room VI.*

Room VI—Greek Beauty in Originals and Copies

Niobid (*Niobide Ferita*, 440 B.C.)

The Romans were astonished by the beauty of Greek statues. Niobid's smooth skin contrasts with the rough folds of her clothing. She twists naturally around an axis running straight up and down. This woman looks like a classical goddess awakening from a beautiful dream, but...

Circle around back. The hole bored in her back, right in that itchy place you can't quite reach, once held a golden arrow. The woman has been shot by Artemis, goddess of hunting, because her mother dared to boast to the gods about her kids. Niobid reaches back in vain, trying to remove the arrow before it drains her of life.

Romans ate this stuff up: the sensual beauty, the underplayed pathos, the very Greekness of it. They crated up centuries-old statues like this and brought them home to their gardens and palaces. Soon there weren't enough old statues to meet the demand. Crafty Greeks began cranking out knock-offs of Greek originals for mass consumption. Rooms VII and VIII contain both originals (like Niobid) and copies—some of extremely high quality, others resembling cheesy fake *David*s in a garden store. Appreciate the beauty of the world's rare, surviving Greek originals.

Rome conquered Greece, but culturally the Greeks conquered the Romans.

• *Move next door to see...*

Room VII—Hellenistic and Classical Bronzes

The Boxer at Rest
(*Pugilatore*, first century B.C.)

An exhausted boxer sits between rounds and gasps for air. Check out the brass knuckles–type Roman boxing gloves. Textbook Hellenistic, this pugilist is realistic and full of emotion. His face is scarred, his back muscles are knotted, and he's got cauliflower ears. He's losing.

Slumped over, he turns with a questioning look ("Why am I losing again?"), and eyes that once held glass now make him look empty indeed. "I coulda been a contender."

Hellenistic Prince *(Principe Elenistico)*

Back then, everyone wanted to be like Alexander the Great. This restored bronze statue—naked and leaning on a spear—shows a prince (probably Attalus II of Pergamon) in the style of a famous statue of his hero from the second century B.C.

• *We've covered Rome's first 500 years. At the end of the hall are the stairs up to the first floor.*

First Floor—
Rome's Peak and Slow Fall

As we saw, Augustus' family did not always rule wisely. Under Nero (ruled A.D. 54–68), the debauchery, violence, and paranoia typical of the Julio-Claudians festered to a head. When the city burned in the great fire of 64, the Romans suspected Nero of torching it himself to clear land for his enormous luxury palace.

Enough. Facing a death sentence, Nero committed suicide with the help of a servant. An outsider was brought in to rule—Vespasian, from the Flavian family.

• *At the top of the stairs, enter Room I. To your right is Vespasian. (Note: If temporary exhibits occupy Room I, you'll find Vespasian and company nearby.)*

NATIONAL MUSEUM

National Museum—First Floor

❶ Vespasian
❷ Domitian
❸ Domitia
❹ Nerva
❺ Trajan

❻ Hadrian
❼ Aphrodite Crouching
❽ Apollo
❾ The Discus Thrower
❿ Hermaphrodite Sleeping

⓫ Septimius Severus
⓬ Caracalla
⓭ Sarcophagus of a Procession
⓮ Seated Statuette of Christ Teaching

Room I—The Flavian Family

Vespasian (*Vespasianus,* ruled A.D. 69–79)

Balding and wrinkled, with a big head, a double chin, and a shy smile, Vespasian was a common man. The son of a tax collector, he rose through the military ranks with a reputation as a competent drudge. As emperor, he restored integrity, raised taxes, started the Colosseum, and suppressed the Jewish rebellion in Palestine.

Domitian (*Domitianus,* ruled A.D. 81–96)

Vespasian's son, Domitian, used his father's tax revenues to construct the massive Imperial Palace on Palatine Hill, home to emperors for the next three centuries. Shown with his lips curled in a sneer, he was a moralistic prude who executed several Vestal ex-Virgins, while in private he took one mistress after another. Until...

Domitia

...his stern wife found out and hired a servant to stab him in the groin. Domitia's hairstyle is a far cry from the "Livia" cut, with a high crown of tight curls.

Nerva (ruled A.D. 96–98)

Nerva realized that the Flavian dynasty was no better than its predecessors. Old and childless, he made a bold, far-sighted move—he adopted a son from outside of Rome's corrupting influence.

• *Entering Room II, Trajan is on the left wall.*

Room II—A Cosmopolitan Culture

Trajan (*Traianus-Hercules,* ruled A.D. 98–117)

Born in Spain, this conquering hero pushed Rome's borders to their greatest extent, creating a truly worldwide empire. The spoils of three continents funneled into a city of a million-plus people. Trajan could dress up in a lion's skin, presenting himself as a "new Hercules," and no one found it funny. Romans felt a spirit of Manifest Destiny: "The gods desire that the City of Rome shall be the capital of all the countries of the world" (Livy).

• *On the opposite wall is...*

Hadrian (*Hadrianus,* ruled A.D. 117–138)

Hadrian was a fully cosmopolitan man. His beard—the first we've seen—shows his taste for foreign things; he poses like the Greek philosopher he imagined himself to be.

Hadrian was a voracious tourist, personally visiting almost every corner of the vast empire, from Britain (where he built Hadrian's Wall) to Egypt (where he sailed the Nile), from Jerusalem (where he suppressed another Jewish revolt) to Athens (where he soaked up classical culture). He scaled Sicily's Mount Etna just to see what made a volcano tick. Back home, he beautified Rome with the Pantheon and his villa at Tivoli, a microcosm of places he'd visited.

Hadrian is flanked here by the two loves of his life. His wife, **Sabina** (left), with modest hairstyle and scarf, kept the home fires burning for her traveling husband. Hadrian was 50 years old when he became captivated by a teenage boy named **Antinous** (right), with his curly hair and full, sensual lips. Together they traveled the Nile, where Antinous drowned. Hadrian wept. Statues of Antinous subsequently went up throughout the Empire, much to the embarrassment of the stoic Romans.

Hadrian spent his last years at his lavish villa outside Rome, surrounded by buildings and souvenirs that reminded him of his traveling days (see Tivoli Day Trip chapter).

• *Backtrack through Room I and turn right, down a hall that leads into the large Room V.*

Rooms V and VI—Rome's Grandeur

Pause at Rome's peak to admire the things the Romans found beautiful. Imagine these statues as they originally stood—in the pleasure gardens of the Roman rich, surrounded by greenery with the splashing sound of fountains, all painted in bright, lifelike colors. Though executed by Romans, the themes are mostly Greek, with godlike humans and human-looking gods.

• *In the center of Room V is...*

Aphrodite Crouching
(Afrodite Accovacciata)

The goddess of beauty crouches while bathing, then turns to admire herself. This sets her whole body in motion—one thigh goes down, the other up; her head turns clockwise while her body goes in reverse—yet she's perfectly still. The crouch creates a series of symmetrical love handles, molded by the sculptor into the marble-like wax. Hadrian had good taste—he ordered a copy of this Greek classic for his bathroom.

• *Two statues down, find the large statue of...*

Apollo

The god of light appears as a slender youth, not as some burly, powerful, autocratic god. He stands *contrapposto*—originally he was leaning against the tree—in a relaxed and very human way. His curled hair is tied with a headband, strands tumbling down his neck. His muscles and skin are smooth. (The rusty stains come from the centuries the statue spent submerged in the Tiber.) Apollo is in a reflective mood, and the serenity and intelligence in his face show off classical Greece as a nation of thinkers.

• *At the far end of the room, connect to Room VI, with...*

The Discus Thrower *(Discobolo)*

An athlete winds up, about to unleash his pent-up energy and hurl the discus. The sculptor has frozen the moment for us so that we can examine the inner workings of the wonder called Man. The perfect pecs and

washboard abs make this human godlike. Geometrically, you could draw a perfect circle around him, with his hipbone at the center. He's natural yet ideal, twisting yet balanced, moving while at rest. For the Greeks, the universe was a rational place, and the human body was the perfect embodiment of the order found in nature.

This statue is the best-preserved Roman copy (not one member is missing—I checked) of the original Greek work by Myron (450 B.C.). (The subtle nubs on his head were aids for a measuring device used when making copies.) Statues of athletes like this commonly stood in the baths, where Romans cultivated healthy bodies, minds, and social skills, hoping to lead well-rounded lives. The Discus Thrower, with his geometrical perfection and godlike air, sums up all that is best in the classical world.

• *Continue into Room VII, where you'll run into a sleeping statue.*

Room VII

Hermaphrodite Sleeping *(Ermafrodito Dormiente)*

After leaving the baths, a well-rounded Roman may head post-haste to an orgy, where he might see a reclining nude like this, be titillated, circle around for a closer look, and say, "Hey! *(Insert your own reaction here)*!"

• *Exit Room VII at the far end and turn left. Then turn right into Room XIII and look to the right to find the bust of Septimius Severus.*

Room XIII—Beginning of the End

Septimius Severus (ruled A.D. 193–211)

Rome's sprawling empire was starting to unravel, and it took a disciplined emperor-warrior like this African to keep it together. Severus' victories on the frontier earned him a grand triumphal arch in the Forum, but here he seems to be rolling his eyes at the chaos growing around him.

• *Near Severus is his son...*

Caracalla (ruled A.D. 211–217)

The stubbly beard, cruel frown, and glaring eyes tell us that

Severus' son was bad news. He murdered his little brother to seize power, then proceeded to massacre thousands of loyal citizens on a whim. The army came to distrust rulers whose personal agenda got in their way, and Caracalla was stabbed in the back by a man whose brother had just been executed. Rome's long slide had begun.

Room XIV—The Fall

There are a lot of serious faces in this room. People who grew up in the lap of luxury and security were witnessing the unthinkable— the disintegration of a thousand years of tradition. Rome never recovered from the chaos of the third century. Disease, corruption, revolts from within, and "barbarians" pecking away at the borders were body blows that sapped Rome's strength.

• *Immediately after entering this long room, find the...*

Sarcophagus of a Procession
(*Sarcofago con Corteo,* etc., A.D. 270)

A parade of dignitaries, accompanying a new Roman leader, marches up Capitol Hill. They huddle together, their backs to the

wall, looking around suspiciously for assassins. Their faces reflect the fear of the age.

By the third century, the Roman army could virtually hand-pick an emperor to be their front man. At one point, the office of emperor was literally auctioned to the highest bidder. In the space of 40 years, 15 different emperors were saluted, then murdered, at the whims of soldiers of fortune.

Rome would stagger on for another 200 years, but the glory of old Rome was gone. The city was becoming a den of thugs, thieves, prostitutes, barbarians...and Christians.

• *Farther along, on the right-hand wall, find the small...*

Seated Statuette of Christ Teaching
(*Cristo Docente,* A.D. 350)

Christ sits like a Roman senator—in a toga, holding a scroll, dispensing wisdom like the law of the land. The statue comes from

those delirious days when formerly persecuted Christians could now "come out" and worship in public. Emperor Constantine (ruled A.D. 306–337) legalized Christianity, and within two generations it was Rome's official religion.

Whether Christianity invigorated or ruined Rome is debated, but the fall was inevitable. Rome's once-great legions backpedaled, until even the city itself was raped and plundered by foreigners (410). In 476, the last emperor sold his title for a comfy pension plan, "Rome" became just another dirty

city with a big history, and the artistic masterpieces now in this museum were buried under rubble.

*(Vertical text at left: NATIONAL MUSEUM)*

The Rest of the Museum

• *For extra credit, consider exploring two more parts of the National Museum.*

Second Floor

This floor contains **frescoes and mosaics** that once decorated the walls and floors of Roman villas. They're remarkably realistic and

un-stuffy, featuring everyday people, animals, flowery patterns, and geometrical designs. The **Villa Farnese frescoes**—in black, red, yellow, and blue—are mostly architectural designs, with fake columns, friezes, and garlands. The **Villa di Livia frescoes,** owned by the wily wife of

Augustus, immerse you in a leafy green garden full of birds and fruit trees, symbolizing the gods.

Basement (Floor -2)

The **"Luxury in Rome"** rooms give a peek into the lives of Rome's well-to-do citizens, featuring fine jewelry, common everyday objects, and an eight-year-old girl's mummy.

Next, enter the **coin collection.** Find your favorite emperor or empress on the coins by using remote-controlled magnifying glasses: Julius Caesar (case 8, #41–44), Augustus (case 8, #65–69, and case 9, #1–38), Augustus' system of denars (case 10), Tiberius (case 10, #1–16), Caligula (case 10, #17–28), and Nero (case 11, #2–33). Evaluate Roman life by studying how Diocletian tweaked the gold standard (glass case 21). In A.D. 300, one denar bought one egg. The rest of the displays trace Europe's money from denars to euros. The final exhibit (case 59) features a monetary unit that is now history—the Italian lira.

CAPITOLINE MUSEUMS TOUR

Musei Capitolini

This enjoyable museum complex claims to be the world's oldest, founded in 1471 when a pope gave ancient statues to the citizens of Rome. Perched on the top of Capitol Hill Square, its two buildings (Palazzo dei Conservatori and Palazzo Nuovo) are connected by an underground passage that leads to the Tabularium and panoramic views of the Roman Forum.

Orientation

Cost: €8-11, depending on temporary exhibition; €8.50–13 combo-ticket with the much less exciting Montemartini Museum (listed on page 81).

Hours: Tue–Sun 9:00–20:00, closed Mon, last entry one hour before closing.

Getting There: From Piazza Venezia or the Forum, walk uphill to the square on top of Capitol Hill (*Campidoglio* in Italian). Enter at the Palazzo dei Conservatori (on your right as you face the equestrian statue).

Information: You'll find some English descriptions within the museum. Tel. 06-8205-9127, www.museicapitolini.org.

Tour: The €5 audioguide is good (€6.20/2 people).

Length of This Tour: Allow two hours.

Baggage Check: Free (mandatory for bags larger than a purse).

Cuisine Art: There's a great view café, called **Caffè Capitolino,** upstairs in Palazzo dei Conservatori (enter from inside museum; also has exterior entrance for the public—facing museum entrance, go to your right around the building to Piazza Caffarelli and through door #4; see map). The pavilion on the terrace outside offers full service; inside is self-service (pay first, then take receipt to bar; good salads and

Capitoline Museums Overview

CAPITOLINE MUSEUMS

- 100 YARDS
- 100 METERS

- ■ Capitoline Museums
- ▬ Underground Passage
- ➜ Entry Point to Sights

- Ⓜ Metro Station
- Ⓣ Taxi Stand
- Ⓑ Bus Stop

- ❶ Entrance & Tickets
- ❷ Palazzo dei Conservatori: Constantine Chunks, Boy Extracting a Thorn, Capitoline She-Wolf, Marcus Aurelius, Temple of Jupiter, Café & View Patio
- ❸ Tabularium: Forum Views
- ❹ Palazzo Nuovo: Dying Gaul, Capitoline Venus
- ❺ "Back Door" to V. E. Monument & Sta. Maria in Aracoeli Church

toasted sandwiches). Piazza Caffarelli is a fine place for a snooze or a picnic.

Starring: The original She-Wolf statue, Marcus Aurelius, the Dying Gaul, the Boy Extracting a Thorn, and Forum views.

The Tour Begins

• *Begin at the square on top of Capitol Hill.*

Overview

Capitol Hill's main square (Campidoglio), home to the museum, began in ancient Rome as a religious center, the site of temples to

the gods Jupiter, Juno, and Minerva. In the 16th century, Michelangelo transformed the square from pagan to papal, while adding a harmonious and refined Renaissance touch. (For more on the square, see page 48.)

To identify the museum's two buildings, face the equestrian statue (with your back to the grand stairway). The museum's layout—with two different buildings connected by an underground passage—can be confusing, but this self-guided tour is easy to follow.

You'll enter at the Palazzo dei Conservatori (on your right), cross underneath the square (beneath the Palazzo Senatorio, or mayoral palace, not open to public—see photo), and exit from the Palazzo Nuovo (on your left).

Palazzo dei Conservatori

• *After your ticket is checked, enter the courtyard.*

In the courtyard, enjoy the massive chunks of Constantine: his head, hand, and foot. When intact, this giant held the place of honor in the Basilica of Constantine in the Forum. Also in the courtyard are reliefs of conquered peoples—not in chains, but new members of an expansive empire.

• *Go up the staircase (the one to the left of the entrance, not the one in the courtyard). On the landing, find...*

Reliefs of Second-Century Imperial Grandeur

These four fine reliefs show great moments in an emperor's daily grind. Find Marcus Aurelius overseeing preparations to sacrifice a bull (with even the bull looking on curiously) on Capitol Hill. Also find Marcus Aurelius in an equestrian pose (like the bronze statue in Capitol Hill Square), with his hand out, offering clemency to his vanquished foes. The detail, with expressive faces and banners blowing in the wind, is impressive. In the relief showing Marcus Aurelius in his chariot, someone's missing...it's Commodus, his wicked son (Russell Crowe's nemesis in *Gladiator*). After the assassination of Commodus, his

memory was damned, so images of him were erased (or, in this case, chiseled out).

• *Continue up the stairs to the first floor. Go through two large frescoed rooms and through the doorway on the right of the far wall to find...*

Boy Extracting a Thorn *(Spinario)*

He's just a boy, intent only on picking a thorn out of his foot. As he bends over to reach his foot, his body sticks out at all angles, like a bony chicken wing. He's even scuffed up, the way small boys get. At this moment, nothing matters to him but that splinter. Our lives are filled with these mundane moments (when we'd give anything for tweezers) rarely captured in art.

Art scholars speculate that the boy's head, tilted unnaturally down, and his body are from two separate statues spliced together.

• *In the next room...*

Capitoline She-Wolf

The original bronze She-Wolf suckles the twins Romulus and Remus. This symbol of Rome is ancient, though the wolf statue itself (long thought to be Etruscan from the fifth century B.C.) was made in the 13th century, and the boys are an invention of the 14th century. Look into the eyes of the wolf. An animal looks back, with ragged ears, sharp teeth, and staring eyes. This wild animal, teamed with the wildest creatures of all—

hungry babies—makes a powerful symbol for the tenacious city/
empire of Rome.

• *In the next room...*

From Michelangelo to Medusa

Along with a bust of Michelangelo, this
room contains Bernini's anguished bust
of Medusa—with writhing snakes on her
head. This goes way beyond a bad hair day.

• *Pass through three small rooms containing
the Artemis of Efenina, followed by Greek
red-figured vases (and the elevator up to the
café). Continue straight to a set of seven stairs
and follow them up to the next room to dis-*
cover the remark-
able bust of...

Commodus as Hercules

This arrogant emperor brat used to run
around the palace in animal skins. Here,
he wears a lion's head over his own, and
drapes the lion's paws over his chest.
This lion king made a bad emperor
(ruled A.D. 180–192).

• *As you are looking at Commodus,
directly behind you is his dad, the
Emperor...*

Marcus Aurelius (C. A.D. 176)

This is the greatest surviving equestrian statue of antiquity.
Marcus Aurelius was a Roman philosopher-emperor (ruled A.D.
161–180) known more for his *Meditations* than his prowess on the
battlefield. Notice that he doesn't use
stirrups. An Asian invention, those
newfangled devices wouldn't arrive in
Europe for another 500 years.

Christians in the Dark Ages
thought that the statue's hand was raised
in blessing, which probably led to their
misidentifying him as Constantine,
the first Christian emperor. While
most pagan statues were destroyed by
Christians, "Constantine" was spared. It
has graced several prominent locations
in medieval Rome, including the papal
palace at San Giovanni in Laterano.

In 1538, this gilded bronze statue was placed in the center of Capitol Hill Square (directly outside the museum), and Michelangelo was hired to design the buildings around it with the statue as the centerpiece. A few years ago, the statue was moved inside and restored, while the copy you see outside today was placed on the square.

Also in the room are a gilded Hercules and more hunks—head, finger, and a globe—of another statue of Constantine. (Or was it the Emperor Sylvestrus Stalloneus?)

• *Descend the ramp to the wall of blocks from the...*

Temple of Jupiter

This is part of the foundation of the ancient Temple of Jupiter (or Giove), once the most impressive in Rome. Study the scale model reconstruction (1:40) to get a sense of the temple's size and where you stand in relation to the ruins.

The King of the Gods resided atop Capitol Hill in this once-classy 10,000-square-foot temple, which was perched on a podium and lined with Greek-style columns, overlooking downtown Rome. The most important rites were performed here, and victory parades through the Forum ended here. The famous temple, known as the Capitolium, gave the hill its name. Replicas of this building were erected in every Roman city. The temple was begun by Rome's last king (the Tarquin), and its dedication in 509 B.C. marks the start of the Roman Republic.

All that remains today of the temple are these ruined foundation stones, made of volcanic tuff, an easily carved rock commonly

used in Roman construction. Although there are hundreds of these blocks here, they represent only a portion of the immense foundation, which is only a fraction of the temple itself. In its prime, the temple rose two stories above our heads. Inside stood a statue of the god of thunder wielding a lightning bolt. The temple was refurbished a number of times over the centuries, often after damage by...lightning bolts.

• *Before heading for the Tabularium and Palazzo Nuovo, consider a break in the café. To do this, backtrack to the room with the Greek red-figured vases (near Michelangelo and Medusa), where you'll find the elevator up to the second floor. The café's huge outdoor view patio overlooks the domes of Rome, representing the religion that remained after Rome fell. When you're ready, go back downstairs to Marcus Aurelius.*

If Marcus trotted a few steps forward, turned left, and went to

CAPITOLINE MUSEUMS

the end of the hall, he'd find a staircase. Go downstairs two flights, to the basement—the piano sotteraneo. *Then cross underneath the square through the long passageway. Near the far end, turn right and climb a set of stairs into the...*

Tabularium

Built in the first century B.C., these sturdy vacant rooms once held the archives of ancient Rome. The word Tabularium comes from "tablet," on which Romans wrote their laws.

The rooms offer a stunning head-on view over the Forum, giving you a more complete picture of the sprawl of ancient

Rome. Panning left to right, find the following landmarks: the Arch of Septimius Severus, the Arch of Titus (in the distance), the lone Column of Phocas, the three columns of the Temple of Castor and Pollux, the three columns (closer to you) of the Temple of Vespasiano, and the eight columns of the Temple of Saturn.

Now do an about-face and look up to see a huge white hunk of carved marble, an overhang from the Temple of Vespasiano.

• *Find more views from this vantage point, plus the remains of another temple, then leave the Tabularium by going back down the stairs. Turn right and go up two flights of stairs. You're now on the first floor of the...*

Palazzo Nuovo

• *From the top of the stairs, the first room you encounter is Room VIII— the "Hall of the Gaul"—with one of the museum's most famous pieces.*

Dying Gaul

A first-century B.C. copy of a Greek original, this was sculpted to celebrate the Greeks' victory over the Galatians. It may have been part of a larger sculpture group (long since lost).

Wounded in battle, the dying Gaul holds himself upright, but barely. Minutes earlier, before he was stabbed in the chest, he'd been in his prime. Now he can only watch helplessly as his life ebbs away. His sword is useless against this last battle. With his messy hair, downcast eyes, and crumpled position, he poignantly reminds us that every victory also means a defeat.

• *In the next few rooms, take a quick look at...*

Ancient Roman Statues and Busts

A reddish faun glories in grapes and life, oblivious to the loss of his penis (at least he still has his tail). The statue, found among a couple of dozen pieces in Hadrian's Villa, was skillfully restored. Check out the chandeliered ceilings in this room and elsewhere; this building is truly a *palazzo* (palace).

The next room, the large hall, features more sculpture from Hadrian's Villa (and elsewhere). Notice the Wounded Amazon (near the window) undoing her delicate dress. This is a Roman copy of a fifth-century B.C. Greek original by Polycletus.

Roll through two rooms lined with busts—the Hall of Philosophers (Socrates, Homer, Euripides, Cicero, and many

more) and the Hall of Emperors (Constantine's mom Helena sits center stage, resting after her journey to Jerusalem to find Christ's cross). In this 3-D yearbook of ancient history, there are few labels. The only purple bust is Caracalla. Infamous for his fervent brutality, he instructed his portraitists to stress his meanness. Directly across on the lower shelf, the smallest bust—of Emperor Gordiano (ruled 238–244 A.D.)—is one of the finest of late antiquity. His expression shows the concerns and consternation of a ruler whose empire is in decline. In this room you can find classic expressions of confidence, brutality, and anguish—human drama through the ages. Don't miss the delicate elegance of the first-century A.D. woman with the complex hairdo by the window.

• *Enter the hallway and start down the hall. The small octagonal room on your left contains one of the museum's treasures.*

Capitoline Venus

This is a Roman copy of a fourth-century B.C. Greek original by the master Praxiteles. Venus, leaving the bath, is suddenly aware that someone is watching her. As she turns to look, she reflexively covers up (nearly). Her blank eyes hold no personality or emotion. Her fancy hairstyle is the only complicated

thing about her. She is simply beautiful—generically erotic.
• *Head to the last room on the left before the stairs. Displayed on the wall is the...*

Mosaic of Doves

Four doves perch on the rim of a bronze bowl as one drinks water from the bowl. Minute bits make up this small, exquisite work. Found in the center of a floor in one of the rooms in Hadrian's Villa, this second-century A.D. mosaic was based on an earlier work done, of course, by the Greeks.

We all know that ancient Rome was grand. But the art in this museum tells us that its culture was exquisite as well.

• *To exit, head down the stairs to the ground floor, and follow signs to the* uscita. *If you checked a bag, cross the courtyard to retrieve it.*

BORGHESE
GALLERY TOUR

Galleria e Museo Borghese

More than just a great museum, the Borghese Gallery is a beautiful villa set in the greenery of surrounding gardens. You get to see art commissioned by the luxury-loving Borghese family displayed in the very rooms for which it was created. Frescoes, marble, stucco, and interior design enhance the masterpieces. This is a place where—regardless of whether you learn a darn thing—you can sit back and enjoy the sheer beauty of the palace and its art.

Orientation

Cost: €8.50, or €12.50 during special exhibits; both prices include basic €2 reservation fee (see "Reservations" below). Credit cards are accepted.

Hours: Tue–Sun 9:00–19:00, ticket office closes one hour earlier, closed Mon.

Reservations: Reservations are mandatory and easy to get in English by booking online (www.ticketeria.it, €1 extra booking fee, user-friendly website) or calling 06-32810. To reach an operator, make sure you're calling during Italian office hours: Mon–Fri 9:00–18:00, Sat 9:00–13:00, office closed Sat in Aug and Sun year-round. If you reach an Italian recording, wait for the English translation to get the most up-to-date information, or press 2 to hear standard information in English. Although the reservation system is easy, plan far enough in advance in case you have any trouble reaching the operator.

    Every two hours, 360 people are allowed to enter the museum. Entry times are 9:00, 11:00, 13:00, 15:00, and 17:00. Reserve a *minimum* of several days in advance for a weekday visit, at least a week ahead for weekends. Reservations are tightest at 11:00 and 15:00, on Tuesdays, and on weekends. For off-season weekdays (but not weekends), your chances of getting a same-day reservation are fairly high if you're flexible about the entry time.

When you reserve, request a day and time, and you'll get a claim number. You'll be advised to pick up your ticket 30 minutes before your appointed time. The ticket office is located on the lower level. If you're paying with a credit card, you can skip the ticket pickup line and head directly to the computer kiosks, enter your reservation number, swipe your credit card, and *pronto*—your tickets are ready.

If you're planning to use a Roma Pass for entry, you still need to make a reservation and pay the €2 fee. Call the reservations number (tel. 06-32810) to make your appointment.

If you don't have a reservation, you can try arriving near the top of the hour, when they sell unclaimed tickets to those standing by. Generally, out of 360 reservations, a few will fail to show (but more than a few may be waiting to grab them). You're most likely to land a stand-by ticket at 13:00 or 17:00.

Getting There: The museum is set idyllically but inconveniently in the vast Villa Borghese

Gardens. To avoid missing your appointment, allow yourself plenty of time to find the place. A taxi drops you 100 yards from the museum. Your destination is the Galleria Borghese (gah-leh-REE-ah bor-GAY-zay). Be sure *not* to tell the cabbie "Villa Borghese"—which is the park, not the museum.

The best public-transportation service is bus #910, which goes from Termini train station to the Via Pinciana stop (a few steps from the villa). Coming from Campo de' Fiori or Via del Corso (at Via Minghetti), bus #116 drops you off at the southern edge of the park. From Largo Argentina, bus #63 takes you to the American Embassy on Via Veneto; walk uphill on Via Veneto to the southern edge of the park.

By Metro, you have two options. From the Spagna Metro stop (or the Spanish Steps), it's a 15-minute walk: From inside the Metro station, follow signs to Via Veneto (not Villa Borghese). You'll continue along an underground labyrinth of escalators and moving sidewalks. Once you hit the supermarket, take a right up the stairs of the exit marked *uscita Villa Borghese*. At the top, turn left and head straight—you'll see signs to the gallery.

From the Barberini Metro stop, walk up Via Veneto, enter the park, and turn right, following signs.

Information: For info on the park or Rome sights in general, visit the nearby park TI (daily 9:00–17:00, maybe later on summer weekends; facing Borghese Gallery, turn left, walk 30 yards down, turn right toward the gate and find the poorly signed TI immediately on the left). Tel. 06-32810 or 06-841-3979, www.galleriaborghese.it.

Tours: €6 guided English tours are offered at 9:10 and 11:10 (may also be offered at 13:10 and 15:10). You can't book a tour when you make your museum reservation—sign up as soon as you arrive. Or consider the excellent 1.5-hour audioguide tour for €5.

Length of This Tour: Two hours is all you get...and you'll want every minute.

Museum Strategy: Visits are strictly limited to two hours. Budget most of your time for the more interesting ground floor, but set aside 30 minutes for the paintings of the Pinacoteca upstairs (highlights are marked by the audioguide icons). Avoid the crowds by seeing the Pinacoteca first. The fine bookshop and cafeteria are best visited outside your two-hour entry window.

Checkroom: Baggage check is free, mandatory, and strictly enforced. Even small purses must be checked. The checkroom does not take coats.

Photography: No photos allowed; you must check your camera.

Cuisine Art: A café is on-site. A picnic-friendly park with benches is just in front of the museum (you can check your picnic with your bags, and feast after your visit).

Starring: Sculptures by Bernini; Canova's *Venus*; paintings by Caravaggio, Raphael, and Titian; and the elegant villa itself.

The Tour Begins

Exterior

As you visit this palace-in-a-garden, consider its purpose. Cardinal Scipione Borghese wanted to create a place just outside of the city where he could showcase his fine art while wining and dining the VIPs of his age. He had the villa built, collected ancient works, and hired the best artists of his day. In pursuing the optimistic spirit of the Renaissance, they invented Baroque.

The cardinal was controversial because he was not religious. But as nepotism was routine in the 17th century, just being a nephew of the pope was justification enough to be made a cardinal. And the power of a cardinal could be parlayed into great wealth, still on incredible display here in the gallery.

Main Entry Hall

The first room that guests would see upon entry is a "theater of the arts"—a multimedia and multi-era extravaganza of art treasures. Baroque frescoes on the ceiling, Greek statues along the walls, and ancient Roman mosaics on the floor capture the essence of the collection—a gathering of beautiful objects from every age and culture inside a lavish 17th-century villa.

Five second- and third-century mosaics from a private Roman villa adorn the floor with colorful, festive scenes of slaughter. Gladiators—as famous in their day as the sports heroes of our age—fight animals and each other with swords, whips, and tridents. The Greek letter Θ marks the dead. Notice some of the gladiators' pro-wrestler nicknames: "Cupid(-o)," "Serpent(-ius)," "Licentious(-us)." On the far left a scene shows how "Alumnusvic" killed "Mazicinus" and left him lying upside down in a pool of blood.

High up on the wall is a thrilling first-century Greek sculpture of a horse falling. The Renaissance-era rider was added by Pietro Bernini, father of the famous Gian Lorenzo Bernini.

Room I

Antonio Canova—*Pauline Bonaparte as Venus* (*Paolina Borghese Bonaparte*, 1808)

Napoleon's sister went the full monty for the sculptor Canova, scandalizing Europe. ("How could you have done such a thing?!" she was asked. She replied, "The room wasn't cold.") With the famous

nose of her conqueror brother, she strikes the pose of Venus as conqueror of men's hearts. Her relaxed afterglow and slight smirk say she's already had her man. The light dent she puts in the mattress makes this goddess human.

Notice the contrasting textures that Canova (1757–1822) gets out of the pure white marble: the rumpled sheet versus her smooth skin, the satiny-smooth pillows and mattress versus the creases in them, her porcelain skin versus the hint of a love handle. Canova polished and waxed the marble until it looked as soft and pliable as cloth.

The mythological pose, the Roman couch, the ancient hairdo, and the calm harmony make Pauline the epitome of the Neoclassical style.

Room II

Gian Lorenzo Bernini—*David* (1624)

Duck! David twists around to put a big rock in his sling. He purses

BORGHESE GALLERY

Borghese Gallery—Ground Floor

Room VI Room V Room IV ❾ Room III
❻   ❹
                     ❺   ❸
                            CHAPEL

Room VII MAIN ENTRY HALL Room II
❼   ❷

Room VIII START Room I
❽   PORTICO ❶

DCH
❿

❶ CANOVA – Pauline Bonaparte as Venus
❷ BERNINI – David
❸ BERNINI – Apollo and Daphne
❹ BERNINI – The Rape of Proserpine
❺ UNKNOWN – Diana the Hunter; Other Marbles
❻ BERNINI – Aeneas
❼ "Theater of the Universe"
❽ CARAVAGGIO – Various
❾ Stairs to Pinacoteca
❿ To Basement (Tickets, Info, Shop, WC)

BORGHESE GALLERY

his lips, knits his brow, and winds his body like a spring as his eyes lock onto the target—Goliath, who's somewhere behind us, putting us right in the line of fire.

In this self-portrait, 25-year-old Bernini (1598–1680) is ready to take on the world. He's charged with the same fighting energy that fueled the missionaries and conquistadors of the Counter-Reformation.

Compared with Michelangelo's *David*, this is unvarnished realism—an unbalanced pose, bulging veins, unflattering face, and armpit hair. Michelangelo's *David* thinks, whereas Bernini's acts—with lips pursed, eyes concentrating, and sling stretched. Bernini slays the pretty-boy *David*s of the Renaissance and prepares to invent Baroque.

Flanking David are two ancient sarcophagi carved with scenes from the *Labors of Hercules* (A.D. 160; find Hercules with his club).

The twisting bodybuilders' poses were the Hellenistic inspiration for Bernini's Baroque. The painting behind them, by a follower of Caravaggio, shows a triumphant David with the giant's head.

Room III

Bernini—*Apollo and Daphne (Apollo e Dafne*, 1625)

Apollo—made stupid by Cupid's arrow of love—chases after Daphne, who has been turned off by the "arrow of disgust." Just

as he's about to catch her, she calls to her father to save her. Magically, her fingers begin to sprout leaves, her toes become roots, her skin turns to bark, and she transforms into a tree. Frustrated Apollo will end up with a handful of leaves.

Stand behind the statue to experience it as Bernini originally intended. It's only when you circle around to the front that he reveals the story's surprise ending.

Walk slowly around the statue. Apollo's back leg defies gravity. Bernini has chipped away more than half of the block of marble, leaving airy, open spaces. The statue spent two years in restoration (described to me as similar to dental work). The marble leaves at the top ring like crystal when struck. Notice the same scene, colorized, painted on the ceiling above.

Bernini carves out some of the chief features of Baroque art. He makes a supernatural event seem realistic. He freezes it at the most dramatic, emotional moment. The figures move and twist in unusual poses. He turns the wind machine on, sending Apollo's cape billowing behind him. It's a sculpture group of two, forming a scene, rather than a stand-alone portrait. And the subject is classical. Even in strict Counter-Reformation times, there was always a place for groping, if the subject matter had a moral—this one taught you not to pursue fleeting earthly pleasures. And, besides, Bernini tends to show a lot of skin, but no genitals.

The cardinal's private chapel (between Rooms III and IV) is the only purely religious room in the palace. It's relatively humble, a reminder that the cardinal probably didn't usually stop in here for much longer than tourists do today.

Room IV

Bernini—*The Rape of Proserpine* (*Il Ratto di Proserpina*, 1622)

Pluto, King of the Underworld, strides into his realm and shows off his catch—the beautiful daughter of the earth goddess. His three-headed guard dog, Cerberus (who guards the gates of hell), barks triumphantly. Pluto is squat, thick, and uncouth, with knotted muscles and untrimmed beard. He's trying not to hurt her, but she pushes her divine molester away and twists to call out for help. Tears roll down her cheeks. She wishes she could turn into a tree.

Bernini was the master of marble. With this work, at the age of 24, he had discovered his Baroque niche. While Renaissance works were designed to be seen from the front, Baroque is theater-in-the-round—full of action, designed to be experienced as you walk around it. Look how Pluto's fingers dig into her frantic body as if it was real flesh. Bernini picked out this Carrara marble, knowing that its relative suppleness and ivory hue would lend itself to a fleshy statue.

• *In a niche over Pluto's right shoulder, find...*

Artist Unknown—Diana the Hunter *(Artemide)*

The goddess has been running through the forest. Now she's spotted her prey, and slows down, preparing to string her (missing) bow with an arrow. Or is she smoking a (missing) cigarette? Scholars debate it.

The statues in the niches are classical originals. Diana the Hunter is a rare Greek original, with every limb and finger intact, from the second century B.C. The traditional *contrapposto* pose (weight on one leg) and idealized grace were an inspiration for artists such as Canova, who grew tired of Bernini's Baroque bombast.

The Marbles in Room IV

The many ancient Roman statues and portrait busts of Roman emperors in this room were intended as a reminder that the pope was essentially a king, the successor to ancient Roman rulers of the past. (Up until around 1800, popes held vast political—and even military—power.)

Appreciate the beauty of the different types of marble in the room: Bernini's ivory Carrara, Diana's translucent white, purple porphyry emperors, granite-like columns that support them, wood-grained pilasters on the walls, and the different colors on the floor—green, red, gray, lavender, and yellow, some grainy, some "marbled" like a steak. Some of the world's most beautiful and durable things have been made from the shells of sea creatures layered in sediment, fossilized into limestone, then baked and crystallized by the pressure of the earth—marble.

Room VI

Bernini—*Aeneas (Enea che fugge,* etc., 1620)

Aeneas' home in Troy is in flames, and he escapes with the three most important things: his family (decrepit father on his shoulder, baby boy), his household gods (the statues in dad's hands), and the Eternal Flame (carried by son). They're all in shock, lost in thought, facing an uncertain future. Aeneas isn't even looking where he's going; he just puts one foot in front of the other. Little do they know that eventually they'll wind up in Italy, where—according to legend—Aeneas will found the city of Rome and house the flame in the Temple of Vesta.

Bernini was just 20 when he started this, his first major work for Cardinal Borghese. He was probably helped by his dad, who nurtured the child prodigy much like Leopold mentored Mozart, but without the rivalry. Bernini's portrayal of human flesh—from baby fat to middle-aged muscle to sagging decrepitude—is astonishing. Still, the flat-footed statue just stands there—it lacks the Baroque energy of his more mature work. More lively are the reliefs up at the ceiling, with their dancing, light-footed soldiers with do-si-do shields.

Room VII

The "Theater of the Universe"

The room's decor sums up the eclectic nature of the villa. There are Greek statues and Roman mosaics. There are fake "Egyptian" sphinxes and hieroglyphs (perfectly symmetrical, in good Neoclassical style). Look out the window past the sculpted gardens at the mesh domes of the aviary, once filled with exotic birds. Cardinal Borghese's vision was to make a place where art, history, music, nature, and science from every place and time would come together..."a theater of the universe."

Room VIII

Caravaggio

This room holds the greatest collection of Caravaggio paintings anywhere. Michelangelo Merisi (1571–1610), nicknamed Caravaggio after his hometown (near Milan), brought Christian saints down to earth with gritty realism. In each of these paintings you see the Baroque innovator Caravaggio's unique style: His saints are balding and wrinkled. His Bacchus (a self-portrait) is pale and puffy-faced. David sticks Goliath's severed head (a self-portrait of the artist) right in your face. The Madonnas

Gian Lorenzo Bernini
(1598–1680)

A Renaissance Man in Counter-Reformation times, Bernini almost personally invented the Baroque style, transforming the city of Rome. If you're visiting Rome, you will see Bernini's work, guaranteed.

Bernini was a child prodigy in his father's sculpting studio, growing up among Europe's rich and powerful. His flamboyant personality endeared him to his cultured employers—the popes in Rome, Louis XIV in France, and Charles I in England. He was extremely prolific, working fast and utilizing an army of assistants.

Despite the fleshiness and sensuality of his works, Bernini was a religious man, seeing his creativity as an extension of God's. In stark contrast to the Protestant world's sobriety, Bernini shamelessly embraced pagan myths and nude goddesses, declaring them all part of the "catholic"—that is, universal—Church.

Bernini, a master of multimedia, was a...
- Sculptor (Borghese Gallery and *St. Teresa in Ecstasy,* pictured above and described on page 59)
- Architect (elements of St. Peter's—see "Bernini Blitz," page 256, and the Church of Sant'Andrea al Quirinale)
- Painter (Borghese Gallery)
- Interior decorator (the *baldacchino* canopy and other works in St. Peter's)
- Civic engineer (he laid out St. Peter's Square, and he designed and renovated Rome's fountains in Piazza Navona, Piazza Barberini, Piazza di Spagna, and more).

Even works done by other artists a century later (such as the Trevi Fountain) can be traced indirectly to Bernini, the man who invented Baroque, the "look" of Rome for the next two centuries.

BORGHESE GALLERY

scarcely glow. The boy Jesus is buck naked. Ordinary people were his models. People emerge from a dark background, lit by a harsh, unflattering light, which highlights part of the figure, leaving the rest in deep shadows. Caravaggio's straightforwardness can be a refreshing change in a museum full of (sometimes overly) refined beauty.

The painting of *La Madonna dei Palafrenieri* was removed from St. Peter's for its lack of decorum. Jesus and Mary step on the snake of evil (i.e., Protestantism). The pope had no problem with that...but the face of Mary is the face of Rome's most famous prostitute of the day. Cardinal Borghese didn't care; he bought it and hung it here.

David with Head of Goliath was painted after Caravaggio killed a man and was forced to flee Rome. By portraying himself as Goliath, he symbolically gives his head to the pope as a request for forgiveness. The pope accepted, but Caravaggio died of yellow fever on his way home.

• *To reach the Pinacoteca, head through the main entry hall back to Room IV, find the entry to the staircase in the far right corner, and spiral up to the...*

Pinacoteca (Painting Gallery)

You must visit the Pinacoteca within the two-hour window of time printed on your Borghese Gallery ticket. Most visitors wait until the last half-hour to see the Pinacoteca, so that's when it's most crowded (and the ground floor is less crowded). If you see the paintings first, remember to save most of your two-hour visit for the ground-floor sculptures.

• *Along the long wall of Room XIV, you'll find the following statues and paintings by Bernini. First, find the two identical white busts set on columns.*

Room XIV

Bernini—*Busts of Cardinal Borghese* (*Ritr. del Card. Scipione Borghese*, 1632)

Say *grazie* to the man who built this villa, assembled the collection, and hired Bernini to sculpt masterpieces. The cardinal is caught turning as though to greet someone at a party. There's a twinkle in his eye, and he opens his mouth to make a witty comment. This man of the cloth was, in fact, a sophisticated hedonist.

Notice that there are two identical versions of this bust. The first one started cracking along the forehead (visible) just as Bernini was finishing it. *No problema*—Bernini whipped out a replacement in just three days.

• *On the left wall above the middle table, find these paintings...*

Two Bernini Self-Portraits (*Autoritratto Giovanile*, 1623, and *Autoritratto in età Matura*, 1630–1635)

Bernini was a master of many media, including painting. The younger Bernini (age 25) looks out a bit hesitantly, as if he's still finding his way in high-class society. His jet-black eyes came from his southern Italian mother who, it's said, also gave him his passionate personality.

In his next self-portrait (age 35), with a few masterpieces under his belt, Bernini shows himself with more confidence and facial hair—the dashing, vibrant man who would rebuild Rome in

Baroque style, from St. Peter's Square to the fountains that dot the piazzas.
• *On the table below, find the smaller...*

Bust of Pope Paul V

The cardinal's uncle was a more sober man, but he was also a patron of the arts with a good eye for talent who hired Bernini's father. When Pope Paul V saw sketches made by little Gian Lorenzo, he announced, "This boy will be the Michelangelo of his age."
• *To the right of the Borghese busts, find a small statue of...*

Two Babies Milking a Goat

Bernini was 11 years old when he did this. That's about the age when I mastered how to make a Play-Doh snake.
• *Room IX is back near the top of the staircase you ascended to get here.*

Room IX
Raphael (Raffaello Sanzio)—*Deposition* (*Deposizione di Cristo,* 1507)

Jesus is being taken from the cross. The men support him while the women support Mary (in purple), who has fainted. Mary

Magdalene rushes up to take Christ's hand. The woman who commissioned the painting had recently lost her son. She wanted to show the death of a son and the grief of a mother. We see two different faces of grief—mother Mary faints at the horror, while Mary Magdalene still can't quite believe he's gone.

In true Renaissance style, Raphael (1483–1520) orders the scene with geometrical perfection. The curve of Jesus' body is echoed by the swirl of Mary Magdalene's hair, and then by the curve of Calvary Hill, where Christ met his fate.

Room X
Correggio—*Danaë* (c. 1531)

Cupid strips Danaë as she spreads her legs, most unladylike, to receive a trickle of gold from the smudgy cloud overhead—this was Zeus' idea of intercourse with a human. The sheets are rumpled, and Danaë looks right where the action is with a smile on her face. It's hard to believe that a supposedly religious family would display such an erotic work. But the Borgheses felt that the Church was truly "catholic" (universal), and that all forms of human expression—including physical passion—glorified God.

• *Backtrack through the room with the two cardinal busts, then turn left and travel to the farthest room.*

Room XX

Titian (Tiziano Vecellio)—*Sacred and Profane Love* (*Amor Sacro e Amor Profano,* c. 1515)

While you might guess that the naked woman on the right embodies profane love, that's actually represented by the material girl on the left—with her box of treasures, fortified castle, and dark, claus-

trophobic landscape. Sacred love is represented by the naked woman who has nothing to hide and enjoys open spaces filled with light, life, a church in the distance, and even a couple of lovers in the field.

The clothed woman at left has recently married, and she cradles a vase filled with jewels representing the riches of earthly love. Her naked twin on the right holds the burning flame of eternal, heavenly love. Baby Cupid, between them, playfully stirs the waters.

Symbolically, the steeple on the right points up to the love of heaven, while on the left, soldiers prepare to "storm the castle" of the new bride. Miss Heavenly Love looks jealous.

This exquisite painting expresses the spirit of the Renaissance—that earth and heaven are two sides of the same coin. And here in the Borghese Gallery, that love of earthly beauty can be spiritually uplifting—as long as you feel it within two hours.

BORGHESE GALLERY

VATICAN MUSEUM TOUR

Musei Vaticani

The glories of the ancient world displayed in a lavish papal palace, decorated by the likes of Michelangelo and Raphael...the Musei Vaticani. Unfortunately, many tourists see the Vatican Museum only as an obstacle between them and its grand finale, the Sistine Chapel. True, this huge, confusing, and crowded megamuseum can be a jungle—but with this book as your vine, you should swing through with ease, enjoying the highlights and getting to the Sistine just before you collapse.

With the Fall of Rome, the Catholic (or "universal") Church became the great preserver of civilization, collecting artifacts from cultures dead and dying. Renaissance popes (15th and 16th centuries) collected most of what we'll see, using it as furniture to decorate their palace (today's museum). Combining the classical and Christian worlds, they found the divine in the creations of man.

We'll concentrate on classical sculpture and Renaissance painting. But along the way (and there's a lot of along-the-way here), we'll stop to leaf through a few yellowed pages from this 5,000-year-old scrapbook of humankind.

The always-crowded museum now has an online reservation system and a website (http://mv.vatican.va) with up-to-date hours and information. Plan ahead for your visit.

Orientation

Cost: €15 plus optional €4 reservation fee. Free on the last Sun of each month (when it's very crowded).

Hours: Mon–Sat 9:00–18:00, last entry at 16:00 (though the official closing time is 18:00, the staff starts ushering you out at 17:30). Closed Sun, except last Sun of the month 9:00–14:00, last entry at 12:30. May be open some Fri nights April–Oct 19:00–23:00 (last entry at 21:30) by reservation only—check the website. Those with reservations can enter the museum as early as 8:00, before the ticket-buying crowds. Hours are notoriously subject to constant change.

The museum is closed on many holidays (mainly religious ones) including, for 2011: Jan 1 (New Year's), Jan 6 (Epiphany), Feb 11 (Vatican City established), March 19 (St. Joseph), April 24 and 25 (Easter Sunday and Monday), May 1 (Labor Day), June 29 (Saints Peter and Paul), Aug 15 plus either Aug 14 or 16—it varies year to year (Assumption of the Virgin), Nov 1 (All Saints' Day), Dec 8 (Immaculate Conception), and Dec 25 and 26 (Christmas). Other holidays and changes in opening hours may pop up—check the hours and calendar at http://mv.vatican.va.

The Sistine Chapel closes before the museum. Individual rooms may close at odd hours, especially in the afternoon. The rooms described here are usually open.

When to Go: The museum is generally hot and crowded, with waits of up to two hours to buy tickets. The worst days are Saturdays, the last Sunday of the month (when it's free), Mondays, rainy days, and any day before or after a holiday closure. Mornings are most crowded. (Stuck in the line? Figure about a 10-minute wait for every 100 yards.)

Avoiding Lines: You can buy a ticket and **reserve an entry time online** at http://mv.vatican.va for €19 (€15 ticket plus €4 booking fee, pay with credit card). You choose your day and time, they email you a confirmation immediately, and you print out the voucher with its reservation bar code. At the Vatican Museum, bypass the ticket-buying line and queue up at the "Entrance with Reservations" line (to the right). Show your voucher to the guard, who will scan it and let you in. Once inside the museum, go to a ticket window (either in the lobby or upstairs), present your voucher and ID, and they'll issue your ticket.

If you book a **guided tour through the Vatican Museum** (see next page), you can also skip the ticket-buying line and approach the guard with your voucher. If you book with a private tour company, you may still have a short wait at crowded times.

If you don't have a reservation, **try arriving after 14:00,** when crowds subside somewhat. Another good time is during the papal audience on Wednesday after 10:30, when many tourists are at St. Peter's Basilica.

Make sure you get in the right line. Generally, individuals without tickets line up against the Vatican City wall (to the left of the entrance as you face it), and individuals with reservations enter on the right.

Dress Code: Modest dress (no short shorts or bare shoulders) is required. While this dress code may not be strictly enforced here, it is at St. Peter's Basilica (which you can visit after leaving the Sistine Chapel).

Getting There: Metro stop Cipro is a 10-minute walk from the entrance, including a climb up a big flight of stairs. The Ottaviano Metro stop is slightly farther from the entrance, but may be closer to the end of the ticket-buying line. Bus #49 from Piazza Cavour stops right at the entrance. Bus #23 from Trastevere hugs the west bank of the Tiber and stops on Via Leone IV, just downhill from the entrance. Bus #64 stops on the other side of St. Peter's Square, a 15- to 20-minute walk (facing the church from the obelisk, take a right through the colonnade and follow the Vatican Wall). Taxis are reasonable (hop in and say, "moo-ZAY-ee vah-tee-KAH-nee").

Information: As you enter the lobby, there's an info desk to your left, and TV screens list what rooms are open or closed. Bookstores are scattered throughout the museum. Some exhibits have English explanations.

At http://mv.vatican.va, you can reserve an entry time, sign up for a tour, get general information, and see what days the museum is closed. Tel. 06-6988-3860 or 06-6988-1662. For more on Vatican City, see page 69.

Tours: The Vatican offers English tours that are easy to book online (€31, includes admission, http://mv.vatican.va). As with individual ticket reservations, present your confirmation voucher to a guard to the right of the entrance, then, once inside, go to the Guided Tours desk (in the lobby, up a few stairs).

Both private tour companies and private guides offer guided English tours of the museum, usually allowing you to skip the long ticket-buying line. For a listing of several companies, see page 36.

Audioguide Tours: If you rent an **audioguide** (€7 plus ID, available at the top of the ramp/escalator), you lose the option of taking the shortcut from the Sistine Chapel to St. Peter's (since audioguides must be returned to the museum entrance/exit). You can download a free **audio tour** of the Sistine Chapel portion of this tour at www.ricksteves.com (or search for "Rick Steves Audio Tours" in iTunes).

Length of This Tour: Until you expire, the museum closes, or 2.5 hours, whichever comes first.

Security and Baggage Check: To enter the museum, you pass through a metal detector (no pocket knives allowed). The baggage check (upstairs from the lobby) takes only big bags; you'll need to carry your day bag with you.

VATICAN MUSEUM

Services: The post office, with stamps that make collectors drool, is upstairs. WCs are mainly at the entrance/exit, plus a few scattered within the collection.

Museum Strategies: There are two exits from the museum, and you'll want to decide which you'll take before you enter. The main exit is right near the entrance. Use this one if you plan on renting an audioguide (which you must return at the entrance) or if you plan on following this self-guided tour exactly as laid out, visiting the Pinacoteca at the end.

The other exit is a shortcut that leads from the Sistine Chapel directly to St. Peter's Basilica (spilling out alongside the church; see map on page 207). This route saves you a 30-minute walk (15 minutes back to the Vatican Museum entry/exit, then 15 minutes to St. Peter's) and lets you avoid the often-long security line at the basilica's main entrance. If you take this route, you'll have to do the following: adhere to St. Peter's stricter dress code (no shorts, miniskirts, or bare shoulders), forgo an audioguide, skip the Pinacoteca or tour it earlier, and be prepared for the odd chance that the shortcut is simply closed (which sometimes happens).

To see the Sistine Chapel with fewer crowds, visit at the end of the day (remember, the chapel closes 1.5 hours before the museum). Add to the experience by slipping directly into St. Peter's Basilica afterward.

Photography: No photos are allowed in the Sistine Chapel. Elsewhere in the museum, photos without a flash are permitted.

Cuisine Art: A self-service cafeteria is inside, near the Pinacoteca, and a smaller café is near the Sistine Chapel. Cheaper choices outside the museum include the great Mercato Trionfale produce market on Via Andrea Doria, three blocks north of the entrance (head across the street, down the stairs, and continue straight). Inexpensive *pizza rustica* shops selling pizza by the slice line Viale Giulio Cesare, and good restaurants are nearby (see page 357).

Starring: World history, Michelangelo, Raphael, *Laocoön*, the Greek masters, and their Roman copyists.

The Tour Begins

This heavyweight museum is shaped like a barbell—two buildings connected by a long hall. The entrance building covers the ancient world (Egypt, Greece, Rome). The one at the far end covers its "rebirth" in the Renaissance (including the Sistine Chapel). The halls there and back are a mix of old and new. Move quickly—don't burn out before the Sistine Chapel at the end—and see how

VATICAN MUSEUM

Vatican Museum Overview

TO OTTAVIANO Ⓜ ↑

TO CIPRO Ⓜ

VIA SEB. VENIERO

VIA D. SCIPIONI

VIA LEONE IV

V. GERMANICO

VIA OTTAVIANO

VIALE VATICANO

❶ →

❷
❹
❺
❸

⓾

CAFETERIA

PIAZZA DEL RISORGIMENTO

VATICAN GARDENS

❻
❼

PAPAL APARTMENTS

VIA DI PORTA ANGELICA

❽
CAFÉ
❾
ELEV.

ST. PETER'S BASILICA

ATRIUM ←

ST. PETER'S SQUARE

OBELISK

200 YARDS
200 METERS

Ⓜ METRO STATION

━━━ VATICAN WALL

▨ VATICAN MUSEUM

VATICAN MUSEUM ENTRY TO OBELISK VIA ROAD IS A 15-MINUTE WALK

❶ Main Entrance & Exit
❷ Egyptian Rooms
❸ Cortile della Pigna
❹ Octagonal Courtyard
❺ Etruscan Wing
❻ Tapestries
❼ Map Gallery & View of Vatican City
❽ Raphael Rooms
❾ Sistine Chapel & Exit to St. Peter's
⓾ Pinacoteca

VATICAN MUSEUM

each civilization borrows from and builds on the previous one.

• *Leave Italy by entering the doors.*

Once you clear the security checkpoint, exchange your printed voucher (on ground floor) or buy your ticket (upstairs). Punch the ticket in the turnstiles, then take the long escalator or spiral stairs up, up, up to a covered courtyard with a view of the St. Peter's dome.

Pause at the courtyard: To your right is the cafeteria and the Pinacoteca painting gallery (consider touring the Pinacoteca now if you plan to take the Sistine-to-St. Peter's shortcut at the end; for a description of the Pinacoteca, see page 234). To your left is the beginning of our tour.

To start our tour, go left, then take another left up a flight of stairs to reach the first-floor Egyptian Rooms (Museo Egizio) on your right. Don't stop until you find your mummy.

Note: Occasionally, the stairs up to Egypt are closed off, and crowds are routed through a spacious open-air courtyard, the Cortile della Pigna (see map on previous page). Just keep following the masses until you reach the *Apollo Belvedere* and *Laocoön* figures. Tour the museum from there to the "Sarcophagi," where you'll find the entrance to the Egyptian rooms.

Egypt (3000–1000 B.C.)

Egyptian art was for religion, not decoration. A statue or painting preserved the likeness of someone, giving him a form of eternal life. Most of the art was for tombs, where they put the mummies.

• *Pass beyond the imitation Egyptian pillars to the left of the case in the center of the room, and you'll find...*

Mummies

This woman died three millennia ago. Her corpse was disemboweled, and her organs were placed in a jar like those you see nearby.

Then the body was refilled with pitch, dried with natron (a natural sodium carbonate), wrapped in linen, and placed in a wood coffin, which went inside a stone coffin, which was placed in a tomb. (Remember that the pyramids were just big tombs.) Notice the henna job on her hair—in the next life, your spirit needed a body to be rooted to...and you wanted to look your best.

Painted inside the coffin lid is a list of what the deceased "packed" for the journey to eternity. The coffins were decorated

Vatican Museum Schematic

ENTRANCE &
MAIN EXIT

EXIT
(SOMETIMES)
CLOSED

ANCIENT
EGYPT
GREECE
ROME
ETRURIA

STATUES   MAPS

TAPESTRIES

RENAISSANCE
RAPHAEL ROOMS
SISTINE CHAPEL

ST.
PETER'S

DCH

with magical spells to protect the body from evil and to act as crib
notes for the confused soul in the netherworld.
• *In the next room are...*

Egyptian Statues

Egyptian statues walk awkwardly, as if they're
carrying heavy buckets, with arms straight down
at their sides. Even these Roman reproduc-
tions (made for Hadrian's Villa) are stiff, two-
dimensional, and schematic—the art is only
realistic enough to get the job done. In Egyptian
belief, a statue like this could be a stable refuge
for the wandering soul of a dead man. Each was
made according to an established set of proportions. Little changed over the centuries—these
had a function, and they worked.
• *Walk through the next small room and into the
curved hallway, and look for...*

Various Egyptian Gods as Animals

Before technology made humans top dogs on earth, it was easier
to appreciate our fellow creatures. Egyptians
saw the superiority of animals and worshipped
them as incarnations of the gods. Wander
through a pet store of Egyptian animal
gods. Find Anubis, a jackal in a toga. In the
curved room, find the lioness, the fierce goddess Sekhmet. The clever baboon is the god of
wisdom, Thot. At the end of the curved hall
on your right is Bes (the small white marble
statue), the patron of pregnant women (and
beer-bellied men).
• *Continue to Room VIII (the third room), pausing
at the glass case, which contains brown clay tablets.*

VATICAN MUSEUM

Sumerian Writing

Even before Egypt, civilizations flourished in the Middle East. The Sumerian culture in Mesopotamia (the ancestors of the ancient

Babylonians and of Saddam Hussein) invented writing in about 3000 B.C. People wrote on clay tablets by pressing into the wet clay with a wedge-shaped (cuneiform) pen. The Sumerians also rolled cylinder seals into soft clay to make an impression used to seal documents and mark property.

• *Pass through the next room, and then turn left, to a balcony with a view of Rome through the window. Then enter the octagonal courtyard.*

Sculpture—Greece and Rome
(500 B.C.–A.D. 500)

This palace wouldn't be here, this sculpture wouldn't be here, and our lives would likely be quite different if it weren't for a few thousand Greeks in a small city about 450 years before Christ. Athens set the tone for the rest of the West. Democracy, theater, economics, literature, and art all flourished in Athens during a 50-year "Golden Age." Greek culture was then appropriated by Rome, and revived again 1,500 years later, during the Renaissance. The Renaissance popes built and decorated these papal palaces, re-creating the glory of the classical world.

Apollo Belvedere

Apollo, the god of the sun and of music, is hunting. He's been running through the woods, and now he spots his prey. Keeping his eye on the animal, he slows down and prepares to put a (missing) arrow into his (missing) bow. The optimistic Greeks conceived of their gods in human form...and buck naked.

The Greek sculptor Leochares, following the style of the greater Greek sculptor Praxiteles, has fully captured the beauty of the human form. The anatomy is perfect, his pose is natural. Instead of standing at attention, face-forward with his arms at his sides (Egyptian-style), Apollo is on the move, coming to rest with his weight on one leg.

The Greeks loved balance. A well-rounded man was both a thinker and an athlete, a poet

The Ancient World

- ❶ Mummies
- ❷ Egyptian Statues
- ❸ Gods as Animals
- ❹ Sumerian Writing
- ❺ Apollo Belvedere
- ❻ Laocoön
- ❼ Belvedere Torso
- ❽ Hercules
- ❾ Porphyry Basin
- ❿ Sarcophagi

and a warrior. In art, the *Apollo Belvedere* balances several opposites. He's moving, but not out of control. Apollo eyes his target, but hasn't attacked yet. He's realistic, but with idealized, godlike features. And the smoothness of his muscles is balanced by the rough folds of his cloak. The only sour note: his left hand, added in modern times. Could we try a size smaller?

During the Renaissance, when this Roman copy of the original Greek work was discovered, it was considered the most perfect work of art in the world. The handsome face, eternal youth, and body that seems to float just above the pedestal made *Apollo Belvedere* seem superhuman, divine, and godlike, even for devout Christians.

• *In the neighboring niche to the right, a bearded old Roman river god lounges in the shade. This pose inspired Michelangelo's* Adam, *in the Sistine Chapel (coming soon). While there are a few fancy bathtubs in this courtyard, most of the carved boxes you see are sarcophagi—Roman coffins and relic holders, carved with the deceased's epitaph in picture form.*

Laocoön

Laocoön (lay-AWK-oh-wahn), the high priest of Troy, warned his fellow Trojans: "Beware of Greeks bearing gifts." The attacking

Greeks had brought the Trojan Horse to the gates as a ploy to get inside the city walls, and Laocoön tried to warn his people not to bring it inside. But the gods wanted the Greeks to win, so they sent huge snakes to crush Laocoön and his two sons to death. We see them at the height of their terror, when they realize that, no matter how hard they struggle, they—and their entire race—are doomed.

The figures (carved from four blocks of marble pieced together seamlessly) are powerful, not light and graceful. The poses are as twisted as possible, accentuating every rippling muscle and bulging vein. Follow the line of motion from Laocoön's left foot, up his leg, through his body, and out his right arm (which some historians used to think extended straight out—until the elbow was dug up early in the 1900s). Goethe would stand here and blink his eyes rapidly, watching the statue flicker to life.

Laocoön was sculpted four centuries after the Golden Age, after the scales of "balance" had been tipped. Whereas *Apollo* is a balance between stillness and motion, this is unbridled motion. *Apollo* is serene, graceful, and godlike, while *Laocoön* is powerful, emotional, and gritty.

Laocoön—the most famous Greek statue in ancient Rome and considered "superior to all other sculpture or painting"—was lost for more than a thousand years. Then, in 1506, it was unexpectedly unearthed in the ruins of Nero's Golden House near the Colosseum. The discovery caused a sensation. They cleaned it off and paraded it through the streets before an awestruck populace. No one had ever seen anything like its motion and emotion, having been raised on a white-bread diet of pretty-boy *Apollo*s. One of those who saw it was the young Michelangelo, and it was a revelation to him. Two years later, he started work on the Sistine Chapel, and the Renaissance was about to take another turn.

• *Leave the courtyard to the right of* Laocoön *and swing around the Hall of Animals, a jungle of beasts real and surreal. Then continue to the limbless torso in the middle of the next large hall.*

Belvedere Torso

My experience with sculpting statues ends with snowmen. But standing face to face with this hunk of shaped rock makes you

appreciate the sheer physical labor involved in chipping a figure out of solid stone. It takes great strength, but at the same time, great delicacy.

This is all that remains of an ancient statue of Hercules seated on a lion skin. Michelangelo loved this old rock. He knew that he was the best sculptor of his day. The ancients were his only peers—and his rivals. He'd caress this statue lovingly and tell people, "I am the pupil of the Torso." To him, it contained all the beauty of classical sculpture. But it's not beautiful. Compared with the pure grace of the *Apollo,* it's downright ugly.

But Michelangelo, an ugly man himself, was looking for a new kind of beauty—not the beauty of idealized gods, but the innate beauty of every person, even so-called ugly ones. With its knotty lumps of muscle, the Torso has a brute power and a distinct personality despite—or because of—its rough edges. Remember this Torso, because we'll see it again later on.

• *Enter the next, domed room.*

Round Room

This room, modeled on the Pantheon interior, gives some idea of Roman grandeur. Romans took Greek ideas and made them big-

ger, like the big bronze statue of Hercules with his club, found near the Theater of Pompey (by modern-day Campo de' Fiori). The mosaic floor once decorated the bottom of a pool in an ancient Roman bath. The enormous Roman basin/hot tub/birdbath/vase decorated Nero's place. It was made of a single block of purple porphyry marble stone imported from the desert of Egypt. Purple was a rare, royal, expensive, and prestigious color in pre-Crayola days. This was the stone of emperors...and then of popes. Now it's all been quarried out, and the only porphyry available to anyone has been recycled.

• *Enter the next room.*

Sarcophagi

These two large porphyry marble coffins were made (though not used) for the Roman emperor Constantine's mother (Helena, on left) and daughter (Constanza, on right). Helena's coffin depicts

a battle game showing dying victims in their barbarian dress. Constanza's is decorated with a mix of Christian and pagan themes. Helena and Constanza were Christians—and therefore outlaws—until Constantine made Christianity legal in

A.D. 312, and they became saints. Both sarcophagi were quarried and worked in Egypt. The technique for working this extremely hard stone (a special tempering of metal was required) was lost after this, and porphyry marble was not chiseled again until Renaissance times in Florence.

• *See how we've come full circle in this building—the Egyptian Rooms are ahead on your left. Go upstairs and prepare for the Long March down the hall lined with statues, toward the Sistine Chapel and Raphael Rooms.*

Overachievers may first choose to pop into the Etruscan wing—labeled Museo Etrusco—*located a few steps up from the Long March level. (Others have permission to save their aesthetic energy for the Sistine.)*

The Etruscans (800–300 B.C.)

Room I

The chariot is from 550 B.C., when crude Romans were ruled by their more civilized neighbors to the north—the Etruscans. Imagine the chariot racing around the dirt track of the Circus Maximus, through the marshy valley of the newly drained Forum, or up Capitol Hill to the Temple of Jupiter—all originally built by Rome's Etruscan kings.

Room II

The golden breastplate (*Pectoral*, 650 B.C., immediately to the right), decorated with tiny winged angels and animals, shows off the sophistication of the Etruscans. Though unwarlike and politically decentralized, these people were able to "conquer" all of central Italy around 650 B.C. through trade, offering tempting metalwork goods like this.

The Etruscan vases done in the Greek style remind us of the other great pre-Roman power—the Greek colonists who settled in southern Italy (Magna Graecia). The Etruscans traded with the

Greeks, adopting their fashions. Rome, cradled between the two, grew up learning from both cultures.

A Greek-style bowl (far corner of the room) depicting a man and woman in bed together would have scandalized early Roman farmers. He's peeing in a chamberpot, she's blowing a flute. Etruscan art often showed husbands and wives at ease together, giving them a reputation among the Romans as immoral, flute-playing degenerates.

Room III

This bronze warrior, whose head was sawed off by lightning, has a rare inscription that's readable (on armor below the navel). It probably refers to the statue's former owner: "Aha! Trutitis gave [this] as [a] gift." Archaeologists understand the Etruscans' Greek-style alphabet and some individual words, but they've yet to fully crack the code. As you look around at beautiful bronze pitchers, candlesticks, shields, and urns, ponder yet another of Etruria's unsolved mysteries—no one is sure where these sophisticated people came from.

Room IV

Most of our knowledge of the Etruscans is from sarcophagi and art in Etruscan tombs. Their funeral art is solemn, but

hardly morbid—check out the sarcopha-guy with the bulging belly, enjoying a banquet for all eternity.

The Etruscans' origins are obscure, but their legacy is clear. In 509 B.C., the Etruscan king's son raped a Roman. The king was thrown out, the republic was declared, Etruscan cities were conquered by Rome's legions, and their culture was swallowed up in Roman expansion. By Julius Caesar's time, the few remaining ethnic Etruscans were reduced to serving their masters as flute players, goldsmiths, surgeons, and street-corner preachers, like the one that Caesar brushed aside when he called out, "Beware the Ides of March..."

• *Browse the remaining dozen rooms of the Etruscan Wing, or backtrack to the long hall (the Gallery of the Candelabra) leading to the Sistine Chapel and Raphael Rooms.*

The Long March—Sculpture, Tapestries, Maps, and Views

This quarter-mile walk gives you a sense of the scale that Renaissance popes built on. Remember, this building was originally a series of papal palaces. The popes loved beautiful things—statues, urns, marble floors, friezes, stuccoed ceilings—and, as heirs of imperial Rome, they felt they deserved such luxury. The palaces and art represent both the peak and the decline of the Catholic Church in Europe. It was extravagant spending like this that inspired Martin Luther to rebel, starting the Protestant Reformation.

Gallery of the Candelabra: Classical Sculpture

In the second "room" of the long hall, stop at the statue Diana the Huntress on the left. Here, the virgin goddess goes hunting. Roman hunters would pray and give offerings to statues like this to get divine help in their search for food.

Farmers might pray to another version of the same goddess, Artemis, on the opposite wall. This billion-breasted beauty stood for fertility. "Boobs or bulls' balls?" Some historians say that bulls were sacrificed and castrated, with the testicles draped over the statues as symbols of fertility.

• *Shuffle along to the next "room." On the left is Bacchus, with a baby on his shoulders.*

Fig Leaves

Why do the statues have fig leaves? Like Bacchus, many of these statues originally looked much different than they do now. First off, they were painted, often in gaudy colors. Bacchus may have had brown hair, rosy cheeks, purple grapes, and a leopard-skin sidekick at his feet. Even the *Apollo Belvedere*, whose cool gray tones we now admire as "classic Greek austerity," may have had

The Long March

❶ Diana the Huntress
❷ Artemis
❸ Bacchus
❹ 3-D Illusion on Ceiling

ETRUSCAN WING

ANCIENT WORLD

CANDELABRA ❶❸ ❷

TAPESTRIES ❹

MAPS

RAPHAEL ROOMS

AND

SISTINE CHAPEL

←——— APPROX. ¼ MILE ———→

DCH

a paisley pink cloak for all we know. Also, many statues had glass eyes like Bacchus.

And the fig leaves? Those came from the years 1550 to 1800, when the Church decided that certain parts of the human anatomy were obscene. (Why not the feet?) Perhaps Church leaders associated these full-frontal statues with the outbreak of Renaissance humanism that reduced their power in Europe. Whatever the cause, they reacted by covering classical crotches with plaster fig

leaves, the same leaves Adam and Eve had used when the concept of "privates" was invented.

Note: The leaves could be removed at any time if the museum officials were so motivated. There are suggestion boxes around the museum. Whenever I see a fig leaf, I get the urge to pick-it. We could start an organ-ized campaign...

• *Cover your eyes in case they forgot a fig leaf or two, and continue to the tapestries.*

Tapestries

Along the left wall are tapestries designed by Raphael's workshop and made in Brussels. They show scenes from the life of Christ: baby Jesus in the manger, being adored by shepherds, and presented in the temple. The Resurrection tapestry, with Jesus coming out of the tomb, is curiously interactive...as you walk, Jesus'

VATICAN MUSEUM

eyes, feet, knee, and even the stone square follow you across the room. Next to it, *The Supper at Emmaus* (with Jesus sitting at a table) seems equally flexible.

Check out the beautiful sculpted reliefs on the ceiling. Admire the workmanship of this relief, then realize that it's not a relief at all—it's painted on a flat surface! Illusions like this were proof that painters had mastered the 3-D realism of ancient statues.

Map Gallery and View of Vatican City

This gallery still feels like a pope's palace. The crusted ceiling of colorful stucco and paint is pure papal splendor. The 16th-century

maps on the walls show the regions of Italy. Popes could take visitors on a tour of Italy, from the toe (entrance end) to the Alps (far end), with east Italy on the right wall, west on the left. The scenes on the ceiling portray exciting moments in Church history in each of those regions.

The windows give you your best look at the tiny country of Vatican City, formed in 1929. It has its own radio station, as you see from the tower on the hill. What you see here is pretty much all there is—these gardens, the palaces you're in, and St. Peter's.

If you have the chance to lean out and look left, you'll see the dome of St. Peter's the way Michelangelo would have liked you to see it—without the bulky Baroque facade.

At the far end, maps show Italy's four ports of entry (including Venice). Also look for maps of Antique Italy (names in Latin, Roman political boundaries in gold) and New Italy.

• *Exit the map room, and take a breather in the next small tapestry hall before turning left into the crowded rooms that lead to the Raphael Rooms. From here, tired visitors can skip the Raphael Rooms and make a beeline to the Sistine Chapel by going straight ahead (unless this route is roped off). But our tour turns left into the Raphael Rooms.*

Renaissance Art

Raphael Rooms: Papal Wallpaper

We've seen art from the ancient world; now we'll see its rebirth in the Renaissance. We're entering the living quarters of the great Renaissance popes—where they slept, worked, and worshipped. The rooms reflect the grandeur of their position. They hired the best artists—mostly from Florence—to paint the walls and ceilings, combining classical and Christian motifs.

Entering, you'll immediately see a huge (non-Raphael) painting that depicts the Polish King Jan III Sobieski liberating Vienna from the Ottomans in 1683, finally tipping the tide in favor of a Christian Europe. See the Muslim tents on the left and the spires of Christian Vienna on the right.

The second room's paintings celebrate the doctrine of the Immaculate Conception, establishing that Mary herself was conceived free from original sin. This medieval idea wasn't actually made dogma until a century ago. The largest fresco shows how the inspiration came straight from heaven (upper left) in a thin ray of light directly to the pope.

• *Next, you'll pass along an outside walkway that overlooks a courtyard (is that the pope's Fiat?), finally ending up in the first of the Raphael Rooms, the...*

Constantine Room

The frescoes (which after Raphael's death were finished by his assistants, notably Giulio Romano) celebrate the passing of the baton from one culture to the next. Remember, Rome was a pagan empire persecuting a new cult from the East—Christianity.

Then, on the night of October 27, A.D. 312 (left wall), as General Constantine (in gold, with crown) was preparing his troops for a coup d'état, he looked up and saw something strange. A cross appeared in the sky with the words, "You will conquer in this sign."

The next day (long wall), his troops raged victoriously into battle with the Christian cross atop their Roman eagle banners. There's Constantine in the center with a smile on his face, slashing through the enemy, while God's warrior angels ride shotgun overhead.

Constantine even stripped (right wall) and knelt before the pope to be baptized a Christian (some say). As emperor, he legalized Christianity and worked hand in hand with the pope (window wall). When Rome fell, its glory lived on through the Dark Ages in the pomp, pageantry, and learning of the Catholic Church.

Look at the ceiling painting. A classical statue is knocked backward, crumbling before the overpowering force of the cross. Whoa! Christianity triumphs over pagan Rome. (This was painted, I believe, by Raphael's surrealist colleague, Salvadorus Dalio.)

• *While viewing these frescoes, ponder the life and times of...*

Raphael

Raphael was only 25 when Pope Julius II invited him to paint the walls of his personal living quarters. Julius was so impressed by Raphael's talent that he had the work of earlier masters scraped off and gave Raphael free rein to paint what he wanted.

Raphael lived a charmed life. He was handsome and sophisticated, and soon became Julius' favorite. He painted masterpieces effortlessly. In a different decade, he might have been thrown out of the Church as a great sinner, but his love affairs and devil-may-care personality seemed to epitomize the optimistic pagan spirit of the Renaissance. His works are graceful but never lightweight or frilly—they're strong, balanced, and harmonious in the best Renaissance tradition. When he died young in 1520, the High Renaissance died with him.

• *Continue on. In a room or two (depending on the current route), you'll reach a room with frescoes arching over the windows. Block the sunlight with your hand to see...*

The Liberation of St. Peter

Peter, Jesus' right-hand man, was thrown into prison in Jerusalem for his beliefs. In the middle of the night, an angel appeared and

rescued him from the sleeping guards (Acts 12). The chains miraculously fell away (and were later brought to the St. Peter-in-Chains Church in Rome), and the angel led him to safety (right), while the guards took hell from their captain (left). This little "play" is neatly divided into three separate acts that make a balanced composition.

Raphael makes the miraculous event even more dramatic with the use of four kinds of light illuminating the dark cell—half-moonlight, the captain's torch, the radiant angel, and the natural

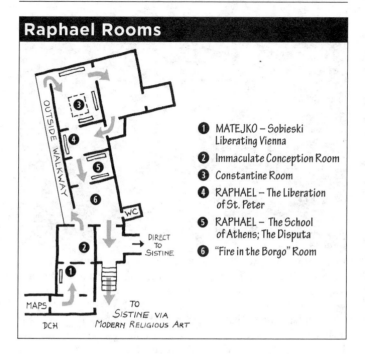

Raphael Rooms

OUTSIDE WALKWAY

1 MATEJKO – Sobieski Liberating Vienna

2 Immaculate Conception Room

3 Constantine Room

4 RAPHAEL – The Liberation of St. Peter

5 RAPHAEL – The School of Athens; The Disputa

6 "Fire in the Borgo" Room

WC

DIRECT TO SISTINE

MAPS

DCH

TO SISTINE VIA MODERN RELIGIOUS ART

---

light spilling through the museum's window. Raphael's mastery of realism, rich colors, and sense of drama made him understandably famous.

Find Pope Julius II (who also commissioned Michelangelo to do the Sistine ceiling) in the role of Peter in *The Liberation,* and as the bearded and kneeling pope in *The Mass of Bolsena* (opposite wall).

• *Enter the next room. Here in the pope's private study, Raphael painted...*

The School of Athens

In both style and subject matter, this fresco sums up the spirit of the Renaissance, which was not only the rebirth of classical art,

but a rebirth of learning, discovery, and the optimistic spirit that man is a rational creature. Raphael pays respect to the great thinkers and scientists of ancient Greece, gathering them together at one time in a mythical school setting.

In the center are Plato and Aristotle, the two greatest Greeks. Plato points up, indicating his philosophy that mathematics and pure ideas are the source of truth, while Aristotle points down, showing preference for hands-on study of the material world. There's their master, Socrates (midway to the left, in green), ticking off arguments on his fingers. And in the foreground at right, bald Euclid bends over a slate to demonstrate a geometrical formula.

Raphael shows that Renaissance thinkers were as good as the ancients. There's Leonardo da Vinci, whom Raphael worshipped, in the role of Plato. Euclid is the architect Donato Bramante, who designed St. Peter's. Raphael himself (next to last on the far right, with the black beret) looks out at us. And the "school" building is actually an early version of St. Peter's Basilica (under construction at the time).

Raphael balances everything symmetrically—thinkers to the left, scientists to the right, with Plato and Aristotle dead center— showing the geometrical order found in the world. Look at the square floor tiles in the foreground. If you laid a ruler over them and extended the line upward, it would run right to the center of the picture. Similarly, the tops of the columns all point down to the middle. All the lines of sight draw our attention to Plato and Aristotle, and to the small arch over their heads—a halo over these two secular saints in the divine pursuit of knowledge.

While Raphael was painting this room, Michelangelo was at work down the hall in the Sistine Chapel. Raphael had just finished *The School of Athens* when he got a look at Michelangelo's powerful figures and dramatic scenes. He was astonished. From this point on, Raphael began to beef up his delicate, graceful style to a more heroic level. He returned to *The School of Athens* and added one more figure to the scene—Michelangelo, the brooding, melancholy figure in front, leaning on a block of marble.

• *On the opposite wall is...*

The Disputa

As if to underline the new attitude that pre-Christian philosophy and Church thinking could coexist, Raphael painted *The Disputa*

facing *The School of Athens*. Christ and the saints in heaven are overseeing a discussion of the Eucharist (the communion wafer) by mortals below. The classical-looking character in blue and gold looks out as if to say, "The pagans had their *School of Athens*, but we Christians (pointing up) have the School of Heaven." These rooms were the papal library, so themes featuring learning, knowledge, and debate were appropriate.

In Catholic terms, the communion wafer miraculously becomes the body of Christ when it's consecrated by a priest, bringing a little bit of heaven into the material world. Raphael's painting also connects heaven and earth, with descending circles: Jesus in a halo, down to the dove of the Holy Spirit in a circle, which enters the communion wafer in its holder. Balance and symmetry reign, from the angel trios in the upper corners to the books littering the floor. Find Dante wearing his poet's laureate in the lower right. (Hint: He's the guy on your €2 coin, modeled after this detail of *The Disputa*.)

Moving along, the last Raphael Room (called the "Fire in the Borgo" Room) shows work done mostly by Raphael's students, who were influenced by the bulging muscles and bodybuilder poses of Michelangelo.

• *Pause here and plan. (WCs are nearby, but sometimes closed.) From here, there are two ways to get to the Sistine Chapel (Capella Sistina). Leaving this final Raphael Room, you'll soon see two arrows. One points to the left—the route that goes directly to the Sistine.*

Bearing right (a five-minute walk and a few staircases longer) leads to quiet rooms at the foot of the stairs, with benches where you can sit in peace and read ahead before entering the hectic Sistine Chapel. Also, you get to stroll through the impressive Modern Religious Art collection on the way (signs will direct you to the Sistine). Your call.

The Sistine Chapel

The Sistine Chapel contains Michelangelo's ceiling and his huge *The Last Judgment*. The Sistine is the personal chapel of the pope and the place where new popes are elected. (The small, old-fash-ioned stove that burns pope-vote ballots—which sends out puffs of telltale smoke—is placed near today's short-cut exit.)

When Pope Julius II asked Michelangelo to take on this important proj-ect, he said, "No, *grazie.*" Michelangelo insisted he was a sculptor, not a painter. The Sistine ceiling was a vast undertaking, and he didn't want to do a half-vast job. But the pope pleaded, bribed, and threatened until Michelangelo finally consented, on the condition that he be able to do it all his own way.

Julius had asked for only 12 apostles along the sides of the ceiling, but Michelangelo had a grander vision—the entire history of the world until Jesus. He spent the next four years (1508–1512) craning his neck on scaffolding six stories up, covering the ceiling with frescoes of biblical scenes.

In sheer physical terms, it's an astonishing achievement: 5,900 square feet, with the vast majority done by his own hand. (Raphael only designed most of his rooms, letting assistants do the grunt work.)

First, he had to design and erect the scaffolding. Any materi-als had to be hauled up on pulleys. Then, a section of ceiling would be plastered. With fresco—painting on wet plaster—if you don't get it right the first time, you have to scrape the whole thing off and start over. And if you've ever struggled with a ceiling light fixture or worked underneath a car for even five minutes, you know how heavy your arms get. The physical effort, the paint dripping in his eyes, the creative drain, and the mental stress from a pushy pope combined to almost kill Michelangelo.

But when the ceiling was finished and revealed to the public,

The Sistine Schematic

GENESIS SCENES + PROPHETS ANCESTORS = THE SISTINE CEILING

it simply blew 'em away. Like the *Laocoön* statue discovered six years earlier, it was unlike anything seen before. It both caps the Renaissance and turns it in a new direction. In perfect Renaissance spirit, it mixes Old Testament prophets with classical figures. But the style is more dramatic, shocking, and emotional than the balanced Renaissance works before it. This is a very personal work—the Gospel according to Michelangelo—but its themes and subject matter are universal. Many art scholars contend that the Sistine ceiling is the single greatest work of art by any one human being.

The Sistine Ceiling: Understanding What You're Standing Under

The ceiling shows the history of the world before the birth of Jesus. We see God creating the world, creating man and woman, destroying the earth by flood, and so on. God himself, in his purple robe, actually appears in the first five scenes. Along the sides (where the ceiling starts to curve), we see the Old Testament prophets and pagan Greek prophetesses who foretold the coming of Christ. Dividing these scenes and figures are fake niches (a painted 3-D illusion) decorated with nude statue-like figures with symbolic meaning.

The key is to see three simple divisions in the tangle of bodies:
1. The central spine of nine rectangular biblical scenes;
2. The line of prophets on either side; and
3. The triangles between the prophets showing the ancestors of Christ.

• *Ready? Within the chapel, grab a seat along the side (if there's room). Face the altar with the big* The Last Judgment *on the wall (more on that later). Now look up to the ceiling and find the central panel of...*

The Creation of Adam

God and man take center stage in this Renaissance version of creation. Adam, newly formed in the image of God, lounges dreamily

The Sistine Ceiling

WALL

DAVID & GOLIATH

ZACHARIAH

JUDITH & HOLOFERNES

EXIT DOOR
TO ST. PETER'S - SOMETIMES OPEN

JOEL | DRUNKENNESS OF NOAH | DELPHICA

ZORO-BABEL

THE FLOOD

JOSIAH

ERYTH-RAEA | SACRIFICE OF NOAH | ISAIAH

EXIT DOOR
TO LONG MARCH BACK TO PINACOTECA & ENTRY LOBBY - A 10·15 MINUTE WALK

OZIAS

TEMPTATION AND EXPULSION

EZEKIAS

EZEKIEL | CREATION OF EVE | CUMAEA

ROBOAM

CREATION OF ADAM

ASA

PERSICA | SEPARATION OF LAND FROM WATER | DANIEL

W A L L

SOLOMON

CREATION OF SUN, MOON & PLANETS

JESSE

SEE PHOTO ON FACING PAGE

JEREMIAH | SEPARATION OF LIGHT FROM DARKNESS | LIBICA

DEATH OF HAMAN

JONAH AND WHALE

MOSES & BRASS SERP.

LAST JUDGMENT WALL

ENTRY DOOR
FROM RAPHAEL ROOMS & MODERN RELIGIOUS ART...

DCH

☆ TO USE THIS DIAGRAM:
FACE THE LAST JUDGMENT &
HOLD THE BOOK UP TO THE CEILING.

VATICAN MUSEUM

in perfect naked innocence. God, with his entourage, swoops in with a swirl of activity (which—with a little imagination—looks like a cross-section of a human brain...quite a strong humanist statement). Their reaching hands are the center of this

work. Adam's is limp and passive; God's is strong and forceful, his finger twitching upward with energy. Here is the very moment of creation, as God passes the spark of life to man, the crowning work of his creation.

This is the spirit of the Renaissance. God is not a terrifying giant reaching down to puny and helpless man from way on high. Here they are on an equal plane, divided only by the diagonal patch of sky. God's billowing robe and the patch of green upon which Adam is lying balance each other. They are like two pieces of a jigsaw puzzle, or two long-separated continents, or like the yin and yang symbols finally coming together—uniting, complementing each other, creating wholeness. God and man work together in the divine process of creation.

• *This celebration of man permeates the ceiling. Notice the Adonises-come-to-life on the pedestals that divide the central panels. And then came woman.*

The Garden of Eden: Temptation and Expulsion

In one panel, we see two scenes from the Garden of Eden. On the left is the leafy garden of paradise where Adam and Eve lie around blissfully. But the devil comes along—a serpent with a woman's

torso—and winds around the forbidden Tree of Knowledge. The temptation to gain new knowledge is too great for these Renaissance people. They eat the forbidden fruit.

At right, the sword-wielding angel drives them from Paradise into the barren plains. They're grieving, but they're far from helpless. Adam's body is thick and sturdy, and we know they'll survive in the cruel world. Adam firmly gestures to the angel, like he's saying, "All right, already! We're going!"

The Nine Scenes from Genesis

Take some time with these central scenes to understand the story that the ceiling tells. They run in sequence, starting at the front:

1. God, in purple, divides the light from darkness.
2. God creates the sun (burning orange) and the moon (pale white, to the right). Oops, I guess there's another moon.
3. God bursts toward us to separate the land and water.
4. *The Creation of Adam.*
5. God creates Eve, who dives into existence out of Adam's side.
6. *The Garden of Eden: Temptation and Expulsion.*
7. Noah kills a ram and stokes the altar fires to make a sacrifice to God.
8. The great flood, sent by God, destroys the wicked, who desperately head for higher ground. In the distance, the Ark carries Noah's family to safety. (The blank spot dates to 1793, when a nearby gunpowder depot exploded, shaking the building.)
9. Noah's sons see their drunken father. (Perhaps Michelangelo chose to end it with this scene as a reminder that even the best of men are fallible.)

Prophets

You'll notice that the figures at the far end of the chapel are a bit smaller than those over *The Last Judgment.*

Michelangelo started at the far end, with the Noah scenes. By 1510, he'd finished the first half of the ceiling. When they took the scaffolding down and could finally see what he'd been working on for two years, everyone was awestruck—except Michelangelo. As powerful as his figures are, from the floor they didn't look dramatic enough for Michelangelo. For the other half, he pulled out all the stops.

Compare the Noah scenes (far end) with their many small figures to the huge images of God at the other end. Similarly, Isaiah (near the lattice screen, marked "Esaias") is stately and balanced,

while Jeremiah ("Hieremias," in the corner by *The Last Judgment*) is a dark, brooding figure. This prophet who witnessed the destruction of Israel slumps his chin in his hand and ponders the fate of his people. Like the difference between the stately *Apollo Belvedere* and the excited *Laocoön*, Michelangelo added a new emotional dimension to Renaissance painting.

The Last Judgment

When Michelangelo returned to paint the altar wall 23 years later (1535), the mood of Europe—and of Michelangelo—was completely different. The Protestant Reformation had forced the Catholic Church to clamp down on free thought, and religious wars raged. Rome had recently been pillaged by roving bands of mercenaries. The Renaissance spirit of optimism was fading. Michelangelo himself had begun to question the innate goodness of mankind.

It's Judgment Day, and Christ—the powerful figure in the center, raising his arm to spank the wicked—has come to find out who's naughty and who's nice. Beneath him,

The Last Judgment

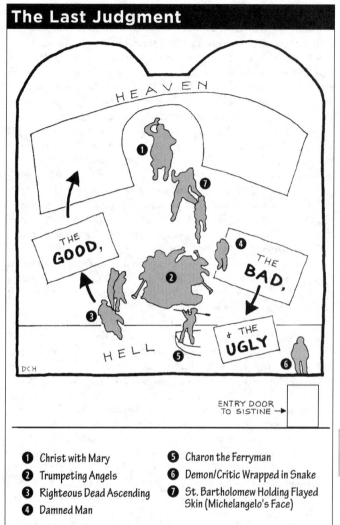

❶ Christ with Mary
❷ Trumpeting Angels
❸ Righteous Dead Ascending
❹ Damned Man
❺ Charon the Ferryman
❻ Demon/Critic Wrapped in Snake
❼ St. Bartholomew Holding Flayed Skin (Michelangelo's Face)

a band of angels blows its trumpets Dizzy Gillespie–style, giving a wake-up call to the sleeping dead. The dead at lower left leave their graves and prepare to be judged. The righteous, on Christ's right hand (the left side of the picture), are carried up to the glories of heaven. The wicked on the other side are hurled down to hell, where demons wait to torture them. Charon, from the underworld of Greek mythology, waits below to ferry the souls of the damned to hell.

It's a grim picture. No one, but no one, is smiling. Even many of the righteous being resurrected (lower left) are either skeletons or cadavers with ghastly skin. The angels have to play tug-of-war with subterranean monsters to drag them from their graves.

Over in hell, the wicked are tortured by gleeful demons. One of the damned (to the right of the trumpeting angels) has an utterly lost expression, as if saying, "Why did I cheat on my wife?!" Two demons grab him around the ankles to pull him down to the bowels of hell, condemned to an eternity of constipation.

But it's the terrifying figure of Christ that dominates this scene. He raises his arm to smite the wicked, sending a ripple of fear through everyone. Even the saints around him—even Mary beneath his arm (whose interceding days are clearly over)—shrink back in terror at loving Jesus' uncharacteristic outburst. His expression is completely closed, and he turns his head, refusing to even listen to the whining alibis of the damned. Look at Christ's bicep. If this muscular figure looks familiar to you, it's because you've seen it before—the Belvedere Torso.

When *The Last Judgment* was unveiled to the public in 1541, it caused a sensation. The pope is said to have dropped to his knees and cried, "Lord, charge me not with my sins when thou shalt come on the Day of Judgment."

And it changed the course of art. The complex composition, with more than 300 figures swirling around the figure of Christ, was far beyond traditional Renaissance balance. The twisted figures shown from every imaginable angle challenged other painters to try and top this master of 3-D illusion. And the sheer terror and drama of the scene was a striking contrast to the placid optimism of, say, Raphael's *School of Athens*. Michelangelo had Baroque-en all the rules of the Renaissance, signaling a new era of art.

With the Renaissance fading, the fleshy figures in *The Last Judgment* aroused murmurs of discontent from Church authorities. Michelangelo rebelled by painting his chief critic into the scene—in hell. He's the jackassed demon in the bottom right corner, wrapped in a snake. Look at how Michelangelo covered his privates. Sweet revenge.

(After Michelangelo's death, prudish Church authorities painted the wisps of clothing that we see today.)

Now move up close. Study the details of the lower part of the painting from right to left. Charon, with Dr. Spock ears and a Dalí moustache, paddles the damned in a boat full of human turbulence. Look more closely at the J-Day band. Are they reading music, or is it the Judgment Day tally? Before the cleaning, these details were lost in murk.

The Last Judgment marks the end of Renaissance optimism epitomized in *The Creation of Adam*, with its innocence and exaltation of man. There, he was the wakening man-child of a fatherly

The Cleaning Project

The ceiling and *The Last Judgment* have been cleaned, removing centuries of preservatives, dirt, and soot from candles, oil lamps, and the annual Papal Barbecue (just kidding). The bright, bright colors that emerged are a bit shocking, forcing many art experts to reevaluate Michelangelo's style. Notice the very dark patches left in the corner above *The Last Judgment,* and imagine how dreary and dark it was before the cleaning.

God. Here, man cowers in fear and unworthiness before a terrifying, wrathful deity.

Michelangelo himself must have wondered how he would be judged—had he used his God-given talents wisely? Look at St. Bartholomew, the bald, bearded guy at Christ's left foot (our right). In the flayed skin he's holding is a barely recognizable face—the twisted self-portrait of a self-questioning Michelangelo.

• *There are two exits from the Sistine Chapel. To return to the main entrance/exit, leave the Sistine through the side door next to the screen. You'll soon find yourself facing The Long March back to the museum's entrance (about 15 minutes away) and the Pinacoteca.*

Or, if you're planning to take the shortcut directly to St. Peter's Basilica (see "Museum Strategies," page 206), exit out the far-right corner of the Sistine Chapel (with your back to the altar). This route saves you a 30-minute walk and the wait in the St. Peter's security line, but you can't get back to the main entrance/exit or the Pinacoteca. Though this corner door is likely labeled "Exit for private tour groups only," you can usually just slide through with the crowds (or protest that your group has left you behind). If for some reason this exit is closed, hang out in the Sistine Chapel for a few more minutes—it'll likely reopen shortly.

The Long March Back

Along this corridor (located one floor below the long corridor that you walked to get here), you'll see some of the wealth amassed by the popes, mostly gifts from royalty. Find your hometown on the 1529 map of the world—look in the land labeled "Terra Incognita." The elaborately decorated library that branches off to the right contains rare manuscripts.

• *The corridor eventually spills out back outside. Follow signs to the...*

Pinacoteca

Like Lou Gehrig batting behind Babe Ruth, the Pinacoteca (Painting Gallery) has to follow the mighty Sistine & Co. But after the Vatican's artistic feast, this little collection of paintings is a delicious 15-minute after-dinner mint.

See this gallery of paintings as you'd view a time-lapse blossoming of a flower, walking through the evolution of painting from medieval to Baroque with just a few stops.

• *Enter, passing a model of Michelangelo's* Pietà *(offering a handy close-up look), and stroll up to Room IV.*

Melozzo da Forli—*Musician Angels*

Salvaged from a condemned church, this playful series of frescoes shows the delicate grace and nobility of Italy during the time known fondly as the Quattrocento (1400s). Notice the detail in the serene faces; the soothing primary colors; the bright and even light; and the classical purity given these religious figures. Rock on.

• *Walk on to the end room (Room VIII), where precious Raphael-designed tapestries that once hung in the Sistine Chapel now surround the highlight of this collection. They've turned on the dark to let Raphael's* Transfiguration *shine. Take a seat.*

Raphael—*The Transfiguration*

Christ floats above a stumpy mountaintop, visited in a vision by the prophets Moses and Elijah. Peter, James, and John, who wanted visual proof that Jesus was Lord, cower in awe under their savior, "transfigured before them, his face shining as the sun, his raiment white as light" (as described by the evangelist Matthew—who can be seen taking notes in the painting's lower left).

Raphael composes the scene in three descending tiers: Christ, the holiest, is on top, then Peter-James-John, and finally, the nine remaining apostles surround a boy possessed by demons. They direct him and his mother to Jesus for healing.

Pinacoteca

❶ DA FORLI – Musician Angels
❷ RAPHAEL – The Transfiguration
❸ LEONARDO DA VINCI – St. Jerome
❹ CARAVAGGIO – Deposition
❺ View of the Dome

PIETÀ MODEL

TO CAFETERIA ←

→ TO EXIT

COURTYARD

DCH

Raphael died in 1520, leaving this final work to be finished by his pupils. The last thing Raphael painted was the beatific face of Jesus, perhaps the most beautiful Christ in existence. When Raphael was buried (in the Pantheon, at age 37), this work accompanied the funeral.

• *Heading back down the parallel corridor, stop in Room IX at the brown unfinished work by Leonardo.*

Leonardo da Vinci—*St. Jerome* (c. 1482)

Jerome squats in the rocky desert. He's spent too much time alone, fasting and meditating on his sins. His soulful face is echoed by his friend, the roaring lion.

This unfinished work gives us a glimpse behind the scenes at

Leonardo's technique. Even in the brown undercoating, we see the psychological power of Leonardo's genius. Jerome's emaciated body on the rocks expresses his intense penitence, while his pleading eyes hold a glimmer of hope for divine forgiveness. Leonardo wrote that a good painter must paint two things: "man and the movements of his spirit." (The patchwork effect is due to Jerome's head having been cut out and used as the seat of a stool in a shoemaker's shop.)

• *Roll on through the sappy sweetness of the Mannerist rooms into the gritty realism of Caravaggio (Room XII).*

Caravaggio—*Deposition* (1604)

Christ is being buried. In the dark tomb, the faces of his followers emerge, lit by a harsh light. Christ's body has a deathlike color. We

see Christ's dirty toes and Nicodemus' wrinkled, sunburned face.

Caravaggio was the first painter to intentionally shock his viewers. By exaggerating the contrast between light and dark, shining a brutal third-degree-interrogation light on his subjects, and using everyday models in sacred scenes, he takes a huge leap away from the Raphael-pretty past and into the "expressive realism" of the modern world.

A tangle of grief looms out of the darkness as Christ's heavy, dead body nearly pulls the whole group with him from the cross into the tomb. After this museum, I know how he feels.

• *Walk through the rest of the gallery's canvas history of art, enjoy one last view of the Vatican grounds and Michelangelo's dome, then follow the grand spiral staircase down. Go in peace.*

VATICAN MUSEUM

ST. PETER'S BASILICA TOUR

Basilica San Pietro

St. Peter's is the greatest church in Christendom. It represents the power and splendor of Rome's 2,000-year domination of the Western world. Built on the memory and grave of the first pope, St. Peter, this is where the grandeur of ancient Rome became the grandeur of Christianity.

Orientation

Cost: Free entry to basilica and Crypt. Dome climb—€5 to climb stairs all the way up, or €7 to take an elevator partway up to the roof, then climb 323 steps to the top of the dome (for details, see "Dome Climb," later). Museum-Treasury—€6.

Dress Code: No shorts or bare shoulders (applies to men, women, and children), and no miniskirts. This dress code is strictly enforced.

Hours of Church: Daily April–Sept 7:00–19:00, Oct–March 7:00–18:00. The church closes on Wednesday mornings during papal audiences. The best time to visit the church is early or late; at 17:00, when the church is fairly empty, sunbeams can work their magic, and the late-afternoon Mass fills the place with spiritual music.

Mass is held daily—Mon–Sat at 8:30, 9:00, 10:00, 11:00, 12:00, and 17:00; Sun and holidays at 9:00, 10:30 (in Latin), 11:30, 12:15, 13:00, 16:00, and 17:45. Confirm the schedule (on-site or at www.saintpetersbasilica.org) and location; it's generally in the south (left) transept.

The **Museum-Treasury** is open daily (April–Sept 9:00–18:15, Oct–March 9:00–17:15), and the **Crypt** closes one hour earlier than the church does. Both are described later in this chapter.

Vatican City

This tiny independent country of little more than 100 acres, contained entirely within Rome, has its own postal system, armed guards, helipad, mini-train station, and radio station (KPOP). Politically powerful, the Vatican is the religious capital of 1.1 billion Roman Catholics. If you're not a Catholic, become one for your visit.

The pope is both the religious and secular leader of Vatican City. For centuries, locals referred to him as "King Pope." Italy and the Vatican didn't always have good relations. In fact, after unification (in 1870), when Rome's modern grid plan was built around the miniscule Vatican, it seemed as if the new buildings were designed to be just high enough so no one could see the dome of St. Peter's from street level. Modern Italy was created in 1870, but the Holy See didn't recognize it as a country until 1929, when the pope and Mussolini signed the Lateran Pact, giving sovereignty to the Vatican and a few nearby churches.

Like every European country, Vatican City has its own versions of the euro coin (with a portrait of Pope Benedict XVI, and before him, of Pope John Paul II). You're unlikely to find one in your pocket, though, as they are snatched up by collectors before falling into actual circulation.

Small as it is, Vatican City has two huge sights: St. Peter's Basilica (with Michelangelo's *Pietà*) and the Vatican Museum (with the Sistine Chapel). The Vatican post office, with offices on St. Peter's Square (next to TI) and in the Vatican Museum, is famous for its stamps (Mon–Sat 8:30–18:30, closed Sun). Vatican stamps are good throughout Rome, but to use the Vatican's mail service, you need to mail your cards from the Vatican; write your postcards ahead of time. (Note that the Vatican won't mail cards with Italian stamps.)

Seeing the Pope: Your best chances for a sighting are on Sunday and Wednesday. The pope usually gives a blessing at noon on Sunday from his apartment on St. Peter's Square (except in July and August, when he speaks at his summer residence at Castel Gandolfo, 25 miles from Rome, reachable by train from Rome's Termini Station). St. Peter's is easiest (just show up) and, for most, enough of a "visit." Those interested in a more formal appearance (though not more intimate) can get a ticket for the Wednesday general audience (at 10:30) when the pope, arriving in his bulletproof Popemobile, greets and blesses the crowds at St. Peter's from a balcony or canopied platform on the square (except in winter, when he speaks at 10:30 in the 7,000-seat Paolo VI Auditorium, next to St. Peter's Basilica). If you only want to see St. Peter's—but not the pope—avoid these times (the basilica closes during papal audiences and crowds are substantial).

For the Wednesday audience, while anyone can observe from a distance, you need a (free) ticket to actually get close to the papal action (and get a seat). To find out the pope's schedule, call 06-6982-3114.

Vatican City Overview

CIPRO
TO
TERMINI
OTTAVIANO
VIA CANDIA
VIALE GIULIO CESARE
VIA LEONE IV
VIALE VATICANO ENTER
VIA OTTAVIANO
VATICAN → MUSEUM
PIAZZA
RISORGIMENTO
SISTINE CHAPEL →
PAPAL APT.
TO
CASTEL
SANT'ANGELO
+ BUS #40 →
EXIT
VIA CONCILIAZIONE
ST. PETER'S →
ST. PETER'S
SQUARE
+ OBELISK
VATICAN
BOUNDARY
BUS
#64
NOT TO VATICAN MUSEUM ENTRY
SCALE: TO OBELISK IS A 15-
MINUTE WALK
T TAXI STAND
M METRO STATION
B BUS STOP
INFO, WC + POST
* POPE VIEWING TICKET PICK-UP
DCH

Santa Susanna Church lets you order tickets online (free, with no booking charge). Pick up your reserved tickets, or check for last-minute availability, at the church the Tuesday before the audience between 17:00 and 18:30, and consider staying for the 18:00 English Mass (Via XX Settembre 15, near recommended Via Firenze hotels, Metro: Repubblica, tel. 06-4201-4554—charming Rosanna speaks English, get all the details at www.santa susanna.org).

Probably less convenient—because of the long line—is getting a ticket at St. Peter's Square from the Vatican guard at their station at the bronze doors (open Tue 12:00–19:30; last-minute tickets may be available Wed morning—just join the line). It's under the "elbow" of Bernini's colonnade, on the right side of the square as you face the basilica (#6 on the map on page 244).

While many visitors come hoping for a more intimate audience, private audiences ended with the death of Pope John Paul II. Pope Benedict doesn't do them.

Dome Climb (Cupola): Daily April–Sept 8:00–18:00, Oct–March 8:00–17:00. Allow one hour for the round-trip to the top of the dome (or a half-hour to the roof). You can take the elevator or stairs to the roof (231 steps up), then climb another 323 steps to the top of the dome. The entry to the elevator is just outside the basilica on the north side of St. Peter's (near the secret exit from the Sistine Chapel—described on page 206). Look for signs to the cupola. For more on the dome, see the end of this chapter.

Getting There: Take the Metro to Ottaviano, then walk 10 minutes south on Via Ottaviano. There are two good bus options: The #40 express bus drops off at Piazza Pio, next to Castel Sant'Angelo—a 10-minute walk to St. Peter's. The more crowded bus #64 is convenient for pickpockets and stops just outside St. Peter's Square to the south (after crossing the Tiber, take the first stop past the tunnel; backtrack toward the tunnel and turn left when you see the rows of columns). A taxi from Termini train station to St. Peter's costs about €10.

Avoiding the Line: To bypass the long security-checkpoint line, visit the Vatican Museum first (though it has its own long lines and checkpoint), then take the shortcut from the Sistine Chapel directly to St. Peter's. (Note, though, that this shortcut isn't always open; you may need to wait a bit.) If you visit the museum first, remember that St. Peter's dress code is stricter than the Vatican Museum's.

Information: The TI on the left (south) side of the square is excellent (Mon–Sat 8:30–18:30, closed Sun, free Vatican and church map, tel. 06-6988-1662, www.saintpetersbasilica.org—has detailed map).

Services: WCs are to the right and left on St. Peter's Square, near baggage storage past the security checkpoint, and on the roof. **Drinking fountains** are at the obelisk and near WCs. The **post office** is next to the TI (you can buy stamps and postcards and drop them into a postbox home).

Tours: The Vatican TI conducts free 1.5-hour tours of **St. Peter's** (depart Mon–Fri from TI, generally at 9:45 and 14:15, confirm schedule at TI, tel. 06-6988-1662). Audioguides can be rented near the checkroom (€5 plus ID, daily 9:00–17:00). You can download a free audio tour at www.ricksteves.com (or search for "Rick Steves Audio Tours" in iTunes).

If you want to see the **Vatican Gardens,** you must book a tour online at least a week in advance at http://biglietteria musei.vatican.va. No response means they're booked up (€31, 2 hours, usually daily except Wed and Sat, includes entry to Vatican Museum; tours start at 9:30 or 10:00 at Vatican Museum tour desk).

To see St. Peter's original grave, you can take a **Scavi "Excavations"** tour into the Necropolis (€12, 1.5 hours, ages 15 and older only, no photos). Book at least a month in advance by email (scavi@fsp.va) or fax (06-6987-3017), following the detailed instructions at www.vatican.va; no response means they're booked up.

Length of This Tour: Allow one hour, plus another hour if you climb the dome.

Checkroom: The free bag check (mandatory for bags larger than a purse or daypack) is outside the basilica (to the right as you face the entrance), and just inside the security checkpoint.

Starring: Michelangelo, Bernini, St. Peter, a heavenly host...and, occasionally, the pope.

The Tour Begins

• *Find a shady spot where you like the view under the columns around St. Peter's oval-shaped "square." If the pigeons left a clean spot, sit on it.*

Background

Nearly 2,000 years ago, this area was the site of Nero's Circus—a huge cigar-shaped Roman chariot racecourse. The tall obelisk you see in the middle of the square once stood about 100 yards from its current location, in the center of the circus course (to the left of where St. Peter's is today). The Romans had no marching bands, so for halftime entertainment they killed Christians. This persecuted minority was forced to fight wild animals and gladiators, or they were simply crucified. Some were tarred up, tied to posts, and burned—human torches to light up the evening races.

One of those killed here, in about A.D. 65, was Peter, Jesus' right-hand man, who had come to Rome to spread the message of love. At his own request, Peter was crucified upside-down, because he felt unworthy to die as his master had. His remains were buried in a nearby cemetery located where the main altar in St. Peter's is today. For 250 years, these relics were quietly and secretly revered.

Peter had been recognized as the first "pope," or bishop of Rome, from whom all later popes claimed their authority as head of the Church. When Christianity was finally legalized in 313, the Christian emperor Constantine built a church on the site of Peter's martyrdom. "Old St. Peter's" lasted 1,200 years (A.D. 329–1500).

By the time of the Renaissance, Old St. Peter's was falling apart and was considered unfit to be the center of the Western Church. The new, larger church we see today was begun in 1506 by the architect Bramante. He was succeeded by Michelangelo and a number of other architects, each with his own designs. Carlo Maderno took Michelangelo's Greek cross–shaped church

ST. PETER'S BASILICA

and lengthened it, adding a long nave. As the construction proceeded, they actually built the new church around the old one (see diagram on opposite page). The project was finally finished 120 years later, and Old St. Peter's was dismantled and carried out of the new church. (A few bits survive from the first church: the central door, some columns in the atrium, eight spiral columns around the tomb from the Jerusalem Temple, the venerated statue of Peter, and Michelangelo's *Pietà*.)

Michelangelo designed the magnificent dome. Unfortunately,

although it soars above St. Peter's, it's barely visible from the center of the square due to Maderno's extended nave. To see the entire dome, you'll need to step outside the open end of the square, where in the 1930s Benito Mussolini opened up the broad boulevard, finally letting people see the dome that had been hidden for centuries by the facade. Though I don't make a habit of thanking fascist dictators, in this case I'll make an exception: *"Grazie, Benito."*

• *More on the church later—for now, let's talk about the square. Ideally, you should head out to the obelisk to view the square and read this. But let me guess—it's 95 degrees outside, right? OK, read on in the shade of these stone sequoias.*

St. Peter's Square

St. Peter's Square, with its ring of columns, symbolizes the arms of the church welcoming everyone—believers and non-believers—with its motherly embrace. It was designed a century after Michelangelo by the Baroque architect Gian Lorenzo Bernini, who did much of the work that we'll see inside. Numbers first: 284 columns, 56 feet high, in stern Doric style. Topping them are Bernini's 140 favorite saints, each 10 feet tall. The "square" itself is actually elliptical, 660 by 500 feet. Though large, it's designed like a saucer, a little higher around the edges, so that even when full of crowds (as it often is), it allows those on the periphery to see above the throngs.

The obelisk in the center is 90 feet of solid granite weighing more than 300 tons. Think for a second about how much history this monument has seen. Originally erected in Egypt more than 2,000 years ago, it witnessed the fall of the pharaohs to the Greeks and then to the Romans. Then the emperor Caligula moved it to imperial Rome, where it stood impassively watching

Old & New St. Peter's

ROMAN CIRCUS COURSE
(1ST C. A.D.)

OLD ST. PETER'S
(A.D. 329-1500)

NEW ST. PETER'S
BRAMANTE & MICHELANGELO
(1506-1590)

MADERNO'S EXTENSION
(1607-1614)

BERNINI'S COLONNADE
(1656-1667)

❶ Current Site of Obelisk
❷ Original Site of Obelisk
❸ Peter's Crucifixion Site
❹ Peter's Tomb (Under Altar)

100 YARDS

100 METERS

the slaughter of Christians at the racecourse and the torture of Protestants by the Inquisition (in the yellow-and-rust building just outside the square, to the left of the church). Today, it watches over the church, a reminder that each civilization builds on the previous ones. The puny cross on top reminds us that Christian culture has cast but a thin veneer over our pagan origins.

• *Now venture out across the burning desert to the obelisk, which provides a narrow sliver of shade.*

St. Peter's Square

ST. PETER'S
BASILICA

1. Obelisk

2. Papal Apartments
   (Top Story, Right)

3. Sistine Chapel
   (in Vatican Museum)

4. "Centro del Colonnato"
   Plaque

5. Swiss Guard at Vatican
   City Entrance

6. Papal Ticket Pick-up
   at Bronze Doors

7. Tourist Info, Vatican Post
   Office, Bookstore & WC

8. Baggage Checkroom,
   Audioguides & WC

9. Exit from Sistine Chapel

10. Elevator to Dome &
    Crypt Entrance

11. To Ottaviano Metro (10 min),
    Cipro Metro (20 min) &
    Vatican Museum (15 min)

ST. PETER'S BASILICA

As you face the church, the gray building to the right at two o'clock, rising up behind Bernini's colonnade, is where the pope lives. The last window on the right of the top floor is his bedroom. To the left of that window is his study window, where he appears occasionally to greet the masses. If you come to the square at night as a Poping Tom, you might see the light on—the pope burns much midnight oil.

On more formal occasions (which you may have seen on TV), the pope appears from the church itself, on the small balcony above the central door.

The Sistine Chapel is just to the right of the facade—the small gray-brown building with the triangular roof, topped by an antenna. The tiny chimney (the pimple along the roofline midway up the left side) is where the famous smoke signals announce the election of each new pope. If the smoke is black, a two-thirds majority hasn't been reached. White smoke means a new pope has been selected.

Walk to the right, five pavement plaques from the obelisk, to one marked *Centro del Colonnato*. From here, all of Bernini's columns on the right side line up. The curved Baroque square still pays its respects to Renaissance mathematical symmetry.

• *Climb the gradually sloping pavement past crowd barriers, the security checkpoint, and the huge statues of St. Paul (with his two-edged sword) and St. Peter (with his bushy hair and keys). Along the way, you'll pass by the dress-code enforcers and a gaggle of ticked-off guys in shorts.*

On the square are two entrances to Vatican City: one to the left of the facade, and one to the right in the crook of Bernini's "arm" (the same entrance that hands out pope-viewing tickets). Guarding this small but powerful country's border crossing are the mercenary guards from Switzerland. You have to wonder if they really know how to use those pikes. Their colorful uniforms are said to have been designed by Michelangelo, though he was not known for his sense of humor.

• *Enter the atrium (entrance hall) of the church.*

The Basilica

The Atrium

The atrium is itself bigger than most churches. The huge white columns on the portico date from the first church (fourth century). Five famous bronze doors lead into the church.

Made from the melted-down bronze of the original door of Old St. Peter's, the central door was the first Renaissance work in Rome (c. 1450). It's only opened on special occasions. The panels (from the top down) feature Jesus and Mary, Paul and Peter, and (at the bottom) how each was martyred: Paul decapitated, Peter crucified upside-down.

The far-right entrance is the **Holy Door,** opened only during Holy Years. On Christmas

Eve every 25 years, the pope knocks three times with a silver hammer and the door opens, welcoming pilgrims to pass through. After Pope John Paul II opened the door on Christmas Eve, 1999, he bricked it up again with a ceremonial trowel a year later to wait another 24 years. (A plaque above the door fudges a bit for effect: it says that Pope "IOANNES PAULUS II" opened the door in the year "MM"—2000—and closed it in "MMI.") On the door itself, note crucified Jesus' shiny knees, polished by pious pilgrims who touch them for a blessing.

• *Now for one of Europe's great "wow" experiences. Enter the church. Gape for a while. But don't gape at Michelangelo's famous* Pietà *(on the right). That's this tour's finale. I'll wait for you at the round maroon pavement stone on the floor near the central doorway.*

The Church

This church is appropriately huge. Size before beauty: The golden window at the far end is two football fields away. The dove in

the window has the wingspan of a 747 (OK, maybe not quite, but it *is* big). The church covers six acres. The babies at the base of the pillars along the main hall (the nave) are adult-size. The lettering in the gold band along the top of the pillars is seven feet high. Really. The church has a capacity of 60,000 standing worshippers (or 1,200 tour groups).

The church is huge and it feels huge, but everything is designed to make it seem smaller and more intimate than it really is. For example, the statue of St. Teresa near the bottom of the first pillar on the right is 15 feet tall. The statue above her near the top looks the same size, but is actually six feet taller, giving the impression that it's not so far away. Similarly, the fancy bronze canopy over the altar at the far end is as tall as a seven-story building. That makes the great height of the dome seem smaller.

Looking down the nave, we get a sense of the splendor of ancient Rome that was carried on by the Catholic Church. The floor plan is based on the ancient Roman basilica, or law-court building, with a central aisle (nave) flanked by two side aisles. In fact, many of the stones used

St. Peter's Basilica

1. Holy Door
2. Charlemagne's Coronation Site
3. Extent of Original "Greek Cross" Plan
4. St. Andrew Statue & View of Dome
5. St. Peter Statue (with Kissable Toe)
6. Pope John XXIII
7. Main Altar (over Peter's Tomb)
8. BERNINI – Dove Window & "Throne of Peter"
9. St. Peter's Crucifixion Site
10. RAPHAEL – The Transfiguration (Mosaic Copy)
11. MICHELANGELO – Pietà
12. Dome & Crypt Entrances
13. Museum-Treasury
14. Blessed Sacrament Chapel

From Pope to Pope

On March 30, 2005, 84-year-old Pope John Paul II appeared at his apartment window overlooking St. Peter's Square, and—

JOAN. PAULUS II

frail and unable to speak—he silently blessed the crowd. It was his final public appearance. He died three days later.

For four days, John Paul II's body lay in state in front of St. Peter's main altar. Outside, hundreds of thousands of pilgrims lined up all the way down Via della Conciliazione, waiting up to 24 hours for one last look at their pope. Some five million people converged on Vatican City during the week.

On the day of the funeral, some 300,000 mourners, dignitaries, and security personnel gathered in windblown St. Peter's Square. As John Paul II's coffin was carried out—decorated with an "M" for Mary—the crowd broke into applause, and many shouted *"Santo subito!"* insisting he be made a saint *(santo)* right now *(subito)*. During the eulogy, Cardinal Josef Ratzinger pointed to the pope's apartment window and told the crowd, "We can be sure that our beloved pope is standing today at the window of the Father's house."

John Paul II was buried in St. Peter's Basilica in the Crypt,

to build St. Peter's were scavenged from the ruined law courts of ancient Rome.

On the floor near the central doorway is a round slab of porphyry stone in the maroon color of ancient Roman officials. This is the spot where, on Christmas night in A.D. 800, the French king Charlemagne was crowned Holy Roman Emperor. Even in the Dark Ages, when Rome was virtually abandoned and visitors reported that the city had more thieves and wolves than decent people, its imperial legacy made it a fitting place to symbolically establish a briefly united Europe.

St. Peter's was very expensive to build and decorate. The popes financed it by selling "indulgences," allowing the rich to buy forgiveness for their sins from the Church. This kind of corruption inspired an obscure German monk named Martin Luther to rebel and start the Protestant Reformation.

The ornate, Baroque-style interior decoration—a riot of marble, gold, stucco, mosaics, columns of stone, and pillars of light—was part of the Church's "Counter-" Reformation. Baroque served as cheery propaganda, impressing followers with the authority of near the tomb of St. Peter and next to the shrine of another popular 20th-century pope, John XXIII. The tomb has no monument—just a simple stone slab with the inscription: Joannes Paulus II (1920-2005).

Then came nine days of mourning—punctuated by a Mass each day in St. Peter's—as cardinals representing Catholics around the globe arrived to elect a new pope.

On April 18, 115 cardinals dressed in crimson were stripped of their mobile phones, given a vow of secrecy, and locked inside the Sistine Chapel for the "conclave" (from Latin *cum clave,* with key). Finally, at 17:50 on April 19, an anxious crowd in St. Peter's Square looked up to see a puff of white smoke emerging from the Sistine Chapel's chimney. The bells in St. Peter's clock towers rang out gloriously (a new tradition) confirming that, indeed, a pope had been elected. The crowd erupted in cheers, and Romans watching on their TVs hailed taxis to hurry to the Square.

On the balcony of St. Peter's facade, a cardinal addressed the crowd below. "Brothers and sisters," he said in several languages, *"Habemus Papam."* We have a pope. As thousands chanted *"Viva il Papa,"* 78-year-old Josef Ratzinger of Germany stepped up, raised his hands, and was introduced as Pope Benedict XVI.

the Church, and giving them a glimpse of the heaven that awaited the faithful.

• *Now, walk straight up the center of the nave toward the altar.*

"Michelangelo's Church"—The Greek Cross

The plaques on the floor show where other, smaller churches of

the world would end if they were placed inside St. Peter's: St. Paul's Cathedral in London (Londinense), Florence's Duomo, and so on.

You'll also walk over circular golden grates. Stop at the second one (at the third pillar from the entrance). Look back at the entrance and realize that if Michelangelo had had his way, this whole long section of the church wouldn't exist. The nave was extended after his death.

Michelangelo was 71 years old when the pope persuaded him to take over the church project and cap it with a dome. He agreed, intending to put the dome over Donato Bramante's original "Greek Cross" floor plan, with four equal arms. In optimistic Renaissance times, this symmetrical arrangement symbolized perfection—the orderliness of the created world and the goodness of man (who was created in God's image). But Michelangelo was a Renaissance man in Counter-Reformation times. The Church, struggling against

Protestants and its own corruption, opted for a plan designed to impress the world with its grandeur—the Latin cross of the Crucifixion, with its nave extended to accommodate the grand religious spectacles of the Baroque period.

• *Continue toward the altar, entering "Michelangelo's Church." Park yourself in front of the statue of St. Andrew to the left of the altar, the guy holding an X-shaped cross. Like Andrew, gaze up into the dome, and also like him, gasp. (Never stifle a gasp.)*

The Dome

The dome soars higher than a football field on end, 448 feet from the floor of the cathedral to the top of the lantern. It glows with

light from its windows, the blue and gold mosaics creating a cool, solemn atmosphere. In this majestic vision of heaven (not painted by Michelangelo), we see (above the windows) Jesus, Mary, and a ring of saints, more rings of angels above them, and, way up in the ozone, God the Father (a blur of blue and red without binoculars).

When Michelangelo died (1564), he'd completed only the drum of the dome—the circular base up as far as the windows—but the next architects were guided by his designs.

Listen to the hum of visitors echoing through St. Peter's and reflect on our place in the cosmos: half animal, half angel, stretched between heaven and earth, born to live only a short while, a bubble of foam on a great cresting wave of humanity.

• *But I digress.*

Peter

The base of the dome is ringed with a gold banner telling us in massive blue letters why this church is so important. According to Catholics, Peter was selected by Jesus to head the church. The banner in Latin quotes from the Bible where Jesus says to him, "You are Peter *(Tu es Petrus)* and upon this rock I will build my church, and to you I will give the keys of the kingdom of heaven" (Matthew 16:18). (Every quote from Jesus to Peter found in the Bible is written out in seven-foot-tall letters that continue around the entire church.)

Peter was the first bishop of Rome. His prestige and that of the city itself made this bishopric more illustrious than all others, and Peter's authority has supposedly passed in an unbroken chain to each succeeding bishop of Rome—that is, the 250-odd popes that followed.

Under the dome, under the bronze canopy, under the altar, some 23 feet under the marble floor, rest the bones of St. Peter, the "rock" upon which this particular church was built. You can't see the tomb, but go to the railing and look down into the small, lighted niche below the altar with a box containing bishops' shawls—a symbol of how Peter's authority spread to the other churches. Peter's tomb (not visible) is just below this box.

Are they really the bones of Jesus' apostle? According to a papal pronouncement: definitely maybe. The traditional site of his tomb was sealed up when Old St. Peter's was built on it in A.D. 326, and it remained sealed until 1940, when it was opened for archaeological study. Bones were found, dated from the first century, of a robust man who died in old age. His body was wrapped in expensive cloth. Various inscriptions and graffiti in the tomb indicate that second- and third-century visitors thought this was Peter's tomb. Does that mean it's really Peter? Who am I to disagree with the pope? Definitely maybe.

If you line up the cross on the altar with the dove in the window, you'll notice that the niche below the cross is just off-center compared with the rest of the church. Why? Because Michelangelo built the church around the traditional location of the tomb, not the actual location—about two feet away—discovered by modern archaeology.

Back in the nave sits a bronze statue of Peter under a canopy. This is one of a handful of pieces of art that were in

Peter

According to the Bible, Peter was a fisherman who was chosen by Christ to catch sinners instead. This "fisher of men" had human weaknesses that have endeared him to Christians. He was the disciple who tried to walk on water—but failed. In another incident, he impetuously cut off a man's ear when soldiers came to arrest Jesus. And he even denied knowing Christ, to save his own skin. But Jesus chose him anyway, and gave him his nickname—Rock (in Latin: *Petrus*).

Legends say that Peter came to the wicked city of Rome after Jesus' death to spread the gospel of love. He may have been imprisoned in the Mamertine Prison near the Roman Forum (see page 44), and other stories claim he had a vision of Christ along the Appian Way (see page 156). Eventually, Peter's preaching offended the Nero administration. Christ's fisherman was arrested, crucified upside-down, and buried here, where St. Peter's now stands.

the earlier church. In one hand he holds the keys, the symbol of the authority given him by Christ, while with the other hand he blesses us. He's wearing the toga of a Roman senator. It may be that the original statue was of a senator and that the bushy head and keys were added later to make it Peter. His big right toe has been worn smooth by the lips of pilgrims and foot-fetishists. Stand in line and kiss it, or, to avoid foot-and-mouth disease, touch your hand to your lips, then rub the toe. This is simply an act of reverence with no legend attached, though you can make one up if you like.

• *Circle to the right around the statue of Peter to find another popular stop among pilgrims: the lighted glass niche with the red-robed body of...*

Pope John XXIII

Pope John XXIII, who reigned 1958–1963, is nicknamed "the good pope." He is best known for initiating the landmark Vatican II Council (1962–1965) that instituted major reforms, bringing the Church into the modern age. The Council allowed Mass to be conducted in the vernacular rather than in Latin. Lay people were invited to participate more in services, Church leadership underwent some healthy self-criticism, and a spirit of ecumenism flourished. Pope John was a populist, referring to people as "brothers and sisters"...a phrase popular today among popes. In 2000, during the beatification process (a stop on the way to sainthood), Church authorities checked his body, and it was surprisingly fresh. So they moved it upstairs, put it behind glass, and now old Catholics who remember him fondly enjoy another stop on their St. Peter's visit.

The Main Altar

The main altar beneath the dome and canopy (the white marble slab with cross and candlesticks) is used only when the pope him-

self says Mass. He sometimes conducts the Sunday morning service when he's in town, a sight worth seeing. I must admit, though, it's a little strange being frisked at the door for weapons at the holiest place in Christendom.

The tiny altar would be lost in this enormous church if it weren't for Gian Lorenzo Bernini's seven-story bronze canopy (God's "four-poster bed"), which "extends" the altar upward and reduces the perceived distance between floor and ceiling. The corkscrew columns echo the marble ones that surrounded the altar/tomb in Old St. Peter's. Some of the bronze used here was taken and melted down from the ancient Pantheon. On the marble base of the columns are three bees on a shield, the symbol of the Barberini family, who commissioned the work and ordered the raid on the Pantheon. As the saying went, "What the barbarians didn't do, the Barberini did."

Starting from the column to the left of the altar, walk clockwise around the canopy. Notice the female faces on the marble bases, about eye level above the bees. Someone in the Barberini family was pregnant during the making of the canopy, so Bernini

put the various stages of childbirth on the bases. Continue clockwise to the last base to see how it came out.

Bernini (1598–1680), the Michelangelo of the Baroque era, is the man most responsible for the interior decoration of the church. The altar area was his masterpiece, a "theater" for holy spectacles. Bernini did: 1) the bronze canopy; 2) the dove window in the apse, surrounded by bronze work and statues; 3) the statue of lance-bearing St. Longinus ("The hills are alive..."), which became

Benedict XVI

When Josef Ratzinger became the 265th pope, he introduced himself as "a simple, humble worker in the vineyard of the Lord."

But the man has a complex history, a reputation for intellectual brilliance, a flair for the piano, and a penchant for controversy for his unbending devotion to traditional Catholic doctrine.

Born in small-town Bavaria in 1927, he lived life under Nazi rule as many Germans did—outwardly obeying leaders while inwardly conflicted. Like all 14-year-old boys, he joined the Hitler Youth and, like most German men, was drafted into the army. During World War II, he trained to spray flak from anti-aircraft guns, saw Jews transported to death camps, and, like many Germans in the final days of the war, he deserted his post.

After the war, he completed his studies in theology and became a rising voice of liberal Catholicism, serving as an advisor at the Second Vatican Council (1962–1965). But after the May 1968 student revolts rocked Europe's Establishment, he became increasingly convinced that Church tradition was needed to offset the growing chaos of the world.

Pope John Paul II appointed him to several positions, and

the model for the other three statues; 4) much of the marble floor decoration; and 5) the balconies above the four statues, incorporating some of the actual corkscrew columns from Old St. Peter's, said to have been looted by the Romans from the Temple of Herod (called "Solomon's Temple") in Jerusalem. Bernini, the father of Baroque, gave an impressive unity to an amazing variety of pillars, windows, statues, chapels, and aisles.

• *Approach the apse, the front area with the golden dove window.*

The Apse

Bernini's dove window shines above the smaller front altar used for everyday services. The Holy Spirit, in the form of a six-foot-high dove, pours sunlight onto the faithful through the alabaster windows, turning into artificial rays of gold and reflecting off swirling gold clouds, angels, and winged babies. During a service, real sunlight passes through real clouds of incense, mingling with Bernini's sculpture. This is the epitome of Baroque—an ornate, mixed-media work designed to overwhelm the viewer.

Beneath the dove is the centerpiece of this structure, the so-

Ratzinger became John Paul II's closest advisor and good friend. Every Friday afternoon for two decades, they met for lunch, intellectual sparring, and friendly conversation.

Under John Paul II, Ratzinger served as the Church's "enforcer" of doctrine, earning the nickname "God's Rottweiler." He spoke out against ordaining women, chastised Latin American priests for fomenting class warfare (Liberation theology), reassigned bishops who were soft on homosexuality, reaffirmed opposition to birth control, and wrote thoughtful papers challenging the secular world's moral relativism. He also punished pedophile priests, though critics charged him with glossing over the issue to preserve the Church's image.

Ratzinger chose the name of "Benedict" to recall both Pope Benedict XV (who tried to bring Europeans together after World War I) and the original St. Benedict (c. 480–543), the monk who symbolizes Europe's Christian roots. A true pan-European who speaks many languages, Ratzinger heads a Church that thrives everywhere except Europe, which is becoming increasingly secular (with the notable exception of an increasing Muslim population). In 2006, Benedict stirred controversy among many Muslims with some unguarded remarks. In 2010, he was criticized for not dealing forcefully enough with pedophile priests. Generally, Benedict XVI has continued John Paul II's two priorities: defending Catholic doctrine in a changing world and building bridges with fellow Christians.

called "Throne of Peter," an oak chair built in medieval times for a king. Subsequently, it was encrusted with tradition and encased in bronze by Bernini as a symbol of papal authority. Statues of four early Church Fathers support the chair, a symbol of how bishops should support the pope in troubled times—times like the Counter-Reformation.

Remember that St. Peter's is a church, not a museum. In the apse, Mass is said daily (Mon–Sat at 17:00, Sun at 17:45—after vespers at 17:00) for pilgrims, tourists, and Roman citizens alike. Wooden confessional booths are available in the north transept (to the right of the main altar) for Catholics to tell their sins to a listening ear and receive forgiveness and peace of mind (daily, usually mornings and late afternoons—see website). The faithful renew their faith, and the faithless gain inspiration. Look at the light streaming through the windows, turn and gaze up

Bernini Blitz

Nowhere is there such a conglomeration of works by the flamboyant genius who remade the church—and the city—in the Baroque style. Here's your scavenger-hunt list. You have 20 minutes. Go!

1. St. Peter's Square: design and statues
2. Constantine equestrian relief (right end of atrium)
3. Decoration (stucco, gold leaf, marble, etc.) of side aisles (flanking the nave)
4. Tabernacle (the temple-like altarpiece) inside Blessed Sacrament Chapel
5. Much of the marble floor throughout church
6. Bronze canopy over the altar
7. St. Longinus statue (holding a lance) near altar
8. Balconies (above each of the four statues) with corkscrew, Solomonic columns
9. Dove window, bronze sunburst, angels, "Throne," and Church Fathers (in the apse)
10. Tomb of Pope Urban VIII (far end of the apse, right side)
11. Tomb of Pope Alexander VII (between the apse and the left transept, over a doorway, with the gold skeleton smothered in jasper poured like maple syrup) Bizarre...Baroque...Bernini.

into the dome, and quietly contemplate your deity (or lack thereof).

• *To the left of the main altar is the south transept. At the far end, left side, find the dark "painting" of St. Peter crucified upside-down.*

South Transept— Peter's Crucifixion Site

This marks the exact spot (according to tradition) where Peter was killed 1,900 years ago. Peter had come to the world's greatest city to preach Jesus' message of love to the pagan, often hostile Romans. During the reign of Nero, he was arrested and brought to Nero's Circus so all Rome could witness his execution. When the authorities told Peter he was to be crucified just like his Lord, Peter said "I'm not worthy" and insisted they nail him on the cross upside-down.

The Romans were actually quite tolerant of other religions, but they required their conquered peoples to worship the Roman emperor as a god. For most religions, this was no problem, but monotheistic Christians refused to worship the emperor even when burned alive, crucified, or thrown to the lions. Their bravery, optimism in suffering, and message of love struck a chord among slaves and members of the lower classes. The religion started by a poor carpenter grew, despite occasional pogroms (persecution of minorities) by fanatical emperors. In three short centuries, Christianity went from a small Jewish sect in Jerusalem to the official religion of the world's greatest empire.

This and all the other "paintings" in the church are actually mosaic copies made from thousands of colored chips the size of your little fingernail. Smoke and humidity would damage real paintings. Around the corner on the right (heading back toward the central nave), pause at the copy of Raphael's huge "painting" (mosaic) of *The Transfiguration*, especially if you won't be seeing the original in the Vatican Museum.

• *Back near the entrance to the church, in the far corner, behind bullet-proof glass, is the...*

Pietà

Michelangelo was 24 years old when he completed this *Pietà* (pee-ay-TAH) of Mary with the dead body of Christ taken from the cross. It was Michelangelo's first major commission (by the French ambassador to the Vatican), done for Holy Year 1500.

Pietà means "pity." Michelangelo, with his total mastery of the real world, captures the sadness of the moment. Mary cradles her crucified son in her lap. Christ's lifeless right arm drooping down lets us know how heavy this corpse is. His smooth skin is accented by the rough folds of Mary's robe. Mary tilts her head down, looking at her dead son with sad tenderness. Her left hand turns upward, asking, "How could they do this to you?"

Michelangelo didn't think of sculpting as creating a figure, but as simply freeing the God-made figure from the prison of marble around it. He'd attack a project like this with an inspired passion, chipping away to find what God put inside.

The bunched-up shoulder and rigor-mortis legs show that Michelangelo learned well from his studies of cadavers. But realistic as this work is, its true power lies in the subtle "unreal" features. Life-size Christ looks childlike compared with larger-than-life Mary. Unnoticed at first, this accentuates the subconscious impression of Mary enfolding Jesus in her maternal love. Mary—the mother of a 33-year-old man—looks like a teenager, emphasizing how Mary was the eternally youthful "handmaiden" of the Lord, always serving him, even at this moment of supreme sacrifice. She accepts God's will, even if it means giving up her son.

The statue is a solid pyramid of maternal tenderness. Yet within this, Christ's body tilts diagonally down to the right and Mary's hem flows with it. Subconsciously, we feel the weight of this dead God sliding from her lap to the ground.

At 11:30 on May 23, 1972, a madman with a hammer entered St. Peter's and began hacking away at the *Pietà*. The damage was repaired, but that's why there's now a shield of bulletproof glass.

This is Michelangelo's only signed work. The story goes that he overheard some pilgrims praising his finished *Pietà*, but attributing it to a second-rate sculptor from a lesser city. He was so enraged that he grabbed his chisel and chipped "Michelangelo Buonarroti of Florence did this" in the ribbon running down Mary's chest.

On your right (covered in gray concrete with a gold cross) is the inside of the Holy Door. It won't be opened until Christmas Eve, 2024, the dawn of the next Jubilee Year. If there's a prayer inside you, ask that St. Peter's will no longer need security checks or bulletproof glass when this door is next opened.

The Rest of the Church

The Crypt (a.k.a. Grottoes, or Tombe)

Visitors can go down to the foundations of Old St. Peter's, containing tombs of popes and memorial chapels. The Crypt entrance is along the right side of the church, but the line starts to form on the church's front steps, near the right door of the main facade. A ramp leads you down to the floor level of the previous church. You can see a few column fragments from Old St. Peter's (a.k.a. "Basilica Costantiniana"). Next come tombs of popes, including Paul VI (1897–1978), who suffered through the church's modernization, and Pope John Paul II (1920–2005)—the flower-filled chapel with the simple tomb. Out of 265 popes, two have been given the title "Great." That elite group may soon grow by 50 percent, as there's talk of calling the pope who died in 2005 "John Paul the Great." The finale is to see the sepulcher of Peter. The visit spills you back inside the church under the dome.

The walk through the Crypt is free and quick (20 minutes)—but you won't see St. Peter's original grave unless you take a Scavi "Excavations" tour (see "Tours" on page 241).

Museum-Treasury (Museo-Tesoro)

The museum, located on the left side of the nave near the altar, contains an original corkscrew column from Old St. Peter's, the room-size tomb of Sixtus IV by Antonio Pollaiuolo, a big pair of Roman pincers used to torture Christians, and assorted jewels, papal robes, and golden reliquaries—a marked contrast to the poverty of early Christians.

Blessed Sacrament Chapel

You're welcome to step through the metalwork gates into this oasis of peace reserved for prayer and meditation. It's located on the right-hand side of the church, about midway to the altar.

Up to the Dome (Cupola)

A good way to finish a visit to St. Peter's is to go up to the dome for the best view of Rome anywhere (daily April–Sept 8:00–18:00, Oct–March 8:00–17:00). The entrance to the dome is along the right side of the church, but the line begins to form out front, at the church's right door (as you face the church).

There are two levels: the rooftop of the church and the very top of the dome. Climb (for €5) or take an elevator (€7) to the first level, on the church roof just above the facade. From the roof, you have a commanding view of St. Peter's Square, the statues on the colonnade, Rome across the Tiber in front of you, and the dome itself—almost terrifying in its nearness—looming behind you.

From here, you can also go inside to the gallery ringing the interior of the dome, where you can look down inside the church. Notice the dusty top of Bernini's seven-story-tall canopy far below.

Study the mosaics up close—and those huge letters! It's worth the elevator ride for this view alone.

From this level, if you're energetic, continue all the way up to the top of the dome. The staircase actually winds between the outer shell and the inner one. It's a sweaty, crowded, claustrophobic 15-minute, 323-step climb, but worth it. The view from the summit is great, the fresh air even better. Admire the arms of Bernini's colonnade encircling St. Peter's Square. Find the big, white Victor Emmanuel Monument, with the two statues on top; and the Pantheon, with its large, light, shallow dome. The large rectangular building to the left of the obelisk is the Vatican Museum, stuffed with art. Survey the Vatican grounds, with its mini–train system and lush gardens. Look down into the square on the tiny pilgrims buzzing like electrons around the nucleus of Catholicism.

ST. PETER-IN-CHAINS TOUR

San Pietro in Vincoli

Michelangelo—Earth's greatest sculptor—died having failed to complete his greatest work, the tomb of Pope Julius II. Today, you can visit the powerful remains of that unfinished masterpiece, including the famous statue of Moses, housed in a historic church that also contains Peter's chains.

Orientation

Cost: Free.

Dress Code: Modest dress is required.

Hours: Daily April–Sept 8:00–12:30 & 15:30–19:00, Oct–March 8:00–12:30 & 15:00–18:00.

Getting There: The church is a 15-minute uphill walk north of the Colosseum. From the Colosseo Metro stop, exit the station to the left and climb the staircase that's roughly 50 yards away, then work your way slowly uphill. For a shorter walk, use the Cavour Metro stop; from that station, go downhill on Via Cavour a half-block, then climb the pedestrian staircase called Via di San Francesco di Paola, which leads right to the church. If asking for directions, say "San Pietro in Vincoli" (sahn pee-AY-troh een VEEN-koh-lee).

Length of This Tour: Allow 30 minutes.

Cuisine Art: See the recommended eateries listed on page 353.

The Tour Begins

• *In the far right corner of the church, you'll find a wall full of marble statues. In the center sits...*

Michelangelo's *Moses* (1515)

Moses has just returned from meeting face-to-face with God. Now he senses trouble back home. Slowly he turns to see his followers worshipping a golden calf. As his anger builds, he glares at them. His physical strength is symbolic of his moral and spiritual fortitude as a leader of his people. His powerful left leg tucks under and tenses, as he's just about to spring up out of his chair and punish the naughty Children of Israel with the Ten Commandments under his arm. Enjoy the cascading beard, one of the greatest in art history.

And if he did stand up, this statue would be 13 feet tall, nearly the height of Michelangelo's famous *David*. This Charlton Heston–with-horns is interesting in photographs...and awe-inspiring when confronted in person. His bare, muscular arms exude power. Michelangelo completed the statue after practicing for four years painting the seated prophets on the Sistine ceiling.

Like other Michelangelo statues, *Moses* is both at rest (seated) and in motion (his tensed leg, turning head, and nervous fingers). This restlessness may reflect Michelangelo's Neo-Platonic belief that the soul is the claustrophobic prisoner of the body. Or it's the statue itself fighting to emerge from the stone around it. A frustrated Michelangelo, working to bring God's statue into existence, reportedly threw his chisel at the thing (some say causing a scar on *Moses*' right knee), yelling at it, "Speak, damn it, speak!"

The horns are the crowning touch. In medieval times, the Hebrew word for "rays of light" (halo) was mistranslated as "horns." Michelangelo knew better but wanted to give the statue an air of *terribilità*, a kind of scary charisma possessed by Moses, Pope Julius II...and Michelangelo. This Moses radiates the smoldering *terribilità* of a borderline-abusive father.

The Tomb Today

In 1542, some of the remnants of the tomb project were brought to St. Peter-in-Chains and pieced together by Michelangelo's assistants. What we see today is a far cry from the original design, which was to have been fully three-dimensional and five times as big. Some of the best statues ended up elsewhere, like the *Prisoners* in Florence, and the *Slaves* in the Louvre. Though the assistants had Michelangelo's original instruction manual, they were trying to assemble it with most of the parts missing.

Moses and the Louvre's *Slaves* are the only statues Michelangelo personally completed for the project. Flanking *Moses* are the Old Testament sister-wives of Jacob, Leah (to our left) and Rachel,

The Tomb of Pope Julius II

Moses sits on the bottom level of a three-story marble wall filled with statues. This is a puny, cobbled-together version of what was to have been a grand tomb for Pope Julius II.

In 1505, Pope Julius II hired young Michelangelo to build his tomb, a huge monument to be placed in St. Peter's Basilica. An excited Michelangelo sketched designs for a three-story wedding-cake mountain of marble studded with 48 statues and bronze reliefs, and topped with a huge statue of the egomaniacal pope. *Moses* was to have been placed on an upper level on the right-hand corner, looking away from the monument.

Michelangelo traveled to Carrara, selected 100 tons of marble for the project, and started working. Then Julius changed his mind. He ordered Michelangelo to work on painting the Sistine Chapel instead. Michelangelo knocked it off in a mere four years so that he could return to his true masterwork. Michelangelo would spend 30 years of his life working in fits and starts on the tomb. But when Julius died (1513), the funding for the project petered out, and Michelangelo eventually moved on to other things. Julius was buried in a simple grave in St. Peter's Basilica at the Vatican.

both begun by Michelangelo but probably finished by pupils. On the second story, a Madonna and Child stand above a reclining, thoughtful-looking Pope Julius II on a coffin.

The sheer variety of decoration we see here gives us a glimpse of the tomb's original scope—nearly 50 statues laced together with Pompeii-esque garlands and proto-Baroque scrolls.

Michelangelo went to his grave thinking that he'd wasted the best years of his life on the tomb. Today, we can only reconstruct it in our minds, imagining a monument intended to exceed (according to Giorgio Vasari) "every ancient or imperial tomb ever made."

The Church

Founded in 440, it's one of Rome's oldest, built to house Peter's chains. Though the church was greatly changed in 1475, the 20 Doric columns flanking the wide nave are from the original church. The central ceiling painting (c. 1700) shows the chains—with their miraculous curative powers in action—healing someone possessed by demons, on the steps of St. Peter's Basilica in the Vatican.

• *On the altar is a gold-and-glass case, containing what tradition claims are...*

Peter's Chains

There are actually two different sets of chains, linked together. One set held Peter (it's said) when he and Paul were in the Mamertine Prison in Rome (near the Forum).

The other dates from when Herod jailed Peter in Jerusalem (Acts 12; see the scene frescoed on the left wall of the apse). During the night, "Peter was sleeping between two soldiers, bound with chains, while sentries were guarding the doors. And behold, an angel of the Lord appeared and a light shone in the cell. The angel struck Peter on the side and woke him, saying, 'Get up quickly.' And the chains fell off his hands." The angel led Peter, who thought he was dreaming, out of the prison to safety. (Raphael's depiction of this is in the Vatican Museum.)

In the waning days of ancient Rome, the Jerusalem chains ended up here as a gift from the Eastern empress to her son-in-law, the Western emperor. When they arrived and were paired with the Mamertine chains, the two sets—chink!—joined together miraculously.

PILGRIM'S ROME TOUR

Pilgrimage Churches

Rome is the "capital" of the world's 1.1 billion Catholics. In Rome, you'll rub elbows with religious pilgrims from around the world—Nigerian nuns, Bulgarian theology students, extended Mexican families, and everyday Catholics returning to their religious roots.

The pilgrim industry helped shape Rome after the fall of the empire. Ancient Rome's population peaked at about 1.2 million. When Rome fell in A.D. 476, barbarians cut off the water supply by breaking the aqueducts, Romans fled the city, and the mouth of the Tiber River filled with silt and became a swamp.

During the Dark Ages, mosquitoes ruled over a pathetic village of 50,000...bad news for pilgrims, bad news for the Vatican. Back then, the Catholic Church was the Christian Church. Because popes needed a place fit for pilgrimages, the Church revitalized the city. Owners of hotels and restaurants cheered.

In 1587, Pope Sixtus V reconnected aqueducts and built long, straight boulevards connecting the great churches and pilgrimage sites. Obelisks served as markers. As you explore the city, think like a pilgrim. Look down long roads and you'll see either a grand church or an obelisk (from which you'll see a grand church).

Orientation

Church of San Giovanni in Laterano: Free, daily 7:00–18:30, €5 audioguide available at info desk near statue of Constantine, €1 discount with this book in 2011 (ID required). The **Holy Stairs** (Scala Santa), in a building across the street from the church, are free and open daily (April–Sept 6:15–12:00 & 15:30–18:30, Oct–March 6:15–12:00 & 15:00–18:00). The church is at Piazza di San Giovanni in Laterano (Metro: San Giovanni, bus #85 or #87, tel. 06-6988-6409).

PILGRIM'S ROME

Pilgrim's Rome

Church of Santa Maria Maggiore: Free, daily 8:30–18:00, skip the
€4 audioguide and €4 museum, Piazza Santa Maria Maggiore,
Metro: Termini or Vittorio Emanuele, tel. 06-6988-6802.

Church of Santa Prassede: Free, bring €0.50 and €1 coins for
lights, daily 7:00–12:00 & 16:00–18:30, 100 yards from Santa
Maria Maggiore.

Church of San Clemente: Upper church—free, lower church—€5,
both open Mon–Sat 9:00–12:30 & 15:00–18:00, Sun 12:00–
18:00, last entry for lower church 20 minutes before closing,
Via di San Giovanni in Laterano, Metro: Colosseo, bus #85 or
#87, tel. 06-774-0021, www.basilicasanclemente.com.

Getting There: Metro line A stops at San Giovanni in Laterano
and Piazza Vittorio. Bus #87 runs from Largo Argentina
to Piazza Venezia to the Colosseum to the Church of San
Clemente to the Church of San Giovanni in Laterano. Bus

#85 does the same route but skips Largo Argentina.

Photography: Generally, photos without flash are allowed in Rome's churches.

The Tour Begins

Overview

Pilgrims to Rome try to visit four great basilicas: St. Peter's Basilica, of course (see tour in this book), St. Paul's Outside the Walls (see page 81), San Giovanni in Laterano, and Santa Maria Maggiore. The last two are covered in this chapter, as well as two other "honorable mentions": For the best Byzantine-style mosaics in Rome, visit the Church of Santa Prassede (near Santa Maria Maggiore). And the fascinating and central San Clemente is not far from San Giovanni in Laterano.

San Giovanni in Laterano

Imagine the jubilation when this church—the first Christian church in the city of Rome—was opened in about A.D. 318. Christians could finally "come out" and worship openly without fear of reprisal. (Still, most Romans were pagan, so this first great church was tucked away from the center of things, near the city wall.) After that glorious beginning, the church served as the center of Catholicism and the home of the popes up until the Renaissance renovation of St. Peter's. Until 1870, all popes were "crowned" here. Even today, it's the home church of the Bishop of Rome—the pope.

The church is located on Piazza di San Giovanni in Laterano (Metro: San Giovanni). From the Metro station, go through the old city walls and look left.

The **Via Sannio** market, selling clothing and some handicrafts every morning except Sunday, is a block south of the church.

Exterior

The massive facade is 18th-century, with Christ triumphant on the top. The blocky peach-colored building adjacent on the right is the Lateran Palace, standing on the site of the old Papal Palace— residence of popes until about 1300. Across the street to your right are the pope's private chapel and the Holy Stairs (Scala Santa), popular with pilgrims (we'll see the stairs later). To the left is a well-preserved chunk of the ancient Roman wall. Pass

San Giovanni in Laterano

20 YDS.
20 m

⑧ APSE
⑦ CHANCEL

PIAZZA DI SAN GIOVANNI IN LATERANO

⑥ TRANSEPT

⑤

TO CLOISTER MOSAICS

N A V E

WC

④

LATERAN PALACE

③

DCH

②

① PORCH

POSTS MARKING WHERE VATICAN CITY CONTROL BEGINS

TO HOLY STAIRS

ENTER

PIAZZA DI PORTA SAN GIOVANNI

① Statue of Constantine
② Central Doorway
③ Baroque Nave
④ Basilica Floor Plan
⑤ Baldacchino
⑥ Golden Columns from Temple of Jupiter
⑦ Bishop's Chair
⑧ Mosaic

the three-foot-high granite posts surrounding the church to leave Italy and enter the Vatican State—Carabinieri must leave their guns at the door.

· *Step inside the portico and look left.*

❶ Statue of Constantine

It's October 28, A.D. 312, and Constantine—sword tucked under his arm and leaning confidently on a (missing) spear—has conquered Maxentius and liberated Rome. Constantine marched to this spot where his enemy's personal bodyguards lived, trashed their pagan idols, and dedicated the place to the god who gave him his victory—Christ. The holes in Constantine's head once held a golden, halo-like crown for the emperor who legalized Christianity. In the relief above the statue, you'll see a beheaded John the Baptist.

At the other end of the portico is the Vatican History Museum (€5). It's worthwhile only if: it's the top of the hour (when visitors are admitted); and you like old paintings by no-name artists.

• *In the portico, take a look at the...*

❷ Central Doorway

These tall green bronze doors, with their floral designs and acorn studs, are the original doors from ancient Rome's Senate House (Curia) in the Forum. The Church moved these here in the 1650s to remind people that from now on, the Church was Europe's lawmaker. The star borders were added to make these big doors bigger. Imagine, those cool little acorns date to the third century.

• *Now go inside the main part of the church. Stand in the back of the nave.*

❸ Baroque Nave

Very little survives from the original church—most of what you see was built after 1600. In preparation for the 1650 Jubilee, Pope Innocent X commissioned architect Francesco Borromini (rival to Bernini) to remake the interior. He redesigned the basilica in the Baroque style, reorganizing the nave, and adding the huge statues of the apostles (stepping out of niches to symbolically bring celestial Jerusalem to our world). The relief panels above the statues depict parallel events from the Old Testament (on the left) and New Testament (on the right). For instance, in the very back you'll see two resurrections: Jonah escaping the whale and Jesus escaping death. Only the ceiling (which should have been a white vault) breaks from the Baroque style—it's Renaissance and the pope wanted it to stay.

❹ Basilica Floor Plan

San Giovanni was the first public church in Rome and the model for all later churches, including St. Peter's. The floor plan—a large central hall (nave) flanked by two side aisles—was based on the ancient Roman basilica (law courts) floor plan. These buildings were big enough to accommodate the large Christian congregations. Note that Roman basilicas came with two apses. You came in through the main entrance, which was designed to stress the authority of the place by slightly overwhelming and intimidating those who entered. When the design was adapted for use as a church, a grand and welcoming entry (the west portal) replaced one of the apses. Upon entering, the worshipper could take in the entire space instantly, and the rows of columns welcomed him to proceed to the altar.

• *The canopy over the altar is called the...*

❺ Baldacchino

In the upper cage are two silver statues of Saints Peter (with keys) and Paul (sword), which contain pieces of their...heads.

The gossip buzzing among Rome's amateur archaeologists is that the Vatican tested DNA from Peter's head (located here) and from his body (located at St. Peter's)...and they didn't match.

• *Standing in the left transept are the...*

❻ Golden Columns from Temple of Jupiter

Tradition says that these gilded bronze columns once stood in pagan Rome's holiest spot—the Temple of Jupiter, dedicated to the King of all Gods, on the summit of Capitol Hill (c. 50 B.C.). Now they support a triangular pediment inhabited by a bearded, Jupiter-like God the Father.

• *In the apse, you'll find the...*

❼ Bishop's Chair

The chair (called a "cathedra") reminds visitors that this is the cathedral of Rome...and the pope himself is the bishop that sits here. Once elected, the new pope must actually sit in this chair to officially become the pope. The ceremonial sitting usually happens within one month of election—Pope Benedict XVI took his seat on May 3, 2005.

• *Under the semicircular dome of the apse, take a close look at the...*

❽ Mosaic

The original design dates from about 450 (although it was made in the 13th century and heavily restored in the 19th century). Pop in

a coin for light. You'll see a cross, animals, plants, and the River Jordan running along the base. Mosaic, of course, was an ancient Roman specialty adapted by medieval Christians. The head of Christ (above the cross) must have been a glorious sight to early worshippers. It was one of the first legal images of Christ ever seen in formerly pagan Rome.

• *Fans of Cosmatesque marble-inlay floor (c. 1100–1300) may want to visit the cloister (€2, free with €5 basilica audioguide rental, enter near left transept).*

The Holy Stairs are outside the church in a building across the street. To get there, exit the church, turn left, and cross the street to the nondescript building that houses the...

Holy Stairs (Scala Santa)

In 326, Emperor Constantine's mother (Sta. Helena) brought home the 28 marble steps of Pontius Pilate's residence in Jerusalem. Jesus climbed these steps on the day he was sentenced to death. Each day, hundreds of faithful penitents climb these steps on their knees (reciting a litany of prayers, available at the desk to the right of the entry). Covered with walnut wood with small glass-covered holes showing stains from Jesus' blood, the steps lead to the "Holy of Holies" (Sancta Sanctorum), the private chapel of the popes in the Middle Ages. With its world-class relics, this chapel was considered the holiest place on earth. The relics were moved to the Vatican in 1905, and the chapel is open only a few hours a week.

In the entry lobby, retrace Jesus' last days on the painting of old Jerusalem; Pilate's House was at the "Pretorio." You can climb the tourist staircases along the sides, look inside the "Holy of Holies" through the grated windows, and buy a souvenir at the gift shop.

On September 20, 1870, as nationalist forces unifying Italy took Rome and ended the pope's temporal power, Pope Pius IX left his Quirinal Palace home for the last time. He stopped here to climb the steps, pray in his chapel, and bless his supporters from the top of the steps. Then he fled to the Vatican, where he spent the rest of his days.

Santa Maria Maggiore

The basilica of Santa Maria celebrates Holy Mary, the mother of Jesus. One of Rome's oldest and best-preserved churches, it was built (A.D. 432) while Rome was falling around it. The city had been sacked by Visigoths (410), and the emperors were about to check out (476). Increasingly, popes stepped in to fill the vacuum of leadership. The fifth-century mosaics give the church the feel

Santa Maria Maggiore

PIAZZA DELL'ESQUILINO

APSE

PAULINE CHAPEL

SIXTUS V CHAPEL

NAVE

GIFT SHOP, MUSEUM & WC

20 YARDS
20 m

PORCH

TO STA. PRASSEDE (100 YDS.)

DCH

ENTER

PIAZZA SANTA MARIA MAGGIORE

1 Manger Fragments
2 Apse Mosaic
3 Mosaics in Chancel Arch
4 Nave Mosaics

5 Tomb of Sixtus V
6 Bernini's Tomb
7 Madonna Painting & Miracle Relief

of the early-Christian community. The general ambience of the church really takes you back to ancient times.

The church is at Piazza Santa Maria Maggiore (Metro: Termini or Vittorio Emanuele).

Exterior

Mary's column originally stood in the Forum's Basilica of Constantine. The fifth-century church built in her honor proclaims she was indeed the Mother of God—a fact disputed by hair-splitting theologians of the day. When you step inside the church, you'll be exiting Italy and entering the Vatican—the Maggiore indicates that this church, a Vatican possession, was much more important than other churches dedicated to the Virgin Mary.

Interior

Despite the Renaissance ceiling and Baroque crusting, you still feel like you're walking into an early-Christian church. The stately rows of columns, the simple basilica layout, the cheery colors, the spacious nave—it's easy to imagine worshipers finding an oasis of peace here as the Roman Empire crashed around them. (The 15th-century coffered ceiling is gilded with gold perhaps brought back from America by Columbus.)

• *In the center of the church is the main altar, under a purple and gold canopy. Underneath the altar, in a lighted niche, are...*

❶ Manger Fragments

A kneeling Pope Pius IX (who established the dogma of the Immaculate Conception in the 19th century) prays before a glass

case with an urn that contains several pieces of wood, bound by iron—these pieces are said to be from Jesus' crib. The church, dedicated to Mary's motherhood, displays these relics as physical evidence that Mary was indeed the mother of Christ. (The church is also built on the site of a former pagan temple dedicated to Rome's mother goddess, Juno.) Is the manger the real thing? Look into the eyes of pilgrims who visit.

• *In the apse, topped with a semi-circular dome, find the...*

❷ Apse Mosaic

This 13th-century mosaic shows Mary being crowned by Jesus, both on the same throne. They float in a bubble representing heaven, borne aloft by angels. By

the Middle Ages, Mary's cult status was secure.
• *Up in the arch that frames the outside of the apse, you'll find some of the church's oldest mosaics.*

❸ Mosaics in Chancel Arch

Colorful panels tell Mary's story in fifth-century Roman terms. Haloed senator-saints in white togas (top panel on left side) attend to Mary, who sits on a throne, dressed in gold and crowned like an empress. The angel Gabriel swoops down to announce to Mary that she'll conceive Jesus, and the Dove of the Holy Spirit follows. Below (the panel in the bottom left corner) are sheep representing the apostles, entering the city of Jerusalem ("Hiervsalem").
• *On the right side of the nave, starting near the altar, take a look at the...*

❹ Nave Mosaics

The church contains some of the world's oldest and best-preserved mosaics from Christian Rome. If the floodlights are on (it doesn't hurt to ask someone), those with good eyesight or binoculars will enjoy watching the story of Moses unfold in a series of surprisingly colorful and realistic scenes—more sophisticated than anything that would be seen for a thousand years.

The small, square mosaic panels are above all the columns, on the right side of the nave. Start at the altar and work back toward the entry.

1. This is a later painting—skip it.
2. Pharaoh's daughter (upper left) and her maids take baby Moses from the Nile.
3. Moses (lower half of panel) sees a burning bush that reconnects him with his Hebrew origins.
4. A parade of Israelites (left side) flee Egypt through a path in the Red Sea, while Pharaoh's troops drown.
5. Moses leads them across the Sinai desert (upper half), and God provides for them with a flock of quail (lower half).
6. Moses (upper half) sticks his magic rod in a river to desalinate it.
7. The Israelites battle their enemies while Moses commands from a hillside.
8. Skip it.
9. Moses (upper left) brings the Ten Commandments, then goes with Joshua (upper right) to lie down and die.
10. Joshua crosses the (rather puny) Jordan River...
11. ...and attacks Jericho...
12. ...and then the walls come a-tumblin' down.

• *If the gate is open, enter the chapel in the right transept (otherwise skip ahead to Bernini's Tomb). On the right wall of the chapel is a statue of a praying pope, atop the...*

❺ Tomb of Sixtus V

The Rome we see today is due largely to Pope Sixtus V (or was it Fiftus VI?). This energetic pope (1585–1590) leveled shoddy medieval Rome and erected grand churches connected by long, broad boulevards spiked with obelisks as focal points (such as the obelisk in Piazza dell'Esquilino behind Santa Maria Maggiore). The city of Rome has 13 Egyptian obelisks—all of Egypt has only five. The white carved-marble relief panels (especially the one in the upper right) show some of the obelisks and buildings he commissioned.

• *Walk back toward the main altar. On a roped-off step between two pillars, you'll find an inscription on the ground marking...*

❻ Bernini's Tomb

The plaque reads, "Ioannes Laurentivs Bernini"—Gian Lorenzo Bernini (1598–1680)—"who brought honor to art and the city, here humbly rests." Next to it is another plaque to the "Familia Bernini." It's certainly humble...a simple memorial for the man who grew up in this neighborhood, then went on to remake Rome in the ornate Baroque style. (For more on Bernini, see page 199.)

• *In the left transept, over the altar, you'll see a...*

❼ Madonna Painting and Miracle Relief

The altar, a geologist's delight, is adorned with jasper, agate, amethyst, lapis lazuli, and gold angels. Amid it all is a simple icon of the lady this church is dedicated to: Mary.

Above the painting is a bronze relief panel showing a pope, with amazed bystanders, shoveling snow. One hot August night in the year 432, Mary appeared to Pope Liberius in a dream, telling him: "Build me a church where the snow falls." The next morning, they discovered a small patch of snow here on the Esquiline Hill—on August 5—and this church, dedicated to Santa Maria, was begun.

• *After looking around Santa Maria Maggiore, fans of mosaics, Byzantines, and the offbeat should consider a visit to the nearby church of Santa Prassede, about 100 yards away.*

Exiting Santa Maria Maggiore, walk away from the church, past Mary on her column, cross the street, and turn right down the small street Via S. Giovanni Gualberto.

Church of Santa Prassede

The mosaics at the Church of Santa Prassede, from A.D. 822, are the best Byzantine-style mosaics in Rome. The Byzantine Empire, with its capital in Constantinople (modern Istanbul), was the eastern half of the Roman Empire. Unlike the western half, it didn't "fall," and its inhabitants remained Christian, Greek-speaking, and cultured for a thousand years while their distant cousins in Italy were fumbling for the light switch in the Dark Ages. Byzantine craftsmen preserved the techniques of ancient Roman mosaicists (who decorated floors and walls of villas and public buildings), then reinfused this learning into Rome during the city's darkest era. Take the time to let your eyes adjust, and appreciate the Byzantine glory glowing out of the dark church.

Bring €0.50 and €1 coins to buy floodlighting. (While €1 feels like a lot for five minutes of light, consider it a donation to maintain the church and treat all those visiting to the full sparkle of the mosaics.) Popping a coin into the box in the Chapel of St. Zeno (described below) saves you a trip to Ravenna.

• *The best mosaics are in the apse (behind the main altar) and in the small Chapel of St. Zeno along the right (north) side of the nave.*

Apse Mosaics

On a blue background is Christ, standing in a rainbow-colored river, flanked by saints. Christ has commanded Peter (to our right

of Christ, with white hair and beard) to spread the Good News to all the world. Beneath Christ, 12 symbolic sheep leave Jerusalem's city gates to preach to the world. Peter came here to the world's biggest city to preach love...and was met with a hostile environment. He turns his palm up in a plea for help. Persecuted Peter was taken in by a hospitable woman named Pudentia (next to him) and her sister, Praxedes (to the left of Christ, between two other saints), whose house was located on this spot. (The church is named for Praxedes.)

The saint on the far left (with the square halo, indicating he was alive at the time this was made) is Pope Paschal I, who built the church in the 800s in memory of these early sisters, hiring the best craftsmen in the known world to do the mosaics.

Chapel of St. Zeno

The ceiling is gold, representing the Byzantine heaven. An icon-like Christ emerges from the background, supported by winged angels in white. On the walls are saints walking among patches of flowers. In the altar niche, Mary and the child Jesus are flanked by the sisters Praxedes and Pudentia. On the side wall, the woman with the square blue halo is Theodora, the mom of the pope who built this.

The chapel, covered completely with mosaics, may be underwhelming to our modern eyes, but in the darkness of Rome's medieval era, it was known as the "Garden of Paradise."

San Clemente

Here, like nowhere else, you'll enjoy the layers of Rome—a 12th-century basilica sits atop a fourth-century Christian basilica, which sits atop a second-century Mithraic Temple and some even earlier Roman buildings.

The church is on Via di San Giovanni in Laterano (Metro: Colosseo). Bus #85 or #87 connects San Clemente and San Giovanni in Laterano, saving a 10-minute walk.

Upper Church—12th Century

The church (at today's ground level) is dedicated to the fourth pope, Clement, who shepherded the small Christian community when the religion was, at best, tolerated, and at worst, a capital offense. Clement himself was martyred by drowning in about A.D. 100—tied to an anchor by angry Romans and tossed overboard. You'll see his symbol, the anchor, around the church. The painting on the ceiling shows Clement being carried aloft to heaven.

While today's main entry is on the side, the original entry was through the courtyard in back, a kind of defensive atrium common in medieval times. To reach the original entry, enter the church through today's main entrance, walk diagonally toward the right, and exit again into this courtyard. Turn around and face the original entry. (This courtyard is inviting for a cool quiet break, as I imagine it was for a visiting medieval pilgrim.)

Back inside the church, step up to the carved marble choir—an enclosure in the middle of the church (Schola Cantorum) where the cantors sat. About 1,200 years ago, it stood in the old church beneath us, before that church was looted and destroyed by invading Normans.

In the apse (behind the altar), study the fine 12th-century mosaics. The delicate Crucifixion—with Christ sharing the cross with a dozen apostles as doves—is engulfed by a Tree of Life richly inhabited by deer, birds, and saints. The message is clear: All life springs from God in Christ. Above it all, a triumphant Christ, one hand on the Bible, blesses the congregation.

St. Catherine Chapel

The chapel near the side (tourists') entrance—considered one of the first great Renaissance masterpieces—is dedicated to St. Catherine of Alexandria, a noblewoman martyred for her defense of persecuted Christians. The fresco on the left wall—which shows an early Renaissance three-dimensional representation of space—is by the Florentine master Masolino (1428), perhaps aided by his young assistant, Masaccio. Studying the left wall, working from left to right, you can follow her story:

1. Catherine (lower left panel), in black, confronts an assembly of the pagan Emperor Maxentius and his counselors. She bravely ticks off arguments on her fingers why Christianity should be legalized. Her powerful delivery silences the crowd.

2. Under the rotunda of a pagan temple (above, on the upper left panel), Catherine, in blue, points up at a statue and tells a crowd of pagans, "Your gods are puny compared to mine."

3. Catherine, in blue (upper right panel, left side), is thrown in prison, where she's visited by the emperor's wife (in green). Catherine converts her.

4. Emperor Maxentius, enraged, orders his own wife killed. The executioner (upper panel, right side), standing next to the empress' decapitated corpse, impassively sheathes his sword.

5. In the most well-known scene (the middle panel on the bottom), Maxentius, in black, looks down from a balcony and condemns Catherine (in black) to be torn apart between two large, spiked wheels turned by executioners. But suddenly, an angel swoops in with a sword to cut her loose.

6. Catherine is eventually martyred (lower right panel). Now dressed in green, she kneels before the executioner, who raises his sword to finish the job.

7. Finally, on the top of holy Mount Sinai (lower right panel, upper right side), two angels bear Catherine's body to its final resting place.

Taking a few steps back, look up at the arch that frames the chapel, topped by the delightful Annunciation fresco (top of the arch) by Masolino. Also notice the big St. Christopher, patron saint of travelers (left pillar), with 500-year-old graffiti scratched in by pilgrims.

Lower Church—Fourth Century

Buy a €5 ticket in the bookshop, and descend 1,700 years to the time when Christians were razzed on their way to church by pagan neighbors. The first room you enter was the original atrium (entry hall)—the nave extends to the right. (Everything you'll visit from here on was buried until the 19th century.)

• *On the flippable stone in the atrium, look for the...*

Pagan Inscription

This two-sided recycled marble burial slab—one side (with leafy decorations) for a Christian, the other for a pagan (you can turn it)—shows how the two Romes lived side by side in the fourth century.

• *In the nave, five yards before the altar, on the left wall, look for the...*

Fresco of St. Clement and Sisinnius

Clement (center) holds a secret Mass for early Christians back when it was a capital crime. Theodora, a prominent Roman (in yellow, to the right), is one of the undercover faithful. Her pagan husband, Sisinnius, has come to retrieve and punish her when— zap!—he's struck blind and has to be led away (right side).

But Sisinnius is still unconvinced. When Clement cures his blindness, Sisinnius (very faded, lower panel, far right) orders two servants to drag Clement off to the authorities. But through a miraculous intervention, the servants mistake a column for Clement (see the shadowy black log) and drag that out of the house instead. The inscription (crossword-style on right, waist-high, very faded) is famous among Italians because it's one of the earliest examples of the transition from Latin to Italian. Sisinnius encourages his servants by yelling *"Fili dele pute, traite!"* ("You sons of bitches, pull!")

• *In the far left corner of the lower church (in the room behind the fresco you just saw), near the staircase leading down, is the...*

Presumed Burial Place of St. Cyril

Cyril, who died in A.D. 869 (see the modern, icon-like mosaic of him), was an inveterate traveler who spread Christianity to the Slavic lands and Russia—today's Russian Orthodox faithful. Along the way, he introduced the Cyrillic alphabet still used by Russians and many other Slavs.

Temple of Mithras (Mithreum)— Second Century

Now descend (through a door immediately to the right of the altar and down steps) farther to the dark, dank Mithraic Temple (Mithreum). Nowhere in Rome is there a better place to experience this weird cult.

• *The barred room to the left is the...*

Worship Hall

Worshippers of Mithras—men only—reclined on the benches on either side of the room. At the far end is a small statue of the god Mithras, in a billowing cape. In the center sits an altar carved with a relief showing Mithras fighting with a bull that contains all life. A scorpion, a dog, and a snake try to stop Mithras, but he wins, running his sword through the bull. The blood spills out, bringing life to the world.

Mithras' fans gathered here, in this tiny microcosm of the universe (the ceiling was decorated with stars), to celebrate the victory with a ritual meal. Every spring, Mithras brought new life again, and so they ritually kept track of the seasons—the four square shafts in the corners of the ceiling represent the seasons, the seven round ones were the great constellations. Initiates went through hazing rituals representing the darkness of this world, then emerged into the light-filled world brought by Mithras.

Rome's official pagan religion had no real spiritual content and did not offer any concept of salvation. As the empire slowly crumbled, people turned more and more to Eastern religions (including Christianity), in search of answers and comfort. The cult of Mithras, stressing loyalty and based on the tenuousness of life, was popular among soldiers. Part of its uniqueness and popularity (in this very class-conscious society) was due to its belief that all were equal before God. It dates back to the time of Alexander the Great, who brought it from Persia. In 67 B.C., soldiers who had survived the bloody conquest of Asia Minor returned to Rome swearing by Mithras. When Christians gained power, they banished the worship of Mithras.

Facing the barred room are two Corinthian columns supporting three arches of the temple's entryway, decorated with a fine stucco coffered ceiling. At the far end of the hallway, another barred door marks the equivalent of a Mithraic Sunday School room. Peeking inside, see a faded fresco of bearded Mithras (right wall) and seven niches carved into the walls representing the seven stages a novice had to go through. Exit signs direct you down. You'll pass a very narrow ancient alleyway separating Roman walls barely three feet across. Step into this and imagine the first Western city to reach one million. Forget the two churches above you, and imagine standing on this exact spot and looking up at the sky 2,000 years ago. Now climb back through the centuries to today's street level.

NIGHT WALK ACROSS ROME

From Campo de' Fiori to the Spanish Steps

Rome can be grueling. But taking an after-dark walk is a fine way to mix romance into all the history, enjoy the cool of the evening, and enliven everything with some of Europe's best people-watching. My favorite nighttime stroll laces together Rome's floodlit night-spots and fine urban spaces with real-life theater vignettes.

Even by day, this walk shows Rome at its most colorful, as it meanders through narrow streets and past important monuments. But, when the sun sets, unexpected magic happens.

Sitting so close to a Bernini fountain that traffic noises evaporate; jostling with local teenagers to see all the gelato flavors; observing lovers straddling more than the bench; jaywalking past *polizia* in flak-proof vests; and marveling at the ramshackle elegance that softens this brutal city for those who were born here and can imagine living nowhere else—these are the flavors of Rome best tasted after dark.

The Walk Begins

• *Start this mile-long walk at Campo de' Fiori, my favorite out-door dining room after dark (see page 346 in the Eating chapter). To lengthen this walk, you can start in Trastevere; see directions on page 73. Alternatively, this walk is equally pleasant in reverse order: You could ride the Metro to the Spanish Steps and finish at Campo de' Fiori, near many recommended restaurants.*

Campo de' Fiori

The center of the great, colorful square is marked with the statue of Giordano Bruno (see sidebar), an intellectual heretic who was burned on this spot in 1600. Bruno overlooks this "Field of Flowers," the site of a busy produce market in the morning and

Giordano Bruno
(1548–1600)

Lauded as a martyr to free thought and reviled as an intellectual con-man and heretic, the philosopher-priest Bruno has a legacy only a Roman could love. Details of his life are sketchy, and his writings range from the sublime to the ridiculous.

The young Dominican priest was nonconformist and outspoken from the start. He had to flee Italy to avoid a charge of heresy, and spent most of his adult life wandering Europe's capitals. In Geneva, he joined the Calvinists, until he was driven out for his unorthodox views. In London, he met with Queen Elizabeth, who found him subversive. In Germany, the Lutherans excommunicated him.

In his writings, Bruno claimed to have discovered the "Clavis Magna" (Great Key) to training the human memory. He published satirical plays tweaking Church morals. He advanced the still-heretical (Copernican) notion that the earth revolved around the sun, and speculated about other inhabited planets in the universe. All his works show a vast-ranging mind aware of the scientific trends of the day.

In 1593, Bruno was arrested by the Inquisition and sent to Rome, where he languished in prison for six years. (Tortured? Lost in bureaucracy? No one knows.) The exact charge against him remains debated by historians.

Bruno was sentenced to death by fire. He replied: "Perhaps you who pronounce this sentence are more fearful than I who receive it." On February 17, 1600, the civil authorities led him to the stake on Campo de' Fiori. As they lit the fire, he was offered a crucifix to hold. He pushed it away.

a favorite of strollers after sundown. This neighborhood is still known for its free spirit and occasional demonstrations. When the statue of Bruno was erected in 1889, local riots overcame Vatican protests against honoring a heretic. Bruno faces his nemesis, the Vatican Chancellory (the big white building just outside the far right corner of the square), while

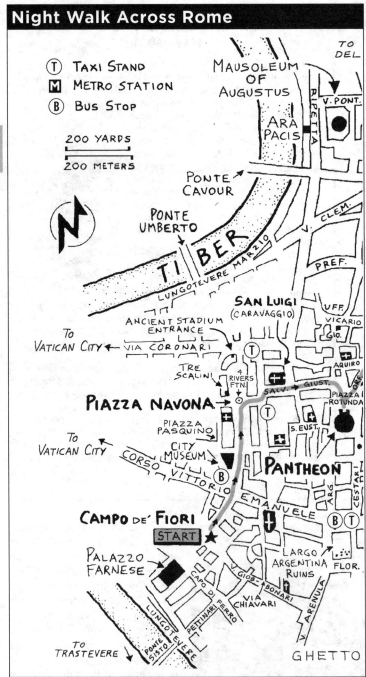

Night Walk Across Rome

(T) TAXI STAND
(M) METRO STATION
(B) BUS STOP

200 YARDS
200 METERS

N

MAUSOLEUM OF AUGUSTUS

ARA PACIS

TO DEL

V. PONT.

RIPETTA

V. CLEM.

PONTE CAVOUR

PONTE UMBERTO

TI BER

LUNGOTEVERE MARZIO

PREF.

SAN LUIGI (CARAVAGGIO)

UFF.

VICARIO

V. CORONARI

ANCIENT STADIUM ENTRANCE

To VATICAN CITY

(T)

AQUIRO

GIO.

TRE SCALINI

4 RIVERS FTN.

SALV. GIUST.

PIAZZA NAVONA

PIAZZA PASQUINO

PIAZZA ROTUNDA

(T)

S. EUST.

PANTHEON

To VATICAN CITY

CITY MUSEUM

(B)

CORSO VITTORIO

EMANUELE

ARG.

CESTARI

(B) (T)

CAMPO DE' FIORI

START

LARGO ARGENTINA RUINS

FLOR.

PALAZZO FARNESE

V. GIOB-

CAPO D FERRO

PETINARI FERRO

VIA CHIAVARI

BONARI

V. ARENULA

To TRASTEVERE

LUNGOTEVERE

PONTE SISTO

GHETTO

NIGHT WALK

his pedestal reads, "And the flames rose up." Check out the reliefs on the pedestal for scenes from Bruno's trial and execution.

At the east end of the square (behind Bruno), the ramshackle apartments are built right into the old outer wall of ancient Rome's mammoth Theater of Pompey. This entertainment complex covered several city blocks, stretching from here to Largo Argentina. Julius Caesar was assassinated in the Theater of Pompey, where the Senate was renting space.

The square is lined with and surrounded by fun eateries. Bruno faces the **Forno** (in the left corner of the square, closed Sun), a popular place for hot and tasty take-out *pizza bianco*. Step in, at least to observe the frenzy as pizza is sold hot out of the oven. You can order *un etto* (100 grams, an average serving) by pointing, then take your snack to the counter to pay. The many bars lining the square are fine for drinks and people-watching. Late at night on weekends, the place is packed with beer-drinking kids, turning what was once a charming medieval square into one vast Roman street party.

• *If Bruno did a hop, step, and jump forward, then turned right on Via dei Baullari and marched 200 yards, he'd cross the busy Corso Vittorio Emanuele; then, continuing another 150 yards on Via Cuccagna, he'd find...*

Piazza Navona

Rome's most interesting night scene features street music, artists, fire-eaters, local Casanovas, ice cream, fountains by Bernini, and outdoor cafés that are worthy of a splurge if you've got time to sit and enjoy Italy's human river.

This oblong square retains the shape of the original racetrack that was built around A.D. 80 by the emperor Domitian. (To see the ruins of the original entrance, exit the square at the far—or north—end, then take an immediate left, and look down to the left 25 feet below the current street level.) Since ancient times, the square has been a center of Roman life. In the 1800s, the city would flood the square to cool off the neighborhood.

The **Four Rivers Fountain** in the center is the most famous fountain by the man who remade Rome in Baroque style, Gian Lorenzo Bernini. Four burly river gods (representing the four continents that were known in 1650) support an Egyptian obelisk. The water of the world gushes everywhere. The Nile has his head covered, since the headwaters were unknown then. The Ganges holds an oar. The Danube turns to admire the obelisk, which Bernini had moved here from a stadium on the Appian Way. And Uruguay's Río de la Plata tumbles backward in shock, wondering how he ever made the top four. Bernini enlivens the fountain with horses plunging through the rocks and exotic flora and fauna from these newly discovered lands. Homesick Texans may want to find the armadillo. (It's the big, weird armorplated creature behind the Plata river statue.)

The Plata river god is gazing upward at the church of St. Agnes, worked on by Bernini's former student–turned-rival, Francesco Borromini. Borromini's concave facade helps reveal the dome and epitomizes the curved symmetry of Baroque. Tour guides say that Bernini designed his river god to look horrified at Borromini's work. Or maybe he's shielding his eyes from St. Agnes' nakedness, as she was stripped before being martyred. But either explanation is unlikely, since the fountain was completed two years before Borromini even started work on the church.

• *Leave Piazza Navona directly across from Tre Scalini (famous for its rich chocolate ice cream), and go east down Corsia Agonale, past rose peddlers and palm readers. Jog left around the guarded building (where Italy's senate meets), and follow the brown sign to the Pantheon, which is straight down Via del Salvatore.*

The Pantheon

Sit for a while under the floodlit and moonlit portico of the Pantheon.

The 40-foot single-piece granite columns of the Pantheon's entrance show the scale the ancient Romans built on. The columns support a triangular Greek-style roof with an inscription that says "M. Agrippa" built it. In fact, it was built *(fecit)* by Emperor Hadrian

Egyptian Obelisks

Rome has 13 obelisks, more than any other city in the world. In Egypt, they were connected with the sun god Ra (like

stone sun rays) and the power of the pharaohs. The ancient Romans, keen on exotic novelty and sheer size, brought the obelisks here and set them up in key public places as evidence and celebration of their occupation of Egypt. Starting from the 1580s, Rome's new rulers—the popes—relocated the obelisks, often topping them with Christian crosses so they came to acquire yet another significance that guaranteed their survival: the triumph of Christianity over all other religions.

The tallest (105 feet) and the most ancient (16th century B.C.) is the one by San Giovanni in Laterano. It once stood in the Circus Maximus next to its sister, which now marks the center of Piazza del Popolo.

The obelisks were carved out of single blocks of granite. Imagine the work, with only man and horsepower, first to quarry them and set them up in Egypt, then—after the Romans came along—to roll them on logs to the river or the coast, sail (or row) them in special barges across the Mediterranean and up the Tiber, and finally hoist them up.

Rome wasn't above cheap imitations, however: A couple of the obelisks are ancient Roman copies. The one at the top of the Spanish Steps has spelling mistakes in the hieroglyphics.

(A.D. 120), who gave credit to the builder of an earlier structure. This impressive entranceway gives no clue that the greatest wonder of the building is inside—a domed room that inspired later domes, including Michelangelo's St. Peter's and Brunelleschi's Duomo (in Florence).

For more information, ✪ see the Pantheon Tour chapter.

• *With your back to the Pantheon, veer to the right, uphill toward the yellow sign that reads* Casa del Caffè *at the Tazza d'Oro coffee shop on Via Orfani.*

From the Pantheon to Piazza Colonna

Tazza d'Oro Casa del Caffè, one of Rome's top coffee shops, dates back to the days when this area was licensed to roast coffee beans. Locals come here for its fine *granita di caffè con panna* (coffee slush with cream).

• *Continue up Via Orfani to...*

Piazza Capranica is home to the big, plain Florentine Renaissance–style Palazzo Capranica (directly opposite as you enter the square). Big shots, like the Capranica family, built towers on their palaces—not for any military use, but just to show off.

• *Leave the piazza to the right of the palace, heading down Via in Aquiro.*

The street Via in Aquiro leads to a sixth-century B.C. **Egyptian obelisk** taken as a trophy by Augustus after his victory in Egypt over Mark Antony and Cleopatra. The obelisk was set up as a sundial. Walk the zodiac markings to the well-guarded front door. This is Italy's **parliament building**, where the lower house meets, and you may see politicians, political demonstrations, and TV cameras.

• *To your right is Piazza Colonna, where we're heading next—unless you like gelato...*

A two-block detour to the left (past Albergo Nazionale) brings you to Rome's most famous *gelateria*. **Giolitti's** is cheap for take-out or elegant and splurge-worthy for a sit among classy locals (open daily until past midnight, Via Uffici del Vicario 40); get your gelato in a cone *(cono)* or cup *(coppetta)*.

Piazza Colonna features a huge second-century column. Its reliefs depict the victories of Emperor Marcus Aurelius over the barbarians. When Marcus died in A.D. 180, the barbarians began to get the upper hand, beginning Rome's long three-century fall. The big, important-looking palace houses the headquarters for the deputies (or cabinet) of the prime minister.

Noisy **Via del Corso** is Rome's main north-south boulevard. It's named for the Berber horse races—without riders—that took place here during Carnevale. This wild tradition continued until the late 1800s, when a series of fatal accidents (including, reportedly, one in front of Queen Margherita) led to its cancellation. Historically the street was filled with meat shops. When it became one of Rome's first gas-lit streets in 1854, these butcher shops were banned and replaced by classier boutiques, jewelers, and antiques dealers.

Nowadays most of Via del Corso is closed to traffic for a few hours every evening and becomes a wonderful parade of Romans out for a stroll (see the "Dolce Vita Stroll" in the Nightlife chapter).

• *Cross Via del Corso to enter a big palatial building with columns, which houses the Galleria del Sordi shopping mall. Inside, take the fork to the right and exit out the back. (If you're here after 22:00, when the mall is closed, circle around the right side of the Galleria on Via dei Sabini.) Once out the back, head up Via de Crociferi, to the roar of the water, lights, and people of...*

The Trevi Fountain

The Trevi Fountain shows how Rome took full advantage of the abundance of water brought into the city by its great aqueducts. This watery Baroque avalanche by Nicola Salvi was completed in 1762. Salvi used the palace behind the fountain as a theatrical back-

drop for the figure of "Ocean," who represents water in every form. The statue surfs through his wet kingdom—with water gushing from 24 spouts and tumbling over 30 different kinds of plants—while Triton blows his conch shell.

The magic of the square is enhanced by the fact that no streets directly approach it. You can hear the excitement as you approach, and then—*bam!*—you're there. The scene is always lively, with lucky Romeos clutching dates while unlucky ones clutch beers. Romantics toss a coin over their shoulder, thinking it will give them a wish and assure their return to Rome. That may sound silly, but every year I go through this tourist ritual...and it actually seems to work.

Take some time to people-watch (whisper a few breathy *bellos* or *bellas*) before leaving. There's a peaceful zone at water level on the far right.

• *From the Trevi Fountain, we're 10 minutes from our next stop, the Spanish Steps. Just use a map to get there, or follow these directions: Facing the Trevi Fountain, go forward, walking along the right side of the fountain on Via della Stamperia. Cross the busy Via del Tritone. Continue 100 yards and veer right at Via delle Fratte, a street that changes its name to Via Propaganda before ending at...*

The Spanish Steps

Piazza di Spagna, with the very popular Spanish Steps, is named for the Spanish Embassy to the Vatican, which has been here for

300 years. It's been the hangout of many Romantics over the years (Keats, Wagner, Openshaw, Goethe, and others). In the 1700s, British aristocrats on the "Grand Tour" of Europe came here to ponder Rome's decay. The British poet John Keats pondered his mortality, then died of tuberculosis at age 25 in the pink building on the right side of the steps. Fellow Romantic Lord Byron lived across the square at #66.

The Sinking Boat Fountain at the foot of the steps, built by Bernini or his father, Pietro, is powered by an aqueduct. Actually, all of Rome's fountains are aqueduct-powered; their spurts are determined by the water pressure provided by the various aqueducts. This one, for instance, is much weaker than Trevi's gush.

The piazza is a thriving night scene. It's clear that the main sight here is not the famous steps, but the people who sit on them. Window-shop along Via Condotti, which stretches away from the steps. This is where Gucci and other big names cater to the trendsetting jet set. Facing the Spanish Steps, you can walk right, about a block, to tour one of the world's biggest and most lavish McDonald's (salad bar, WC).

• *Our walk is finished. If you'd like to reach the top of the steps sweat-free, there's a free elevator just outside the Spagna Metro stop (elevator closes at 21:00; Metro stop is to the left of the Spanish Steps). Afterward, you can zip home on the Metro (usually open until 22:00) or grab a taxi at either the north or south side of the piazza.*

TRASTEVERE WALK

From the Tiber to the Church of Santa Maria in Trastevere

Trastevere—the colorful neighborhood across the river from downtown—is *the* place to immerse yourself in the crustier side of Rome. This half-mile walk is designed to train your eye to see Rome more intimately. You'll discover a secret, hidden city of heroic young martyrs, lovers kissing on Vespas, party-loving Renaissance bankers, and feisty "Trasteverini"—old-timers who pride themselves on never setting foot on the opposite bank of the Tiber River.

Orientation

Getting There: Trastevere (trahs-TAY-veh-ray) is on the west side of the Tiber River, south of Vatican City and across the river from the Forum and Capitol Hill area. To get there by foot from Capitol Hill, cross the Tiber on Ponte Cestio (which goes over Isola Tiberina). You can also reach it on tram #8 from Largo Argentina, or on express bus #H from Termini train station and Via Nazionale; if taking either of these, get off at Piazza Belli, just after crossing the Tiber. From the Vatican (Piazza del Risorgimento), take bus #23 or #271.

Church of St. Cecilia: Free, Mon–Sat 9:30–13:00 & 16:00–18:30, Sun 11:30–12:30 & 16:00–18:30; crypt-€2.50; loft with frescoes-€2.50, may be open only in the morning, ask the nuns to open the door.

Church of Santa Maria in Trastevere: Free, daily 7:30–21:00.

Villa Farnesina: €5; April–June and mid-Sept–Oct Mon–Sat 9:00–16:00, closed Sun; July–mid-Sept and Nov–March Mon–Sat 9:00–13:00, closed Sun.

Audio Tour: You can download a free audio version of this walk at www.ricksteves.com or from iTunes (search for "Rick Steves Audio Tours").

When to Go: This walk can work well at any time of day. Mornings are cool and relatively quiet. Note that many churches are closed at midday, and Villa Farnesina closes as early as 13:00 (and as late as 16:00). Strolling through Trastevere at dusk is especially atmospheric. Consider combining this walk with a meal—several recommended restaurants are on the map and described in the Eating chapter. This walk can be a prelude to the ❂ Night Walk Across Rome described in the previous chapter.

The Walk Begins

• *Start halfway across the Ponte Cestio (Cestius Bridge)—called the "Ponte Fabricio" on the east side of the river—which connects Isola Tiberina ("Island in the Tiber") to Trastevere.*

Isola Tiberina and the Tiber River

Rome got its start 3,000 years ago along the Tiber River at this point. This was as far upstream as big boats could sail and the first place the river could be crossed by bridge. As a center of river trade, Rome connected the interior of the Italian peninsula with the Mediterranean. The area below you would have been bustling in ancient times. Look down and imagine small ports, water mills, ramshackle boats, and platforms for fishing.

The island itself was once the site of a temple dedicated to Asclepius, the god of medicine. Ancient Romans who were ill spent the night here and left little statues of their healed body parts (feet, livers, hearts...) as thank-you notes. This tradition survives: Today, throughout Italy, Catholic altars are often encrusted with votive offerings, symbolizing gratitude for answered prayers. During plagues and epidemics, the sick were isolated on the island. These days, the island's largest building is the Fatebenefratelli, the public hospital favored by Roman women for childbirth. The island's reputation for medical care lives on.

The high point of the bridge (upon which you're probably leaning) is an ancient stone with a faded inscription dating from about A.D. 370, when this then-400-year-old bridge was rebuilt. The eroding plaque is stapled into the balustrade like a piece of recycled scrap. Run your fingers over the word "Caesar" (top line, just right of center). This part of the Tiber River flooded frequently, which

Trastevere Walk

Walk

❶ Ponte Cestio & Isola Tiberina
❷ Piazza in Piscinula
❸ Church of St. Cecilia
❹ Church of Santa Maria in Trastevere

Hotel/Restaurants

❺ Hotel Santa Maria
❻ Residenza Arco dei Tolomei & Arco del Lauro B&B
❼ Relais le Clarisse
❽ Casa San Giuseppe
❾ Trattoria da Lucia
❿ Trattoria da Olindo
⓫ Dar Poeta Pizzeria
⓬ Osteria Ponte Sisto da Oliviero
⓭ Ristorante Checco er Carettiere
⓮ Pizzeria "Ai Marmi"
⓯ To Cantina Paradiso
⓰ Gelateria alla Scala

unfortunately made the land on the north bank the ideal location for the medieval Jewish ghetto (now long gone, but Rome's synagogue remains—❶ see Jewish Ghetto Walk, next chapter).

In the 1870s, the Romans removed the threat of flooding by practically walling off the Tiber, building the tall, anonymous embankments that continue to isolate the river from the city today.

• *Head south to leave the bridge. The green riverside Sora Mirella kiosk on the right (if it's open) is the most famous vendor of Rome's summer refresher called a* grattachecca *(pronounced grah-tah-kek-kah, €4), a concoction of shaved ice with fruit-flavored syrup and chopped fruit (similar to an American granita). Cross the street and go down the steps into the car-filled piazza.*

Piazza in Piscinula

This square is famous for its church bell tower (the cute little thing directly across from the bridge); dating from 1069, it's the oldest working one in the city. Study the brown building on the riverside and spot faint traces of Renaissance decoration. Today's earth-tone shades of the city echo this original Roman brown.

• *Facing the tower, exit the square from the far right corner, opposite where you entered, going uphill on Via dell'Arco de' Tolomei.*

Trastevere Back Lanes

Look up and directly ahead to the top of the hill to see the elegantly restored, freshly painted tower sandwiched between apartments. In medieval times, the city skyline had 300 of these towers (about 50 survive). Each noble family competed for the tallest one until, in about 1250, city authorities got fed up and had them all lopped off. Later—mainly Baroque—construction incorporated most of the remaining "stumps," and you can still see these remnants of medieval Rome all over the old center. Incorporating old structures into new ones was always considered more economical and practical than demolishing and starting again from scratch. In the Middle Ages, Rome had regressed to being a big village; any idea of town planning was lost until the Renaissance.

Notice the plants spilling over the many rooftop terraces—the Roman equivalent of a leafy backyard. An *attico con terrazzo* (penthouse with a terrace) is every Roman's dream.

Continue on, walking under the low arch. Lots of aristocratic buildings were connected by these elevated passages. Imagine herds of sheep shuffling through here in medieval times while smoke billowed from the windows and doors of homes that lacked chimneys.

Turn left and walk along Via dei Salumi ("Cold Cuts Street"). Because of its vicinity to the river, Trastevere was always a commercial neighborhood, and many of its alleys were named after businesses based here. The streets—rarely paved—were clogged by shop stalls.

The red-brown building on your right (pretty ugly unless you're a fascist) is a school from the Mussolini era. The fascist leader believed in the classical motto *mens sana in corpore sano* ("a healthy mind in a healthy body"), and loved being seen fencing, boxing, swimming, and riding. He endowed school buildings with lots of gyms.

After passing the school, turn right again, heading up Vicolo dell'Atleta ("Alley of the Athlete"). Check out the latest fashions in underwear hanging out to dry. Apartments in Rome tend to be quite small, and electricity is more expensive than in the US, so few have clothes dryers.

Strolling here, you'll understand why the Italian language has no word for "privacy" (they use our word and roll the *r*). Reading a letter on the Metro attracts a crowd. If someone has a fight (or a particularly good orgasm), the entire neighborhood knows. Young lovers with no place to go are adept at riding *motorini*...while parked.

All around, ancient fragments are recycled ingloriously into medieval buildings. Halfway down the alley on the right is a restaurant that, a thousand years ago, was a synagogue. Find the Hebrew faintly inscribed on the base of the columns of the exposed brick structure. A large part of Rome's Jewish community, the most ancient outside Palestine, lived in Trastevere until the popes moved them into the ghetto on the other side of the river in the 1500s.

• *Continue, turning left on Via dei Genovesi, then right on Via di Santa Cecilia to reach Piazza di Santa Cecilia. Enter the convent courtyard of the church, sit by the fountain, and take a moment to enjoy the peace and quiet.*

Church of St. Cecilia

Trastevere has many early Christian churches like St. Cecilia. This is because in the second and third centuries, a large community

of foreigners lived here, including early Christians from Greece and Judaea, who introduced their cultures and religions to the neighborhood.

Notice the church's eclectic exterior. Its mismatched columns were recycled from pagan temples. The typical medieval bell tower sports an 18th-century facade. This church, dedicated to Cecilia, patron saint of musicians and singers, is popular for weddings. Of Rome's 40 medieval churches, many have two-year waiting lists for weekend weddings. While most young Roman couples favor the more sober elegance of medieval churches over Baroque (usually dismissed as *troppo pesante*—"too heavy"), the typical Italian wedding gowns are far from understated.

Inside the church, find the statue of St. Cecilia by Stefano Maderno (in the case below the altar). A Christian convert from a wealthy family in a time of persecution, Cecilia revealed her faith to her pagan husband on their wedding night and told him of her aspiration to remain chaste (uh-oh...). An angel appeared to reason with the frustrated groom. Once converted, he devoted himself to carrying out Christian burials in the catacombs, until he himself was killed. Cecilia was soon condemned as well. The Romans, who tried unsuccessfully for three days to suffocate her with steam in her bath to make it appear accidental, finally lost patience and beheaded her. Cecilia bequeathed her house to the neighborhood community, and this spot has been a place of worship ever since.

In the days when Christianity was illegal, wealthy converts hosted Mass for the local community in their homes. When Christians were finally allowed to build churches, they often did so on the sites of these homes for the sake of continuity. While the Church of St. Cecilia originated in the third century, what we see today was built in the ninth century and extensively restored in the 18th century.

Viewing Maderno's statue of Cecilia, remember that during the Catholic Counter-Reformation, art charged with great emotional impact was used to enhance faith. The new appetite for relics led to a search for Cecilia's remains. When her tomb was opened, Maderno was present and claimed, along with other bystanders, to have seen her body perfectly preserved for an unforgettable instant before it turned to dust. He created this touching statue from his memory of that scene. Cecilia lies with her face turned and hidden, the violence of her death suggested only by the gash in her neck, the position of her fingers indicating the oneness of the Trinity. (Like Italians today, she counted starting with her thumb.)

The canopy above the altar, dating from the 1200s, represents an innovative fusion of Roman and French Gothic architecture and sculpture, showing that the artist (Arnolfo di Cambio) knew his classics and had also been to Paris.

The mosaic in the apse dates from the ninth century. Pope Paschal (on the left), who built the church, holds a little model of it in his hands. His square halo signifies that he was alive when the mosaic was made. His small head suggests he was less important than the others in the scene.

If you visit mid-morning, you have two options before leaving: Go downstairs to see the crypt, which contains the ancient remains of Cecilia's house, or go upstairs to the loft to view fancy frescoes. Cecilia's house is pretty bare, but it does have some early Christian iconography, original mosaic floors, and grain storage bins (follow sign to *crypt*, €2.50).

In the loft, where cloistered nuns would view the Mass while hidden behind a screen, are some extraordinary frescoes of angels painted by Pietro Cavallini, a contemporary of Giotto (c. 1300). Scholars debate who influenced whom: Giotto or Cavallini. But there's no debate that the art here shows cutting-edge realism in the expressive faces of angels who sit believably in their chairs (loft-€2.50; may be open only in the morning, you'll need to ask the nuns to open the door on the left side of the facade). If you're here at 18:00 on a Saturday, you're welcome to read the Lectio Divina with the nuns.

• *Leaving the church, backtrack left, take the first left onto Via de Genovesi, and hike straight ahead to where it meets a busy street.*

Viale Trastevere to Piazza Santa Maria

The wide, modern boulevard called Viale Trastevere bisects Trastevere, which was otherwise spared most of the demolishing and rebuilding suffered by other traditional neighborhoods when Rome became the capital of united Italy in 1870. Cross to the other side of Viale Trastevere and turn right, then left into Largo San Giovanni de Matha. Pass by the TI and the textbook Baroque facade of the faded yellow church and continue to Via Lungaretta. You'll notice a change in atmosphere—the quiet, mystical charm of the first part of your walk has given way to livelier, more colorful, more touristy (and higher-rent) surroundings. Look up. Now, along with underwear...you see art. Walk to the big square and sit down on the fountain steps.

Piazza Santa Maria in Trastevere

You're in the heart of the neighborhood. Piazza Santa Maria is the district's most important meeting place. The 17th-century fountain was actually designed to be the "sofa" of the neighborhood with its broad and inviting steps. During major soccer games, a large screen is set up here so that everybody can share in the tension and excitement. At other times, children gather here with a ball and improvise matches of their own. For more on soccer, see the sidebar on the next page.

• *Dominating the square is the...*

Church of Santa Maria in Trastevere

One of Rome's oldest churches, this was built on the site of a home where early Christians worshipped illegally until the year 312. It

was made a basilica—the first church dedicated to the Virgin Mary—in the fourth century, when Christianity was legalized (free, daily 7:30–21:00). The tower survives from the 12th-century church. The portico (covered area just outside the door) is decorated with ancient fragments filled with early Christian symbolism. Many of these stones were lids to burial niches from catacombs. Notice how early Christians prayed as evangelical Christians do today.

Step inside. Immediately to the left of the entry, a plaque on the wall is dedicated to "Olea Sancta." The "holy oil" was actually a small petroleum deposit discovered here in 30 B.C. This black

Soccer: The National Obsession

One of Rome's most local "sights" is a soccer match. Winston Churchill said that Italians lose wars like soccer matches and soccer matches like wars; soccer, or *calcio,* is the national obsession. Everyone, regardless of age or social class, is an expert, quick with an opinion on a coach's lousy decision or a referee's unprofessional conduct. Fans love to insult officials: A favorite is *"arbitro cornuto!"*—the referee is a cuckold (i.e., his wife sleeps around). The country's obsession turned into jubilation on July 9, 2006, when Italy won the World Cup, and Rome—along with every other city, town, and village in Italy—went crazy with joy.

Rome has a special passion for soccer. It has two teams, Roma (representing the city) and Lazio (the region), and the rivalry is fanatic. When Romans are introduced, they ask each other, *"Laziale o romanista?"* The answer can compromise a relationship. Both Roma (jersey: yellow and red; symbol: she-wolf) and Lazio (jersey: light blue and white; symbol: imperial eagle) claim to be truly Roman. Lazio is older (founded in 1900), but Roma has more supporters. Lazio is supposed to be more upper-class, Roma more popular, but the social division is blurred.

liquid was almost magical in its ability to power lamps and was incorporated into the lore of this church.

Grab a pew. Most of what you see dates from around the 12th century, although the granite columns are from ancient Roman buildings. Later architects tried hard to match them, but notice how the shorter columns have taller bases and how the capitals are mismatched. (Some have tiny pagan heads of Egyptian gods.) The ancient basilica floor plan (and ambience) survives. The intricate coffered ceiling has an unusual image of Mary painted on copper at the center.

Step up behind the main altar (left side) for a closer look at the fine mosaic work. Pop a coin in the box for light. The central scene is one of the few surviving examples of an early medieval mosaic (8th to 10th century) in Rome. It's rich in symbolism. Christ is flanked by the first two

The most eagerly awaited sporting event of the year is the derby, when the two teams fight it out at the Olympic Stadium. All of Italy acknowledges that team spirit is most fervent in Rome. Fans prepare months in advance, and on the day of the match they fill the entire stadium with team colors, flags, banners, and smoke candles.

Witty slogans on banners work like dialogues: A Roma banner proclaimed, "Roma: Only the sky is higher than you." The Lazio banner replied, "In fact, the sky is blue and white" (like its team colors). The exchange revealed that there had been a Lazio informer on the Roma side, which traumatized Roma fans

for weeks. Tourists go to a match more for the action in the stands than the action on the field—it's one of the most Roman of all experiences.

Both teams call the Stadio Olimpico home, so you can catch a game most weekends from September to May (Metro line A to Flaminio, then catch tram #2 to the end of the line, Piazza Mancini, and cross the bridge to the stadium). If you're coming from Termini train station, take bus #910; from the Vatican, take bus #32 from Piazza Risorgimento.

popes. Notice the stature Mary is given. Tour guides claim this is the first mosaic to show her at the throne with Jesus in heaven. He has his arm around his mother as if introducing her to us. Sitting below Jesus, Mary, and the popes is the throne-like chair of the bishop, giving legitimacy to the Church leadership. The flock of sheep is not just any flock—it represents Jesus in the middle (marked by a halo with a cross in it) and the 12 apostles.

The more "modern" mosaic panels show scenes from the life of Mary. These mosaics from the 1300s (by Cavallini) are impressively realistic and expressive, yet predate the Renaissance by a hundred years. The first of six panels (to the left of the curved apse) shows the birth of Mary. A servant in the corner checks the temperature of the water with her hand before she bathes the baby, introducing an element of tenderness that breaks the abstract rigidity of medieval art. Next comes the angel announcing Jesus' coming to Mary, Jesus' birth, the adoration of the Magi, the presentation of Jesus in the temple, and Mary's eternal sleep (not death). The gold mosaic backgrounds show buildings that, while still unrealistic, are a good step toward accurate 3-D representation.

The incredibly expensive 13th-century floor is a fine example of Cosmati mosaic work—a style of mosaic featuring intricate geometric shapes (in this case, made with marble scavenged from Roman ruins).

As you leave, spend a moment with St. Anthony (in the back corner, opposite the entry). He was a favorite of the poor and is inundated with prayer requests on scraps of paper. The Community of St. Egidio operates from this church. They feed the local poor and care for young drug addicts. Each Christmas they take out all the pews, move in tables and chairs, and put on a huge dinner for those in need.

Tour Over

From here, enjoy simply exploring Rome's most colorful district. Saunter around the streets to the left of the church as you leave. The farther you venture from the square, the less touristy and more rustic the neighborhood becomes. Wandering the back lanes and pondering the earthy enthusiasm people seem to have for life here, I can imagine that bygone day when proud Trastevere locals would brag that they never crossed the river.

To cap off your Trastevere stroll with one more sight, consider visiting **Villa Farnesina,** a Renaissance villa decorated by Raphael (see the description and self-guided tour on page 74). To get there, face the Church of Santa Maria in Trastevere and leave the piazza by walking along the right side of the church, following Via della Paglia to Piazza di S. Egidio. Exit the piazza near the church and you'll be on Via della Scala. Follow through the Porta Settimiana, where it changes names to Via della Lungara. On your right, you'll pass John Cabot University. Look for a white arch that reads Accademia dei Lincei. The villa is through this gate.

If you're in the mood to extend this walk, head to the river, cross the pedestrian bridge, Ponte Sisto, and make your way to Campo de' Fiori where the **Night Walk Across Rome** begins (see that chapter for details).

JEWISH GHETTO WALK

North Bank of the Tiber

For centuries, Rome's Jewish ghetto has been the site of both relentless persecution and the undying pride and solidarity of a tight-knit community. Built in 1555 on the banks of a frequently flooded bend of the Tiber River, the ghetto was the forced home of the Roman Jewish population for more than 300 years, between the Counter-Reformation (16th century) and Italian unification (1870). Though most of the old ghetto has been torn down, you can still find a few reminders of the Roman Jews' storied past and lively present.

Orientation

Getting There: The Jewish ghetto was—and Rome's main synagogue still is—on the east bank of the Tiber, near the Isola Tiberina ("Island in the Tiber") and the ancient ruins of the Theater of Marcellus (Teatro di Marcello). It's a three-minute walk from Largo Argentina.

When to Go: If you want to visit the synagogue and museum, avoid this walk on a Saturday, when they're closed.

Synagogue and Jewish Museum: €7.50 ticket includes both; June–Sept Sun–Thu 10:00–19:00, Fri 10:00–16:00, closed Sat; Oct–May Sun–Thu 10:00–17:00, Fri 9:00–14:00, closed Sat; last entrance 45 minutes before closing; on Lungotevere dei Cenci, tel. 06-6840-0661, www.museoebraico.roma.it. Modest dress is required. The only way to visit the synagogue (if you're not there for a prayer service) is with an hourly **tour** (included in admission, English tours usually at :15 past the hour, 30 minutes, check schedule at ticket counter).

Walking Tour: The museum conducts walking tours of the Jewish Ghetto at least once a day Sun–Fri (€8, usually at 13:15, no tours on Sat). Ask for the schedule at the museum entry and sign up at least 30 minutes prior to the tour departure time (minimum of three required).

Local Guide: Micaela Pavoncello is uniquely equipped to guide visitors through the neighborhood that her family has lived in since ancient Roman times (€130/2 hours, ask for Ghetto Tour, tel. 328-863-8128, www.jewishroma.com, info@jewish roma.com).

Audio Tour: You can download a free audio tour of this walk at www.ricksteves.com (or search for "Rick Steves Audio Tours" in iTunes).

Cuisine Art: One of the stops near the end of this tour is at a Jewish bakery. A restaurant is nearby: **Sora Margherita Associazione Culturale,** offering traditional Roman and Jewish fare, hides without a sign on a square a block from the end of this tour (closed Mon except in winter when it's closed Sat–Sun instead, Piazza delle Cinque Scole 30; see page 346 in the Eating chapter).

History

Today, of Italy's 35,000 Jews, nearly half call Rome home. Jews here have a uniquely Roman style of worship, and even preserve remnants of their own Judaic-Roman dialect.

That's because, unlike most of the world's Jewish people, Roman Jews are neither Sephardic (descended from Spain) nor Ashkenazi (descended from Eastern Europe). Italy's Jews came directly from the Holy Land before the Diaspora, first arriving in Rome in the second century B.C. as esteemed envoys (hoping to establish business ties), and then, after Rome invaded Judaea in the first century A.D., as POWs sold into slavery. These first Jews lived, like other foreigners, outside the city—across the river, in Trastevere.

Julius Caesar favored the Jews because they were well-networked throughout the empire, and they didn't push their religion on others. As Christianity enveloped Rome and the pope became literally the king of Rome's Jews, the Jews experienced discrimination, with laws intended to limit the spread of Judaism (e.g., no proselytizing, no new synagogues, no intermarriage). The severity of these laws varied from pope to pope. Through most of the Middle Ages, Rome's Jews prospered and were often held in high regard as physicians, businessmen, and confidants of popes. The community in Trastevere was even allowed to spill across to the opposite bank of the Tiber.

In the Ghetto

The word "ghetto" is Italian, first used in Venice in the 1600s to describe the part of town where Jews lived—near the copper foundry (*geto* was the word for foundry). Initially the term meant only Jewish neighborhoods, but as the word spread through Europe and beyond, it was used generically to mean any neighborhood where a single ethnic group is segregated.

Starting in the eighth century, anti-Semitism began increasing throughout Europe. Then, in 1492, all of Spain's Jews were either baptized or expelled, with similar decrees following in other European countries. Rome's Jewish population doubled, swelling with refugees. By the 1500s, the Catholic Counter-Reformation—begun to combat rising Protestantism—turned its attention to anything deemed a "heresy" or simply not Catholic, including Judaism. In 1555, Pope Paul IV forcibly moved all of Rome's Jews into the undesirable flood zone inside the bend of the Tiber River, creating a ghetto of some 4,000 Jews packed into a miserable seven acres of mucky land. There they lived—in cramped conditions, behind a wall, with a curfew—for three centuries. They could go out by day, but had to return before the gates were locked at night. Jews were forced to wear yellow scarves and caps, and were prohibited from owning property or holding good jobs. During Carnevale (Mardi Gras), they were forced to parade down Via del Corso while Christians lined the streets and shouted insults. Through this long stretch of oppression, the synagogue was the only place Jews could feel respected and dignified. It's no wonder such loving attention was given to the Jewish tools of worship.

Rome's Jews enjoyed a little boost in freedom when Napoleon occupied the city (1805–1814) and after the ghetto walls were torn down in 1848. But it was only after Italian unification in 1870—when a secular government replaced the religious rule of the Vatican—that the ghetto's inhabitants were granted full rights and citizenship. When Rome became the country's capital, the city—ashamed of its shoddy Jewish quarter—destroyed the old ghetto and modernized the district, giving it the street plan we see today.

Then came the rise of fascism. Even though Mussolini wasn't rabidly anti-Semitic, he instituted a slew of anti-Jewish laws as he allied himself more strongly with Hitler. When Mussolini was deposed and the Nazis occupied Rome late in the war, the ghetto community was suddenly in even greater danger. Of the 13,000

Jewish Ghetto Walk

TO PANTHEON

LARGO ARGENTINA

VIA D. BOTTEGHE OSCURE

N

100 YARDS

100 METERS

PIAZZA MATTEI

TURTLE FOUNTAIN

PIAZZA COSTAGUTI

VIA DEI FUNARI

END

VIA SAN AMBROGIO

VIA ARENULA

S.M. PIANTO

Jewish BAKERIES

School

CATALANA

PIAZZA DELLE CINQUE SCOLE

TEMPIO

SYNAGOGUE & MUSEUM

VIA REGINELLA

VIA DEL PORTICO D'OTTAVIA

S. ANG. PESCH.

TRIB. CAMP.

SANT' ANGELO

PISCARIO

TEATRO DI MARCELLO

VIA D. TEATRO MARCELLO

TO CAPITOL HILL & FORUM

LUNGOTEVERE DEI CENCI

TIBER

ISOLA TIBERINA Hospital

PONTE FABRICIO

START

PIERLEONI

RIVER

LUNGO D. ANGUILLARA

PONTE CESTIO

TRASTEVERE

PONTE ROTTO

DCH

① Ponte Fabricio
② Synagogue & Jewish Museum
③ Santa Maria della Pietà
④ Largo 16 Ottobre 1943
⑤ Portico d'Ottavia
⑥ Via del Portico d'Ottavia
⑦ Turtle Fountain
⑧ Carmelite Convent
⑨ Hotel Arenula
⑩ Sora Margherita Assoc. Culturale (Eatery)

JEWISH GHETTO WALK

ghetto-dwellers, 2,000 were sent off to concentration camps. Only a handful came back.

A measure of healing and reconciliation came with Pope John Paul II, who took a special interest in fostering relations with the Jewish community. It was the late pope who finally acknowledged that the Church should have intervened more forcefully to defend the Jews during the Holocaust. He was also the first pope in history to enter a synagogue (here in this neighborhood in 1986—described later on this walk). In his last letter, John Paul II thanked Rome's emeritus rabbi for allowing him to initiate this Catholic-Jewish rapprochement he felt was so long overdue. In 2010, Pope Benedict followed up with a visit here, where he also condemned the persecutions of the past.

The Walk Begins

• *Start at the north end of Ponte Fabricio, which connects central Rome with the Isola Tiberina and the neighborhood of Trastevere. You'll see the big synagogue with its square dome. The former ghetto consists of the synagogue and the several blocks behind it.*

Ponte Fabricio
Ponte Fabricio is nicknamed Ponte Quattro Capi ("Bridge of the Four Heads") for its statues of the four-faced pagan god Janus. In ancient times, it was called Pons Judaeocum ("Jews' Bridge") because foreigners, immigrants, and Jews—who weren't allowed to live in central Rome—would commute across this bridge to get into town. Some 30,000 Jews once lived in a thriving community in Trastevere. Look down at the river. The embankment was only built in the late-19th century. Before then, this was the worst flood zone along the Roman riverbank—just right for a ghetto for the politically powerless.
• *With your back to the river, at your left is the...*

Synagogue (Sinagoga) and
Jewish Museum (Museo Ebraico)
In the 16th century, when Pope Paul IV forced the Jews to reside within a walled ghetto, the center was this synagogue. When Italy became unified in 1870, the ghetto was essentially demolished, replaced with the modern blocks you see today.

The Jews were initially offered better real estate for their synagogue, but chose instead to rebuild here, on the original site. This new "Synagogue of Emancipation" was built in a remarkable three years (completed 1904) with the enthusiastic support of the entire Roman community. This is where Pope John Paul II made his historic visit in 1986.

Enter the synagogue via the main door on the riverside. The admission price includes the museum entrance and a guided synagogue visit.

Inside the synagogue, take in the impressive dome, which is square to distinguish it from a Christian church. Ponder the inside of the dome, painted with the colors of the rainbow—symbolic of God's promise to Noah that there would be no more floods. The stars on the ceiling recall God's pledge that Abraham's descendants would flourish and be as many as the stars in the sky. As there were no Jewish architects and no models to study when it was built, this churchlike synagogue is Art Nouveau with a dash of Tiffany. The sandy color tones are a reminder of the community's desert heritage.

The museum shows off historically significant artifacts described in English. You'll see second-century B.C. reliefs with Jewish symbols, finely worked Judaica (religious items), and other relics of the Jewish past. As the Jews were not allowed to be craftsmen during the ghetto period, they had to commission many of the pieces you'll see from some of the finest Christian artists of that time—the same artists working for the kings and aristocracy of Europe—making these items historically and artistically significant. Note that Jewish historians don't use "B.C." (Before Christ) or "A.D." (Anno Domini), but rather "B.C.E." (Before the Common Era) and "C.E." (Common Era). The museum also shows a film in English of the Nazi occupation of Rome.

Back outside, you may notice security measures around the synagogue: heavy concrete planter boxes (that double as car-bomb barriers), policemen in kiosks, and video cameras on the fences.

• *Look for the yellow church across from the Ponte Fabricio...*

Santa Maria della Pietà (a.k.a. San Gregorio)

When the ghetto was a walled-in town, Catholics built churches at each gate to try and spread their faith to the Jews. Notice the Hebrew script under the crucifix. It quotes the Jewish prophet Isaiah—"All day long, I have stretched out my hands to a disobedient and faithless nation that has lost its way" (Isaiah 65:2)—but misuses the quote to give it an anti-Semitic twist.

• *Walk away from the river behind the synagogue toward the ancient Roman ruins. The small square in front of the ruins is called...*

Largo 16 Ottobre 1943

This square is named for the day when Nazi trucks parked here and threatened to take the Jews to concentration camps unless the community came up with 50 kilos (110 pounds) of gold in 24 hours. Everyone, including non-Jewish Romans, tossed in their precious gold, and the demand was met. The Nazis took the gold—and later, they took the Jews as well.

• *The big ancient ruin is the...*

Portico d'Ottavia

This monumental gateway—with columns supporting a triangular pediment—was built by soon-to-be-emperor Augustus. Once flanked by temples and libraries, the passageway served as a kind of cultural center. After Rome's fall, the portico housed a thriving fish market. In the eighth century, the ruins of the portico became incorporated into the Church of Sant'Angelo in Pescheria.

For centuries, this Christian church was packed every Saturday with Jews—forced by decree to listen to Christian sermons. Notice the faded bits of Christian fresco on the arch. Locals love to tell of the poor old woman who refused to sell her land and now owns this priceless bit of real estate that includes the ancient arch (at #25 under the arch).

To the left is the main drag of today's ghetto. We'll head there soon, but first go to the bridge on your right to look down at the level of the street in Roman times. Just past the bridge, the former oratory is now a wedding-registry shop. (If it's open, pop in and see who's getting married when and admire their choice of table setting.) From the bridge, you get a fine view of Teatro di Marcello (which predates the Colosseum). Beyond it is the tree-capped Capitol Hill.

• *Now walk around the arch to the main street of the ghetto to...*

Via del Portico d'Ottavia

This main drag is a fine place to get a taste of yesterday's ghetto and today's Rome. From the start (near the Roman arch), look down the street. On the left is the new building from 1911. On the right, in the distance, is the only surviving line of old ghetto building fronts. Imagine today's street as it was then: much narrower (as it is at the far end today). Walking down the street, notice kosher restaurants proudly serving *carciofi* (artichokes, which only

Jewish grandmothers can cook properly) and shops of fine, locally produced Judaica. You might see posters for community events, a few men wearing yarmulkes, and political graffiti, both pro- and anti-Israel. The Palestine Liberation Organization attacked this area in 1982, and a police presence still lingers.

After a block, you reach the center of the district. Look right, down Via San Ambrogio, to see an old surviving street. Looking down this lane, imagine the dense population, flood muck, and squalor of the past. The pedestrianized square ahead is where older folks hang out together and shoot the breeze, sometimes even bringing their favorite chairs from home. Though the Jewish community has long since dispersed all over Rome, most Roman Jews

continue to spend time in this neighborhood to enjoy the strong feeling of community that survives. The big yellow building (on the left) houses the Jewish school.

This neighborhood has become trendy recently, and apartment prices are now beyond the means of most members of the Jewish community. Ironically, only the richest Jews could afford to relocate after 1870—and because the poor had to stay, their descendants have enjoyed healthy real-estate appreciation.

At #7, there's a gallery that generally features modern Israeli artists. At its door is a prayer capsule—residents touch it as they come and go to recall their Jewish creed.

Opposite the big school, take a one-block detour down Via della Reginella. At #28, notice where the six-floor buildings end and more elegant and spacious (but no taller) three-floor buildings begin...marking the end of the ghetto. In the square (Piazza Mattei) at the end of the lane is a fun fountain—an old Mannerist work, later embellished with turtles by Bernini. It's said that Bernini cared about the Jews and honored them with the symbol of a turtle—an ancient creature that carries all its belongings on its back.

Returning back to the main drag (Via del Portico Ottavia), continue to Bar Toto, where you'll see a slot in the wall—a ghetto-era charity box for orphans that still accepts donations for worthy causes. The ancient relief above the box marks the home of a big shot who, at the start of the Renaissance age (before the ghetto's establishment in 1555), plugged this chunk of ancient Rome into his facade for prestige. A bit farther down (at #1), another bit of ancient marble depicts a lion attacking a gazelle. Notice the big stone inset with a Latin inscription dated "MMCCXX." Yes, that's

2220, and no, it's not from the future. It marks the years since the birth of Rome in 753 b.c.—meaning it was carved in a.d. 1467.

At the next intersection (Piazza Costaguti), stand in the white decorative square in the cobbles. The recommended Sora Margherita Associazione Culturale, a restaurant with no sign, is

located on the car-filled square— Piazza delle Cinque Scole—30 yards to the left, at #30 (described on page 346). On your right is a traditional Jewish bakery. Go inside to check out the braided challah bread, cheesecakes, almond paste–filled macaroons, and "Jewish Pizzas"—like little €2 fruitcakes. Just beyond that, the curving, white-columned structure is part of a former Carmelite convent. Imagine the outrage of the Jewish community when the Church built a convent and a Catholic school here in the ghetto to preach to their children, and forced locals to attend Mass.

Pop into the tunnel-like alleyway next to it, and—in the evocative little courtyard—imagine the tight conditions of thousands of Jews living in this small seven-acre area. Then head back to the main square and consider how times are much better today.

SLEEPING

For hassle-free efficiency, I favor accommodations and restaurants handy to your sightseeing activities. Rather than listing hotels scattered throughout Rome, I describe my favorite neighborhoods and recommend the best-value accommodations in each, ranging from hotels to less-expensive hostels and convents.

A major feature of this book is its extensive listing of good-value rooms—especially in Rome, where hotels are generally pricey, the cheaper hotels can be depressing, and the TI isn't allowed to give opinions on quality. I like places that are clean, small, central, quiet at night, traditional, inexpensive, family-run, friendly, and not listed in other guidebooks. In Rome, for me, a hotel with six out of these nine attributes means it's a keeper.

As you look over the listings, you'll notice that some hotels promise special prices to my readers who book direct (without using a TI room-finding service or hotel-booking website, which take a commission). To get these rates, mention this book when you reserve, then show the book upon arrival. During slow times or online promos, rooms might be offered for even less than listed.

Given the economic downturn, hoteliers are willing and eager to make a deal. I'd suggest emailing several hotels to ask for their best price. Comparison-shop and make your choice. In general, prices can soften up if you do any of the following: offer to pay cash, mention this book, stay at least three nights, offer to skip breakfast, or ask if there are cheaper rooms. Haggle if you arrive late in the day during off-season (roughly mid-July through August and November through mid-March). It's common for hotels in Rome to lower their prices 10–35 percent in the off-season, although prices at hostels and the cheaper hotels won't fluctuate much. Room rates are lowest in sweltering August.

Reserve your hotel room well in advance if you'll be in Rome over a holiday (see list of "Major Holidays and Weekends" on page 6).

Types of Accommodations

Hotels

Double rooms listed in this book will range from about €65 (very simple, toilet and shower down the hall) to €480 (maximum plumbing and more), with most clustering around €150 (with private bathrooms). I've favored these pricier options, because intense and grinding Rome is easier to enjoy with a welcoming oasis to call home.

Solo travelers find that the cost of a *camera singola* is often only 25 percent less than a *camera doppia.* Three or four people can save money by requesting one big room. (If a Db is €110, a Qb would be about €150.) Most listed hotels have rooms for anywhere from one to five people. If there's room for an extra cot, they'll cram it in for you (charging you around €25). English works in all but the cheapest places.

Traffic in Rome roars. With the recent arrival of double-paned windows and air-conditioning, night noise is not the problem it once was. Even so, light sleepers who ask for a *tranquillo* room will likely get a room in the back...and sleep better.

Nearly all places offer private bathrooms. Generally rooms with a bath or shower also have a toilet and a bidet (which Italians use for quick sponge baths). The cord that dangles over the tub or shower is not a clothesline. You pull it when you've fallen and can't get up.

Double beds are called *matrimoniale,* even though hotels aren't interested in your marital status. Twins are *due letti singoli.*

When you check in, the receptionist will normally ask for your passport and keep it for a couple of hours. Hotels are legally required to register each guest with the police. Relax. Americans are notorious for making this chore more difficult than it needs to be.

Assume that breakfast is included in the prices I've listed, unless otherwise noted. If breakfast is included but optional, you may want to skip it. While convenient, it's usually expensive— €5-8 for a simple continental buffet with ham, cheese, yogurt, and unlimited *caffè latte.* A picnic in your room followed by a coffee at the corner café can be lots cheaper.

More pillows and blankets are usually in the closet or available on request. In Italy, towels and linen aren't always replaced every day. Hang your towel up to dry. Budget hotels often use "waffle" or very thin tablecloth-type towels which take less water and electricity to launder.

Chill Out

All but the cheapest hotels have air-conditioning. Because Europeans are generally careful with energy use, you'll find government-enforced limits on air-conditioning and heating. There's a one-month period each spring and fall when neither is allowed. Air-conditioning sometimes costs an extra per-day charge, is worth seeking out in summer (though it may be on only at certain times of the day), and is rarely available from fall through spring. Fancier hotel rooms usually include air-conditioning in the price. Conveniently, many business-class hotels drop their prices in July and August, just when the air-conditioned comfort they offer is most important.

Most hotel rooms with air conditioners come with a control stick (like a TV remote) that generally has the same symbols and features: fan icon (click to toggle through wind power, from light to gale); louver icon (choose steady airflow or waves); snowflake and sunshine icons (cold air or heat, depending on season); clock ("O" setting: run x hours before turning off; "I" setting: wait x hours to start); and the temperature control (20 or 21 degrees Celsius is comfortable).

Most hotel rooms have a TV and telephone, and Internet access (usually Wi-Fi) is increasingly common. Simpler places rarely have a phone. Pricier hotels usually come with a small stocked fridge called a *frigo bar* (FREE-goh bar; pay for what you use).

Almost no hotels have parking, but nearly all have a line on spots in a nearby garage (about €24/day).

Hoteliers can be a great help and source of advice. Most know Rome well, and can can assist you with everything from public transit and airport connections to finding a good restaurant, the nearest launderette, or an Internet café.

Even at the best hotels, mechanical breakdowns occur: air-conditioning malfunctions, sinks leak, hot water turns cold, and toilets gurgle and smell. Report your concerns clearly and calmly at the front desk. For more complicated problems, don't expect instant results.

If you suspect night noise will be a problem, ask for a quiet room in the back or on an upper floor. To guard against theft in your room, keep valuables out of sight. Some rooms come with a safe, and other hotels have safes at the front desk. Use them if you're concerned.

Checkout can pose problems if surprise charges pop up on your bill. If you settle up your bill the night before you leave, you'll have time to discuss and address any points of contention.

Bed-and-Breakfasts (B&Bs)

B&Bs offer double the cultural intimacy for a good deal less than most hotel rooms. Roman B&Bs are small—most have no more than three rooms, and the owner generally lives on-site. (Be aware that small hotels sometimes erroneously use the term "B&B.") You'll pay in cash rather than by credit card. Expect few services and no amenities such as public lounges, in-room phones, private bathrooms, and daily bed-sheet changes (though the basics, such as sheets and towels, are provided). After picking up your keys, you can come and go as you wish. When reserving, confirm what kind of breakfast is included—some less-expensive B&Bs simply give you a voucher for a pastry and coffee at a nearby bar.

Doubles with breakfast start at €65, with prices increasing along with the number of amenities. Due to our large volume of readers and the small size of Roman B&Bs, it isn't practical to include many B&B listings here. To find a B&B in Rome, start your search with a website such as www.bedandbreakfast.com or www.b-b.rm.it. You'll get better prices, however, by booking directly with the B&B. Some websites connect you directly with the B&B owner, including www.wheninromebandb.com and www.gulliverslodge.com (see listing on page 323).

Convents

Although I list only four, Rome has many convents that rent out rooms. See the Church of Santa Susanna's website for a list (www.santasusanna.org, select "Coming to Rome"). At convents, the beds are twins and English is often in short supply, but the price is right.

Consider these nun-run places, all listed in this chapter: the expensive but divine **Casa di Santa Brigida** (near Campo de' Fiori), the **Suore di Santa Elisabetta** (near Santa Maria Maggiore), the **Casa Il Rosario** (near Piazza Venezia), and the user-friendly **Casa per Ferie Santa Maria alle Fornaci** (near the Vatican).

Hostels

For easy communication with young, friendly entrepreneurs, €20–30 dorm beds, and some inexpensive doubles—within a 10-minute hike of Termini train station—consider the various hostels I've listed, or check www.backpackers.it for more listings.

Apartments

Many locals rent out their apartments in downtown Rome, a great value for families or multiple couples traveling together. Rentals are generally by the week, with prices around €120 per day. Apartments typically offer a couple of bedrooms, a sitting area, and a teensy *cucinetta* (kitchenette), usually stocked with dishes

Sleep Code

(€1 = about $1.25)

Price Rankings

To help you easily sort through these listings, I've divided the rooms into three categories based on the price for a standard double room with bath during high season:

$$$ Higher Priced—Most rooms €180 or more.
$$ Moderately Priced—Most rooms between €130–180.
$ Lower Priced—Most rooms €130 or less.

I always rate hostels as $, whether or not they have double rooms, because they have the cheapest beds in town. Prices can change without notice; verify the hotel's current rates online or by email. For other updates, see www.rick steves.com/update.

Abbreviations

To give maximum information in a minimum of space, I use the following code to describe accommodations. Prices listed are per room, not per person. When a price range is given for a type of room (such as double rooms listing for €100–150), it means the price fluctuates with the season, size of room, or length of stay.

S = Single room (or price for one person in a double).
D = Double or Twin room. "Double beds" are often two twins sheeted together and are usually big enough for nonromantic couples.
T = Triple (generally a double bed with a single).
Q = Quad (usually two double beds).
b = Private bathroom with toilet and shower or tub.
s = Private shower or tub only (toilet is down the hall).

According to this code, a couple staying at a "Db-€140" hotel would pay a total of €140 (about $175) for a double room with a private bathroom. Unless otherwise noted, breakfast is included, hotel staff speaks basic English, and credit cards are accepted.

If I mention "Internet access," there's a public terminal in the lobby for guests to use. If I specify "Wi-Fi" or "cable Internet," you can generally access it in your room, but only if you have your own laptop.

and flatware. After you check in, you're basically on your own. While you won't have a doorman to carry your bags or a maid to clean your room each day, you will get an inside peek at a Roman home, and you can save lots of money—especially if you take advantage of the cooking facilities—with no loss of comfort. Most places are rented through booking agencies, the TI, or websites. Browse through www.craigslist.org (select "Rome," then "Vacation Rentals"), www.vrbo.com, and www.wantedinrome.com. Steve and Linda of The Beehive also run a booking service for private rooms and apartments in the old centers of Rome, Florence, and Venice; rates start at €30 per person (see listing on page 323, www.cross-pollinate.com).

Practicalities

Phoning

To call Italy from the US or Canada, dial 011-39 and then the local number. (The 011 is our international access code, and 39 is Italy's country code.) If calling Italy from another European country, dial 00-39-local number. (The 00 is Europe's international access code.) To call a Rome hotel from anywhere in Italy (including Rome), simply dial the 10-digit local number. For more tips on calling, see page 436.

Making Reservations

Given the quality of the accommodations I've found for this book, I'd recommend that you reserve your rooms in advance, particularly if you'll be traveling during peak season. Book several weeks ahead, or as soon as you've pinned down your travel dates. Note that some national holidays jam things up and merit your making reservations far in advance (see "Major Holidays and Weekends" sidebar on page 6). Just like at home, holidays that fall on a Monday, Thursday, or Friday can turn the weekend into a long holiday, so book the entire weekend well in advance.

Requesting a Reservation: To reserve, contact hotels directly by email, phone, or fax. Email is the clearest and most economical way to make a reservation. Or you can go straight to the hotel website; many have secure online reservation forms and can instantly inform you of availability and any special deals. But be sure you use the hotel's official site and not a booking agency's site—otherwise you may pay higher rates than you should. If you're phoning from the US, be mindful of time zones (see page 7). Most recommended hotels are accustomed to guests who speak only English.

Your hotelier wants to know these key pieces of information (also included in the sample request form on page 468 and at www.ricksteves.com/reservation):

- number and type of rooms
- number of nights
- date of arrival
- date of departure
- any special needs (e.g., bathroom in the room or down the hall, twin beds vs. double bed, air-conditioning, quiet, view, ground floor, etc.)

When you request a room, use the European style for writing dates: day/month/year. Hoteliers need to know your arrival and departure dates. For example, for a two-night stay in July, I would request: "1 double room for 2 nights, arrive 16/07/11, depart 18/07/11." (Consider carefully how long you'll stay; don't just assume you can tack on extra days once you arrive.)

If you don't get a reply to your email or fax, it usually means the hotel is already fully booked (but you can try sending the message again, or call to follow up). If they say they're booked up, mention that you're using this book.

Confirming a Reservation: If the hotel's response tells you its room availability and rates, it's not a confirmation. You must tell them that you want that room at the given rate. Many hoteliers will request your credit-card number for a one-night deposit to hold the room. While you can email your credit-card information (I do), it's safer to share that personal info via phone call, fax, or secure online reservation form (if the hotel has one on its website).

Canceling a Reservation: If you must cancel your reservation, it's courteous to do so with as much advance notice as possible—at least three days. Simply make a quick phone call or send an email. Family-run hotels and B&Bs lose money if they turn away customers while holding a room for someone who doesn't show up. Understandably, many hoteliers bill no-shows for one night.

Cancellation policies can be strict: For example, you might lose a deposit if you cancel within two weeks of your reserved stay, or you might be billed for the entire visit if you leave early. Ask about cancellation policies before you book.

If canceling via email, request confirmation that your cancellation was received to avoid being billed.

Reconfirm Your Reservation: Always call to reconfirm your room reservation a day or two in advance from the road. If you'll be arriving late (after 17:00), alert your hotelier. On the small chance that a hotel loses track of your reservation, bring along a hard copy of their emailed or faxed confirmation.

Reserving Rooms as You Travel: If you enjoy having a flexible itinerary, you can make reservations as you travel, calling hotels or B&Bs a few days to a week before your visit. If you'd rather travel without any reservations at all, you'll have greater success snaring rooms if you arrive at your destination early in the day. When you anticipate crowds (weekends are worst), call hotels at about 9:00 on the day you plan to arrive, when the hotel clerk knows who'll be checking out and just which rooms will be available. If you encounter a language barrier, ask the fluent receptionist at your current hotel to call for you.

Accommodations

Near Termini Train Station

While not as atmospheric as other areas of Rome, the hotels near Termini train station are less expensive, restaurants are plentiful, and the many public-transportation options link it easily with the entire city. The city's two Metro lines intersect at the station, and most buses leave from here. Piazza Venezia is a 20-minute walk down Via Nazionale.

Via Firenze

Via Firenze is safe, handy, central, and relatively quiet. It's a 10-minute walk from Termini Station and the airport train, and two blocks beyond Piazza della Repubblica and the TI. The Defense Ministry is nearby, so you've got heavily armed guards watching over you all night.

The neighborhood is well-connected by public transportation (with the Repubblica Metro stop nearby). Virtually all the city buses that rumble down Via Nazionale (#64, #70, #115, #640, and the #40 express) take you to Piazza Venezia (Forum) and Largo Argentina (Pantheon). From Largo Argentina, both the #64 bus (jammed with people and thieves) and the #40 express bus continue to the Vatican. Or, at Largo Argentina, you can transfer to electric trolley #8 to Trastevere (get off at first stop after crossing the river).

Phone and Internet Center is a cute and handy little hole-in-the-wall cybercafé within a block or so of several recommended hotels (€3/hour, daily 8:30–20:30, Via Modena 48, tel. 06-482-8850). To stock your closet pantry, pop over to **Despar Supermarket** (daily 8:00–21:00, Via Nazionale 211, at the corner of Via Venezia). A 24-hour **pharmacy** near the recommended hotels is Farmacia Piram (Via Nazionale 228, tel. 06-488-4437).

$$$ Residenza Cellini feels like the guest wing of a gorgeous Neoclassical palace. It offers 11 rooms, "ortho/anti-allergy beds," four-star comforts and service, and a breezy breakfast terrace (Db-€185, larger Db-€205, extra bed-€25, prices good through 2011 with this book and cash, air-con, elevator, Internet access and Wi-Fi, Via Modena 5, tel. 06-4782-5204, fax 06-4788-1806, www.residenzacellini.it, residenzacellini@tin.it, Barbara, Gaetano, and Donato).

SLEEPING

Hotels near Termini Train Station

TO VILLA BORGHESE GARDENS

¼ MILE
400 METERS

T TAXI STAND
M METRO STATION
B BUS STOP

U.S. EMB.

TO SPANISH STEPS

SANTA MARIA VITTORIA

BATHS OF DIOCLETIAN

STA. MARIA DEGLI ANGELI

VIA VENETO

CAPPUCCIN CRYPT

VIA BARBERINI

SANTA SUSANNA

QUIRINALE PALACE

SAN CARLINO

TO TREVI & PANTHEON

NATIONAL MUSEUM

PIAZZA REP.

PIAZZA CINQUE-CENTO

TERMINI STATION

TO COLOSSEUM & FORUM

CAVOUR

SANTA MARIA MAGGIORE

STA. PRASSEDE

TO VITTORIO EMANUELE

LARGO MAGNA

1 Residenza Cellini, Hotel Adler & Internet Center
2 Hotel Modigliani
3 Hotels Oceania & Nardizzi Americana
4 Hotel Aberdeen
5 Hotel Margaret
6 Hotel Opera Roma
7 Hotel Sonya
8 Hotel Selene
9 Hotel Montreal

10 Hotel Italia Roma
11 Suore di Sta. Elisabetta
12 Gulliver's Lodge B&B
13 The Beehive
14 Hotel Select Garden
15 Hotel Sileo & Fawlty Towers Hostel
16 Funny Palace Hostel, Launderette & Internet Café
17 Yellow Hostel

SLEEPING

$$$ **Hotel Modigliani,** a delightful 23-room place, is energetically run in a clean, bright, minimalist yet in-love-with-life style that its artist namesake would appreciate. There's a very generous lounge, a garden, and a newsletter introducing you to each of the staff (Db-€195, but check website for deals and ask for a 10 percent Rick Steves discount; air-con, Wi-Fi; northwest of Via Firenze—from Tritone Fountain on Piazza Barberini, go 2 blocks up Via della Purificazione to #42; tel. 06-4281-5226, www.hotel modigliani.com, info@hotelmodigliani.com, Giulia and Marco).

$$ Hotel Oceania is a peaceful slice of air-conditioned heaven. This 23-room manor house–type hotel is spacious and quiet, with spotless, tastefully decorated rooms, run by Stefano, who still maintains his father Armando's tradition of serving delicious "world-famous" coffee. He works hard to maintain a caring family atmosphere with a fine staff, and provides lots of thoughtful extra touches (Sb-€125, Db-€158, Tb-€190, Qb-€212, these prices good through 2011 with this book and cash, large roof terrace, family suite, Internet access and Wi-Fi, videos in the TV lounge, Via Firenze 38, third floor, tel. 06-482-4696, fax 06-488-5586, www.hoteloceania.it, info@hoteloceania.it; Anna and Radu round out the staff).

$$ Hotel Aberdeen, which perfectly combines high quality and friendliness, is warmly run by Annamaria, with support

from cousins Sabrina and Cinzia and sister Laura. The 37 comfy, modern, air-conditioned rooms are a terrific value. Enjoy the frescoed breakfast room (Sb-€102, Db-€160, Tb-€170, Qb-€200, for these rates—or better—book direct via email or use the "Rick Steves reader reservations" link on their website, much cheaper rates off-season, Internet access and Wi-Fi, Via Firenze 48, tel. 06-482-3920, fax 06-482-1092, www.hotelaberdeen.it, info@hotel aberdeen.it).

$ Hotel Adler, which serves breakfast on its garden patio, has wide halls and eight quiet, simple rooms in a good location (plus six more rooms in their slightly pricier Bellesuite wing). It's run the old-fashioned way by a charming family (Db-€130, Tb-€170, Qb-€195, Quint/b-€220, 5 percent off these prices through 2011 with this book, air-con, elevator, Internet access and Wi-Fi, Via Modena 5, second floor, tel. 06-484-466, fax 06-488-0940, www.hoteladler-roma.com, info@hoteladler-roma.com, Alessandro).

$ Hotel Nardizzi Americana, with 33 pleasant, air-conditioned rooms and a delightful rooftop terrace, is an excellent value (Sb-€95, Db-€125, Tb-€155, Qb-€175, email them or use "Rick Steves readers reservations" link on their website to get these special rates in 2011, normal website sometimes has even lower rates, additional 10 percent off any time with cash, air-con, elevator, Internet access and Wi-Fi, Via Firenze 38, fourth floor, tel. 06-488-0035, fax 06-488-0368, www.hotelnardizzi.it, info @hotelnardizzi.it, Stefano, Fabrizio, Mario, and Samy).

$ Hotel Margaret, basic but welcoming, fills its walls with Impressionist prints and offers 12 decent rooms at a good price

(Db-€95, big Db-€120, Tb-€140, Qb-€170, mention this book for their best rate, air-con, elevator, Wi-Fi, northeast of Via Firenze at Via Antonio Salandra 6, fourth floor, tel. 06-482-4285, fax 06-482-4277, www.hotelmargaretrome.com, info@hotelmargaret .net, friendly Monica).

Between Via Nazionale and Santa Maria Maggiore

$$ **Hotel Opera Roma,** with contemporary furnishings and marble accents, boasts 15 fresh and spacious but somewhat dark rooms. It's located a stone's throw from the Opera House (Db-€165, Tb-€190, these prices good through 2011 with this book, 5 percent less with cash, air-con, elevator, Internet access and loaner laptop on request, Via Firenze 11, tel. 06-487-1787, www.hoteloperaroma .com, info@hoteloperaroma.com, Rezza and Federica).

$$ **Hotel Sonya** offers 28 well-equipped, high-tech rooms, a central location, and decent prices. Farhad, a member of the multi-talented staff, bakes cakes and other goodies daily for the better-than-usual breakfast (Sb-€90, Db-€150, Tb-€165, Qb-€185, Quint/b-€200, 5 percent discount with this book and cash, air-con, elevator, loaner laptops in room and Wi-Fi, faces the Opera House at Via Viminale 58, Metro: Repubblica or Termini, tel. 06-481-9911, fax 06-488-5678, www.hotelsonya.it, info@hotel sonya.it, Francesca and Ivan).

$$ **Hotel Selene** spreads its rooms out on a few floors of a big palazzo. With elegant furnishings and room to breathe, its 40 rooms are a good value (Db-€145, Tb-€165, €10 less with cash, air-con, elevator, Via del Viminale 8, tel. 06-482-4460, www.hotel seleneroma.it, reception@hotelseleneroma.it).

$ **Hotel Montreal,** run with care, is a bright, solid business-class place with 27 rooms on a big street a block southeast of Santa Maria Maggiore (Sb-€95, Db-€120, Tb-€150, may be less if you email direct and ask for a Rick Steves discount, air-con, elevator, Internet access, communal garden terrace, good security, Via Carlo Alberto 4, 1 block from Metro: Vittorio Emanuele, 3 blocks west of Termini train station, tel. 06-445-7797, fax 06-446-5522, www.hotelmontrealroma.com, info@hotelmontrealroma.com, Pasquale).

$ **Hotel Italia Roma,** in a busy, interesting, and handy locale, is located safely on a quiet street next to the Ministry of the Interior. Thoughtfully run by Andrea, Sabrina, Nadine, and Gabriel, it has 35 comfortable, clean, and bright rooms (Sb-€80, Db-€120, Tb-€160, Qb-€180, 30 percent cheaper July–Aug, air-con-€10 extra per day, elevator, Internet access and Wi-Fi, Via Venezia 18, just off Via Nazionale, Metro: Repubblica, tel. 06-482-8355, fax 06-474-5550, www.hotelitaliaroma.it, info@hotelitaliaroma.com). Request one of the four "residenza" rooms upstairs on the third floor, which are newer, quiet, and the same price. They also have eight decent annex rooms across the street.

$ Suore di Santa Elisabetta is a heavenly Polish-run convent with a peaceful garden and 70 beds in tidy twin-bedded (only) rooms. Often booked long in advance, with such tranquility it's a super value (S-€40, Sb-€48, D-€66, Db-€85, Tb-€106, Qb-€128, Quint/b-€142, no air-con, elevator serves top floors only, fine view roof terrace and breakfast hall, 23:00 curfew, a block southwest of Santa Maria Maggiore at Via dell'Olmata 9, Metro: Termini or Vittorio Emanuele, tel. 06-488-8271, fax 06-488-4066, www .elzbietanki-roma.eu, ist.it.s.elisabetta@libero.it).

$ Gulliver's Lodge B&B has four fun, colorful rooms on the ground floor of a large, secure building. Well-located on a busy street, the rooms are nevertheless quiet. Although the public spaces are few, in-room extras like DVD players (and DVDs, including my Italy shows) make it a nice home base (Db-€110, Tb-€120, cash only, air-con, Internet access and Wi-Fi, a 15-minute walk southwest of Termini train station at Via Cavour 101, Metro: Cavour, tel. 06-9727-3789, www.gulliverslodge.com, stay@gulliverslodge .com, Sara and Mary).

Sleeping Cheaply, Northeast of Termini Train Station

The cheapest beds in town are northeast of Termini train station (Metro: Termini). Some travelers feel this area is weird and spooky after dark, but these hotels feel plenty safe. With your back to the train tracks, turn right and walk two blocks out of the station. **Splashnet** launderette/Internet café is handy if you're staying in this area (€6 full-serve wash and dry, Internet access-€1.50/hour, €2 luggage storage per day—or free if you wash and go online, daily 8:30–24:00, just off Via Milazzo at Via Varese 33, tel. 06-4470-3523).

$ The Beehive gives vagabonds—old and young—a cheap, clean, and comfy home in Rome, thoughtfully and creatively run by Steve and Linda, a friendly young American couple. They offer six great-value artsy-mod double rooms (D-€80, T-€105) and an eight-bed dorm (€25 bunks, Internet access and Wi-Fi, private garden terrace, 2 blocks north of Termini train station at Via Marghera 8, tel. 06-4470-4553, www.the-beehive.com, info@the -beehive.com).

$ Hotel Select Garden, a modern and comfortable 19-room hotel run by the cheery Picca family, boasts lively modern art adorning the walls and a beautiful lemon-tree garden. It's a welcome refuge from the bustling eternal city, located on a quiet street just a couple of blocks from the train station (Sb-€85, Db-€100, Tb-€120, these prices good through 2011 with this book, air-con,

Wi-Fi, Via V. Bachelet 6, tel. 06-445-6383, fax 06-444-1086, www
.hotelselectgarden.com, info@hotelselectgarden.com, Armando).

$ Hotel Sileo, with shiny chandeliers in dim rooms, has a
contract to house train conductors who work the night shift—so
two of its doubles are rentable only from 18:30 to 9:00 for €60.
The rest of their 10 rooms are available any time of day (Db-€75,
Tb-€90, air-con, elevator, Via Magenta 39, fourth floor, tel. & fax
06-445-0246, www.hotelsileo.com, info@hotelsileo.com). Friendly
Alessandro and Maria Savioli don't speak English, but daughter
Anna does.

$ Funny Palace Hostel, adjacent to Splashnet and run by
its entrepreneurial owner Mabri, rents dorm beds in quiet four-
person rooms and 18 stark-but-clean private rooms (dorm beds-€30,
Db-€100, cash only, reception in the launderette—described earlier, Via Varese 33/31, tel. 06-4470-3523, www.hostelfunny.com).

$ Yellow Hostel rents 130 beds in 4-, 6-, and 12-bed coed
dorms to 18- through 39-year-olds only. Hip yet sane, it's well-
run with fine facilities, including lockers. There's no curfew, and a
late-night bar is next door (€24-34 per bed depending on plumbing, size, and season; reserve via email—no telephone reservations
accepted, no breakfast, Wi-Fi and laptop rental available, 6 blocks
from station, just past Via Vicenza at Via Palestro 44, tel. 06-493-
82682, www.the-yellow.com).

$ Fawlty Towers Hostel is alright, and works for backpackers
arriving by train. It offers 50 beds and lots of fun, games, and extras
(4-bed dorms-€25 per person, S-€55, D-€65, Db-€80, Q-€90,
includes sheets, elevator, free Internet access, kitchenette, peaceful
sun terrace, from station walk a block down Via Marghera and
turn right to Via Magenta 39, tel. 06-445-0374, fax 06-4543-5942,
www.fawltytowers.org, info@fawltytowers.org). Their nearby
annex, **Bubbles,** offers similar beds and rates and shares the same
reception desk.

Near Ancient Rome
Stretching from the Colosseum to Piazza Venezia, this area is
central. Sightseers are a short walk from the Colosseum, Roman
Forum, and Trajan's Column.

Near the Colosseum
$$$ Hotel Lancelot is a comfortable yet elegant refuge—a
60-room hotel with the ambience of a B&B. It's quiet and safe,
with a shady courtyard, restaurant, bar, and tiny communal sixth-
floor terrace. Well-run by Faris and Lubna Khan, it's popular with
returning guests (Sb-€125, Db-€196, Tb-€222, Qb-€260, €20 extra
for sixth-floor terrace room with a Colosseum view, 5 percent off
these rates with this book, air-con, elevator, wheelchair-accessible,

Hotels near Ancient R...

IIII STAIRS
↓ ENTRANCES TO SIGHTS
M METRO STATION
B BUS STOP

200 YARDS
200 METERS

DCH

1. Hotel Lancelot
2. Hotel Paba
3. Nicolas Inn B&B,
   Hotel Pensione Rosetta
   & Enoteca Cavour 313

4. Hotel Nerva
5. Hotel Giardino
6. Casa Il Rosario
7. Caffè dello Studente &
   Hostaria da Nerone Rest.

Wi-Fi, parking-€10/day, 10-minute walk behind Colosseum near San Clemente Church at Via Capo d'Africa 47, tel. 06-7045-0615, fax 06-7045-0640, www.lancelothotel.com, info@lancelothotel.com). Faris and Lubna speak the Queen's English.

$$ Hotel Paba has seven fresh rooms, chocolate-box–tidy and lovingly cared for by Alberta Castelli. Though it overlooks busy Via Cavour just two blocks from the Colosseum, it's quiet enough (Db-€135, extra bed-€40, 5 percent cash discount, huge beds, breakfast served in room, air-con, elevator, Wi-Fi, Via Cavour

Cavour, tel. 06-4782-4902, fax 06-4788-1225, www .com, info@hotelpaba.com).

Nicolas Inn Bed & Breakfast, a delightful little four-room with thoughtful touches, is spacious and bright. It's run by rançois and American expat Melissa, who make you feel like you have caring friends in Rome (Db-€100–170, extra bed-€30, 10 percent Rick Steves discount with this book and cash, included breakfast served at neighboring bar, air-con, Wi-Fi, Via Cavour 295, tel. 06-976-18483, www.nicolasinn.com, info@nicolasinn.com).

$ Hotel Pensione Rosetta, homey and family-run, rents 20 rooms. It's pretty minimal, with no lounge and no breakfast, but has a good location and reasonable prices (Sb-€65, Db-€90, Tb-€105, air-con, Wi-Fi, Via Cavour 295, tel. 06-478-23069, www.rosettahotel.com, info@rosettahotel.com).

Near Piazza Venezia
To locate these hotels, see the map on page 325.

$$$ Hotel Nerva is a three-star slice of tranquility with 19 small, overpriced (but often discounted) rooms on a surprisingly quiet back street just steps away from the Roman Forum (Sb-€140, Db-€190, extra bed-€45, ask for Rick Steves discount, rates very soft—especially off-season, air-con, elevator, Via Tor de' Conti 3, tel. 06-678-1835, fax 06-6992-2204, www.hotelnerva.com, info @hotelnerva.com, Antonio, Paolo, Anna).

$ Hotel Giardino, true to its name, has a small garden area and offers 11 pleasant rooms in a central location three blocks northeast of Piazza Venezia. With a tiny central lobby and a small breakfast room, it suits travelers who prize location over big-hotel amenities (Sb-€85, Db-€130, one smaller Db for 15 percent less; these prices good through 2011 with this book, cash only, check website for specials, air-con, effective double-paned windows, on a busy street off Piazza di Quirinale at Via XXIV Maggio 51, tel. 06-679-4584, fax 06-679-5155, www.hotel-giardino-roma.com, info@hotel-giardino-roma.com, helpful Gianluca).

$ Casa Il Rosario is a peaceful, well-run Dominican convent renting 40 rooms with monastic simplicity to both pilgrims and tourists in a good neighborhood (reserve several months in advance, S-€42, Sb-€54, Db-€94, Tb-€120, single beds only, fans, free Internet access, roof-terrace picnics welcome, 23:00 curfew, midway between the Quirinale and Colosseum near bottom of Via Nazionale at Via Sant'Agata dei Goti 10, bus #40 or #170 from Termini, tel. 06-679-2346, fax 06-6994-1106, irodopre@tin.it).

In the Pantheon Neighborhood
Winding, narrow lanes filled with foot traffic and lined with boutique shops and tiny trattorias...this is village Rome at its best.

and pearly gates instead of doors, this lavish 20-room convent makes exhaust-stained Roman tourists feel like they've died and gone to heaven. If you don't need a double bed, it's worth the splurge (Sb-€110, twin Db-€190, 3 percent extra if you pay with credit card, can pay with personal check for no extra charge, book well in advance, air-con, elevator, Internet access, tasty €25 dinners, roof garden, plush library, Monserrato 54, tel. 06-6889-2596, fax 06-6889-1573, piazzafarnese@brigidine.org, many of the sisters are from India and speak English). If you get no response to your fax or email within three days, consider that a "no."

$ Hotel Smeraldo, with 50 rooms, is strictly run, clean, and a great deal (Sb-€100, Db-€130, Tb-€160, rooms €30 less off-season, buffet breakfast free with this book in 2011, air-con, elevator, flowery roof terrace, midway between Campo de' Fiori and Largo Argentina at Vicolo dei Chiodaroli 9, tel. 06-687-5929, fax 06-6880-5495, www.smeraldoroma.com, albergosmeraldoroma @tin.it, Massimo and Walter). Their **Dipendenza Smeraldo,** 10 yards around the corner at Via dei Chiavari 32, has 16 similar rooms (same price and free breakfast, same reception and contact info).

In the Jewish Ghetto

$$ Hotel Arenula, with 50 decent rooms, is the only hotel in Rome's old Jewish ghetto. While it has the ambience of a gym and attracts lots of students, it's a good value in the thick of old Rome (Sb-€75–98, Db-€133, €100 July–Aug, 5 percent off with this book in high season of 2011, extra bed-€21, air-con, no elevator, Wi-Fi, opposite the fountain in the park on Via Arenula at Via Santa Maria de' Calderari 47, tel. 06-687-9454, fax 06-689-6188, www.hotelarenula.com, info@hotelarenula .com, Rosanna).

Close to the Pantheon

These places are buried in the pedestrian-friendly heart of ancient Rome, each within a four-minute walk of the Pantheon. You'll pay more here—but you'll save time and money by being exactly where you want to be for your early and late wandering.

$$$ Hotel Nazionale, a four-star landmark, is a 16th-century palace that shares a well-policed square with the Parliament building. Its 100 rooms are accentuated by lush public spaces, fancy bars, a uniformed staff, and a marble-floored restaurant. It's a big, stuffy hotel with a revolving front door, but it's a worthy splurge if you want security, comfort, and ancient Rome at your doorstep (Sb-€220, Db-€350, giant deluxe Db-€480, extra person-€70, ask for 10 percent Rick Steves discount, check online for summer and weekend discounts, air-con, elevator, Piazza Montecitorio 131, tel.

Hotels in the Pantheon Neighborhood

1 Casa di Santa Brigida
2 Hotel Smeraldo
3 Dipendenza Smeraldo
4 Hotel Arenula

5 Hotel Nazionale
6 Albergo Santa Chiara
7 Hotel Due Torri
8 Hotel 939 Rome & Hotel Marcus

You'll pay for the atmosphere, but this is where you want to be—especially at night, when Romans and tourists gather in the flood-lit piazzas for the evening stroll, the *passeggiata*.

Near Campo de' Fiori

You'll pay a premium (and endure a little extra night noise) to stay in the old center. But each of these places is romantically set deep in the tangled back streets near the idyllic Campo de' Fiori and, for many, worth the extra money.

$$$ Casa di Santa Brigida overlooks the elegant Piazza Farnese. With soft-spoken sisters gliding down polished hallways and pearly gates instead of doors, this lavish 20-room convent makes exhaust-stained Roman tourists feel like they've died and gone to heaven. If you don't need a double bed, it's worth the splurge (Sb-€110, twin Db-€190, 3 percent extra if you pay with credit card, can pay with personal check for no extra charge, book well in advance, air-con, elevator, Internet access, tasty €25 dinners, roof garden, plush library, Monserrato 54, tel. 06-6889-2596, fax 06-6889-1573, piazzafarnese@brigidine.org, many of the sisters are from India and speak English). If you get no response to your fax or email within three days, consider that a "no."

$ Hotel Smeraldo, with 50 rooms, is strictly run, clean, and a great deal (Sb-€100, Db-€130, Tb-€160, rooms €30 less off-season, buffet breakfast free with this book in 2011, air-con, elevator, flowery roof terrace, midway between Campo de' Fiori and Largo Argentina at Vicolo dei Chiodaroli 9, tel. 06-687-5929, fax 06-6880-5495, www.smeraldoroma.com, albergosmeraldoroma @tin.it, Massimo and Walter). Their **Dipendenza Smeraldo,** 10 yards around the corner at Via dei Chiavari 32, has 16 similar rooms (same price and free breakfast, same reception and contact info).

In the Jewish Ghetto
$$ Hotel Arenula, with 50 decent rooms, is the only hotel in Rome's old Jewish ghetto. While it has the ambience of a gym and attracts lots of students, it's a good value in the thick of old Rome (Sb-€75–98, Db-€133, €100 July–Aug, 5 percent off with this book in high season of 2011, extra bed-€21, air-con, no elevator, Wi-Fi, opposite the fountain in the park on Via Arenula at Via Santa Maria de' Calderari 47, tel. 06-687-9454, fax 06-689-6188, www.hotelarenula.com, info@hotelarenula .com, Rosanna).

Close to the Pantheon
These places are buried in the pedestrian-friendly heart of ancient Rome, each within a four-minute walk of the Pantheon. You'll pay more here—but you'll save time and money by being exactly where you want to be for your early and late wandering.

$$$ Hotel Nazionale, a four-star landmark, is a 16th-century palace that shares a well-policed square with the Parliament building. Its 100 rooms are accentuated by lush public spaces, fancy bars, a uniformed staff, and a marble-floored restaurant. It's a big, stuffy hotel with a revolving front door, but it's a worthy splurge if you want security, comfort, and ancient Rome at your doorstep (Sb-€220, Db-€350, giant deluxe Db-€480, extra person-€70, ask for 10 percent Rick Steves discount, check online for summer and weekend discounts, air-con, elevator, Piazza Montecitorio 131, tel.

Hotels in the Pantheon Neighborhood

❶ Casa di Santa Brigida	❺ Hotel Nazionale
❷ Hotel Smeraldo	❻ Albergo Santa Chiara
❸ Dipendenza Smeraldo	❼ Hotel Due Torri
❹ Hotel Arenula	❽ Hotel 939 Rome & Hotel Marcus

You'll pay for the atmosphere, but this is where you want to be—especially at night, when Romans and tourists gather in the flood-lit piazzas for the evening stroll, the *passeggiata*.

Near Campo de' Fiori

You'll pay a premium (and endure a little extra night noise) to stay in the old center. But each of these places is romantically set deep in the tangled back streets near the idyllic Campo de' Fiori and, for many, worth the extra money.

$$$ Casa di Santa Brigida overlooks the elegant Piazza Farnese. With soft-spoken sisters gliding down polished hallways

06-695-001, fax 06-678-6677, www.hotelnazionale.it, info@hotel nazionale.it).

$$$ Albergo Santa Chiara is big, solid, and hotelesque. Flavia, Silvio, and their fine staff offer marbled elegance (but basic furniture) and all the hotel services in the old center. Its ample public lounges are dressy and professional, and its 99 rooms are quiet and spacious (Sb-€138, Db-€190, Db-€215 April–June and Oct, Tb-€262, check website for discounts, book online direct and request special Rick Steves rates, elevator, behind Pantheon at Via di Santa Chiara 21, tel. 06-687-2979, fax 06-687-3144, www .albergosantachiara.com, info@albergosantachiara.com).

$$$ Hotel Due Torri, hiding out on a tiny quiet street, is beautifully located. It feels professional yet homey, with an accommodating staff, generous public spaces, and 26 small rooms. While the location and lounge are great, the rooms are overpriced (Sb-€125, Db-€195, family apartment-€230 for 3 and €260 for 4, check website for frequent discounts, air-con, elevator, pay Internet access, a block off Via della Scrofa at Vicolo del Leonetto 23, tel. 06-6880-6956, fax 06-686-5442, www.hotelduetorriroma.com, hotelduetorri@mclink.it, Cinzia).

$ Hotel 939 Rome and **Hotel Marcus** are two hotels that seem like one (same entrance, lobby, and contact info). The 939 has renovated rooms, while the Marcus is more utilitarian. Together they offer 17 rooms on the second floor in the old center of Rome above noisy Via della Scrofa (Db-€100–140, extra bed-€30, check website for frequent discounts, air-con, elevator; from Via della Scrofa, turn right at Piazza Nicosia and head to Via del Clementino 94, tel. 06-6830-0312, www.hotel939.com, hotel939@hotmail.it, helpful Aurora).

In Trastevere

Colorful and genuine in a gritty sort of way, Trastevere is a treat for travelers looking for a less touristy and more bohemian atmosphere. Choices are few here, but by trekking across the Tiber, you can have the experience of being comfortably immersed in old Rome. To locate the following two places, see the map on page 294.

$$$ Hotel Santa Maria sits like a lazy hacienda in the midst of Trastevere. Surrounded by a medieval skyline, you'll feel as if you're on some romantic stage set. Its 18 small but well-equipped, air-conditioned rooms—former cells in a cloister—are all on the ground floor, as are a few suites for up to six people. The rooms circle a gravelly courtyard of orange trees and stay-awhile patio furniture (Db-€180, Tb-€220; prices good through 2011 with this book, cash, and minimum stay of three nights; family rooms, free loaner bikes, Internet access and Wi-Fi, face church on Piazza Maria Trastevere and go right down Via della Fonte d'Olio 50 yards to Vicolo del Piede 2, tel. 06-589-4626, fax 06-589-4815, www.hotelsantamaria.info, info@hotelsantamaria.info, Stefano). Some rooms come with family-friendly fold-down bunks for €30 extra per person. Their freshly renovated six-room **Residenza Santa Maria** is a couple of blocks away (same prices and contact info).

$$$ Residenza Arco dei Tolomei has six small, unique, antique-filled rooms in a quiet and elegant setting—you can pretend you're visiting aristocratic relatives (Db-€200, discounts for cash and for stays of three days or more, reserve well in advance, Internet access and Wi-Fi, from Piazza Piscinula a block up Via dell'Arco de' Tolomei at #27, tel. 06-5832-0819, www.bbarcodei tolomei.com, info@bbarcodeitolomei.com; Marco, Gianna Paola, and dog Pixel).

$$$ Relais le Clarisse retains the tranquil feel of its former life as a convent. Its five tastefully furnished rooms, which vary in size and amenities, surround a leafy courtyard—a little slice of the countryside in the city (Db-€205, Db suite-€195–220, Tb suite-€220–250, Qb suite-€260–290, prices vary with season, just off Viale Trastevere at Via Cardinale Merry del Val 20, tel. & fax 06-5833-4437, www.leclarisse.com, info@leclarisse.com, Maria and Toy).

$$ Casa San Giuseppe is down a characteristic laundry-strewn lane with views of Aurelian Walls. While convent-owned, it's a secular place renting 29 plain but peaceful, spacious, and spotless rooms (Sb-€115, Db-€155, Tb-€185, Qb-€215, garden-facing rooms are quiet, air-con, elevator, Internet access, parking-€15, just north of Piazza Trilussa at Vicolo Moroni 22, tel. 06-5833-3490, fax 06-5833-5754, www.casasangiuseppe.it, info@casasangiuseppe .it, Germano).

$$ Arco del Lauro B&B rents six white, minimalist rooms in a good location. Facing a courtyard (no views but little noise), the friendly welcome and good value make up for the lack of public spaces (Db-€135, Qb-€185, prices good if booked direct, cash only, included breakfast served in a café, Internet access and Wi-Fi, from Piazza Piscinula a block up Via dell'Arco de' Tolomei at #27, tel. 06-9784-0350, www.arcodellauro.it, info@arcodellauro.it, Lorenza and Daniela).

Near Vatican City

Sleeping near the Vatican is expensive, but some enjoy calling this neighborhood home. Even though it's handy to the Vatican (when the rapture hits, you're right there), everything else is a long way away.

$$$ Hotel Alimandi Vaticano, facing the Vatican Museum, is beautifully designed. Run by the Alimandi family (Enrico,

Hotels & Restaurants near Vatican City

200 YARDS
200 METERS

VIA D MILIZIE
VIA ANDREA DORIA
VIA OTRANTO
OTTAVIANO
CESARE
To ❸
PIAZZA EROI
MARKET
VIA PISANI
VIA LEONE IV
V. GIULIO
VIA OTTAVIANO
VIA SCIPIONI
VIA CANDIA
❾
VIA GERMANICO
❷
SEB. VEN.
❺
CIPRO
VIA
ENTRY
❻
❽
PIAZZA RISORGI-MENTO
WALL
VIA COLA
VIA CRES.
VATICANO WALL
VATICAN MUSEUM
PAPAL APT.
ITALIAN POST
BORGO PIO
PED. ZONE
TO ❼, CASTEL SANT' ANGELO + BUS #40→
VIALE
GARDENS
SISTINE CHAPEL
VIA CORRIDORI
VIA CONCILIAZIONE
RADIO VAT.
ST. PETER'S
OBELISK
N
WALL
AUDIENCE HALL
BUS #64
PORTA CAV.
ST. PETER'S SQUARE
VIA AURELIA
TUNNEL
DCH
VIA STAZIONE
TO SAN PIETRO TRAIN STN. + ❹

Ⓣ TAXI STAND
Ⓜ METRO STATION
Ⓑ BUS STOP

❶ Hotel Alimandi Vaticano
❷ Hotel Alimandi Tunisi
❸ To Hotel Gerber & Casa Valdese
❹ To Casa per Ferie Rooms
❺ Hostaria dei Bastioni Rest.

❻ La Rustichella Buffet & Gelateria Millennium
❼ To Tre Pupazzi & Vecchio Borgo Rest.
❽ L'Insalata Ricca, Duecento Gradi & Gelateria Old Bridge
❾ Supermarket

SLEEPING

Irene, Germano), it features four stars, 24 spacious rooms, and all the modern comforts you can imagine (Sb-€170, standard Db-€170–200, big Db with 2 double beds-€240–260, Tb-€230–260, 5 percent less with cash, air-con, elevator, Viale Vaticano 99, Metro: Cipro, tel. 06-397-45562, fax 06-397-30132, www.alimandi .it, alimandivaticano@alimandi.com).

$$ Hotel Alimandi Tunisi is a good value, run by other members of the friendly and entrepreneurial Alimandi family—Paolo, Grazia, Luigi, Marta, and Barbara. Their 27 perfumed rooms are air-conditioned, modern, and marbled in white (Sb-€90, Db-€130–175, 5 percent less with cash, grand buffet breakfast served in great roof garden, elevator, small gym, pool table, piano lounge, down the stairs directly in front of Vatican Museum, Via Tunisi 8, Metro: Cipro, reserve by phone at tel. 06-3972-3941, fax 06-3972-3943, www.alimandi.it, alimandi@tin.it). They offer a €15/person airport shuttle.

$$ Hotel Gerber, set in a quiet residential area, is family-run with 27 well-polished, businesslike, air-conditioned rooms (Sb-€120, Db-€170, Tb-€190, Qb-€200, 10 percent high-season discount and 15 percent low-season discount off these prices with this book in 2011 if you book direct, elevator, Wi-Fi, leafy terrace, Via degli Scipioni 241, at intersection with Via Ezio, a block from Metro: Lepanto, tel. 06-321-6485, fax 06-321-7048, www.hotel gerber.it, info@hotelgerber.it; Peter, Simonetta, and friendly dog Kira).

$ Casa Valdese is an efficient, well-managed, church-run hotel just over the Tiber River and near the Vatican, with 35 big, quiet rooms. It feels safe if a bit institutional, with the bonus of two breezy, communal roof terraces with incredible views (two external Sb-€58, Db-€130, Tb-€180, Qb-€210, discounts for 3-night stays, Internet access and Wi-Fi; from Lepanto Metro station, go one block down Via M. Colonna, turn left on Via degli Scipioni, then continue for a block to the intersection with Via Alessandro Farnese 18; tel. 06-321-5362, fax 06-321-1843, www .casavaldeseroma.it, reception@casavaldeseroma.it).

$ Casa per Ferie Santa Maria alle Fornaci houses pilgrims and secular tourists with simple class just a short walk south of the Vatican in 54 identical stark, utilitarian, mostly twin-bedded rooms. This is the most user-friendly convent-type place I've found. Reserve at least three months in advance (Sb-€70, Db-€98, Tb-€130, air-con, elevator; take bus #64 from Termini train station to San Pietro train station, then walk 100 yards north along Via della Stazione di San Pietro to Piazza Santa Maria alle Fornaci 27; tel. 06-393-67632, fax 06-393-66795, www.trinitaridematha.it, cffornaci@tin.it).

EATING

The Italians are masters of the art of fine living. That means eating...long and well. Lengthy, multi-course lunches and dinners and endless hours sitting in outdoor cafés are the norm. Americans eat on their way to an evening event and complain if the check is slow in coming. For Italians, the meal is an end in itself, and only rude waiters rush you. When you want the bill, mime-scribble on your raised palm or ask for it: *"Il conto?"* You may have to ask for it more than once. To save time, you could ask for the check when you receive the last item you order.

Even those of us who liked dorm food will find that the cafés, cuisine, and wines become a highlight of our Italian adventure. Trust me: This is sightseeing for your palate, and even if the rest of you is sleeping in cheap hotels, your taste buds will relish an occasional first-class splurge. You can eat well without going broke. But be careful: You're just as likely to blow a small fortune on a disappointing meal as you are to dine wonderfully for €25.

Restaurants

When restaurant-hunting, choose places filled with locals, not the place with the big neon signs boasting, "We speak English and accept credit cards." Restaurants parked on famous squares generally serve bad food at high prices to tourists. Locals eat better at lower-rent locales. Family-run places operate without hired help and can offer cheaper meals.

Good restaurants don't open for dinner before 19:00. Restaurants in Rome seem touristy in the early evening because tourists generally eat early, and Romans often eat late. Dinnertime is generally 20:00 to 22:00, and in restaurants it is a multi-course affair. A trattoria or *osteria* (which historically meant a simple restaurant) can now be just as elegant and pricey as a *ristorante*.

Tipping

In Italy, the "service" charge *(servizio)* is usually built into your bill's grand total in one of two ways: if the menu says *servizio incluso*, the listed prices already include this fee; if it says *servizio non incluso*, a fixed percentage (usually 10-15 percent of the total) will be added as a line item to the bottom of the bill. In either case, the total you pay already includes a basic tip. If you're pleased with the service, you can round up the bill by a euro or two (though many Italians rarely add this additional tip). Even if you pay your bill with a credit card, it's best to tip in cash—leave it on the table or hand it directly to your server.

Tipping is an issue only at restaurants that have waiters and waitresses. If you order your food at a counter, don't tip.

For unexciting but basic values, look for a *menù turistico*, a three- or four-course set-price meal (also called *menù del giorno*—menu of the day); the price includes a service charge, and there's no need to tip. While set-price meals can be cheap and easy, galloping gourmets order à la carte with the help of a menu translator. (*Rick Steves' Italian Phrase Book & Dictionary* has a menu decoder with enough phrases for intermediate eaters.) When going to an especially good restaurant with an approachable staff, my favorite strategy is to simply say, "Make me happy" (in this case, it's just fine to set a price limit).

A full meal consists of an appetizer (antipasto, €4–6), a first course (*primo piatto*, pasta or soup, generally €5–12), and a second course (*secondo piatto*, an expensive meat or fish dish, typically €6–15). Vegetables *(contorni, verdure)* rarely come with the *secondo* and cost extra (€4–6) as a side dish (an ample size for two people).

The euros can add up in a hurry. Light and budget eaters get a *primo piatto* each and share an antipasto. (Italians admit that the *secondo* is the least interesting aspect of their cuisine.) Another good option is sharing an array of *antipasti*—either several specific dishes or a plate of mixed delights assembled from a buffet. When Americans hear "buffet," we think it's a pile-the-plate-high, go-back-for-more, all-you-can-eat deal; but in Italy, an *antipasti* buffet is designed and priced as an appetizer—locals visit it once, taking a moderate amount. Watch others and imitate.

Some special dishes come in large quantities meant for two people; the shorthand way of showing this on a menu is "X2" (meaning "for two people"). The price listed generally indicates the cost per person.

Note that steak and seafood are often sold by weight (priced by the kilo—1,000 grams, or just more than 2 pounds; or by the *etto*—100 grams). The letters "s.q." means according to quantity. Fish is usually served whole with the head and tail; you can't just get half a fish or a filet unless it already comes prepared as just a filet (*filetto,* sometimes *trancio*—slice, as in tuna or swordfish). However, you can ask your waiter to select a smaller fish for you. Sometimes, especially for steak, restaurants require a minimum order of four or five *etti.* Beware, or be shell-shocked by €50 entrées. Make sure you're really clear on the price before ordering.

Restaurants often add a cover charge (*pane e coperto*—"bread and cover charge," €1–2) and a service charge (*servizio,* 10–15 percent); these charges are listed on the menu. As mentioned earlier, fixed-price tourist deals *(menù turistico)* include the service charge. If service is included, you don't need to tip.

Wine Bars *(Enoteche)*

An *enoteca* is a popular, fast, and inexpensive option for lunch. Surrounded by the office crowd, you can get a salad, plate of meats and cheeses, and a glass of good wine (see blackboards for the day's selection and price per glass). The area around the Pantheon and Piazza Parlamento (popular with politicians and bureaucrats) has plenty of *enoteche* handy for a sightseeing lunch break or evening destination. For more on wines, see page 342.

Bars/Cafés

Italian "bars" are not taverns but cafés. These neighborhood hangouts serve coffee, mini-pizzas, sandwiches, and drinks from the cooler. Many dish up plates of fried cheese and vegetables from under the glass counter, ready to reheat. This budget choice is the Italian equivalent of English pub grub.

For quick meals, bars usually have trays of cheap, ready-made sandwiches (*panini* or *tramezzini*). Some kinds are delightful grilled. To save time for sightseeing and room for dinner, consider a ham-and-cheese *panino* at a bar (called *toast;* have it grilled twice if you want it really hot) for lunch. To get food "to go," say, *"Da portar via"* (for the road). All bars have a WC *(toilette, bagno)* in the back, and customers (and the discreet public) can use it.

Bars serve great drinks: hot, cold, sweet, caffeinated, or alcoholic. Chilled bottled water, still *(naturale)* or carbonated *(frizzante),* is sold cheap to go.

Coffee: Coffee is as important as wine in Rome, and Italian coffee is some of the world's best. If you ask for *"un caffè,"* you'll get espresso. If you ask for a latte, you'll get just that—a glass of hot milk. Cappuccino is served to locals before noon and to tourists any time of day. (To an Italian, cappuccino is a breakfast drink and a travesty after eating anything with tomatoes.) Italians like their coffee only warm. To get it hot, request *"Molto caldo"* (MOHL-toh

EATING

KAHL-doh; very hot) or *"Più caldo, per favore"* (pew KAHL-doh pehr fah-VOH-ray; hotter, please).

Romans like iced coffee in the summer. It's slightly diluted, sugared espresso, called *caffè freddo;* to get it with ice, say *"con ghiaccio"* (kohn ghee-AH-choh, with a hard g). *Cappuccino freddo* is cold cappuccino served in a tall glass.

Experiment with a few of the hot options:
• Cappuccino: Espresso with foamed milk on top
• *Caffè latte:* Tall glass with espresso and hot milk mixed, no foam
• *Caffè hag:* Instant decaf (you can order decaffeinated versions of any coffee drink—ask for it *decaffeinato*)
• *Macchiato* (mah-kee-AH-toh): Espresso with only a little milk
• *Caffè americano:* Espresso diluted with water
• *Caffè corretto:* Espresso with a shot of liqueur

Juice: *Spremuta* means freshly squeezed as far as *succo* (fruit juice) is concerned; it's usually orange juice, and February through April it's almost always made from blood oranges. (Note: *Spumante* means champagne.)

Beer: Beer on tap is *alla spina.* Get it *piccola* (33 cl, 11 oz), *media* (50 cl, about a pint), or *grande* (a liter, about 2 pints).

Wine: To order a glass (*bicchiere;* bee-kee-AY-ree) of red *(rosso)* or white *(bianco)* wine, say, *"Un bicchiere di vino rosso/bianco."* *Corposo* means full-bodied. House wine *(vino della casa)* often comes in a quarter-liter carafe (8.5 oz, *un quarto*), half-liter pitcher (17 oz, *un mezzo*), or one-liter pitcher (34 oz, *un litro*). For more on wine, see page 342.

Other Drinks: A common *digestivo* in Rome is an *amaro,* which means "bitter." These alcoholic brews are often homemade by restaurants from a secret combination of herbs to aid digestion. Popular commercial brands are Fernet Branca and Montenegro. If your tastes run sweeter, try an anise-flavored liqueur called Sambuca, served *con moscha* (with three "flies"—coffee beans).

Prices: You'll notice a two- or three-tiered price system. It's cheapest to drink a cup of coffee while standing at the bar; you'll pay more for that same cup to sit at an indoor table, and often still more at an outdoor table. If you're on a budget, don't sit without first checking out the financial consequences. Ask, "Same price if I sit or stand?" by saying, *"Costa uguale al tavolo o al banco?"* (KOH-stah oo-GWAH-lay ahl TAH-voh-loh oh ahl BAHN-koh?). A cup of coffee at any bar generally costs only a euro if you stand. While coffee may cost €5 at a table, you can stand at the fanciest place in town and sip your coffee at the bar for the same price as at a simple café.

If the bar isn't busy, just order, and then pay when you leave.

Otherwise: 1) Decide what you want; 2) Find out the price by checking the price list on the wall, the prices posted near the food, or by asking the barista; 3) Pay the cashier; and 4) Give the receipt to the barista (whose clean fingers handle no dirty euros) and tell him or her what you want.

Budget Options

Rome offers many budget options for hungry travelers. Stop by a *rosticceria* for great cooked deli food. Self-service cafeterias (called "free flow" in Italian) offer the basics without add-on charges.

Pizza is cheap and everywhere. Key pizza vocabulary: *capricciosa* (generally ham, mushrooms, olives, and artichokes), *funghi* (mushrooms), *marinara* (tomato sauce, oregano, garlic, no cheese), *quattro formaggi* (four different cheeses), and *quattro stagioni* (different toppings on each of the four quarters, for those who can't choose just one menu item). If you ask for *peperoni* on your pizza, you'll get green or red peppers, not sausage. Kids like the simple *margherita* (cheese with tomato sauce) or *diavola* (the closest thing in Italy to American pepperoni). At take-out shops, pizza is sold either by the slice *(pizza a taglio)* or by the weight *(pizza rustica;* 100 grams, or *un etto*, is a cheap snack; 200 grams, or *due etti*, makes a light meal).

For a fast, cheap, and healthy lunch, find a *tavola calda* ("hot table") bar with a buffet spread of meat and vegetables, and ask for a mixed plate of vegetables with a hunk of mozzarella *(piatto misto di verdure con mozzarella)*. Don't be limited by what you can see. If you'd like a salad with a slice of cantaloupe and a hunk of cheese, they'll whip that up for you in a snap. Belly up to the bar and, with a pointing finger and key words in the chart in this chapter, you can get a fine mixed plate of vegetables. If something's a mystery, ask for a small taste *(un assaggio;* oon ah-SAH-joh).

Many places sell sandwiches of rustic bread and roasted pork with herbs (look for *porchetta*, por-KET-ah).

You might see döner kebab places selling slow-roasted veal, chicken, or falafel and salad fixings wrapped in pita bread, offering a cheap break from Italian food.

Beware of cheap eateries sporting big color photos of pizza and piles of different pastas. They have no kitchens and simply microwave disgusting prepackaged food. Unless you like lasagna with ice in the center, avoid these.

Ordering Food at Tavola Caldas

plate of mixed veggies	*piatto misto di verdure*	pee-AH-toh MEES-toh dee vehr-DOO-ray
"Heated, please."	*"Scaldare, per favore."*	skahl-DAH-ray, pehr fah-VOH-ray
"A taste, please."	*"Un assaggio, per favore."*	oon ah-SAH-joh, pehr fah-VOH-ray
artichoke	*carciofi*	kar-CHOH-fee
asparagus	*asparagi*	ah-spah-RAH-jee
beans	*fagioli*	fah-JOH-lee
breadsticks	*grissini*	gree-SEE-nee
broccoli	*broccoli*	BROH-koh-lee
cantaloupe	*melone*	may-LOH-nay
carrots	*carote*	kah-ROT-ay
green beans	*fagiolini*	fah-joh-LEE-nee
ham	*prosciutto*	proh-SHOO-toh
mushrooms	*funghi*	FOONG-ghee
potatoes	*patate*	pah-TAH-tay
rice	*riso*	REE-zoh
spinach	*spinaci*	speen-AH-chee
tomatoes	*pomodori*	poh-moh-DOH-ree
zucchini	*zucchine*	zoo-KEE-nay

(Excerpted from *Rick Steves' Italian Phrase Book & Dictionary*)

Picnics

In Rome, picnicking saves lots of euros and is a great way to sample regional specialties. In the process of assembling your meal, you get to deal with the Romans in the market scene. For a colorful experience, gather your ingredients in the morning at one of Rome's open-air produce markets (see the Shopping chapter); you'll probably visit several small stores or market stalls to put together a complete meal, and many close around noon.

While it's fun to visit the small specialty shops, an *alimentari* is your one-stop corner grocery store. A *supermercato* gives you more efficiency with less color for less cost. At busier supermarkets, you'll need to take a number for deli service. You'll find handy late-night supermarkets near the

Pantheon (Via Giustiniani), Spanish Steps (Via della Vittoria), Trevi Fountain (Via del Bufalo), and Campo de' Fiori (Via di Monte della Farina). Many *alimentari* and even supermarkets will gladly make you a fresh sandwich, charging you only for the weight of what you take and the piece of bread. And *rosticcerie* sell cheap food to go—you'll find options such as lasagna, rotisserie chicken, and sides like roasted potatoes and spinach.

Juice-lovers can get a liter of O.J. for the price of a Coke or coffee. Look for "100% *succo*" (juice) on the label. Hang on to the half-liter mineral-water bottles (sold everywhere for about €1). Buy juice in cheap liter boxes, then drink some and store the extra in your water bottle. Tap water—*acqua del rubinetto*—is fine; like the Romans do, I refill my water bottle from the public taps found all over the city (often near fountains).

Picnics can be an adventure in high cuisine. Be daring. Try the fresh mozzarella, *presto* pesto, shriveled olives, and any regional specialties the locals are excited about. Shopkeepers are happy to sell small quantities of produce. They seem to enjoy giving you a taste *(un assaggio)*. It is customary to let the merchant choose the produce for you. Say *"Per oggi"* (pehr OH-jee; "For today,") and

he or she will grab you something ready to eat, weigh it, and make the sale. A typical picnic for two might be fresh rolls, 100 grams of meat (*un etto* = 100 grams = about a quarter pound), 100 grams of cheese, two tomatoes, three carrots, two apples, yogurt, and a liter box of juice. Total cost: about €10.

Note that Rome discourages people from picnicking or drinking at historic monuments (such as on the Spanish Steps) in the old center. Technically violators can be fined, though it rarely happens. You'll be fine if you eat *with* a view rather than *on* the view.

Roman Cuisine

In ancient times, the dinner party was the center of Roman social life. It was a luxurious affair, set in the *triclinium* (formal dining room). Guest lists were small (3–9 people), and the select few reclined on couches during the exotic multi-course meal. Today the couches are gone, and the fare may not include jellyfish, boiled tree fungi, and flamingo, but the *cucina Romana* influence remains. It's fair to say that while French cuisine makes an art of the preparation, Italian (and Roman) cuisine is simpler and all about the ingredients.

Roman meals are still lengthy social occasions. Simple, fresh,

Eating with the Seasons

Italian cooks love to serve you fresh produce and seafood at its tastiest. If you must have porcini mushrooms outside of October and November, they'll be frozen. To get the freshest veggies at a fine restaurant, request *"Un piatto di vedure della stagioni, per favore"* ("A plate of veggies in season, please"). Here are a few examples of what's fresh when:

April-May:	Calamari, squid, green beans, asparagus, artichokes, and zucchini flowers
April-May and Sept-Oct:	Black truffles
May-June:	Mussels, asparagus, zucchini, cantaloupe, and strawberries
May-Aug:	Eggplant
Oct-Nov:	Mushrooms, white truffles, and chestnuts
Fresh year-round:	Clams and meats

seasonal ingredients dominate the dishes. The *cucina* is robust, strongly flavored, and unpretentious—much like the people who've created it over the centuries. It is said that Roman cooking didn't come out of emperors' or popes' kitchens, but from the *cucina povera*—the home cooking of the common people. This may explain the fondness Romans have for meats known as the *quinto quarto* ("fifth quarter"), such as tripe, tail, brain, and pigs' feet, as well as their interest in natural preservatives like chili peppers and garlic. Rome belongs to the warm, southern region of Lazio, which produces a rich variety of flavorful vegetables and fruit that are the envy of American supermarkets. Rome's proximity to the Mediterranean also allows for a great variety of seafood (especially on Fridays) that can be pricey if you're dining out.

Today, eating like a Roman means stopping at the neighborhood bar each morning for a pastry and coffee (usually cappuccino or espresso). Lunch (between 13:00 and 15:00) is traditionally the largest meal of the day, eaten at home, although work habits have changed this for many people who don't want to spend time commuting. Instead, they grab a quick meal in a *tavola calda* (cafeteria) buffet or a *panino* or *tramezzino* (sandwich).

EATING

When it's hot outside, a shaved-ice-with-fruit-syrup concoction called a *grattachecca* (grah-tah-KEK-kah) cools you down fast. The vendors at the little booths scrape shavings off ice blocks and then flavor them with syrups. Try the combo-flavors such as *limon-cocco*—lemon and coconut syrups with fresh chunks of coconut.

Specialties you may find on a menu include the following:

Antipasti (Appetizers)

Antipasto misto: A plate of marinated or grilled vegetables (eggplant, artichokes, peppers, mushrooms), cured meats, or seafood (anchovies, octopus).

Bruschetta: Toast brushed with olive oil and garlic or chopped tomatoes.

Fiori di zucca fritti: Squash blossoms filled with mozzarella and anchovies, then battered and fried.

Prosciutto e melone: Thin slices of ham wrapped around pieces of cantaloupe.

Supplí Fried oval-shaped rice balls with tomato sauce and mozzarella.

Primi Piatti (First Courses)

Spaghetti alla carbonara: Any type of pasta with a sauce made from beaten eggs, fried *pancetta* (bacon) or *guanciale* (cured pork cheek), cheese (*pecorino romano* or *parmigiano reggiano*), and black pepper.

Bucatini all'amatriciana: Thin pasta tubes with a sauce of tomatoes, onion, pork, and pecorino cheese on top.

Gnocchi alla romana: Small dumpling-like disks made from semolina, instead of potato, and baked with butter and cheese.

Penne all'arrabbiata: "Angry quills"—quill-shaped pasta topped with a spicy tomato sauce of chili peppers *(pepperoncini)* and garlic.

Rigatoni con la pajata: Medium-size wide pasta tubes topped with a stew of milk-fed calf intestines.

Stracciatella alla romana: Meat broth with whipped eggs, topped with parmesan cheese.

Spaghetti alle vongole veraci: Small clams in the shell sautéed with white wine and herbs, served over pasta.

Secondi Piatti (Second Courses)

Saltimbocca alla romana: "Jump-in-the-mouth"—thinly sliced veal layered with prosciutto and sage, then lightly fried.

Abbacchio alla scottadito: Baby lamb chops grilled and eaten as finger food.

Trippa alla romana: Tripe braised with onions, carrots, and mint.

Coda alla vaccinara: Oxtail braised with garlic, wine, tomato, and celery.

Involtini al sugo: Veal cutlets rolled with prosciutto, celery, and cheese in a tomato sauce.

Anguillette in umido: Stewed baby eels from nearby Lake Bracciano.

Filetti di baccalà: Dried cod fried in a batter.

Contorni (Side Dishes)

Sometimes the second course is not served with a vegetable, and you may want to order a side dish separately. If you get a salad, note that olive oil and wine vinegar are the only dressings.

Carciofi alla giudia: Small artichokes flattened and fried.

Fave al guanciale: Fava beans simmered with *guanciale* (cured pork cheek) and onion.

Misticanza: Mixed green salad of arugula *(rucola)* and curly endive *(puntarelle)* with anchovies.

Dolci (Desserts)

Dessert can be a seasonal fruit, such as *fragole* (strawberries) or *pesche* (peaches), or even cheese, such as *pecorino romano* (made from ewe's milk) or *caciotta romana* (made from a combination of ewe's and cow's milk).

Crostata di ricotta: A cheesecake-like dessert with ricotta, Marsala wine, cinnamon, and bits of chocolate.

Bignè: Cream puff–like pastries filled with *zabaglione* (egg yolks, sugar, and Marsala wine).

Tartufo: Rich dark-chocolate gelato ball with a cherry inside. **Con panna** gets you whipped cream on top.

Gelato: Rather than order dessert in a restaurant, I like to stroll with a cup or cone of gelato picked up at one of Rome's popular *gelaterie*.

Vini (Wines)

No large meal in Italy is complete without wine. Choosing a wine can be intimidating, but the Italian government tries to help you choose something decent, even if you're clueless. In general, wines are designated by one of the following categories:

Vino da Tavola (table wine) is the lowest grade. While inexpensive, Italy's wines are so good that, for many people, a basic *vino da tavola* is just fine with a meal. Many restaurants, even modest ones, take pride in their house wine (*"vino della casa"*), bottling their own or working with wineries.

Words to Live by, or...
How to Describe Wine in Italian

dry	*secco*	SAY-koh
sweet	*dolce*	DOHL-chay
earthy	*terroso*	tay-ROH-zoh
tannic	*tannico*	TAH-nee-koh
young	*giovane*	joh-VAH-nay
mature	*maturo*	mah-TOO-roh
sparkling	*spumante*	spoo-MAHN-tay
fruity	*fruttoso*	froo-TOH-zoh
full-bodied	*corposo*	kor-POH-zoh
elegant	*elegante*	ay-lay-GAHN-tay

Denominazione di Origine Controllata (DOC), a cut above table wine, is usually cheap, and can be very good. More than 700 wines have earned the DOC designation.

Denominazione di Origine Controllata e Garantita (DOCG) is the highest grade, and can be identified by the pink or green label on the neck and the scary price tag on the shelf. Only a limited number of wines in Italy can be called DOCG. They're generally a good bet if you want a quality wine, but you don't know anything else about the winemaker.

Riserva is a DOC or DOCG wine matured for a longer, more specific time.

The newest category is *Indicazione Geografica Tipica* (IGT), encompassing a broad group of wines that range from basic to some of Italy's best. It includes the "Super Tuscans"—wines that don't follow the strict "recipe" required for DOC or DOCG status, but that give vintners more opportunity to be creative.

Visit a Roman *enoteca* (wine bar) and sample some wines side-by-side to figure out what you like—and what suits your pocketbook. Although Lazio is not the most notable wine region in Italy, it produces several pleasant white wines and a few reds. **Frascati,** probably the best-known wine of the region, is an inexpensive dry white made from Trebbiano and Malvasia grapes. **Castelli Romani,** from the hills just south of Rome, is also from the Trebbiano grape and is similar to **Marino, Colli Albani,** and **Velletri,** all light and fairly dry. **Torre Ercolana** is known as Lazio's finest red. This dense wine is made from the regional Cesanese grape, as well as Cabernet and Merlot. Produced in small quantities, it must be aged for at least five years.

Restaurants

I've listed a number of restaurants I enjoy. While most are in quaint and therefore pricey and touristy areas (Piazza Navona, the Pantheon neighborhood, Campo de' Fiori, and Trastevere), many are tucked away just off the tourist crush.

In general, I'm impressed by how small the price difference is from a mediocre restaurant to a fine one. You can pay about 20 percent more for double the quality. If I had $90 for three meals in Rome, I'd spend $50 for one and $20 each for the other two, rather than $30 on all three. For splurge meals, I'd consider Gabriello, Fortunato, and Al Bric (in that order).

Rome's fabled nightspots (most notably Piazza Navona, near the Pantheon, and Campo de' Fiori) are lined with the outdoor tables of touristy restaurants with enticing menus and formal-vested waiters. The atmosphere is super-romantic: I, too, like the idea of dining under floodlit monuments, amid a constantly flowing parade of people. But you'll likely be surrounded by tourists, and noisy English-speakers can kill the ambience of the spot...leaving you with just a forgettable and overpriced meal. Restaurants in these areas are notorious for surprise charges, forgettable food, microwaved ravioli, and bad service.

I enjoy the view by savoring just a drink or dessert on a famous square, but I dine with locals on nearby low-rent streets, where the proprietor needs to serve a good-value meal and nurture a local following to stay in business. If you're set on eating—or just drinking and snacking—on a famous piazza, you don't need a guide-book listing to choose a spot; enjoy the ritual of slowly circling the square, observing both the food and the people eating it, and just sit where the view and menu appeals to you.

In Trastevere

Colorful Trastevere is now pretty touristy. Still, Romans join the tourists to eat on the rustic side of the Tiber River. Start at the central square (Piazza Santa Maria). Then choose: Eat with tourists enjoying the ambience of the famous square, or wander the back streets in search of a mom-and-pop place with barely a menu. My recommendations are within a few minutes' walk of each other (between Piazza Santa Maria Trastevere and Ponte Sisto; see map on page 294).

Trattoria da Lucia lets you enjoy simple, traditional food at a good price in a great scene. It's the quintessential rustic, 100 percent Roman Trastevere dining experience, and has been family-run since World War II. You'll meet four generations of the family, including Giuliano and Renato, their uncle Ennio, and Ennio's mom—pictured on the menu in the 1950s. The family specialty is *spaghetti alla Gricia,* with pancetta bacon (€9 pastas, €11 *secondi,* Tue–Sun 12:30–15:00 & 19:30–23:00, closed Mon, cash only, comfy indoor or evocative outdoor seating, just off Via del Mattonato on Vicolo del Mattonato 2, tel. 06-580-3601, some English spoken).

Trattoria da Olindo takes homey to extremes. You really feel like you dropped in on a family that cooks for the neighborhood to supplement their income. Don't expect any smiles here (€7 pastas, €9 *secondi,* Mon–Sat dinner served 20:00–22:30, closed Sun, cash only, indoor and funky outdoor seating, on the corner of Vicolo della Scala and Via del Mattonato at #8, tel. 06-581-8835).

Dar Poeta Pizzeria, tucked in a back alley, cranks out some of the best wood-fired pizza I've had in Rome. It's run by four friends—Marco, Paolo, Enrico, and another Marco—who welcome you into the informal restaurant beneath exposed brick arches. If you're in a spicy mood, order *lingua di fuoco* (tongue of fire). If you're extra hungry, pay an extra euro for *pizza alto* (thicker crust). Choose between their classic, cramped interior and lively tables outside on the cobblestones. Their chocolate dessert calzone is a favorite (€6–9 pizzas, daily 12:00–24:00, Vicolo del Bologna 45, tel. 06-588-0516).

Osteria Ponte Sisto da Oliviero, small and Mediterranean, specializes in traditional Roman cuisine, but has frequent Neapolitan specials as well. Just outside the tourist zone, it caters mostly to Romans and offers beautiful desserts and a fine value (€10 pastas, €14 *secondi,* Thu–Tue 12:30–15:30 & 19:30–24:00, closed Wed, Via Ponte Sisto 80, tel. 06-588-3411, Oliviero). Crossing Ponte Sisto (pedestrian bridge) toward Trastevere, continue across the little square (Piazza Trilussa) and you'll see it on the right.

Ristorante Checco er Carettiere is a big, family-run place that's been a Trastevere fixture for four generations. With white tablecloths, well-presented food, and dressy local diners, this is *the* place for a special meal in Trastevere. While it's overpriced, you'll eat well amidst lots of fun commotion. Reservations are smart, especially on weekends (€16 pastas, €22 *secondi,* daily 12:30–15:00 & 19:30–23:15, Via Benedetta 10, tel. 06-580-0985). Their *osteria* next door (#13) shares the same kitchen and offers less ambience, lower prices, and a more basic menu that changes daily (€11 pastas). Romans consider their *gelateria* (next door at #7) to be among the best on this side of the river.

Pizzeria "Ai Marmi" is a bright and noisy festival of pizza, where the oven and pizza-assembly line are surrounded by marble-slab tables (hence the nickname "the Morgue"). It's a classic Roman scene, with famously good €8 pizzas and very tight seating. Expect a long line between 20:00 and 22:00 (Thu–Tue 18:30–24:00, closed Wed, cash only, outdoor seating on busy Viale Trastevere, tram #8 from Largo Argentina to first stop over bridge, just beyond Piazza Sonnino at Viale Trastevere 53, tel. 06-580-0919).

Cantina Paradiso Wine and Cocktail Bar, a block over Viale Trastevere from the touristy action, has a simple romantic charm. During happy hour (18:00–21:00), the €6 drinks come with a well-made little buffet that can turn into a cheap, light dinner (€8 pastas, daily 12:00–24:00, lunch buffet, vegetarian options, Via San Francesco a Ripa 73, tel. 06-5899-799, Kiki).

And for Dessert: **Gelateria alla Scala** is a terrific little ice-cream shop that dishes up delightful cinnamon *(cannella)* and oh-wow pistachio (daily 12:00–24:00, Piazza della Scala 51, across from church on Piazza della Scala).

In the Jewish Ghetto

The Jewish Ghetto sits just across the river from Trastevere (see map on page 306).

Sora Margherita, hiding without a sign on a cluttered square, has been a rustic neighborhood favorite since 1927. Amid a picturesque commotion, families chow down on old-time Roman and Jewish dishes for a decent price. As it's technically not a real restaurant (it avoids red tape by being officially designated as an *associazione culturale*), you'll need to sign a card to join the "cultural association" when you order (don't worry; membership has no obligations except that you enjoy your meal). The menu's crude term for the fettuccini gives you some idea of the mood of this place: *nazzica culo* ("shaky ass"—what happens while it's made). Reservations are almost always necessary (June-Aug Mon–Fri 12:30–15:00, dinner seatings on Thu and Fri only at 20:00 and 21:30, closed Sat-Sun; Sept–May Mon–Sat 12:30–15:00, dinner seatings on Fri and Sat at 20:00 and 21:30, closed Sun; just south of Via del Portico d'Ottavia at Piazza delle Cinque Scole 30—look for the red curtain, tel. 06-687-4216, Ivan doesn't speak English).

In the Pantheon Neighborhood

For the restaurants in this central area, I've listed them based on which landmark they're closest to: Campo de' Fiori, Piazza Navona, the Trevi Fountain, or the Pantheon itself.

On and near Campo de' Fiori

While it is touristy, Campo de' Fiori offers a sublimely romantic setting. And, since it's so close to the collective heart of Rome, it remains popular with locals, even though its restaurants offer greater atmosphere than food value. The square is lined with popular and interesting bars, pizzerias, and small restaurants—all great for people-watching over a glass of wine. Later at night it's taken over by a younger clubbing crowd.

Osteria da Giovanni ar Galletto is nearby, on the more elegant and peaceful Piazza Farnese. Angelo entertains an upscale Roman crowd and has magical outdoor seating. Regrettably, service can be horrible, you need to double-check the bill, and single diners aren't treated very well. Still, if you're in no hurry and ready to savor my favorite al fresco setting in Rome (while humoring the waiters), this is a good bet (€10 pastas, €15 *secondi*, Mon–Sat 12:15–15:00 & 19:30–23:00, closed Sun, reservations smart for outdoor seating, tucked in corner of Piazza Farnese at #102, tel. 06-686-1714).

Osteria Enoteca al Bric is a mod bistro-type place run by Roberto and Barbara, who love to cook, serve good wine, and listen to jazz. Wine-case lids decorate the wall like happy memories (daily from 19:30 for dinner, closed Mon, reserve if dining after 20:30, can be pricey, 100 yards off Campo de' Fiori at Via del Pellegrino 51, tel. 06-687-9533).

Filetti di Baccalà is a cheap and basic Roman classic, where nostalgic regulars cram into wooden tables savoring their old-school favorites—fried cod finger-food fillets (€5 each) and raw *puntarelle* greens (slathered with anchovy sauce in spring and winter). Study what others are eating, and order from your grease-stained server by pointing at what you want. Sit in the fluorescently lit interior or try to grab a seat out on the little square, a quiet haven a block east of Campo de' Fiori (Mon–Sat 17:30–23:00, closed Sun, cash only, Largo dei Librari 88, tel. 06-686-4018).

Trattoria der Pallaro, an eccentric and well-worn eatery that has no menu, has a slogan: "Here, you'll eat what we want to feed you." Paola Fazi—with a towel wrapped around her head turban-style—and her gang dish up a rustic five-course meal of bland but typically Roman food for €25, including wine and coffee, and capped with a thimble of mandarin juice. While the service is odd and the food is forgettable, the experience can be fun (Tue–Sun 12:00–15:30 & 19:00–24:00, closed Mon, cash only, indoor/outdoor seating on quiet square, a block south of Corso Vittorio Emanuele, down Largo del Chiavari to Largo del Pallaro 15, tel. 06-6880-1488).

Pizzeria da Baffetto 2 makes pizza Roman-style: thin crust, crispy, and wood-fired. Eat in the cramped informal interior, or outside on the busy square (€7–9 pizzas, Wed–Mon 12:00–15:30 & 18:30–24:00, closed Tue, a block north of Campo de' Fiori at Piazza del Teatro di Pompeo 18, tel. 06-6821-0807).

Near Piazza Navona

Piazza Navona is the most quintessential setting for dining on a Roman square. Whether you eat here or not, you'll want to stroll the piazza before or after your evening meal. This is where many

Restaurants in the

T Taxi Stand **M** Metro Station
B Bus Stop → Entry Point to Sights

① Osteria da Giovanni ar Galletto
② Osteria Enoteca al Bric
③ Filetti di Baccalà
④ Trattoria der Pallaro
⑤ Pizzeria da Baffetto 2
⑥ Pizzeria da Baffetto
⑦ Ciccia Bomba
⑧ Cul de Sac & L'Insalata Ricca
⑨ L'Insalata Ricca
⑩ Rist. Pizzeria "da Francesco"
⑪ L'Antica Birreria Peroni
⑫ Rist. Pizzeria Sacro e Profano

Pantheon Neighborhood

13 Ristorante da Fortunato
14 Ristorante Enoteca Corsi
15 Miscellanea
16 Osteria da Mario
17 Le Coppelle Taverna
18 Trattoria dal Cav. Gino

19 Antica Salumeria
20 Super Market Di per Di
21 Supermercato Despar
22 Gelateria Caffè Pasticceria Giolitti
23 Crèmeria Monteforte
24 Gelateria San Crispino

EATING

people fall in love with Rome. The tangled streets just to the west are lined with popular eateries of many stripes.

Pizzeria da Baffetto, buried deep in the old quarter behind Piazza Navona, is a Roman favorite, famous for its rustic charm and tasty pizza. Its tables are tightly arranged amid the commotion of photos and sketches littering the walls. The pizza-assembly kitchen keeps things energetic, and the pizza oven keeps the main room warm (you can opt for a table on the cobbled street). Come early or late, or be prepared to wait (€7 pizzas, cash only, daily from 18:30, order "P," "M," or "D"—small, medium, or large; west of Piazza Navona on the corner of Via Sora at Via del Governo Vecchio 114, tel. 06-686-1617).

Ciccia Bomba is a traditional trattoria where Gianpaolo and crew serve up well-priced homemade pasta, wood-fired pizza, and other Roman specialties. With a name like "Fatso," this place had better have good food...and it does (€7 pastas, €9 *secondi*, Mon–Sat 12:00–15:00 & 19:00–24:00, closed Sun, off-season open Sun and closed Wed, Via del Governo Vecchio 76, a block west of Piazza Navona, just north from Piazza Pasquino, tel. 06-6880-2108).

Cul de Sac is a corridor-wide trattoria lined with wine bottles and packed with enthusiastic locals. Come early for an excellent tasting plate of salami and one of their many bottles of wine (they've got more than 1,000), or come later for a full meal of nicely cooked Roman dishes (daily 12:00–16:00 & 18:00–24:00, tel. 06-6880-1094, a block off Piazza Navona on Piazza Pasquino).

L'Insalata Ricca is a popular chain that specializes in hearty and healthy €8 salads and less-healthy pastas (daily 12:00–15:45 & 18:45–24:00). They have a handy branch on Piazza Pasquino (next to Cul de Sac, tel. 06-6830-7881), and a more spacious and enjoyable location a few blocks away, on a bigger square next to busy Corso Vittorio Emanuele (near Campo de' Fiori at Largo dei Chiavari 85, tel. 06-6880-3656).

Ristorante Pizzeria "da Francesco" is a bustling, unpretentious place with hardworking young waitstaff, great indoor seating, and classic outdoor seating on a cluttered little square that makes you want to break out a sketch pad. Their blackboard explains the daily specials (€7 pizzas, €8 pastas, €10 *secondi*, open daily, 3 blocks west of Piazza Navona at Piazza del Fico 29, tel. 06-686-4009).

Near the Trevi Fountain

L'Antica Birreria Peroni is Rome's answer to a German beer hall. Serving hearty mugs of the local Peroni beer and lots of just plain fun beer-hall food and Italian classics, the place is a hit with Romans for a cheap night out (Mon–Sat 12:00–24:00, closed Sun, midway between Trevi Fountain and Capitol Hill, a block off Via del Corso at Via di San Marccllo 19, tel. 06-679-5310).

Ristorante Pizzeria Sacro e Profano fills an old church with spicy southern Italian (Calabrian) cuisine and satisfied tourists. Run with enthusiasm by Francesco and friends, this is just far enough away from the Trevi mobs. Their pizza oven is wood-fired, and their hearty €15 *antipasti* plate is a filling montage of Calabrian taste treats (daily 12:00–15:00 & 18:00–24:00, a block off Via del Tritone at Via dei Maroniti 29, tel. 06-679-1836).

Close to the Pantheon

Eating on the square facing the Pantheon is a temptation (there's even a McDonald's that offers some of the best outdoor seating in town), and I'd consider it just to relax and enjoy the Roman scene. But if you walk a block or two away, you'll get less view and better value. Here are some suggestions.

Ristorante da Fortunato is an Italian classic, with fresh flowers on the tables and white-coated, black-tie waiters politely serving good meat and fish to politicians, foreign dignitaries, and tourists with good taste. Don't leave without perusing the photos of their famous visitors—everyone from former Iraqi Foreign Minister Tariq Aziz to Bill Clinton seems to have eaten here. All are pictured with the boss, Fortunato, who, since 1975, has been a master of simple edible elegance. The outdoor seating is fine for watching the river of Roman street life flow by, but the atmosphere is inside. For a dressy night out, this is a reliable and surprisingly reasonable choice—but be sure to reserve ahead (plan to spend €45 per person, Mon–Sat 12:30–15:00 & 19:30–23:30, closed Sun, a block in front of the Pantheon at Via del Pantheon 55, tel. 06-679-2788).

Ristorante Enoteca Corsi is a wine shop that grew into a thriving lunch-only restaurant. The Paiella family serves straightforward, traditional cuisine at great prices to an appreciative crowd of office workers. Check the blackboard for daily specials (gnocchi on Thursday, fish on Friday, and so on). Friendly Giuliana, Claudia, and Manuela welcome eaters to step into their wine shop and pick out a bottle. For the cheap take-away price, plus €2–4 (depending on the wine), they'll uncork it at your table. With €8 pastas, €11 main dishes, and fine wine at a third of the price you'd pay in normal restaurants, this can be a superb value. And guests with this book finish their meal with a free glass of the family's homemade *limoncello* (Mon–Sat 12:00–15:00, closed Sun, a block toward the Pantheon from the Gesù Church at Via del Gesù 87, no reservations possible, tel. 06-679-0821).

Miscellanea is run by much-loved Mikki, who's on a mission to keep foreign students well-fed. You'll find hearty and fresh €4 sandwiches and a long list of €6 salads, along with pasta and other staples. Mikki (and his son, Romero) often tosses in a fun little extra, including—if you have this book on the table—a free glass

EATING

of Mikki's "sexy wine" (homemade from *fragoline*—strawberry-flavored grapes). This place is popular with American students on foreign-study programs (daily 8:00–24:00, indoor/outdoor seating, facing the rear of the Pantheon at Via della Palombella 34, tel. 06-6813-5318).

Osteria da Mario, a homey little mom-and-pop joint with a no-stress menu, serves traditional favorites in a fun dining room or on tables spilling out onto a picturesque old Roman square (€8 pastas, €10 *secondi,* Mon–Sat 13:00–15:30 & 19:00–23:00, closed Sun, from the Pantheon walk 2 blocks up Via Pantheon, go left on Via delle Coppelle, take first right to Piazza delle Coppelle 51, tel. 06-6880-6349, Marco).

Le Coppelle Taverna is simple, basic, family-friendly, and inexpensive—especially for pizza—with a checkered-tablecloth ambience (€9 pizzas, daily 12:30–15:00 & 19:30–23:30, Via delle Coppelle 39, tel. 06-6880-6557, Alfonso).

Trattoria dal Cav. Gino, tucked away on a tiny street behind the Parliament, has been a favorite since 1963. Photos on the wall recall the days when it was the haunt of big-time politicians. Grandpa Gino shuffles around grating the parmesan cheese while his sister and son serve up traditional Roman favorites and make sure things run smoothly. Reserve ahead, even for lunch (€8 pastas, €11 *secondi,* cash only, Mon–Sat 13:00–14:45 & 20:00–22:30, closed Sun, fish on Friday, behind Piazza del Parlamento and just off Via di Campo Marzio at Vicolo Rosini 4, tel. 06-687-3434, Fabrizio and Carla—Gino's son and daughter—both speak English).

Picnicking Close to the Pantheon

It's fun to munch a picnic with a view of the Pantheon. (Remember to be discreet.) Here are some options.

Antica Salumeria is an old-time *alimentari* (grocery store) on the Pantheon square. Eduardo speaks English and will help you assemble your picnic: artichokes, mixed olives, bread, cheese, meat (they're proud of their Norcia prosciutto), and wine (with plastic glasses). Just set a price (figure €10 per person), and Eduardo will assemble it. Their pastries are fresh from their own bakery. While you can create your own sandwiches (sold by the weight, more fun, and cheaper), they also sell quality ready-made sandwiches for around €5 (daily 8:00–21:00, mobile 334-340-9014).

Supermarkets near the Pantheon: Food is relatively cheap at Italian supermarkets. **Super Market Di per Di** is a convenient place for groceries a block from Gesù Church (Mon–Sat 8:00–21:00, Sun 9:00–19:30, 50 yards off Via del Plebiscito at Via del Gesù 59). Another place, **Supermercato Despar,** is a half a block from the Pantheon toward Piazza Navona (daily 9:00–22:00, Via Giustiniani 18).

Gelato Close to the Pantheon

Three fine *gelaterie* are within a two-minute walk of the Pantheon.

Gelateria Caffè Pasticceria Giolitti, Rome's most famous and venerable ice-cream joint, has reasonable take-away prices and elegant Old World seating (daily 7:00–24:00, just off Piazza Colonna and Piazza Monte Citorio at Via Uffici del Vicario 40, tel. 06-699-1243).

Crèmeria Monteforte is known for its traditional, quality gelato and super-creamy sorbets (*cremolati*). The fruit flavors are especially refreshing—think gourmet slushies (Tue–Sun 10:00–24:00, off-season closes earlier, closed Mon and Dec, faces the west side of the Pantheon at Via della Rotonda 22, tel. 06-686-7720).

Gelateria San Crispino, well-respected by Romans, serves small portions of particularly tasty gourmet gelato using creative ingredients. Because of their commitment to natural ingredients, the colors are muted; gelato purists consider bright colors a sign of unnatural chemicals used to attract children. They serve cups, but no cones (daily 12:00–24:00, a block in front of the Pantheon on Piazza della Maddalena, tel. 06-6889-1310).

In North Rome: Near the Ara Pacis and Spanish Steps

To locate these restaurants, see the "Dolce Vita Stroll" map on page 368.

Ristorante il Gabriello is inviting and small—modern under medieval arches—and provides a peaceful and local-feeling respite

from all the top-end fashion shops in the area. Claudio serves with charisma, while his brother Gabriello cooks creative Roman cuisine using fresh, organic products from his wife's farm. Italians normally just trust the waiter and say, "Bring it on." Tourists are understandably more cautious, but you can be trusting here. Simply close your eyes and point to anything on the menu. Or invest €45 in "Claudio's Extravaganza" (not including wine), and he'll shower you with edible kindness. Specify whether you'd prefer fish, meat, or both. (Note that Romans think raw shellfish is the ultimate in fine dining. If you differ, make that clear.) When finished, I stand up, hold my belly, and say, *"Ahhh, la vita è bella"* (€10 pastas, €15 *secondi,* dinner only, Mon–Sat 19:00–23:00, closed Sun, reservations smart, air-con, dress respectfully—no shorts please, 3 blocks from Spanish Steps at Via Vittoria 51, tel. 06-6994-0810).

Osteria Gusto is thriving with trendy locals. While pricey,

EATING

it's untouristy, gives a glimpse of today's Roman scene, and is fine for a glass of good wine over an artisanal cheese plate or a complete dinner (€13 pastas, €20 *secondi*, daily 12:30–15:30 & 19:00–24:00, opens at 18:30 for drinks and appetizers only, reservations recommended after 20:00 and on weekends, on the corner of Via Soderini at Via della Frezza 16, tel. 06-3211-1482).

L'EnotecAntica, an upbeat, atmospheric 200-plus-year-old *enoteca,* has around 60 Italian-only wines by the glass (€4 to €10), and a fresh €14 *antipasti* plate of veggies, salami, and cheese. It's very crowded on summer evenings (daily 11:00–24:00, Via della Croce 76b, tel. 06-679-0896).

In Ancient Rome: Eating Cheaply near the Colosseum

You'll find good views but poor value at the restaurants directly behind the Colosseum. To get your money's worth, eat at least a block away. Here are three handy eateries, all shown on the map on page 325: one at the foot of Via Cavour, and two at the top of Terme di Tito (a long block uphill from the Colosseum, near St. Peter-in-Chains church—of Michelangelo's *Moses* fame; for directions, see page 261).

Enoteca Cavour 313 is a wine bar with a mission: to offer good wine and quality food with an old-fashioned commitment to value and friendly service. It's also a convenient place for a good lunch near the Forum and Colosseum. Angelo and his three partners enjoy creating a mellow ambience under lofts of wine bottles (daily specials and fine wines by the glass, daily 12:30–14:45 & 19:30–24:00, 100 yards off Via dei Fori Imperiali at Via Cavour 313, tel. 06-6785-496).

Caffè dello Studente is popular with engineering students attending the nearby University of Rome. Pina, Mauro, and their perky daughter Simona (speaks English) give my readers a royal welcome and serve typical *bar gastronomia* fare—toasted sandwiches, salads, and pizzas (stick to any of the aforementioned fare to avoid frozen dishes). If they have a "Rick Steves menu," give it a miss. You can get your food to go *(da portar via),* eat standing at the crowded bar, or wait for table service outside. If it's not busy, show this book when you order at the bar and sit without paying extra at a table (Mon–Sat 7:30–22:30, April–Oct Sun 9:00–22:30, Nov–March closed Sun, Via delle Terme di Tito, tel. 06-488-3240).

Hostaria da Nerone, next door, is a more formal restaurant with much better food and homemade pasta dishes. Their €9 *antipasti* plate—with a variety of veggies, fish, and meat—is a good value for a quick lunch. While the *antipasti* menu indicates specifics, you can have a plate of whatever's out—just direct the waiter to assemble the €9 *antipasti* plate of your lunchtime dreams (Mon–Sat 12:00–15:00 & 19:00–23:00, closed Sun, indoor/outdoor seating, Via

EATING

Restaurants near Termini Train Station

① Ristorante del Giglio
② Ristorante Da Giovanni
③ Ristorante La Pentolaccia
④ Ricci Est Est Est Pizzeria
⑤ Hostaria Romana
⑥ Bar Tavola Calda
⑦ Snack Bar
⑧ Panificio Firenze
⑨ Flann O'Brien Irish Pub

delle Terme di Tito 96, tel. 06-481-7952, run by Teo and Eugenio).

Near Termini Train Station

You have several eating options near my recommended hotels on Via Firenze.

Dining

Ristorante del Giglio is an elegant circa-1900 place with a long tradition of serving traditional Roman dishes. You'll eat pricey dishes in a big hall of about 20 tables with dressy locals and tourists following the recommendations of nearby hotels. While not a particularly good value, the space is nice and it's stress-free (€12 pastas, €15 *secondi*,

Mon 19:00–23:00, Tue–Sat 12:15–15:00 & 19:00–23:00, closed Sun, alluring dessert cart, Via Torino 137, tel. 06-488-1606, Fiorella).

Ristorante Da Giovanni is a well-worn old-time eatery that makes no concessions to tourism or the modern world—just hard-working cooks and waiters serving standard dishes at great prices to a committed clientele. It's simply fun to eat in the middle of this high-energy, old-school diner (€6–9 pastas and *secondi*, daily specials, Mon–Sat 12:00–15:00 & 19:00–22:00, closed Sun and Aug, corner of Via XX Settembre at Via Antonio Salandra 1, tel. 06-485-950).

Ristorante La Pentolaccia, pricier and more romantic than the nearby Da Giovanni, is a dressy, tourist-friendly place with tight seating and classic Roman cooking (Mon–Sat 12:00–15:00 & 17:30–23:00, Sun 17:30–23:00, a block off Via XX Settembre at Via Flavia 38, tel. 06-483-477).

Ricci Est Est Est Pizzeria, a venerable family-run pizzeria, has plenty of historical ambience, good €8 pizzas, and danger-ously tasty *fritti,* such as fried *baccalà* (cod) and zucchini flowers (Tue–Sun 19:00–24:00, closed Mon and Aug, Via Genova 32, tel. 06-488-1107).

Hostaria Romana is a busy bistro with a hustling and fun-loving gang of waiters and noisy walls graffitied by happy eat-ers. While they specialize in fish and traditional Roman dishes, their €10 *antipasti* plate can make a good meal in itself (Mon–Sat 12:15–15:00 & 19:15–23:00, closed Sun, a block up the lane just past the entrance to the big tunnel near the Trevi Fountain at Via de Boccaccio 1, tel. 06-474-5284).

Fast, Simple Meals near Termini Train Station

Bar Tavola Calda is a workers' favorite for a quick, cheap lunch. They have good, fresh, hot dishes ready to go for a fine price. Head back past the bar to peruse their enticing display, point at what you want, then grab a seat and the young waitstaff will serve you (Mon–Fri 6:00–18:00, closed Sat–Sun, Via Torino 40).

Snack Bar puts out a lunchtime display of inexpensive pastas, colorful sandwiches, fresh fruit, and salad. Their loyal customers love the *caffè con crema* whipped with sugar (daily 6:00–24:00, Via Firenze 33, mobile 339-393-1356, Enrica).

Panificio Firenze has take-out pizza, sandwiches, and an old-fashioned *alimentari* (grocery) with everything you'd need for a picnic (Mon–Fri 7:00–19:00, Sat 7:00–14:00, closed Sun, Via Firenze 51–52, tel. 06-488-5035).

Flann O'Brien Irish Pub is an entertaining place for a light meal of pasta...or something *other* than pasta, such as grilled meats and giant salads, served early and late, when other places are closed. They have Irish beer, live sporting events on TV, and per-haps the most Italian crowd of all. Walk way back before choosing a table (daily 7:00–24:00, Via Nazionale 17, at intersection with Via Napoli, tel. 06-488-0418).

Near Vatican City

Avoid the restaurant-pushers handing out fliers near the Vatican: bad food and expensive menu tricks. Try any of these instead (see map on page 331).

Hostaria dei Bastioni, run by Emilio, is conveniently located midway on your hike from St. Peter's to the Vatican Museum, with noisy street-side seating and a quiet interior (€7 pastas, €12 *secondi,* no cover charge, Mon–Sat 12:00–15:30 & 19:00–23:00, closed Sun, Via Leone IV 29, at corner of Vatican wall, tel. 06-3972-3034).

La Rustichella serves tasty wood-fired pizza and the usual pasta in addition to their famous and sprawling *antipasti* buffet (€8 for a single plate). Arrive when it opens at 19:30 to avoid a line and have the pristine buffet to yourself. Do like the Romans do—take a moderate amount and make one trip only (Tue–Sun 12:30–15:00 & 19:30–24:00, closed Mon, near Metro: Cipro, opposite church at end of Via Candia, Via Angelo Emo 1, tel. 06-3972-0649). Consider the fun and fruity **Gelateria Millennium** next door.

L'Insalata Ricca is another branch of the popular chain that serves salads and pastas (daily 12:30–15:30 & 18:30–23:45, across from Vatican walls at Piazza Risorgimento 5, tel. 06-3973-0387).

Duecento Gradi is a good bet for fresh and creative €5 sandwiches (daily 12:00–23:00, Piazza Risorgimento 3, tel. 06-3975-4239).

Viale Giulio Cesare: This street is lined with cheap *pizza rustica* shops, self-serve places, and inviting eateries.

Along Borgo Pio: The pedestrians-only Borgo Pio—a block from Piazza San Pietro—has restaurants worth a look, such as **Tre Pupazzi** (Mon–Sat 12:00–15:00 & 19:00–23:00, closed Sun, at corner of Via Tre Pupazzi and Borgo Pio, tel. 06-686-8371). At **Vecchio Borgo,** across the street, you can get pasta, pizza slices, and veggies to go (Mon–Sat 9:00–21:00, closed Sun, Borgo Pio 27a, tel. 06-8117-3585).

Picnic Supplies: Turn your nose loose in the wonderful **Mercato Trionfale** covered market, one of the best in the city, three blocks north of the Vatican Museum (Mon–Sat roughly 7:00–14:00, closed Sun, corner of Via Tunisi and Via Andrea Doria). If the market is closed, try several nearby supermarkets; the most convenient is **GS Di per Di** (Mon–Sat 8:00–20:00, Sun 9:00–20:00, Via Sebastiano Veniero 16).

Gelato: **Gelateria Old Bridge** scoops up hearty portions of fresh gelato for tourists and nuns alike. The quality, quantity, and value can't be beat (daily 10:00–23:00, just off Piazza Risorgimento across from Vatican walls at Via Bastioni 3).

ROME WITH CHILDREN

Sorry, but Rome is not a great place for little kids. Parks are rare. Kid-friendly parks are rarer. Most of the museums are low-tech and lack hands-on fun.

The good news for kids? Pizza and gelato. And Italians are openly fond of kids, so you'll probably get lots of friendly attention from locals.

Sights and Activities

Rome's many squares are traffic-free, with plenty of space to run and pigeons to feed while Mom and Dad enjoy a coffee at an outdoor table.

When visiting the ancient sites, have some fun with *Rome: Past and Present,* a book with plastic overlays showing how the ruins used to look. It's available at stalls near the entrance of ancient sites.

The following sights, which are fun for kids, are covered in more detail elsewhere in this book: the **Montemartini Museum** for ancient statuary (in an old power plant with art at kids' level, and no crowds—see page 81); **Time Elevator Roma** (like a Disney ride trying to teach Roman history—see page 57); the **Planetarium** and **Astrological Museum** (especially the "Machine of Space and Time") at the Museum of Roman Civilization in E.U.R. (see page 84); and the climb to the top of **St. Peter's dome** (it'll tire them out, plus it includes a dizzy railing view into the church from halfway up the dome—see page 259). The topless double-decker **Trambus 110 tour** offers a two-hour swing past all of the major sights (see page 38).

Older children may want to **rent a bike** at the Ancient Appian Way (see Ancient Appian Way Tour chapter); use the bike/

Family Travel Tips

- Take advantage of local information. Ask at Rome's TIs about kid-friendly activities. TIs often have a helpful "kid's pack."

- Don't overdo it. Tackle only one or two key sights a day (Vatican Museum, or Colosseum and Forum) and mix in a healthy dose of fun activities, like exploring Rome's great public sites (Piazza Navona, Trevi Fountain, and Villa Borghese Gardens).

- Rome's hotels often give price breaks for kids. (Air-conditioning can be worth the splurge.)

- Eat dinner early (around 19:00) and you'll miss the romantic crowd. While kids may do best in self-serve cafeterias or even fast-food places, if you eat early you'll find that kids are comfortable and welcome in better restaurants. Eating *al fresco* is great with kids. For ready-made picnics that can please adults and kids, try the *rosticcerie* (delis). *Pizza rustica* shops sell cheap take-out pizza; kids like *margherita* (tomato and cheese) and *diavola* (similar to pepperoni).

- Public WCs are hard to find: Try museums, bars, gelato shops, and fast-food restaurants.

- Follow this book's crowd-beating tips. Kids don't want to stand in a long line for a museum (which they might not even want to see).

- Any person under 39 inches tall travels free on Rome's public transit.

- If you're taking the train to another city, ask for the family discount ("Offerta Familia") when buying tickets at a counter; or, at a ticket machine, click "Yes" to the "Do you want ticket issue?" cue, then click "Familia." With the discount, families of three to five people with at least one kid (age 12 or under) get 50 percent off the kids' tickets, and 20 percent off the adults'. The deal doesn't apply to all trains at all times, but it's certainly worth asking about.

pedestrian path to avoid the traffic. The spooky tunnels of the **Catacombs** are goblin-pleasers (the Catacombs of Priscilla offer half-off entry for kids 15 and under; for Catacombs, see pages 66 and 88). The macabre **Cappuccin Crypt,** decorated with bones, fascinates children and adults alike (see page 62).

The **Vatican Museum** comes with mummies and cool statues (in particular, my kids were very entertained by the entire hall of statues with their penises broken off). Nearby, **Castel Sant'Angelo**—with Vatican views and weapon displays—appeals to young knights (see page 71).

The **Church of San Ignazio,** with its false dome, fascinates kids and adults (see page 148). Your children can get a whiff of Egypt by visiting Rome's funky little **pyramid** (free and always viewable, Metro: Piramide—see page 78). Check out the cat hospice in the adjacent park and climb on the chunk of old Roman wall across the street.

The **Villa Borghese Gardens** are Rome's sprawling central park. The best kids' zones are near Porta Pinciana, where you'll find rental bikes, pony rides, and other amusements (Metro: Barberini or Spagna). Summer weekends at the gardens, sure to be a hit with kids, include classic Roman puppet shows at Teatro dei Burattini. Rome's **zoo,** Bioparco, in the northeast section of the park, houses about 900 animals—including the endangered black lemur, pygmy hippopotamus, Gila monster, and painted hunting dog (kids under 3-free, kids 4–12-€10.50, adults-€12.50, April–Oct 9:30–18:00, Nov–March 9:30–17:00, last entry one hour before closing, café and picnic areas, Piazzale del Giardino Zoologico 1, Metro: Flaminio, tel. 06-360-8211, www.bioparco.it).

Explora, a children's museum, is a hands-on wonderland for kids 12 and under. Descriptions are in Italian, but younger kids probably won't care (kids 1–3-€3, kids 4–99-€7, parent must accompany child; four 1.75-hour sessions/day: Tue–Sun at 10:00, 12:00, 15:00, and 17:00; closed Mon, confirm session times in advance by checking website—www.mdbr.it—or calling 06-361-3776, helpful English-speaking staff; 10-minute walk from Piazza del Popolo at Via Flaminia 82, Metro: Flaminio).

Bocca della Verità, the legendary "Mouth of Truth" at the Church of Santa Maria in Cosmedin, is fun for kids and parents with cameras (see page 45). Liars beware.

Rome has a big water park called **Hydromania** (€16.50 June–Aug Mon–Fri, €18 Sat–Sun, cheaper for kids 12 and under and anyone arriving after 14:00, open June–Aug daily 9:30–18:30, Sat–Sun until 19:00, closed Sept–May, Vicolo Casal Lumbroso 200, exit 33 off ring freeway west of the city, tel. 06-6618-3183, www.hydromania.it).

Aquapiper, another water park, is near Tivoli (Via Maremmana Inferiore, in Guidonia, 15-minute drive east of Rome, tel. 0774-326-538, www.aquapiper.it); ask about the free shuttle bus from the center of Rome (leaves from Piazza della Repubblica).

Rome feels safe at night, and you can easily take your kids on the walks suggested in this book, such as the "Dolce Vita Stroll" on page 367. On the Night Walk Across Rome (page 282), children like slurping up chocolate gelato at the Tre Scalini *gelateria* on Piazza Navona and tossing coins in the Trevi Fountain. Consider letting your child act as tour guide for an hour by actually leading one of the walks. *Buona fortuna!*

SHOPPING

Traditionally, shops are open from 9:00 to 13:00 and from 16:00 to 19:00. They're often closed on Sundays, summer Saturday afternoons, and winter Monday mornings. But in the city center, you'll find that many are now staying open through lunch (generally 10:00–19:00).

For information on VAT refunds and customs regulations, see page 13.

If all you need are souvenirs, a surgical strike at any souvenir shop will do. Otherwise, try...

Department Stores

To conveniently peruse clothes, bags, shoes, and perfume at several major Italian chain stores, wander the shopping complex under Termini Station (most stores open daily 8:00–22:00).

Large department stores offer relatively painless one-stop shopping. A good upscale department store is **La Rinascente** (like Nordstrom or Macy's). Its main branch is on Piazza Fiume, and there's a smaller store on Via del Corso in the **Galleria Alberto Sordi,** an elegant 19th-century "mall" (across from Piazza Colonna). **UPIM** is the Roman JC Penney (many branches, including inside Termini Station, Via Nazionale 111, Piazza Santa Maria Maggiore, and Via del Tritone 172). **Oviesse,** a cheap clothing outlet, is near the Vatican Museum (on the corner of Via Candia and Via Mocenigo, Metro: Cipro).

Shopping Neighborhoods

A good, midrange shopping area is all along **Via del Corso,** with prices increasing as you head toward Piazza di Spagna. **Via Nazionale** also features a range of affordable shops, especially for clothes and shoes. Cheapskates scrounge through the junky but dirt-cheap shops in the gritty area around **Piazza Vittorio.**

Boutiques

For top fashion, stroll the streets around the Spanish Steps, including **Via Condotti, Via Borgognona** (for the big-name shops), and **Via del Babuino** (trendy design shops and galleries). For antiques, stroll **Via de Coronari** (between Piazza Navona and the bend in the river), **Via Giulia** (between Campo de' Fiori and the river), and **Via Margutta** (classier, with art galleries too, from Spanish Steps to Piazza del Popolo). For funkier, unique items, try **Via Giubbonari**—it's packed with artsy little boutiques—and other streets near Campo de' Fiori.

Flea Markets

For antiques and fleas, the granddaddy of markets is the **Porta Portese** *mercato delle pulci* (flea market). This Sunday-morning market is long and spindly, running between the actual Porta Portese (a gate in the old town wall) and the Trastevere train station. Starting at Porta Portese, walk through the long, tacky parade of stalls selling cheap bras and shoes. Along the way, check out the con artists with the shell games. Each has shills in the crowd "winning big money" to get suckers involved. Hang on to your wallet—literally, in your front pocket (and make sure your money belt is tucked in). This is a den of thieves. The heart of the market for real flea-market junk (hiding a few little antique treasures) is the square in the center near Via Cesare Pascarella. I find that a slow stroll through the entire market and back to the Porta Portese takes about an hour and a half. While the shopping gets old (and the vendor food will make you sick), the people-watching is endlessly entertaining (6:30–13:00 Sun only, on Via Portuense and Via Ippolito Nievo; to get to the market, catch bus #75 from Termini station or tram #8 from Largo Argentina, get off the bus or tram on Viale Trastevere, and walk toward the river—and the noise).

At the **Via Sannio** market, you'll find new and used clothing and leather goods, some handicrafts, and random items that were probably stolen. You won't find antiques (Mon–Sat 9:00–13:30, closed Sun, behind Coin department store, a couple of blocks south of San Giovanni in Laterano, Metro: San Giovanni).

Open-Air Produce Markets

Rome's outdoor markets provide a fun and colorful dimension of the city that even the most avid museumgoer should not miss. Wander through the easygoing neighborhood produce markets, which clog certain streets and squares every morning (7:00–13:00) except Sunday. Consider the huge **Mercato Trionfale** (three blocks in front of Vatican Museum at Via Andrea Doria). Another great food market is the **Mercato Esquilino** (Via Turati near Piazza Vittorio). Smaller but equally charming slices of everyday Roman life are at markets on these streets and squares: **Piazza delle Coppelle** (near the Pantheon), **Via Balbo** (near Termini Station and recommended hotels off Via Nazionale), and **Via della Pace** (near Piazza Navona). The covered **Mercato di Testaccio** sells mostly produce and is a hit with photographers and people-watchers (Piazza Testaccio, near Metro: Piramide). And **Campo de' Fiori,** despite having become quite touristy, is still a fun scene.

Airport Souvenirs

Fiumicino (a.k.a. Leonardo da Vinci) Airport sells Italian specialty foods vacuum-packed to clear US customs. Most shops are near the departure gates (after you check your bags and pass through security). Try *parmigiano reggiano* cheese, dried porcini mushrooms or peppers, and better olive oil than you can buy at home. Don't bother buying any salami or prosciutto unless it's canned; you're not allowed to bring fresh meat into the US. Remember, if you're flying to the US and transferring before your final destination, you'll likely be required to pack purchased liquids in your checked luggage after clearing customs (a potential recipe for disaster).

NIGHTLIFE

Romans get dressed up and eat out in casual surroundings for their evening entertainment. For most visitors, the best after-dark activity is simply to grab a gelato and stroll the medieval lanes that connect the romantic, floodlit squares and fountains. Head for Piazza Navona, the Pantheon, Campo de' Fiori, Trevi Fountain, Spanish Steps, Via del Corso, Trastevere (around the Santa Maria in Trastevere Church), or Monte Testaccio.

○ See my Night Walk Across Rome chapter and "Dolce Vita Stroll," page 367.

Performances

Get a copy of the entertainment guide *Evento* (free at TIs). Look at the current listings of concerts, operas, dance, and films. Posters around town also advertise upcoming events. For the most up-to-date events calendar, check these English-language websites: www.inromenow.com, www.wantedinrome.com, and http://rome.angloinfo.com.

Classical Music: Music-lovers will seek out the mega-music complex of the **Rome Auditorium** (Parco della Musica), designed by contemporary architect Renzo Piano (€20–60 tickets, check availability in advance as concerts often sell out, Via Vittorio Veneto 96, take Metro to Flaminio and then catch tram #2, box office tel. 06-8024-1281, www.auditorium.com). Nicknamed the Park of Music, it's a place where many Romans go just for the scene—music store, restaurants, cafés, and fresh modern architecture with three state-of-the-art auditoriums (known as "the beetles" for their appearance). If you want to see today's Rome enjoying today's culture, an evening here is the best you'll do. As it's quite a ways out of the city center, shuttle buses get everyone back downtown after the concerts are over.

The **Teatro dell'Opera** has an active schedule of opera and classical concerts. You'll see locals in all their finery, so pull your finest outfit from your backpack (near Via Firenze/Via Nazionale hotels at Via Firenze 72, tel. 06-4816-0255, www.operaroma.it).

Musical events at the Anglican **Church of St. Paul's Within the Walls** range from orchestral concerts (usually Tue and Fri) to full operatic performances, which are usually on Saturdays (€20–30, performances at 20:30, arrive 30–45 minutes early for a good seat, lasts between 1.5–2.5 hours, Via Napoli 58, near Termini train station and recommended hotels, tel. 06-482-6296, www .imusiciveneziani.com). On Sunday evenings at 18:30, the church often hosts hour-long candlelit *Luminaria* concerts (€15–20, buy tickets at the church on Sunday, or in advance at NapNet Internet Point just behind the church at Via Napoli 26, tel. 06-4890-7461).

Movies

Some theaters around town run movies in their original language (look for "V.O."—*versione originale*). Check out www.inromenow .com for current English-language film showings. **Warner Village Moderno** shows some films in English (Piazza della Repubblica, near Termini train station and recommended hotels), as does the **Nuovo Olimpia** (3 blocks north of Piazza Colonna, just off the Via del Corso at Via in Lucina 16, tel. 06-686-1068). Also try Monday nights at the Trastevere's retro **Alcazar** (Via Cardinale Merry del Val 14, tel. 06-588-0099).

Nightclubs

An interesting place for club-hopping is **Monte Testaccio.** After 21:00, ride the Metro to the Piramide stop and follow the noise. Monte Testaccio, once an ancient trash heap, is now a small hill whose cool caves house funky restaurants and trendy clubs. (It stands amid a pretty rough neighborhood, though.)

Other Evening Activities

Some **museums** have later opening hours (especially on Sat in summer), offering a good chance to see art in a cooler, less-crowded environment. See the "Rome at a Glance" sidebar on page 52, and ask the TI if any museums are currently open late.

The **Scuderie del Quirinale** stays open late when it's hosting major art exhibitions (Sun–Thu 10:00–20:00, Fri–Sat 10:00–22:30, last admission one hour before closing, Via XXIV Maggio 16, tel. 06-696-271, www.scuderiequirinale.it).

Pub crawls, offered year-round by several companies, attract a boisterous crowd. I tried one, and had never seen 50 young, drunk people having so much fun. Look for fliers locally. Late on Friday and Saturday evenings, entire quarters of old Rome seem to be overtaken by young beer-drinking revelers. Campo de' Fiori becomes one big, rude street party.

Dolce Vita Stroll

This is the city's chic stroll, from Piazza del Popolo (Metro: Flaminio) down a wonderfully traffic-free section of Via del Corso, and up Via Condotti to the Spanish Steps each evening around 18:00. Saturdays and Sundays are best; leave earlier than 18:00 if you plan to visit the Ara Pacis, which closes at 19:00 (and is closed Mon).

Shoppers, people-watchers, and flirts on the prowl fill this neighborhood of some of Rome's most fashionable stores (open after siesta 16:30–19:30). While both the crowds and the shops along Via del Corso have gone downhill recently, elegance survives in the grid of streets between this street and the Spanish Steps.

Throughout Italy, early evening is time to stroll. While elsewhere in Italy this is called the *passeggiata,* in Rome it's a cruder, big-city version called the *struscio.* (*Struscio* means "to rub.") Unemployment among Italy's youth is very high; many stay with their parents even into their thirties. They spend a lot of time being trendy and hanging out. Hard-core cruisers from the suburbs, which lack pleasant public spaces, congregate on Via del Corso to make the scene. The hot *vroom-vroom* motorscooter is their symbol; haircuts and fashion are follow-the-leader. They are called the *coatto.* In a more genteel small town, the *passeggiata* comes with sweet whispers of "*bella*" and "*bello*" ("pretty" and "handsome"). In Rome, the admiration is stronger, oriented toward consumption—they say "*buona*" and "*buono*"—meaning roughly "tasty." But despite how lusty this all sounds, you'll see as many chunky, middle-aged Italians on this walk as hormone-charged youth. If you get hungry during your stroll, see page 353 for descriptions of neighborhood wine bars and restaurants.

To get to **Piazza del Popolo,** where the stroll starts, take Metro line A to Flaminio and walk south to the square. Delightfully car-free, Piazza del Popolo is marked by an obelisk that was brought to Rome by Augustus after he conquered Egypt. (It used to stand in the Circus Maximus.) In medieval times, this area was just inside Rome's main entry (for more background on the square, see page 64).

The Baroque church of **Santa Maria del Popolo** is worth popping into (Mon–Sat until 19:00, Sun until 19:30, next to gate in old wall on north side of square). Inside, look for Raphael's Chigi Chapel (KEE-gee, second chapel on left) and two paintings by Caravaggio (the side paintings in the Cerasi Chapel, left of altar; see listing on page 65).

From Piazza del Popolo, shop your way down **Via del Corso.**

NIGHTLIFE

Dolce Vita Stroll

FLAMINIO

VILLA BORGHESE GARDENS

PIAZZA FLAMINIO

V. G. WASH.

V. TIAM

V. L. SAVOIA

V. MURO TORTO

STA. MARIA DEL POPOLO

START

FERD. SAVOIA

PIAZZA DEL POPOLO

PONTE MARGHERITA

LUNG. AUG.

VIA RIPETTA

VIA PIETTA

VIA BABUINO

MARGUTTA

M SPAGNA

MAUSOLEUM OF AUGUSTUS

FREZZA

VITTORIA

TRINITÀ DEI MONTI

PONTE.

❶

❸

CROCE

FOUNTAIN

SPANISH STEPS

ARA PACIS

❷

CARROZE

CONDOTTI

T

END FOR (WINDOW) SHOPPERS

PONTE CAVOUR

V. BORGOGNONA

V. FRATTINA

V. SCROFA

V. FONT. BORG.

Pza. S. LOR.

V. VITE

POST

V. DUE MACELLI

TIBER

PREFETTI

ROSINI

❹

V. CON.

V. MERCEDE

V. SAND.

B

V. S. AND.

VIA

TRITONE

T

TREVI FOUNTAIN

PIAZZA PARLAMENTO

T

PIAZZA COLONNA

SABINA

MURATTE

DATA

TO PANTHEON

PIETRA

CARAVITA M

SAN IGNAZIO

DCH

GALLERIA DORIA PAMPHILJ

B

V. IV

NOV.

PIAZZA VENEZIA

T

TO COLOSSEUM & M

VICTOR EMMANUEL MONUMENT

FOR. IMP.

CAPITOL HILL

END FOR HISTORIANS

GRAND STAIRCASE

200 YARDS

200 METERS

Ⓣ TAXI STAND

Ⓜ METRO STATION

Ⓑ BUS STOP

❶ Ristorante il Gabriello

❷ Osteria Gusto

❸ L'EnotecAntica

❹ Trattoria dal Cav. Gino

Historians side-trip right down Via Pontefici past the fascist architecture to see the massive, rotting, round-brick **Mausoleum of
Augustus,** topped with overgrown cypress trees. Beyond it, next
to the river, is Augustus' **Ara Pacis** (Altar of Peace), enclosed
within a protective glass-walled museum (described on page 67).

From the mausoleum, return to Via del Corso and the 21st
century, continuing straight until **Via Condotti.** Window shoppers should take a left to join the parade to the **Spanish Steps.** The
streets that parallel Via Condotti to the south (Borgognona and
Frattini) are more elegant, and filled with high-end boutiques.

Historians: Ignore Via Condotti and forget the Spanish Steps.
Stay on Via del Corso, which has been straight since Roman times,
a half-mile down to the Victor Emmanuel Monument. Climb
Michelangelo's stairway to his glorious (especially when floodlit) square atop Capitol Hill. Stand on the balcony (just past the
mayor's palace on the right), which overlooks the Forum. As the
horizon reddens and cats prowl the unclaimed rubble of ancient
Rome, it's one of the finest views in the city.

CONNECTIONS

Rome is well-connected with the rest of the planet: by train, bus, plane, car, and cruise ship. This chapter addresses your arrival and departure from the city. It explains the various options and gives a rundown on their points of departure.

By Train

Rome's main train station is the centrally located **Termini** Station, which has connections to the airport. Rome's other major station is **Tiburtina** bus/train station, which is starting to get a few high-speed rail connections. Smaller stations include **Ostiense** (useful for going to South Rome and Testaccio) and its neighbor, **Porta San Paolo** (with connections to Ostia Antica). If you're staying near the Vatican and taking a regional train, it saves time to get off at **San Pietro** Station rather than at Termini.

Minimize time in the station—the banks of user-friendly automated ticket machines (marked *Biglietto Veloce/Fast Ticket*) are handy. They take euros and credit cards, display schedules, issue tickets, and even make reservations for railpass-holders. Still, it can be quicker to get tickets and train info from travel agencies in town. For more on train travel in Italy—including your ticket-buying options—see page 447.

Termini Train Station

Termini, Rome's main train station, is a buffet of tourist services. While information desks are jammed with travelers, very handy red info kiosks at the head of the tracks can answer your simple questions.

Along track 24, about 100 yards down, you'll find the **TI** (daily 8:00–20:30), a **post office** (Mon–Fri 8:30–14:00, Sat 8:30–13:00, closed Sun), a **hotel booking** office, and **car rental** desks. The **baggage storage** (*deposito bagagli*) is downstairs (€4/5 hours, then cheaper, daily 6:00–24:00).

The **"Leonardo Express" train** to Fiumicino Airport runs from track 25; access is at the very far end of track 24 (see "By Plane," later). A good self-service **cafeteria,** Ciao, is near the head of track 24, upstairs, with fine views (daily 11:00–22:30).

Near track 1, you'll find a **pharmacy** (daily 7:30–22:00); along the same track is a **waiting room** and **train information** office (daily 6:00–24:00). The handy **Drugstore Conad,** selling everything from groceries to electronics, is just downstairs (daily 6:00–24:00).

Elsewhere in the station are **ATMs,** late-hours banks, and 24-hour thievery. In the station's main entrance lobby, **Borri Books** sells books in English, including popular fiction, Italian history and culture, and kids' books, plus maps upstairs (daily 7:00–23:00).

Termini is also a local transportation hub. The city's two Metro lines (A and B) intersect at Termini Metro station (downstairs). Buses (including Rome's hop-on, hop-off bus tours—see page 38) leave across the square directly in front of the main station hall. The Metro and bus areas are under construction until sometime in 2011—look for signs directing you to the Metro platform or bus stop. Taxis queue in front; avoid con men hawking "express taxi" services in unmarked cars (only use ones marked with the word *taxi* and a phone number). To avoid the long taxi line, simply hike out past the buses to the main street and hail one.

From Termini, most of my recommended hotels are easily accessible by foot (for those near this train station) or by Metro (for those in the Colosseum and Vatican neighborhoods).

The station has some sleazy sharks with official-looking business cards; avoid anybody selling anything unless they're in a legitimate shop at the station.

Since virtually all of the most convenient connections for travelers depart from Termini, I've listed those below. (But as a precaution, it's always smart to confirm whether your train departs from Termini or Tiburtina.)

From Rome's Termini Station by Train to: Venice (roughly hourly, 3.5 hours, overnight possible), **Florence** (at least hourly, 1.5 hours, some stop at Orvieto en route), **Orvieto** (hourly, 1.25 hours), **Assisi** (hourly, 2–3.5 hours, 5 direct, most others change in Foligno), **Pisa** (hourly, 3–4 hours, many change in Florence), **La Spezia** (8/day direct, more with transfers in Pisa, 4 hours), **Milan** (hourly, 3.5–8 hours, overnight possible), **Naples** (at least hourly, 1.25 hours on Frecciarossa trains, otherwise 2–2.5 hours), **Civitavecchia** cruise-ship port (2/hour, 1.25 hours), **Brindisi** (6/day, 3 direct, 6–9 hours, overnight possible), **Amsterdam** (6/day, 20 hours), **Bern** (6/day, 9 hours, several overnight options), **Frankfurt** (7/day, 12 hours, several overnight options), **Munich** (4/day, 11 hours, several overnight options), **Nice** (6/day, 10 hours), **Paris** (3/day, 12–15 hours, several overnight options, important to reserve ahead, 19:00 railpass rule works for 18:20 night train), **Vienna** (3/day, 12 hours, several overnight options).

Tiburtina Train and Bus Station

Tiburtina, Rome's second-largest train station, is located in the city's northeast corner. In general, slower trains (from Milan, Bolzano, Bologna, Udine, and Reggio di Calabria) and some night trains (from Munich, Milan, Venice, Innsbruck, and Udine) use Tiburtina, as does the night bus to Fiumicino Airport. Direct night trains from Paris and Vienna use Termini Station instead. In 30 years of visits, I've never had occasion to use Tiburtina, but that may change—Tiburtina is currently being redeveloped for high-speed rail. At least one Eurostar Italia train stops here already, and a new company—Nuovo Trasporto Viaggiatori (NTV)—is expected to start running its Italo high-speed trains from Tiburtina sometime in 2011 (for details, see www.ntvspa.it).

Tiburtina is better known as a hub for bus service to destinations all across Italy. Buses depart from the piazza in front of the station. Ticket offices are located in the piazza and around the corner on Circonvallazione Nomentana.

Within the train station are a currency-exchange office and a 24-hour grocery. Tiburtina Station is on Metro line B, with easy connections to Termini (a straight shot, four stops away) and the entire Metro system. Or take bus #492 from Tiburtina to various city-center stops (such as Piazza Barberini, Piazza Venezia, and Piazza Cavour) and the Vatican neighborhood.

By Bus

Long-distance buses (such as from Siena and Assisi) arrive at Rome's **Tiburtina Station** (described above).

From Rome by Bus to: Assisi (2/day, 3 hours—the train makes much more sense), **Siena** (8/day, 3 hours), **Sorrento** (1–2/day, 4 hours; this is the quickest and easiest way to go straight to Sorrento).

By Plane

Rome's two airports—**Fiumicino** (a.k.a. Leonardo da Vinci) and the small **Ciampino**—share the same website (www.adr.it). For budget flights within Europe, easyJet uses both airports, while Ryanair only uses Ciampino. Vueling and Blue Express only use Fiumicino.

Fiumicino Airport

Rome's major airport has a TI (in terminal 3, daily 8:00–19:00), ATMs, banks, luggage storage, shops, and bars. The Rome Walks website (www.romewalks.com) has a useful video on options for getting into the city from the airport.

A slick, direct **"Leonardo Express" train** connects the airport and Rome's central Termini train station in 30 minutes for €15. Trains run twice hourly in both directions from roughly 6:00 to 23:00 (leaving the airport at :06 and :36). From the airport's arrival gate, follow signs to *Stazione/Railway Station*. Buy your ticket from a machine, the Biglietteria office, or a newsstand at the platform, then validate it in a yellow machine near the track. Make sure the train you board is going to the central "Roma Termini" station, not "Roma Orte" or others.

Going from Termini train station to the airport, trains depart at about :22 and :52 past the hour, from track 25 (located way down at the far end of track 24; allow 10 minutes for the hike, moving walkways downstairs). Check the departure boards for "Fiumicino Aeroporto"—the local name for the airport—and confirm with an official or a local on the platform that the train is indeed going to the airport (€15, buy ticket from any *tabacchi* or newsstand in the station, or at the self-service machines, Termini–Fiumicino trains run 5:52–22:52). Read your ticket: If it requires validation, stamp it in the yellow machine near the platform before boarding. From the train station at the airport, you can access all of the terminals—1, 2, 3, or 5.

Allow lots of time going in either direction; there's a fair amount of transportation involved, including moving walkways, escalators, and walking (e.g., getting from your hotel to Termini, from Termini to the train platform, the ride to the airport, getting from the airport train station to check-in, etc.). Flying to the US involves an extra level of security—plan on getting to the airport even earlier (I like to arrive 2.5 hours ahead of my flight).

Shuttle van services run to and from the airport and can be economical for one or two people. Consider Rome Airport Shuttle (€25/1 person, extra people-€6 each, by reservation only, tel. 06-4201-4507 or 06-4201-3469, www.airportshuttle.it).

A **taxi** between Fiumicino and downtown Rome takes 45

minutes in normal traffic (for tips on taxis, see page 32). If you're catching a taxi at the airport, be sure to wait at the taxi stand. Avoid unmarked, unmetered taxis; these guys will try to tempt you away from the taxi-stand lineup by offering an immediate (rip-off) ride. Rome's official taxis have a fixed rate to and from the airport (€45 for up to four people with bags). If your cab driver tries to charge you more than €45 from the airport into town, say, *"Quarantacinque euro—È la legge"* (kwah-RAHN-tah CHEENG-kway AY-oo-roh—ay lah LEJ-jay; which means, "Forty-five euros—It's the law"), and they should back off.

A new law allows cabbies not based in Rome to charge €60 for the ride. That sign is posted next to the €45-fare sign—confusing many tourists and allowing dishonest cabbies to overcharge. Only use a Rome city cab (with the "SPQR" shield on the door). They can only charge €45 for the ride to anywhere in the historic center (within the old city walls, where most of my recommended hotels are located).

To get from the airport into town cheaply by taxi, try teaming up with any tourist also just arriving (most are heading for hotels near yours in the center). When you're departing Rome, your hotel can arrange a taxi to the airport at any hour.

For **airport information,** call 06-65951. To inquire about flights, call 06-6595-3640 (Alitalia: tel. 06-2222; British Airways: tel. 199-712-266; Continental: tel. 06-6605-3030; Delta: tel. 848-780-376; Swiss International: tel. 848-868-120; United: tel. 848-800-692).

Ciampino Airport

Rome's smaller airport (tel. 06-6595-9515) handles charter flights and some budget airlines (including all Ryanair and some easyJet flights).

To get to downtown Rome from the airport, you can take the Cotral bus, which leaves every 40 minutes (€1.20, 20-minute ride, toll-free tel. 800-174-471, www.cotralspa.it), to the Anagnina Metro stop, where you can connect by Metro to the stop nearest your hotel. Rome Airport Shuttle (listed earlier) also offers service to and from Ciampino. The Terravision Express Shuttle connects Ciampino and Termini, leaving every 20 minutes (€4 one-way, €8 round-trip, www.terravision.eu). The SIT Bus Shuttle also connects Termini train station to Ciampino (€6, about 2/hour, 30–60 minutes, runs 7:45–23:15 Ciampino to Termini, 4:30–21:30 Termini to Ciampino, pick-up on Via Marsala just outside the train exit closest to track 1, tel. 06-591-7844, www.sitbusshuttle.it). A taxi should cost €35 to downtown (within the old city walls, including most of my recommended hotels).

By Car

Driving and Parking in Rome

The Grande Raccordo Anulare circles greater Rome. This ring road has spokes that lead you into the center. Entering from the north, leave the autostrada at the Settebagni exit. Following the ancient Via Salaria (and the black-and-white *Centro* signs), work your way doggedly into the Roman thick of things. This will take you along the Villa Borghese Gardens and dump you right on Via Veneto in downtown Rome. Avoid rush hour and drive defensively: Roman cars stay in their lanes like rocks in an avalanche.

Parking in Rome is dangerous. Park near a police station or get advice at your hotel. The Villa Borghese underground garage is handy (Metro: Spagna). Garages charge about €24 per day.

Consider this: Your car is a worthless headache in Rome. Avoid a pile of stress and save money by parking at the huge, easy, and relatively safe lot behind the train station in the hill town of Orvieto (follow *P* signs from autostrada) and catching the train to Rome (hourly, 60–90 minutes).

If you absolutely must drive and park a car in Rome, try to avoid commuter traffic by arriving Friday evening, or anytime during the weekend, and by leaving town during the weekend. Park your car at Tiburtina station (€1/hour, www.atac.roma.it) and take a 10-minute ride on the Metro line B into the center.

For more information on car rental and driving in Italy, see page 452.

By Cruise Ship

Hundreds of cruise chips—including Carnival, Royal Caribbean, Princess, and Celebrity lines—dock each year at the Port of **Civitavecchia,** about 45 miles northwest of Rome. Port facilities include a waiting room, ATMs, bag storage, and snack bar.

Getting Between Civitavecchia and Downtown Rome

Twice-hourly **trains** connect Civitavecchia and Rome's Termini Station (€5–9, 1–1.25 hours, regional and pricier IC options, get tickets at ticket window). The best deal: ask for the €9 BIRG ticket, which covers all-day, unlimited travel on regional trains in second class and on the Metro and bus system in Rome. Be sure to write your name on the back and validate it in the yellow box before getting on train.

To reach Civitavecchia's train station from the ship, take the free shuttle bus to the port entrance, and walk about 10–15 minutes straight along the seaside road. Some shuttle buses may take you

CONNECTIONS

all the way to the station—ask. The Rome Walks website (www .romewalks.com) has a useful video on taking the train from the port into the city.

To reach the port from Civitavecchia train station, turn right after you exit and walk 10–15 minutes along the waterfront road. Or you can take either bus #C or #F from in front of the train station; buy your ticket at the *tabacchi* shop before you board. Local taxis also run between the port and the train station (often meeting the ship or call 076-626-121).

The road traffic between Civitavecchia and Rome is terrible, making trains faster and more economical than any of your other options. **Taxis** can run €200–400 between Civitavecchia and Rome. A slightly less expensive option is to hire a **private limousine** (figure €150 for up to three people).

Getting Between Civitavecchia and Fiumicino Airport

You'll need to take two **trains** to link Civitavecchia and Fiumicino Airport: one between the airport and Rome's Termini Station, and another between Termini and Civitavecchia. See "By Plane," earlier.

Shuttle van services run between the port and Rome's Fiumicino Airport. Try **Rome Airport Shuttle** (€90/1–2 people, €15 each additional person up to 8, share with others and save, much more for pickup between 21:00 and 7:00, tel. 06-4201-4507 or 06-4201-3469, www.airportshuttle.it).

Day Trips to Rome from Civitavecchia

Do-it-yourselfers will find it easy to visit Rome for a day using the **train** (see details earlier). Consider disembarking the train at Rome's San Pietro Station instead of more-central Termini Station, in order to start your sightseeing with St. Peter's Basilica and the Vatican. (Most regional, but not InterCity, trains stop at San Pietro; be sure you take the right train.) Then take the Metro to the Spanish Steps to explore Rome's other sights. If you return to the port from Rome's Termini Station, note that Civitavecchia trains generally leave from tracks 27–30, a 10-minute walk from the station entrance.

If your cruise ship stops in Civitavecchia for the day, you may be offered a **shore excursion** to Rome. Many of Civitavecchia's private limousine companies and the Rome Airport Shuttle also offer Rome **tours.** Look for a tour that is a minimum eight hours in length: six hours for sightseeing and two-plus hours of travel time. On shorter tours you'll see most of Rome from the bus window. Plan to spend about €200 per person.

DAY TRIPS
FROM ROME

There's so much to see and do in Rome that you could easily fill a vacation without ever leaving the city limits. But here are several nearby sights that might match your particular interest.

Ostia Antica is similar to Pompeii, but without the crowds. This excavated ancient Roman city is located an easy 45 minutes by Metro and train from Rome.

Tivoli is less accessible (consider seeing it via private tour), but you're rewarded with the ruins of Hadrian's Villa and with the lush gardens and recently restored fountains of a Renaissance mansion, the Villa d'Este.

Thanks to Italy's excellent train system, it's 1.5 hours to **Naples** on a direct high-speed train (or 2–3 hours on cheaper trains), landing you right in the middle of town. Visit Roman statues and mosaics at the wonderful Archaeological Museum, stroll colorful Spaccanapoli street, and have lunch in the city where pizza was born, sampling the exotic chaos of southern Italy.

History hounds can venture an hour farther south of Naples to see the ultimate in ruined Roman cities—**Pompeii**—frozen in time by the eruption of Mt. Vesuvius.

Arrive back in Rome for a late dinner at a sidewalk café to recount your busy day over a glass of wine.

OSTIA ANTICA DAY TRIP

For an exciting day trip, pop down to the Roman port of Ostia, which is similar to Pompeii but a lot closer and, in some ways, more interesting. Because Ostia was a working port town, it shows a more complete and gritty look at Roman life than wealthier Pompeii. Wandering around today, you'll see warehouses, apartment flats, mansions, shopping arcades, and baths that served a once-thriving port of 60,000 people.

Orientation

Cost: €6.50 for the site and museum.

Hours: Tue–Sun April–Oct 8:30–19:00, Nov–Feb 8:30–17:00, March 8:30–18:00, last entry one hour before closing, closed Mon. The museum closes from 13:30 to 14:15 for lunch.

Getting There: Getting to Ostia Antica from downtown Rome is a snap—it's a 45-minute combination Metro/train ride. (Since the train is part of the Metro system, it only costs one Metro ticket each way—€2 total round-trip.)

From Rome, take Metro line B to the Piramide stop, which is also the Roma Porta San Paolo train station, so the train tracks are just a few steps from the Metro tracks. Follow signs to *Lido*—go up the escalator, turn left, and go down the steps into the Roma-Lido station. All trains depart in the direction of Lido, leave every 15 minutes, and stop at Ostia Antica along the way. The lighted schedule reads something like, "*Treno in partenza alle ore 13.25, bin 3*," meaning, "Train departing at 13:25 from track 3." Look for the next train, hop on, ride for about 30 minutes (keep your Metro ticket handy), and get off at the Ostia Antica stop. (If you don't have a ticket to get back, purchase one at the ticket window at the station, or from the nearby snack bar.)

Leaving the train station in Ostia Antica, cross the road via the blue skybridge and walk straight down Via della Stazione di Ostia Antica, continuing straight until you reach the parking lot. The entrance is to your left.

Tip: If you're using the Metro and want to maximize sightseeing efficiency on your Ostia day trip, consider visiting the sights in south Rome on your return. The Piramide Metro stop—where you'll change trains—really *is* next to a pyramid, and in the middle of the Testaccio neighborhood, which has several interesting sights. Other south Rome sights include St. Paul's Outside the Walls and the Montemartini Museum (for more on all of these, see page 78).

Information: A map of the site with suggested itineraries is available for €2 from the ticket office. Although you'll see little audioguide markers throughout the site, there are no audioguides. However, you can download a **free Rick Steves audio tour** version of this walking tour at www.ricksteves.com or from iTunes (search for "Rick Steves Audio Tours"). Tel. 06-5635-8099; www.itnw.roma.it/ostia/scavi (Italian website), www.ostiaantica.info (English summary), or www.ostia-antica.org.

Length of This Tour: Allow two hours inside the site. Add in your round-trip train rides, and it's at least a four-hour excursion from Rome.

Cuisine Art: A good cafeteria is next to Ostia's museum.

History

Located at (and named for) the mouth *(ostium)* of the Tiber, Ostia was founded in the fourth century B.C. Gobbled up early by Rome, its main industry was the salt gleaned from nearby salt flats, which was a precious preserver of meat in ancient times. Ostia—often called Rome's first colony—served as a naval base, protecting Rome from any invasion by river. By 150 B.C., when Rome controlled the Mediterranean, Ostia's importance became commercial rather than military. Rome eventually outgrew the port of Ostia, and a vast new port was dug nearby (where Rome's airport now stands). But Ostia remained a key administrative and warehousing center, busy with the big business of keeping more than a million Romans fed and in sandals.

Eventually things really soured for Ostia. Rome fell. The river changed course. The port was abandoned, silted up, became a malaria-infested swamp, and was eventually forgotten. The mud that buried Ostia actually protected it from the ravages of time—and stone-scavenging medieval peasants.

Ostia Antica

1. Necropolis
2. Porta Romana
3. Republican Warehouses
4. Baths of Neptune
5. Theater
6. Square of the Guilds
7. Mill
8. Via Casa di Diana
9. Forum
10. Forum Baths
11. Ostia Museum

The Tour Begins

Overview

Consider your visit a three-part affair:

1. Follow this tour, which leads you straight down Decumanus Maximus (the town's main drag), with a couple of slight detours, finishing at the forum (the main square).

2. Pop into the museum and consider getting a bite to eat at the cafeteria.

3. Explore the back lanes—going on a visual scavenger hunt—as you wander your way back to the entry point.

• *Find the map (30 yards inside the gate, on the right) for an orientation. The pale green shows the ancient coast and course of the river—which eventually abandoned its city. Notice how the core of Ostia is a rectangular Roman military camp, with two major roads crossing at the forum. One of four city gates lies ahead, and on your left is the...*

❶ Necropolis

Ancient Romans buried their dead outside the city walls. Ostia was a famously pagan town, slow to become Christian. To a pagan, the closest thing to an afterlife was to be remembered. If their families could afford it, they'd have the tomb on the roadside with a thumbnail bio carved into the stone that all could read as they came and went (e.g., "My name was Caius. I was a baker."). This area was called a necropolis (city of the dead); Christians preferred the term cemetery (from the Greek for resting place). Detour to find family sepulchers (marked by arches)—private open-air rooms lined with niches for ash-filled urns. Until the first century A.D., cremation was common. In the second and third centuries A.D., the Romans here buried their dead in marble and terra-cotta sarcophagi in tombs.

• *Ahead (where the road narrows) you enter the ancient city of Ostia through the scant remains of the gate called...*

❷ Porta Romana

Just as Rome's Porta Ostiense faced Ostia, Ostia's Porta Romana faced Rome. Inside the gate (which was locked at night) you'd find a place to leave your animal (on the left) and a warehouse (on the right). To the left (under the big tree), you can see on the gate the bits of the Latin inscription that proclaimed to all who entered.

It reads: "The Senate and the people of the colony of Ostia constructed the walls." The "colony" reference is a reminder that Ostia was the first bit of the Roman Empire. The big basin, once fed by a fountain, was where animals could be watered. Information panels like the one here are generally helpful only for the artist's reconstruction of the sight. The verbiage is what locals refer to as *aria fritta* (fried air—greasy and heavy but containing nothing of value).

From the gate, Ostia's main street (named Decumanus Maximus) leads straight to the forum, where this walk ends. Note that this road was elevated above some buildings' foundations. Over the centuries, Ostia's ground level rose. You can actually identify buildings from the republic (centuries before Christ) and the empire (centuries after Christ) by their level. Anything you walk down into is from the earlier period.

• *Just inside the gate and to the right are the...*

❸ Republican Warehouses (Magazzini Repubblicani)

The first century B.C. was busy with activities relating to the river port. Walking along the main street, you pass vast warehouses on the right. The goods of the port—such as grain from Sicily, Egypt, and all of North Africa—were processed and stored in

warehouses here (which had elevated floors to keep things dry) before being consumed by Rome.

Ahead, a series of stubby brick columns are the remains of a roofed portico that provided a shaded walkway into town. Notice the bricks—generally, rough bricks are

original, while smooth bricks are part of the reconstruction. Ostia has been picked clean since ancient times. The ports' treasures ended up gracing buildings as far away as Constantinople.

• *Continue straight ahead about 100 yards. The little well in the road is medieval—a remnant from Dark Age squatters who found shelter in these ruins. From here, you'll see a viewpoint (with railings, above on the right). Climb up for a view of the...*

OSTIA ANTICA

❹ Baths of Neptune (Terme di Nettuno)

Examine the fine mosaic with Neptune riding four horses through the sea. Apart from the cupid riding the dolphin, the sea looks

frightening—which it was. The large square to the left of the mosaic would have been busy with people wrestling, stretching, doing jumping jacks, and getting rubdowns. The niches that ring the square housed small businesses. The row of umbrella pines in the distance marks the original

channel of the river before it changed course, abandoning the town.

• *Climb back down to the main drag, and continue to the right until you reach the theater on your right. Enter the theater through its main central gate.*

❺ Theater (Teatro)

The scant remains of the stucco decor under the entry arch give a hint of the elegance of this place 2,000 years ago. At the end of the tunnel, men would bid their women farewell (before the women went to sit in the higher seats—typical of the gender division in public Rome).

Before you is a typically Roman complex mixing religion, business, and entertainment: a grand theater facing a temple surrounded by a commercial square. Up to 4,000 residents could gather in this theater. Plays were rowdy daytime events—like going to a day game at the ballpark—with lots of audience participation. And heaven help a bad actor. The three rows of marble steps near the orchestra were reserved for the chairs of big shots. In its day, a wall rose behind the stage, enclosing the theater. Even today, this place—one of the oldest brick theaters anywhere—is used for concerts. Climb to the top of the theater for a fine view.

• *From the theater, continue (farther away from the main street) behind the stage into the big square. Head to the right and walk counterclockwise around the square, ending up back at the theater. Most of the notable mosaics line the right side of the square.*

❻ Square of the Guilds (Piazzale delle Corporazioni)

This grand square evolved from a simple place—where businessmen would stroll and powwow together—to become a monu-

mental square lined with more than 60 offices of ship owners and traders. This was the bustling center of Rome's import-export industry. Along the sidewalk, second-century A.D. mosaics advertise the services offered by the various shops. Walking counterclockwise, circle the square to "read" the mosaics that advertised in Latin and in pictograms for illiterate or non-Latin-reading sailors. The most common symbol—the lighthouse—was the sign of the port of Ostia. Grain containers are reminders that grain was the major import of Ostia. The elephant marking the office of the Sabratans (a place in present-day Libya) symbolized the sale of ivory or perhaps of exotic animals (great for parties and private spectacles and Colosseum events). The fine mosaic in the corner shows the innovative Roman ships. When ship technology enabled boats to tack and sail against the wind, commerce moved more readily, making the Mediterranean a thriving Roman free-trade zone.

Statues of notable local guild members and business leaders decorated the courtyard. The temple in the center was likely related to Ceres, the goddess of harvest and abundance (prosperity from good business).

At the end of the square, as you leave, notice the small white altar on the right. This would have been used to sacrifice animals—such as the rams carved into the corners—to ask for favor from the gods. The entrails would be read to divine the future, and to determine whether the gods were for or against a particular business venture. This altar is a copy; the original is in Rome. (Consider the burden on Italy of protecting and preserving what is actually the cultural heritage of all of Europe against illegal digging, exportation, vandalism, weather, and pollution. There's a special branch of the Carabinieri dedicated to art theft.)

• *Continue down the main street. About two blocks down (look for Tempio Repubblicano on the corner to the right), Via dei Molini marks the wall of the original military* castrum *(rectangular camp). Before continuing straight into that oldest part of Ostia, turn right, down Via dei Molini (but don't take the left onto Via Casa di Diana—we'll get to that next). Walk about a block and a half until you see Molino del Silvano on the left.*

OSTIA ANTICA

❼ Mill (Molino)

This mill building *(panificio)* dates from A.D. 120. The lava millstones in front of you were used to grind grain. Study the work-

ings: A bowl-like lower structure carefully cupped a moving upper section. Grain would be sprinkled in from a sack hanging from the ceiling. Mules or workers would power the grinding by walking in circles, pushing inserted wood poles. Powdery flour (with not much grit) would eventually tumble out of the bottom of the mill, ready to be made into bread.

• *Now, backtrack half a block down Via dei Molini in the direction of the main street. At the big tree, take the first right onto...*

❽ Via Casa di Diana

There are two places of interest along this street: a tavern (halfway down on the left) and a typical apartment building with stairs leading to a commanding rooftop view (across the street from the tavern, on the right).

At the **Insula of the Thermopolium,** step past the grooved threshold—which once held a sliding wooden door—and belly up to the tavern's bar. You'll see display shelves with food and drinks for sale, a small sink, and a cute fresco advertising food, drink, and music. Too smoky and noisy? Step out back and enjoy the quiet courtyard with the fountain.

The **Insula of the Paintings** is across the street. Climb all the way to the open rooftop for a good view and a chance to imagine life as an apartment dweller in ancient Rome. An *insula* was a multistoried tenement complex where the lower-middle class lived. In ancient times, the lower classes lived in miserable, cramped apartment buildings up to 10 floors high (the average was 5 floors). People living on the higher floors climbed treehouse-type stairs to get to their rooms. There was no plumbing. It was stinky. "Windows" just had shutters or curtains of cloth dipped in grease, which let in the street noise.

Buildings were made cheaply of wood, with weak foundations, so many burned or collapsed. The apartments had no heat and no kitchen (food was cooked or purchased elsewhere). Garbage was tossed out the windows. Chariot and cart traffic were allowed only at night. There was lots of night noise.

The wealthier classes, on the other hand, lived in sprawling and luxurious homes. These were generally built on one floor, with a series of rooms facing a central open courtyard. Decorative pools collected rainwater. Statues, mosaics, and frescoes were everywhere. Rome's wealthy were as comfortable as the poor were wretched.

From this rooftop perch, find the museum (the modern building). Behind the museum, see modern pleasure boats where today's Tiber leaves Ostia. The temporary arched roofing protects rooms warehousing lots of ancient bits and pieces (worth a look).

• *Now, walk (from street level, of course) to the end of the street, toward the high brick temple that marks Ostia's...*

❾ Forum

Whenever possible, Rome imposed a grid road plan on its conquered cities. After Rome conquered Ostia in about 400 B.C., it built a military camp, or *castrum*—a rectangular fort with east, west, north, and south gates and two main roads converging on the forum. Throughout the empire, Romans found comfort in this familiar city plan. While people found it no fun to be conquered, the empire brought order and stability to their lives through laws and the creation of grid-planned cities and grand squares such as this one.

Ostia's main square became a monumental forum in the imperial period. And dominating this square, like most Roman towns, was the **grand temple** (from A.D. 120). The marble veneer was scavenged in the Middle Ages, leaving only the core brickwork. Note the reinforcement arches in the brick. The temple, called the Capitolium (after the original atop Capitol Hill in Rome), was dedicated to the pagan trinity of Jupiter, Juno, and Minerva. A forum dominated by a Capitolium temple was a standard feature of colonies throughout the empire. The purpose: to transport the Roman cult of Jupiter, Juno, and Minerva to the newly conquered population.

On the opposite side of the square, distinguished by its sawed-off column, is the Temple of Roma and Augustus. Its position is powerfully symbolic. The power of the emperor stands equal, facing the power of the Capitolium Triad.

The basilica also faces the forum square. Dating from about A.D. 100, this was where legal activities and commercial business took place. (With your back to the Capitolium temple, it's to your right and consists of little more than the footprint of the building.) Its central nave and two side aisles lead to the "high altar" where the judge sat.

Behind the Capitolium temple—and a little to the right— the pink modern building houses the fine little Ostia Museum. Behind that is a shop and a modern cafeteria. From the forum, the Decumanus Maximus continues into a vast urban expanse, great for simply wandering (see "Archaeological Scavenger Hunt" at the end of this chapter).

• *But first, make one more stop. Walk to the front left corner of the Temple of Roma and Augustus. As you're facing it, look left for a street marked by a grand arch. This leads to Ostia's best and largest baths (entrance on right).*

❿ Forum Baths (Terme del Foro)

As you wander around this huge complex, try to imagine it peopled, steaming, and busy. Government-subsidized baths were a popular social and business meeting place in any Roman city. Roman engineers were experts at radiant heat. A huge furnace heated both the water and air that flowed through pipes under the floors and in the walls (you can see the hollow bricks in the walls). Notice the fine marble steps—great for lounging—that led into the pools. People used olive oil rather than soap to wash, so the water needed to be periodically skimmed by servants. Like a high-end spa, there was a *laconicum* (sweating room), two *tepidaria* (where Romans were rubbed down by masseuses), and the once-steamy *caldarium* with three pools.

From the baths (across the street and a bit to the right from

the entry), find the 20-hole latrine. You can still see the pivot hole in the floor that once supported its revolving door. The cutout below each seat was to accommodate the washable sponge on a stick, which was used rather than toilet paper. Rushing water below each seat (brought in by aqueduct) did the flushing. So much for privacy—even today, there's no word in Italian for it.

⓫ Ostia Museum

This small museum offers a delightful look at some of Ostia's finest statuary. Without worrying too much about exactly what's what, just wander and imagine these fine statues—tangled wrestlers, kissing cupids, playful gods—adorning the courtyards of wealthy

Ostia families. Most of the statues are second- and third-century A.D. Roman pieces inspired by rare and famous Greek originals. The portrait busts are of real people—the kind you'd sit next to in the baths (or on the toilets).

A forte of Roman sculptors was realistic busts. Roman religion revered the man of the house (and his father and grandfather). A statue of daddy and grandpa was common in the corner of any proper house. Also, with the emperor considered a god, you'd find his bust in classrooms, at the post office, and so on. The sarcophagi (marble coffins) generally show mythological scenes.

Perhaps the most interesting room (to the left as you enter, just before the steps) features statuary from religions of foreign lands. Being a port town, Ostia accommodated people (and their worship needs) from all over the known world. The large statue of a man sacrificing a bull is a Mithraic altarpiece (see page 280).

The **cafeteria** and **shop** are in a modern building just behind the museum.

Archaeological Scavenger Hunt

As you return to the entry gate, get off the main drag and explore Ostia's back streets. Wandering beyond the forum and then taking the back lanes as you return to the entry, see if you can find:

- Tarp- and sand-protected mosaic flooring.
- White cornerstones put into buildings to fend off wild carts and reflect corners in the dark.
- Fast-food fish joint (on Decumanus Maximus, just beyond the forum).
- Hidden bits of fresco (clue: under hot tin roofs).
- Republican buildings and buildings dating from the empire.
- Stucco roughed up for fresco work (before applying the wet plaster of a fresco, the surface needs to be systematically gouged so the plaster can grip the wall).
- Mill stones for grinding grain (Ostia's big industry).
- Floor patterns made colorful with inlaid marble.
- A *domus* (single-family dwellings always faced a fancy, central open-air courtyard).

TIVOLI DAY TRIP

At the edge of the Sabine Hills, 18 miles east of Rome, sits the medieval hill town of Tivoli, a popular retreat since ancient times. Today, it's famous for two very different villas: Hadrian's Villa (the emperor's Versailles-like place of government, which enabled him to rule from outside but still near the capital city), and the restored Villa d'Este (the lush and watery 16th-century residence of a cardinal in exile).

The town of Tivoli, with Villa d'Este in its center, is about 2.5 miles from Hadrian's Villa ("Villa Adriana" in Italian). The TI is on Largo Garibaldi, near the bus stop (Tue–Sun 9:30–17:30, closed Mon, tel. 0774-313-536).

Note that Hadrian's Villa is open daily, and Villa d'Este is closed on Monday.

Getting to Tivoli

Reaching the town of Tivoli is easy, and Villa d'Este is in the town center. Getting to Hadrian's Villa is complicated and time-consuming—you'll go into Tivoli, then backtrack on another bus—but many find it well worth the trouble (see map on page 377). To return to Rome from Tivoli, simply reverse the connections—*no problema*.

From Rome, take a Metro/bus combination. Ride Metro line B to Ponte Mammolo, and then take the local blue Cotral bus to Tivoli (3/hour, direction: Tivoli).

For **Villa d'Este,** get off in downtown Tivoli, near the central square and the big park with amusements. Cross the road and follow signs (for about a block) that lead to the villa.

To get to **Hadrian's Villa** from downtown Tivoli, catch orange city bus #4X. Buy your ticket at a nearby *tabacchi* shop. When you're ready to leave Hadrian's Villa to go back to Tivoli, catch bus #4 or #4X in the direction of Tivoli. If you're continuing on to Rome, get off at the main road and change to a Cotral bus (ask the bus driver for help—he knows what you need to do). Departures after 16:30 can be sparse.

Several Rome tour companies—including Context Rome, Rome Walks, and Through Eternity—offer private tours of the villas (see their respective websites for specifics; tour companies listed on page 37).

Hadrian's Villa

Built at the peak of the Roman Empire by Hadrian (ruled A.D. 117–138), this was a retreat from the political complexity of court life. The Spanish-born Hadrian—an architect, lover of Greek culture (nick-

named "The Little Greek"), and great traveler—created a microcosm of the lands he ruled as emperor, which at that point stretched from England to the Euphrates and encompassed countless diverse cultures. In the spirit of Legoland, Epcot, and Las Vegas, he re-created famous structures from around the world, producing a kind of diorama of his empire in the form of the largest and richest Roman villa anywhere. Just as Louis XIV governed France from Versailles rather than Paris, Hadrian ruled Rome from this villa of more than 300 evocative acres. He basically spent his last decade here.

Start your visit at the plastic model of the villa (the WC is nearby). Find the Egyptian Canopus (sanctuary of the god Serapis, a canal lined with statues), the Greek Pecile (from Athens), and the Teatro Marittimo (a circular palace, Hadrian's favorite retreat on an island, where he did his serious thinking). Regrettably, this "Versailles of Ancient Rome" was plundered by barbarians and Renaissance big shots who all wanted something classical in their courtyards. They burned the marble to make lime for cement. The art was scavenged and wound up in the Vatican Museum, the Louvre, and other museums throughout Europe.

Cost and Hours: €10, audioguide-€4, April–Sept daily 9:00–19:00, closes earlier off-season, last entry 1.5 hours before closing, tel. 0774-382-733, www.pierreci.it/en/museums-and-monuments/villa-adriana.aspx.

Villa d'Este

Ippolito d'Este's grandfather, Alexander VI, was the pope. Ippolito was fast-tracked for church service from birth and became a cardinal. His claim to fame: his pleasure palace at Tivoli. In the

1550s, he destroyed a Benedictine monastery to build this fanciful late-Renaissance palace. Like Hadrian's Villa, it's a large residen-

tial estate. But this one features hundreds of Baroque fountains, all gravity-powered. The Aniene River, frazzled into countless threads, weaves its way entertainingly through the villa. At the bottom of the garden, the exhausted little streams once again team up to make a sizable river. As Pirro Ligorio, Tivoli's architect, was also the archaeologist in charge of excavating Hadrian's Villa, that sight provided much in both inspiration and raw material for the fancy fountains of Tivoli. He could basically use Hadrian's Villa as a quarry to provide statuary and decorative stone work for his vision in making Tivoli.

The cardinal had a political falling-out with Rome, and was exiled. With this watery wonderland on a cool hill with fine views, he made sure Romans would come to visit. It's symbolic of the luxury and secular interests of the cardinal.

After years of neglect, the villa has been completely restored.

TIVOLI

All the most eye-popping fountains have been put back in operation, and—with the exception of the two highest jets of the central fountain, which are electric-powered—everything still operates on natural hydraulics. A terrace restaurant has been installed on the highest level of the garden, opportunely placed to catch cool afternoon sea breezes coming in across the plain of Rome. Expect lots of stairs.

Cost and Hours: €6.50, audio-guide-€4, Tue–Sun 8:30–18:30, closed Mon, closes earlier off-season, last entry one hour before closing, tel. 0774-312-070, www.villadestetivoli.info. Upon arrival, note the posted schedule listing when the water organ *(l'organo ad acqua)* will play—a cute 10-minute performance every two hours.

NAPLES AND POMPEII DAY TRIP

While the Eternal City can keep you busy for ages, here are two excuses to leave Rome for a day. The trip south to Naples and Pompeii is demanding (four to five hours of train travel round-trip). But you'll be rewarded for your time, given the chance to wander ancient Rome's most evocative ruins and go on an urban safari in what is perhaps Europe's most intense city.

If you have a week in Rome and are interested in maximum travel thrills, take a day trip to Naples and Pompeii. (See map on page 377.) Note that Naples' Archaeological Museum is closed on Tuesday. Pompeii is open daily.

Naples (Napoli)

If you like Italy as far south as Rome, go farther south. It gets better. If Italy is getting on your nerves, don't go farther. Italy intensifies as you plunge deeper. Naples is Italy in the extreme—its best (birthplace of pizza and Sophia Loren) and its worst (home of the Camorra, Naples' "family" of organized crime).

Neapolis ("new city") was a thriving Greek commercial center 2,500 years ago. Today, it remains southern Italy's leading city, offering a fascinating collection of museums, churches, and eclectic architecture. Walking through its colorful Old Town is one of my favorite sightseeing experiences anywhere in Italy.

Naples—Italy's third-largest city, with more than one million people—has almost no open spaces or parks, which makes its position as Europe's most densely populated city plenty evident. Watching the police try to enforce traffic sanity is almost comical in Italy's grittiest, most polluted, and most crime-ridden city.

But Naples surprises the observant traveler with its impressive knack for living, eating, and raising children in the streets with good humor and decency.

Overcome your fear of being run down or ripped off long enough to talk with people. Enjoy a few smiles and jokes with the man running the neighborhood tripe shop, or the woman taking her day-care class on a walk through the traffic.

The pulse of Italy throbs in Naples. Like Cairo or Mumbai, it's appalling and captivating at the same time, the closest thing to "reality travel" that you'll find in Western Europe. But this tangled mess still somehow manages to breathe, laugh, and sing—with a captivating Italian accent.

Planning Your Time

A blitz visit to Naples and Pompeii looks something like this:

7:35   Catch the express train from Rome to Naples, where you'll transfer to the commuter train to Pompeii.

10:00 Tour Pompeii, grab a quick lunch (it's best to bring a picnic), then catch the commuter train back to Naples.

14:30 Visit Naples' Archaeological Museum during the heat of the day (closed Tue).

15:30 Take my self-guided "Slice of Neapolitan Life" walk.

18:30 Finish with a pizza dinner as the city comes to life in the early evening.

20:30 Hop on the train back to Rome.

22:30 Arrive in Rome.

Orientation to Naples

Tourist Information

The most convenient of Naples' three TIs is in Centrale train station (daily 9:00–19:00, near track 23, tel. 081-268-779, www.ept napoli.info or www.inaples.it). Pick up a map and the *Qui Napoli* booklet, which lists the latest museum hours, events, and transportation info. If they say they're "finished," ask for an old one. In town, you'll find TIs at the Galleria Umberto I shopping mall, across from the entrance to the Teatro di San Carlo (Mon–Sat 9:00–19:00, Sun 9:00–14:00, tel. 081-402-394), and across from the Church of Gesù Nuovo (same hours as Galleria Umberto I, tel. 081-551-2701).

Naples

PIAZZA CAVOUR

CENTRALE STATION (F.S.)

PIAZZA CAPUANA MKT.

ARCHAEO-LOGICAL MUSEUM

MUSEO

CAPPELLA SANSEVERO

DUOMO

VIA FORIA

VIA CARBONARA

CASANOVA

VIA S.S. APOST.

FIRENZE

AIRPORT BUS

PIAZZA GARI-BALDI

MONTESANTO METRO + FUNICULAR

PIAZZA DANTE

VIA TARSIA

PESSINA

GESÙ NUOVO

VIA B. CROCE

S. BIAGIO

"SPACCA-NAPOLI"

FORCELLA

PIZZA!

UMB.I.

FISH MKT.

CORSO GARI.

CIRCUM-VESUVIANA TERMINUS STATION (TO POMPEII)

TO POMPEII

EMAN.

VOMERO

VIT.

CORSO

VIA P. SCURA

TOLEDO

MORG.

S. CHIARA

PIAZZA CARITÀ

VIA PIGNASECCA

VIA ROMA

VIA DIAZ

DEPRETIS

CORSO

VIA COLOMBO

N. MARINA

PORT

SPANISH QUARTER

GALLERIA UMBERTO I

PZZA. MUNI.

BUS TO TRAIN STN.

STAZIONE MARITTIMA

TEATRO DI SAN CARLO

PIAZZA DEL PLEBISCITO

CASTEL NUOVO

BEVE-RELLO

CAR FERRIES TO SICILY + SARDINIA

CHIAIA

S. FRAN E PAOLO

VITTORIO TUNNEL

N. SAURO

ROYAL PALACE

TO SORRENTO, CAPRI, ISCHIA + PROCIDA

TO LUNGOMARE

VIA PARTENOPE

800 YARDS

800 METERS

"SPACCANAPOLI"

METRO STATION

BUS STOP

VIEW

CASTEL DELL'OVO

BORGO MARINARO

DCH

NAPLES AND POMPEII

Arrival in Naples

By Train: Trains run at least hourly from Rome (1.25 hours on Frecciarossa express trains, otherwise 2–2.5 hours). There are several Naples train stations, but all trains coming into town stop at either Napoli Centrale or Garibaldi—essentially the same stop, one on top of the other.

Centrale is the busiest station, facing Naples' main square, Piazza Garibaldi. You'll find all the administrative facilities in Centrale, including a TI, the Circumvesuviana stop (in the basement) for commuter trains to Pompeii, an ATM (at Banco di Napoli near track 24), and a baggage check (€4/5 hours, then €0.60/hour, daily 7:00–23:00, near track 5, marked *deposito bagagli*). Warning: Services in this station tend to change location frequently.

Garibaldi is a subway station used by trains to make a quick stop as they barrel through. It's connected to Centrale by escalators. Any train listed on the schedule as leaving *Napoli PG* or *Napoli-Garibaldi* departs not from the actual Centrale train station, but from the Piazza Garibaldi subway station below.

Continuing to Pompeii on the Circumvesuviana

Naples and Pompeii are connected by a **commuter train**—the Ferrovia Circumvesuviana—handy for tourists, commuters...and pickpockets (www.vesuviana.it).

At Naples' Centrale Station, follow the signs to the Circumvesuviana (across from track 14, downstairs), where you'll find the ticket office and info booth. There are two trains per hour to Pompeii (about 35 minutes, €2.40 one-way, final destination: Sorrento, not covered by railpasses). When you buy your ticket, purchase a round-trip ticket if you'll be returning to Naples: Ask for *"Pompeii, andata e ritorno"* (ahn-DAH-tah ay ree-TOR-noh). Ask which track your train will depart from (*"Quale binario?"*; KWAH-lay bee-NAH-ree-oh). Just beyond, you'll find the gate where you insert your ticket. The train platforms are downstairs. Before boarding, check the schedule carefully or confirm with a native to make sure the train is going to Pompeii. You want the *Pompei Scavi, Villa dei Misteri* stop.

The Circumvesuviana also has its own terminal (one Metro stop or a 10-minute walk beyond Centrale Station), but there's no reason to use it unless you're nearby. When returning to Naples' Centrale Station on the Circumvesuviana, get off at Garibaldi— the next-to-the-last stop (Centrale Station is just up the escalator).

If you're coming **from Rome,** note that a different (non-Circumvesuviana) train—run by the national rail company—goes from Rome to Naples, then continues to the ugly modern city of Pompei. There is almost no reason to go to Pompei city, where you'll face a long walk to the actual site. Therefore, from Rome, it's better to simply get off at Naples' Centrale Station and transfer to the Circumvesuviana (to the *Pompei Scavi* stop).

Helpful Hints

Theft Alert: Err on the side of caution. Don't venture into neighborhoods that make you uncomfortable. Walk with confidence, as if you know where you're going and what you're doing. Assume able-bodied beggars are thieves.

Stick to busy streets and beware of gangs of hoodlums. A third of the city is unemployed, and past local governments have set an example that the Mafia would be proud of. Assume con artists are more clever than you. Any jostle or commotion

NAPLES AND POMPEII

is probably a thief-team smokescreen. To keep bags safe, it's probably best to store them at Centrale Station.

Perhaps your biggest risk of theft is while catching or riding the Circumvesuviana commuter train. Remember, if you're connecting from a major train, you'll be stepping from a relatively secure compartment into a crowded Naples subway filled with thieves hunting disoriented tourists with luggage. While I ride the Circumvesuviana comfortably and safely, each year I hear of many who get ripped off on this ride. You won't be mugged—just conned or pickpocketed. Especially late at night, the Circumvesuviana train is plagued by intimidating ruffians. For maximum safety and peace of mind, sit in the front car, where the driver will double as your protector.

Con artists may say you need to "transfer" by taxi to catch the Circumvesuviana; you don't. Anyone offering to help you with your bags is likely a thief, despite displayed credentials. There are no porters at Centrale Station or in the basement where the Circumvesuviana station is located. Wear your money belt, hang on to your bag, and don't display any valuables.

Traffic: In Naples, red lights are discretionary, and pedestrians need to be wary, particularly of motor scooters. Smart tourists jaywalk in the shadow of bold and confident locals, who generally ignore crosswalks. Wait for a break in traffic, cross with confidence, and make eye contact with approaching drivers. The traffic will stop.

Local Guides: Roberta Mazzarella, who sorts through the wonders of Naples as only a local can, is excellent for a city walk (about €50/hour depending on itinerary, private tours only, mobile 339-135-7619, robertamazzarella@yahoo.it). **Pina Esposito** specializes in art and archaeology, and does fine tours of Naples' excellent but somewhat hard-to-appreciate Archaeological Museum (€120/2 hours, 10 percent off with this book, confirm one week in advance, sometimes available on shorter notice, mobile 349-596-8251, annamariaesposito1@virgilio.it). Both are flexible and also lead tours of Capri, Pompeii, and the surrounding area.

Getting Around Naples

By Subway: Naples' subway, the Metropolitana, has two lines. Line 2, the main line, runs from Centrale Station (catch it downstairs at the Garibaldi stop) through the center of town (direction: Pozzuoli), stopping at Piazza Cavour (a 5-minute walk from the Archaeological Museum) and Montesanto (top of Spanish Quarter and Spaccanapoli street). Line 1 runs from Piscinola/Scampia (suburbs) into the city center, stopping at the Museo station, near the Archaeological Museum (connects to Line 2's Piazza Cavour subway stop). Tickets cost €1.10 and are good for 1.5 hours. All-day tickets cost €3.10. Validate tickets either at the turnstile (if there is one), or in the small yellow boxes you'll see before you reach the track.

By Taxi: If you can afford a taxi, don't mess with the buses. A short taxi ride costs about €10 (insist on the meter—*tassametro*, €2 supplement after 22:00, €1.50 supplement on Sun, extra for baggage and holidays).

On a Hop-on, Hop-off Bus Tour: The "Sightseeing Napoli" tour bus makes three loops through the city, allowing ticket-holders to get on and off as they lace the city's sights together (€22, tickets good for 24 hours, buy from driver or from kiosk in front of Castel Nuovo near the port, scant recorded narration; for details, see the brochure at hotels and TI).

Sights in Naples

▲▲▲Archaeological Museum (*Museo Archeologico*)

For lovers of antiquity, this museum alone makes Naples a worthwhile stop. Considering its popularity and the importance of the collection, it's remarkable how ramshackle, unkempt, and dumpy its displays are. Still, if you can overlook the dust bunnies, this museum offers the best possible peek into the artistic jewelry boxes of Pompeii and Herculaneum. When Pompeii was excavated in the early 1800s, Naples' Bourbon king bellowed, "Bring me the best of what you find!" The actual sites are impressive but barren; the finest art and artifacts ended up here.

Cost and Hours: €6.50, but often €10 with mandatory charge for special exhibits, cash only, Wed–Mon 9:00–19:30, closed Tue.

Getting There: To take the subway from Centrale Station, follow signs to the Metro, called *Metropolitana* (near track 14, downstairs). Buy your ticket at the kiosk or a *tabacchi* and ask which track—"*Quale binario?*" (KWAH-lay bee-NAH-ree-oh)— to Piazza Cavour (direction: Pozzuoli, usually track 4). Validate your ticket in the small yellow boxes near the escalator going down to the tracks. Ride the subway one stop. As you leave the Metro, you can exit and hike uphill, or follow *Linea 1 Museo* signs through a long series of underground moving sidewalks to the *Museo* stop (on a different line), where you'll exit a bit closer to the museum. No matter where you emerge, look for a grand old red building located up a flight of stairs at the top of the block.

Figure on €10 for a taxi from the train station to the museum—insist on the meter *(tassametro)*.

Secret Room Appointment: Depending on how packed the

museum is, you may need to make an appointment on arrival to visit the Secret Room (Gabinetto Segreto), which contains erotic art from Pompeii (included in admission, you get a 15-minute window; to schedule a time, go to the information counter—on your immediate right as you enter). When it's not crowded, an appointment is unnecessary.

Information: Tel. 081-442-2149. For the basics, you can follow my self-guided tour (below). If you want a **guided tour,** look for Pina Esposito at the museum (see "Helpful Hints," earlier, €120/2-hour tour, 10 percent less with this book; help her assemble a group of up to 10 to split the fee). **Audioguides,** which haven't been updated for years, cost €4 (at ticket desk). The shop sells a worthwhile *National Archaeological Museum of Naples* guidebook— at €12, it's still a better value than the audioguide. Bag check is obligatory and free. Photos are allowed without a flash.

The museum seems to be in constant chaos due to ongoing renovations. If you can't find a particular work, ask a museum custodian, *"Dov'è?"* (DOH-vay, meaning "Where is?"), followed by the item's name.

Self-Guided Tour: Overview

Entering the museum, stand at the base of the grand staircase. To your right, on the ground floor, are larger-than-life statues from the Farnese Collection, starring the *Toro Farnese*. Up the stairs on the mezzanine level (turn left at the lion) are mosaics and frescoes from Pompeii, including the *Battle of Alexander* and the Secret Room of erotic art. On the top floor is a scale model of Pompeii and bronze statues from Herculaneum (a nearby town destroyed in the same eruption that devastated Pompeii). You'll find WCs by circling behind the staircase.

• *From the base of the grand staircase, turn right and head to the far end.*

Ground Floor: The Farnese Collection

The museum's ground floor alone has enough Greek and Roman art to put any museum on the map. Its highlight is the Farnese Collection, a grand hall of huge, bright, and wonderfully restored statues excavated from Rome's Baths of Caracalla.

The tangled *Toro Farnese* depicts a woman being tied to a bull. At 13 feet, it's the tallest ancient marble group ever found, and the

largest intact statue from antiquity. A
third-century A.D. copy of a lost bronze
Hellenistic original, it was carved out
of one piece of marble. Michelangelo
and others "restored" it at the pope's
request—meaning that they integrated
surviving bits into a new work. Panels on
the wall show which pieces were actually
carved by Michelangelo (in blue on the
chart): the head of the woman in back,
the torso of the aunt under the bull, and
the dog. (Imagine how the statue would
stand out if it was thoughtfully lit and
not surrounded by white walls.)

Here's the story behind the statue: Once upon an ancient
Greek time, King Lycus was bewitched by Dirce. He abandoned
his pregnant wife, Antiope (standing regally in the background).
The single mom gave birth to twin boys (shown here). When
they grew up, they killed their deadbeat dad and tied Dirce to the
horns of a bull to be bashed against a mountain. Captured in marble,
the action is thrilling: cape flailing, dog snarling, hooves in the air.
You can almost hear the bull snorting. And in the back, Antiope

oversees this harsh ancient justice with
satisfaction.

At the far end of the hall stands
Hercules. In a small room behind him is a
glass case with the sumptuous **Farnese Cup**
(*Tazza Farnese*, second century B.C., from
Egypt). This large, ancient cameo made of
agates looks less like a cup than a cereal bowl.
Its decorations are both Egyptian (the Nile
toting a lush cornucopia) and, on the flip side,
Greek (Medusa's head).

• *Backtrack a bit, then head up to the mezzanine
level.*

Mezzanine: Pompeiian Mosaics and the Secret Room

Most of these mosaics—of animals,
musicians, and geometric designs—
were taken from Pompeii's House
of the Faun (see page 423). The
house's delightful centerpiece is a
20-inch-high statue of the ***Dancing
Faun.*** This rare surviving Greek
bronze statue (from the fourth cen-

tury B.C.) is surrounded by some of the best mosaics of that age.

A highlight is the grand ***Battle of Alexander,*** a second-century

B.C. copy of the original Greek fresco, done a century earlier. It decorated a floor in the House of the Faun and was found intact; the damage you see occurred as this treasure was moved from Pompeii to the king's collection here. The painting (on left, made before it was moved) shows how it once looked. Alexander (left side of the scene, with curly hair and side-burns) is about to defeat the Persians under Darius (central figure, in chariot with turban and beard). This pivotal victory allowed Alexander to quickly overrun much of Asia (331 B.C.). Alexander is the only one without a helmet...a confident master of the battle-field while everyone else is fighting for their lives, eyes bulging with fear. Notice how the horses, already in retreat, add to the scene's propaganda value. Notice also the shading and perspective, which Renaissance artists would later work so hard to accomplish. (A modern reproduction of the mosaic is now back in the House of the Faun.)

The **Secret Room** *(Gabinetto Segreto)* contains a sizable assortment of erotic frescoes, well-hung pottery, and perky statues that once decorated bedrooms, meeting rooms, brothels, and even shops at Pompeii and Herculaneum. (On crowded days, you may have to make an appointment on arrival to view the room, though this is rare—see "Secret Room Appointment," page 398.) These bawdy statues and frescoes—many of them once displayed in Pompeii's grandest houses—were entertainment for guests. (By the time they made it to this museum, in 1819, the frescoes could be viewed only with permission from the king—see the letters in the glass case just outside the door.) The Roman nobles commis-sioned the wildest scenes imaginable. Think of them as ancient dirty jokes.

Circulating counterclockwise through this section, look for: 1) a faun playfully pulling the sheet off a beautiful woman, only to be grossed out by the plumbing of a hermaphrodite (perhaps the original *"Mamma mia!"*); 2) horny pygmies from Africa in action; 3) Venus, the patron goddess of Pompeii, a favorite pin-up girl; 4) a particularly high-quality statue of a goat and a satyr illustrating the act of sodomy; and 5) a toga with an embarrassing bulge.

The next room is furnished and decorated the way an ancient brothel might have been. The 10 frescoes on the wall functioned as both a menu of services offered and as a kind of *Kama Sutra* of sex positions. The walls feature big stone penises that once projected over Pompeii's doorways. A massive phallus was not necessarily a sexual symbol, but a magical amulet used against the "evil eye." It symbolized fertility, happiness, good luck, riches, straight A's, and general well-being. The glass cases contain more phallic art.

• *So, now that your travel buddy is finally showing a little interest in art...finish up your visit by climbing the stairs to the top floor.*

Top Floor: Statues, Artifacts, and a Model of Pompeii

At the top of the stairs, you'll enter a grand, empty hall. This was the great hall of the university (17th and 18th centuries) until the building became the royal museum in 1777. The sundial (from 1791) still works. At noon, a sunray strikes the spot, indicating today's date...if you know your zodiac.

To your right are rooms containing **bronze statues** from Herculaneum—of racers, dancers, and fauns (first-century B.C.

copies of fourth-century B.C. originals). They once decorated the holiday home (Villa dei Papyri in Herculaneum) of Julius Caesar's father-in-law. Look into the lifelike blue eyes of the intense *atleta* (athletes), bent on doing their best. The *Five Dancers*, with their inlaid-ivory eyes and graceful poses, decorated a portico. *Resting Hermes* (with his tired little heel wings) is taking a break. The *Drunken Faun* (singing and snapping his fingers to the beat, a wineskin at his side) is clearly living for today—true to the *carpe diem* preaching of the Epicurean philosophy. Caesar's father-in-law was an Epicurean philosopher, and his library—containing 2,000 papyrus scrolls—supported his outlook.

Return to the grand hall and continue to the other side, passing through several rooms of vases, statuettes, spoons, glassware, and other objects found at Pompeii. Keep going to the far end, where you'll find a **scale model** of the archaeological site of Pompeii, circa 1879 *(plastico di Pompeii)*. Belly up to the railing and find the Porta Marina entrance and the large rectangle of the town's Forum. Another model on the wall shows the site in 2004, after more excavations.

The Rest of the Museum

After years in restoration, the museum's large collection of **frescoes** taken from the walls of Pompeii villas is back (in Rooms LXVI to LXXVIII). Pompeiians loved to decorate their homes with scenes from mythology (Hercules' Labors, Venus and Mars in love), landscapes, everyday market scenes, and faux architecture. The display is roughly chronological.

For extra credit, visit **Doriforo**. (Ask a guard, *"Dov'è il Doriforo?"* He was last spotted on the ground floor, in the hall to

the left, as you face the staircase.) This seven-foot-tall "spear-carrier" (the literal translation of *doriforo*) just stands there, as if holding a spear. What's the big deal about this statue, which looks like so many others? It's a marble replica made by the Romans of one of the most-copied statues of antiquity, a fifth-century B.C. bronze Greek original by Polyclitus. This copy once stood in a Pompeii gym, where it inspired ancient athletes with the ideal proportions of Greek beauty. So full of motion, and so realistic in its *contrapposto* pose (weight on one foot), the *Doriforo* would later inspire Donatello and Michelangelo, triggering the Renaissance. And so the glories of ancient Pompeii, once buried and forgotten, live on today.

Self-Guided Walk

▲▲▲A Slice of Neapolitan Life Walk

Walk from the Archaeological Museum through the heart of town and back to Centrale Station. Allow at least three hours, plus pizza and sightseeing stops. If you have limited time, do a shorter, hour-long version by walking briskly and skipping the sights south of Spaccanapoli (including the Royal Palace, Teatro di San Carlo, and Galleria Umberto I).

Naples, a living medieval city, is its own best sight. Couples artfully make love on Vespas surrounded by more fights and smiles per cobblestone than anywhere else in Italy. Rather than seeing Naples as a list of sights, visit its one great museum and then capture its essence by taking this walk through the core of the city. Should you become overwhelmed or lost, step into a store and ask for directions: "Where is the central station?" in Italian is *"Dov'è la stazione centrale?"* (DOH-vay lah staht-zee-OH-nay chen-TRAH-lay). Or point to the next sight in this book.

Part 1: Via Pessina, Via Toledo, and the Spanish Quarter

The first part of this walk is a straight one-mile ramble down a boulevard to Galleria Umberto I, near the Royal Palace. Ideally, begin by touring the Archaeological Museum (at the top of Piazza Cavour, Metro: Cavour or Museo).

• *Leaving the Archaeological Museum, turn right and go one block, to the head of Via Pessina. This busy street leads downhill to Piazza*

"A Slice of Neapolitan Life" Walk

Dante—see his statue in the distance.

Piazza Dante: This square is marked by a statue of Dante, the medieval poet. Here you can feel Italy...but many Neapolitans merely feel the repression of the central state. When Napoleon was defeated, Naples became its own independent kingdom. But with Italian unification in 1861, Naples went from being a thriving cultural and political capital to a provincial town, its money used to help establish the industrial strength of the North. Originally, a statue of a Spanish Bourbon king stood here. The grand red-and-gray building is typical of Bourbon structures from that period. With the unification of Italy, the king, symbolic of Italy's colonial subjugation, was replaced by Dante—considered the father of the Italian language and a strong symbol of nationalism.

Old Dante looks out over an urban area that was once grand, then chaotic, and is now slowly becoming grand again. Behind Dante's right shoulder is Port'Alba, part of Naples' old wall and the entrance to a small street lined with book vendors. Via Pessina, the long, straight street that you're walking, originated as a military road built by Spain in the 16th century. It skirted the old town wall to connect the Spanish military headquarters (now the museum) with the Royal Palace (down by the bay). A subway station called Dante (with a modern-art flair) was recently built here on Piazza Dante. Construction was slowed by the city's rich underground history: 13 feet down—Roman ruins; 23 feet down—Greek ruins; and every inch of the way—big headaches for construction workers.

Across the street, **Caffè Mexico** (at #86) is an institution known for its espresso, which is served already sweetened—ask for *senza zucchero* if you don't want sugar (pay first, then take receipt to the counter; locals tip €0.10). Most Italians agree that Neapolitan coffee is the best anywhere.

Continue walking downhill, remembering that here in Naples, red lights are considered "decorations." When crossing a street, try to tag along with a native. The people here are survivors: A long history of corrupt and greedy colonial overlords has taught Neapolitans to deal creatively with authority. Many credit this aspect of Naples' past for the advent of organized crime here.

Via Pessina becomes Via Toledo (another reminder of Spanish rule), Naples' principal shopping street. In 1860, from the white marble balcony of the Neoclassical building overlooking Piazza Sette Settembre, the famous revolutionary Giuseppe Garibaldi declared Italy united and Victor Emmanuel II its first king. Not until 1870, when Rome fell to the unification forces, was the dream of Italian unity fully realized.

• *Continue straight on Via Toledo. At the next left (Via Maddaloni), about three blocks below Piazza Dante and a block past Piazza Sette*

Settembre, you'll come to the long, straight street called...

Spaccanapoli: Before crossing the street—whose name trans-

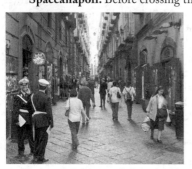

lates as "split Naples"—look left. Look right. Since ancient times, this thin street (which changes names several times: Maddaloni, Via B. Croce, Via S. Biagio dei Librai, Forecella, and Vicaria) has bisected the city. We'll return to this intersection later. (If you want to abbreviate this walk, turn left here and skip ahead to "Part 2.")

• *Stay on Via Toledo, which runs through...*

Piazza Carità: Surrounded by fascist architecture from 1938, this square is full of stern, straight, obedient lines. (For the best fascist architecture in town, take a slight detour from here—with your back to Via Toledo, leave Piazza Carità downhill on the right-hand corner and walk a block to the Poste e Telegrafi building. There you'll see several government buildings with stirring reliefs singing the praises of a totalitarian society.)

• *From Piazza Carità, wander south down Via Toledo for a few blocks, looking to your left for more examples of...*

Fascist Architecture (Banks): Notice the two banks. Try robbing the Banco di Napoli (Via Toledo 178). Step across the street and check out its architecture: typical fascist arches and reliefs, built to celebrate the bank's 400th anniversary (est. 1539—how old is *your* bank?).

On the next corner, **Banca Intesa Sanpaolo** fills an older palace—take a free peek at the opulent interior. On the second floor is a great late Caravaggio painting. *The Martyrdom of Saint Ursula* shows a terrible scene: His marriage proposal rejected, the king of the Huns flings an arrow into Ursula's chest. Blood spurts, Ursula is stunned but accepts her destiny sweetly, and Caravaggio himself (far right, his last self-portrait) screams to symbolize the rejection of evil (€3, Mon–Sat 10:00–18:00, closed Sun; includes 40-minute audioguide, a look at old Naples paintings, and a fine WC).

• *From here, side-trip uphill three blocks into the...*

Spanish Quarter: This is a classic world of *basso* (low) living. In such tight quarters, families generally do it in the road. This is *the* cliché of life in Naples, as shown in so many movies. The Spanish Quarter is Naples at its rawest, poorest, and most characteristic. The only predictable things about this Neapolitan tide pool are the ancient grid plan of its streets (which survives from

Greek times), the friendliness of its shopkeepers, and the boldness of its mopeds. Concerned locals will tug on their lower eyelids, warning you to be wary. Hungry? Pop into a grocery shop and ask the man to make you his best prosciutto and mozzarella sandwich (the price should be about €4).

• *Return to Via Toledo (clogged with more people than cars) and work your way down to the immense...*

Piazza del Plebiscito: This square celebrates the 1861 vote (*plebiscito,* plebiscite), when Naples chose to join Italy. Walk to the middle of the square. From here, you'll see the Church of San Francesco di Paola, with its Pantheon-inspired dome and broad, arcing colonnades.

• *Opposite is the...*

Royal Palace *(Palazzo Reale)*: Having housed Spanish, French, and even Italian royalty, this building displays statues of all those who stayed here. Look for eight kings in the niches, each from a different dynasty (left to right): Norman, German, French, Spanish, Spanish, Spanish, French (Napoleon's brother-in-law), and, finally, Italian—Victor Emmanuel II, King of Savoy. The statues were done at the request of V. E. II's son, so his dad is the most dashing of the group. This huge, lavish palace welcomes the public (€4, more with special exhibits, Thu–Tue 9:00–20:00, closed Wed, last entry one hour before closing, audioguide-€4, or €5/2 people, tel. 848-800-288).

The palace's grand Neoclassical staircase leads up to a floor with 30 plush rooms. You'll follow a one-way route (with some English descriptions) featuring paintings by "the Caravaggio Imitators," Neapolitan tapestries, fine inlaid-stone tabletops, and more. Don't miss the huge Hercules room and the chapel with a fantastic Nativity scene (a commotion of 18th-century ceramic figurines).

The **Gran Caffè Gambrinus,** facing the piazza, takes you back to the elegance of 1860. It's a classic place to sample a unique Neapolitan treat called *sfogliatella* (crispy scallop-shell-shaped pastry filled with sweet ricotta cheese). Or you might prefer the mushroom-shaped, rum-soaked bread-like cakes called *babà,* which come in a huge variety. Stand at the bar *(banco),* pay double to sit *(tavola),* or just wander around as you imagine the café buzzing with the ritzy intellectuals, journalists, and artsy bohemian types who munched on *babà* here during Naples' 19th-century heyday (daily 7:00–24:00, Piazza del Plebiscito 1, tel. 081-417-582).

• *Continue 50 yards past the Royal Palace to enjoy a...*

NAPLES AND POMPEII

Fine Harbor View: While boats busily serve Capri and Sorrento, Mount Vesuvius smolders ominously in the distance. Look back to see the vast "Bourbon red" palace—its color inspired by Pompeii. On the hilltop above Piazza del Plebiscito is Naples' Carthusian Monastery and the Castle of St. Elmo. This street continues to Naples' romantic harborfront—the fishermen's quarters or Borgo Marinaro—a fortified island connected to the mainland by a stout causeway, with its fanciful Castel dell'Ovo ("castle of the egg") and trendy harborside restaurants. Farther along the harborfront stretches the Lungomare promenade and Santa Lucia district. (The long harborfront promenade, Via Francesco Caracciolo, is a delightful people-watching scene on balmy nights.)

• *Head back to the piazza and go behind the palace, where you can peek inside the Neoclassical...*

Teatro di San Carlo: Built in 1737, 41 years before Milan's La Scala, this is Europe's oldest opera house and Italy's second-most-respected (after La Scala). The theater burned down in 1816, and was rebuilt within the year. Guided 40-minute visits basically just show you the fine auditorium with its 184 boxes—each with a big mirror to reflect the candlelight (€5, Mon–Sat 10:00–17:30, tours every 40 minutes, closed Sun, tel. 081-553-4565, www.teatrosancarlo.it).

Beyond Teatro di San Carlo and the Royal Palace is the huge, harborfront Castel Nuovo, which houses government bureaucrats and the **Civic Museum,** featuring 14th- to 16th-century art (€5, Mon–Sat 9:00–19:00, closed Sun, last entry one hour before closing, tel. 081-795-5877).

Across the street from Teatro di San Carlo, go through the tall yellow arch into the Victorian iron and glass of the 100-year-old shopping mall, **Galleria Umberto I.** Gawk up.

• *For Part 2 of this walk, double back up Via Toledo to Piazza Carità, veering right on Via Morgantini to Via Maddaloni (to avoid the backtracking and uphill walk, catch an €8 taxi to the church of Gesù Nuovo—JAY-zoo noo-OH-voh).*

Part 2: Spaccanapoli Back to the Station

You're back at the straight-as-a-Greek-arrow Spaccanapoli, formerly the main thoroughfare of the Greek city of Neapolis.

• *Stop at...*

Piazza Gesù Nuovo: This square is marked by a towering 18th-century Baroque monument to the Counter-Reformation. Although the Jesuit order was powerful in Naples because of its

Spanish heritage, locals never attacked Protestants here with the full fury of the Spanish Inquisition. The square also has a handy little TI and is the starting point for electric bus #E1, which makes a 40-minute loop through the characteristic old quarter and ends up back here (€1.10, buy ticket at nearby newsstand before boarding, 2/hour, daily 7:00–24:00).

• *Now visit two bulky old churches, starting with the austere, fortress-like, 17th-century...*

Church of Gesù Nuovo: The unique pyramid-grill facade survives from a fortified 15th-century noble palace. Step inside for a brilliant Neapolitan Baroque interior. The second chapel on the right features a much-adored statue of Giuseppe Moscati (1880–1927), a Christian doctor famous for helping the poor. In 1987, Moscati became the first modern doctor to be canonized.

Continue on to the third chapel and enter the **Sale Moscati.** This huge room is filled with "Ex Votos"—tiny red-and-silver plaques of thanksgiving for prayers answered with the help of St. Moscati (each has a symbol of the ailment cured). Naples' practice of using Ex Votos, while incorporated into its Catholic rituals, goes back to its pagan Greek roots. Rooms from Moscati's nearby apartment are on display, and a glass case shows possessions and photos of the great doctor. As you leave the Sale Moscati, notice the big bomb casing that hangs in the left corner. It fell through the church's dome in 1943, but caused almost no damage...yet another miracle (daily 7:00–12:30 & 16:00–19:30).

• *Head across the street, to the simpler...*

Church of Santa Chiara: Dating from the 14th century, this church is from a period of French royal rule under the Angevin dynasty. Consider the stark contrast between this church (Gothic) and the Gesù Nuovo (Baroque). Notice the huge, inlaid-marble, Angevin coat of arms on the floor. The faded Trinity on the back wall, to the left of the entry, shows a dove representing the Holy Spirit between the heads of God the Father and Christ (c. 1414). This is an example of the fine frescoes that once covered the walls. Most were stuccoed over during Baroque times or destroyed in 1943 by WWII bombs. The altar is adorned with four finely carved Gothic tombs of Angevin kings. A chapel stacked with Bourbon royalty is just to the right (daily 7:00–12:30 & 16:30–20:00).

• *Leaving the church, take a right and head to the back of the building. Continue through the archway straight ahead, and pass all the parked cars to reach the farthest door on the right. Here you'll find the bright, ornate, majolica-tiled...*

Cloistered Courtyard of Santa Chiara: Note the sprawling nativity scene immediately on your right as you enter—a cartoonish 3-D snapshot of Old World Napoli. Stop in at its museum (€5, Mon–Sat 9:30–17:30, Sun 9:30–14:30, last entry 30

minutes before closing).
• *Now return to the main drag, turn right, and continue straight down traffic-free Via B. Croce. A good little lunch spot, Trattoria da Titina e Gennaro, is just down the street across from the church (Via Santa Chiara 6).*

Since this is a university district, you'll see lots of students and bookstores. This neighborhood is also extremely superstitious. Look for incense-burning women with carts full of good-luck charms for sale.
• *Farther down Spaccanapoli, you'll see the next square...*

Piazza San Domenico Maggiore: This square is marked by an ornate 17th-century monument built to thank God for ending the plague. But more important is the well-loved **Scaturchio Pasticceria,** another good place to try *sfogliatella* (€1.50 to go, costs double at a table in the square, daily 7:20–20:40, tel. 081-551-7031).
• *From this square, detour left along the right side of the castle-like church, then follow yellow signs, taking the first right and walking one block to...*

Cappella Sansevero: This small chapel is a Baroque explosion mourning the body of Christ, who lies on a soft pillow under an incredibly realistic veil. It's also the personal chapel of Raimondo de Sangro, an eccentric Freemason. The monuments to his relatives have a second purpose: to share the Freemason philosophy of freedom through enlightenment (€6, Mon and Wed–Sat 10:00–18:00, Sun 10:00–13:30, closed Tue, last entry 20 minutes before closing, no photos but postcards are sold in gift shop, Via de Sanctis 19, tel. 081-551-8470).

Study the incredible *Veiled Christ* in the center. Carved out of marble, it's like no other statue I've seen (by Giuseppe "Howdeedoodat" Sammartino, 1753). The Christian message (Jesus died for our salvation) is accompanied by a Freemason message (the veil represents how the body and ego are obstacles to real spiritual freedom). As you walk from Christ's feet to his head, notice how the expression on Jesus' face goes from suffering to peace.

Raimondo de Sangro lies buried at the far (altar) end. An inventor, he created the deep-green pigment used on the ceiling fresco. The inlaid M. C. Escher–esque maze on the floor around de Sangro's tomb is another Freemason reminder of how the quest for knowledge gets you out of the maze of life.

To the right of the altar, the statue *Despair* struggles with a marble rope net (carved out of a single piece of stone), symbolic of a troubled mind. The Freemason symbolism shows how knowledge—in the guise of an angel—frees the human mind. On the opposite side of the altar from *Despair,* a veiled woman fingers a broken plaque, symbolizing...something.

Your Sansevero finale is downstairs: two mysterious...

skeletons. Perhaps another of the mad inventor's fancies: Inject a corpse with a fluid to fossilize the veins so that they'll survive the body's decomposition. While that's the legend, it was most likely created to illustrate how the circulatory system works.

• *Return to Via B. Croce (a.k.a. Spaccanapoli), turn left, and continue your cultural scavenger hunt. At the intersection of Via Nilo, find the...*

Statue of the Nile (on the left): A reminder of the multi-ethnic make-up of Greek Neapolis, this statue is in what was the Egyptian quarter. Locals like to call this statue *The Body of Naples*, with the overflowing cornucopia symbolizing the abundance of their fine city. (I once asked a Neapolitan man to describe the local women, who are famous for their beauty, in one word. He replied simply, "Abundant.") This intersection is considered the center of old Naples.

A few blocks farther, at the tiny square, Via San Gregorio Armeno leads left into a colorful district (and also to the underground Napoli Sotterranea archaeological site). You'll see many shops that sell tiny components of fantastic *presepi* (nativity scenes), including figurines caricaturing local politicians and celebrities. Just as many Americans keep an eye out year-round for Christmas tree ornaments, Italians regularly add pieces to the family *presepe*, the centerpiece of their holiday celebrations.

• *As Via B. Croce becomes Via S. Biagio dei Librai, notice the...*

Gold and Silver Shops: Some say stolen jewelry ends up here, is melted down immediately, and gets resold in some other form as soon as it cools. The inimitable Sr. Grassi runs the Ospedale delle Bambole (doll hospital) at #81.

• *Cross busy Via Duomo.*

Here, the street and side-street scenes along Via Vicaria intensify. This is known as a center of the Camorra (organized crime).

Paint a picture with these thoughts: Naples has the most intact street plan of any ancient Roman city. Imagine this city during those times (and retain these images as you visit Pompeii), with streetside shop fronts that close up after dark, turning into private homes. Today, it's just one more page in a 2,000-year-old story of a city: all kinds of meetings, beatings, and cheatings; kisses, near misses, and little-boy pisses.

You name it, it occurs right on the streets today, as it has since ancient times. People ooze from crusty corners. Black-and-white death announcements add to the clutter on the walls. Widows sell cigarettes from buckets. For a peek behind the scenes in the shade of wet laundry, venture

Pizza in Naples

Naples—whose pizzerias bake just the right combination of fresh dough, mozzarella, and tomatoes in traditional wood-burning ovens—is the birthplace of pizza. Drop by one of the two most venerable pizzerias in town (both a few long blocks from the station, at the end of the "A Slice of Neapolitan Life Walk").

Antica Pizzeria da Michele is for pizza purists. Filled with locals (and tourists), it serves just two varieties: *margherita* (tomato sauce and mozzarella) and *marinara* (tomato sauce, oregano, and garlic, no cheese). Come early to sit and watch the pizza artists in action. A pizza with beer costs €6 (Mon-Sat 10:00–24:00, closed Sun; look for the vertical red *Antica Pizzeria* sign at the intersection of Via Pietro Colletta and Via Cesare Sersale at #1; tel. 081-553-9204).

Pizzeria Trianon, across the street, has been da Michele's archrival since 1923. It offers more choices, slightly higher prices (€5–7), air-conditioning, and a cozier atmosphere. For less chaos, head upstairs. While waiting for your meal, you can survey the evolution of a humble wad of dough into a smoldering bubbly feast in their entryway pizza kitchen (daily 11:00–15:30 & 19:00–23:00, Via Pietro Colletta 42, tel. 081-553-9426, Giuseppe).

down a few side streets. Buy two carrots as a gift for the woman on the fifth floor if she'll lower her bucket to pick them up. The neighborhood action seems best at about 18:00.

A few blocks on, at the tiny fenced-in triangle of greenery, hang out for a few minutes to just observe the crazy motorbike action and teen scene.

• *From here, veer right onto Via Forcella (which leads to the busy boulevard that takes you to Centrale Station). A tiny, round traffic island protects a chunk of the ancient Greek wall of Neapolis (fourth century B.C.). But first, turn right on busy Via Pietro Colletta, walk 50 yards, and step into the North Pole, at the...*

Polo Nord Gelateria: The oldest *gelateria* in Naples has had four generations of family working here since 1931. Before you order, sample a few flavors, including their *bacio* or "kiss" flavor (chocolate and hazelnut)—all are made fresh daily (Mon–Sat 10:00–24:00, Sun 10:00–14:00 & 17:00–24:00, Via Pietro Colletta 41, tel. 081-205-431). Via Pietro Colletta leads past Napoli's two most competitive **pizzerias** (see "Pizza in Naples" sidebar) to Corso Umberto I.

• *Turn left on the grand-boulevard-like Corso Umberto I. From here to Centrale Station, it's at least a 10-minute walk (if you're tired, hop on a bus; they all go to the station). To finish the walk, continue on*

Corso Umberto I—past a gauntlet of purse/CD/sunglasses salesmen and shady characters hawking stolen camcorders—to the vast, ugly Piazza Garibaldi. On the far side is the station. You made it.

Open-Air Fish Market

For those with a little more time, Naples' fish market squirts and stinks as it has for centuries under the Porta Nolana (gate in the city wall) just four blocks from Centrale train station. Of

the town's many boisterous outdoor markets, this will net you the most photos and memories. From Piazza Nolana, wander under the medieval gate and take your first left down Vico Sopramuro, enjoying this wild and entirely edible cultural scavenger hunt (Tue–Sun 8:00–14:00, closed Mon).

Two other markets with more clothing and less fish are at Piazza Capuana (several blocks northwest of Centrale Station and tumbling down Via Sant'Antonio Abate, Mon–Sat 8:00–18:00, Sun 9:00–13:00) and a similar cobbled shopping zone along Via Pignasecca (just off Via Toledo, west of Piazza Carità).

Pompeii

Stopped in its tracks by the eruption of Mount Vesuvius in A.D. 79, Pompeii offers the best look anywhere at what life in Rome must

have been like 2,000 years ago. An entire city of well-preserved ruins is yours to explore. A once-thriving commercial port of 20,000, Pompeii (worth ▲▲▲) grew from Greek and Etruscan roots to become an important Roman city. Then, at about noon on August 24, A.D. 79, everything changed

as the city became buried under waves of hot volcanic ash. For archaeologists, this was a shake-and-bake windfall, teaching them volumes about daily Roman life. Pompeii was rediscovered in the 1600s; excavations began in 1748.

Pompeii

NAPLES AND POMPEII

SEE POMPEII WALK MAP

1 Main Entrance
2 Forum
3 Cafeteria & Baths
4 House of the Faun
5 House of the Vetti
6 Brothel
7 Theater
8 Amphitheater

UNEXCAVATED AREAS

200 YARDS
200 METERS

VILLA DEI MISTERI

VIA SEPOLCRI

PORTA DI ERCOLANO

CITY WALLS

PORTA DEL VESUVIO

PORTA DI NOLA

VIA NOLA

VIA DELL' ABBONDANZA

PORTA DI SARNO

PALESTRA

VIA STABIANA

VIA DEI TEATRI

PORTA DI STABIA

PORTA DI NOCERA

PIAZZA ANFITEATRO ENTRANCE

PIAZZA ANFITEATRO

VIA

ROMA TO POMPEI TOWN (MODERN)

VIA GIUSEPPE SS 18

DCH

PATH

PORTA MARINA MAIN ENTRANCE

TRAIN STATION

CIRCUM-VESUVIANA

TICKETS

VIA MARINA

EXIT

FORUM

VIA PLINIO SS 18

PIAZZA ESEDRA

+ BUS STOP FOR VESUVIUS

TO NAPLES

A-3

SS 18

TO NAPLES

TO SALERNO

A-3

TO SORRENTO

TO SALERNO

Orientation to Pompeii

Cost: €11.

Hours: Daily April–Oct 8:30–19:30, Nov–March 8:30–17:00 (last entry 1.5 hours before closing).

Getting There: Pompeii is about 35 minutes from Naples on the Circumvesuviana train line that continues to Sorrento (2/hour, €2.40 from Naples, one-way, not covered by railpasses, www.vesuviana.it). Get off at the *Pompei Scavi, Villa dei Misteri* stop (it's the stop after *Torre Annunziata*). Store your bag at the train station's bar for a small fee (€2, confirm last pick-up time—bar often closes early), or, better yet, use the free baggage check at the site. From the Pompei Scavi train station, turn right and walk down the road about a block to the entrance (first left turn). The TI is farther down the street, but it's not a necessary stop for your visit. Parking is available at Camping Zeus near the Circumvesuviana train station (€2.50/hour).

Information: A good map and a helpful information booklet (which describes the most important stops within the site), when available, are included with your admission, but you must pick them up at the information window (to the left of the WCs). Tel. 081-857-5347, www.pompeiisites.org.

The bookshop sells the small Pompeii and Herculaneum *Past and Present* book. Its helpful text and plastic overlays allow you to recreate the ruins (€12 in bookstores, pay no more than that if you buy from a street vendor; look for the current year's edition).

Tours: My self-guided tour covers the basics. **Live guides** (around €115/2 hours) of varying quality can be risky—there really is no guarantee of what you're getting. They cluster near the ticket booth and may try to herd you into a group with other travelers, which makes the price more reasonable for you. For a private tour, hire the knowledgeable **Gaetano Manfredi,** who brings energy, intensity, and theatricality to his tours. He's a joy to follow for two hours as he brings the dusty ruins to life. Avoid impersonators. The real Gaetano takes bookings only in advance, preferably by email (tel. 338-725-5620, rates vary with season and group size, www.pompeiitourguide.com, gaetanoguide@hotmail.it). Parents, note that some sexually explicit frescoes are included on tours.

For evening visitors, Pompeii offers a "Moons of Pompeii" **sound-and-light show** that's partly a walking tour, with video footage projected onto the ruins (€20, summers only, check website for schedule, tel. 081-1930-3885, www.lelunedi pompei.it).

Audioguide Tours: These are available from a kiosk near the ticket booth at the Porta Marina entrance (€6.50, €10/2 people, ID required), but they offer basically the same info as your free booklet. If you have an iPod or other MP3 player, you can download my free audio tour of this walk at www.ricksteves .com (or search for "Rick Steves Audio Tours" in iTunes).

Length of This Tour: Allow three hours.

Baggage Check: A free baggage check is near the turnstiles at the site entrance (retrieve bags by 19:00).

Services: The site has two WCs—one near the entrance and another in the cafeteria.

Cuisine Art: Your best bet is to bring your own food. The restaurant within the site serves edible sandwiches, pizza, and pasta at a reasonable price. A few mediocre restaurants cluster between the entrance and the train station.

Starring: Roofless (collapsed) but otherwise intact Roman buildings, plaster casts of hapless victims, a few erotic frescoes, and the dawning realization that these ancient people were no different from us.

Background

Pompeii, founded in 600 B.C., eventually became a booming Roman trading city. Not rich, not poor, it was middle class—a

perfect example of typical Roman life. Most streets would have been lined with stalls and jammed with customers from sunup to sundown. Chariots vied with shoppers for street space. Two thousand years ago, Rome controlled the entire Mediterranean—making it a kind of free-trade zone—and Pompeii was a central and bustling port.

There were no posh neighborhoods in Pompeii. Rich and poor mixed it up as elegant houses existed side by side with simple homes. While nearby Herculaneum would have been a classier place to live (traffic-free streets, fancier houses, far better drainage), Pompeii was the place for action and shopping. It served an estimated 20,000 residents with more than 40 bakeries, 30 brothels, and 130 bars, restaurants, and hotels. With most of its buildings covered by brilliant, white, ground-marble stucco, Pompeii in A.D. 79 was an impressive town.

As you tour Pompeii, remember that its best art is in the Archaeological Museum in Naples (described earlier in this chapter).

Self-Guided Tour

• *Just past the ticket-taker, start your approach up to the…*

❶ Porta Marina

The city of Pompeii was born on the hill ahead of you. This was the original town gate. Before Vesuvius blew, the sea came nearly to here.

Look to the left in the distance to see the stone rings where ships were tied to the dock. Also notice the two openings in the gate (ahead, up the ramp). Both were left open by day to admit major traffic. At night, the larger one was closed for better security.

• *Pass through the Porta Marina and continue up the street, pausing at the three large stepping-stones in the middle.*

❷ Pompeii's Streets

Every day, Pompeiians flooded the streets with gushing water to clean them. These stepping-stones let pedestrians cross without

getting their sandals wet. Chariots traveling in either direction could straddle the stones (all had standard-size axles). A single stepping-stone in a road means it was a one-way street, a pair indicates an ordinary two-way, and three (like this) signifies a major thoroughfare. The basalt stones are the original Roman pavement. The sidewalks (elevated to hide the plumbing) were paved with bits of broken pots (an ancient form of recycling) and studded with reflective bits of white marble. These "cats' eyes" helped people get around after dark, either by moonlight or with the help of lamps.

• *Continue straight ahead, don your mental toga, and enter the city as the Romans once did. The road opens up into the spacious main square: the Forum. Stand at the end of this rectangular space and look toward Mount Vesuvius.*

❸ The Forum (Foro)

Pompeii's commercial, religious, and political center stands at the intersection of the city's two main streets. While it's the most ruined part of Pompeii, it's grand nonetheless. Picture the piazza

The Eruption of Vesuvius

At about noon on August 24, A.D. 79, Mount Vesuvius blew, sending a mushroom cloud of ash, dust, cinders, and rocks 12 miles into the air. It spewed for 18 hours straight, as winds blew the cloud southward. The white-gray ash settled like snow on Pompeii, collapsing roofs and floors, but leaving the walls intact. Two thousand of the town's 20,000 residents were entombed under eight feet of fine powder.

The next morning, Vesuvius' upper portion collapsed, picking up speed as it fell to earth, creating a cloud of ash, pumice, and gas. The red-hot avalanche (a "pyroclastic flow") sped down the side of the mountain at nearly 100 miles per hour. Four minutes later, it engulfed the city of Herculaneum (four miles away), burying it in nearly 60 feet of hot mud. The mud cooled into stone, freezing the moment in time.

surrounded by two-story buildings on all sides. The pedestals that line the square once held statues (now safely displayed in the museum in Naples). In its heyday, Pompeii's citizens gathered here in the main square to shop, talk politics, and socialize. Business took place in the important buildings that lined the piazza.

The Forum was dominated by the **Temple of Jupiter,** at the far end (marked by a half-dozen ruined columns atop a stair-step base). Jupiter was the supreme god of the Roman pantheon—you might be able to make out his little white marble head at the center-rear of the temple.

At the near end of the Forum (where you're standing) is the **curia,** or city hall. Like many Roman buildings, it was built with brick and mortar, then covered with marble walls and floors. To your left (as you face Vesuvius and the Temple of Jupiter) is the **basilica,** or courthouse.

Since Pompeii was a typical town, it has the same layout and components that you'll find in any Roman city—main square, curia, basilica, temples, axis of roads, and so on. All power converged at the Forum: religious (the temple), political (the curia), judicial (the basilica), and commercial (this piazza was the main marketplace). Even the power of the people was expressed here, since this where they gathered to vote. Imagine the hubbub of this town square.

Look beyond the Temple of Jupiter. Five miles to the north

NAPLES AND POMPEII

Pompeii Walk

ORIGINAL SHAPE

VESUVIUS (IN DISTANCE)

PORTA DEL VESUVIO

WALLS

UNEXCAVATED AREA

TO PORTA DI ERCOLANO

C I T Y

VIA VETTI

VIA VESUVIO

VIA NOLA

VIA

HOUSE OF THE VETTI (MAY BE CLOSED) ⑬

VICOLO DI MERCURIO

VIA DI FORTUNA

HOUSE OF THE FAUN

VICOLO

⑫

⑪

TABERNA HEDONES

VIA CONSULARE

⑨

⑧

⑩ VIA FORO

⑭

VIA STABIANA

TO ⑱

VIA

⑦

VIA AUGUSTALI

⑮

CAFETERIA + WC

⑥

TEMPLE OF JUPITER

Forum

③

PORTA MARINA **START** ①

②

④

⑤

VIA DELL' ABBONDANZA

VIA TEATRI

⑯

TEATRO PICCOLO

⑰

RAMP

EXIT

C I T Y   W A L L S

THEATER (MAY BE CLOSED) **FINISH**

TO MAIN ENTRANCE, TICKETS & CIRCUMVESUVIANA TRAIN STATION

TO PIAZZA ESEDRA

DCH

⬎ VIEW

NAPLES AND POMPEII

❶ Porta Marina
❷ Pompeii's Streets
❸ Forum
❹ Basilica
❺ Via Abbondanza
❻ Fish & Produce Market; Plaster Casts of Victims
❼ Baths of the Forum
❽ Fast-Food Joint
❾ House of the Tragic Poet
❿ Aqueduct Arch
⓫ House of the Faun
⓬ Original Lead Pipes
⓭ House of the Vetti
⓮ Bakery & Mill
⓯ Brothel
⓰ Temple of Isis
⓱ Theater & Piccolo Theater
⓲ Amphitheater

looms the ominous backstory to this site: **Mount Vesuvius.**
Mentally draw a triangle up from the two remaining peaks to
reconstruct the mountain before the eruption. When it blew,
Pompeiians had no idea that they were living under a volcano,
since Vesuvius hadn't erupted for 1,200 years. (Still active, its last
eruption was in 1944.) Imagine the wonder—then the horror—as
the column of smoke roared upward, and then began to fall like
hail, rain, and snow, collapsing roofs and burying everything in a
blanket of ash.

• *As you face Vesuvius, the basilica is to your left, lined with stumps of
columns. Step inside and see the layout.*

❹ Basilica

Pompeii's basilica was a first-century palace of justice. This ancient
law court has the same floor plan later adopted by many Christian
churches (which are also called basilicas). The big central hall (or
nave) is flanked by rows of columns marking off narrower side
aisles. Along the side walls are traces of the original marble.

The column stumps—all about the same height—were not
ruined by the volcano. Rather, they were left unfinished when
Vesuvius blew. Pompeii had been
devastated by an earthquake in
A.D. 62, and was just in the process of rebuilding the basilica
when Vesuvius erupted 17 years
later. The half-built columns
show off the technology of the
day. Uniform bricks were stacked
around a cylindrical core. Once
finished, they would have been

coated with marble dust stucco to simulate marble columns—an
economical construction method found throughout Pompeii (and
the Roman Empire).

Besides the earthquake and the eruption, Pompeii's buildings
have suffered other ravages over the years, including Spanish plun-
derers (c. 1800), 19th-century souvenir hunters, WWII bombs,
wild vegetation, and another earthquake in 1980. The fact that the
entire city was covered by the eruption of A.D. 79 actually helped
preserve it, saving it from the sixth-century barbarians who plundered many other towns into oblivion.

• *Exit the basilica and cross the square to the far side, where the city's
main street hits the Forum.*

❺ Via Abbondanza

Look down Via Abbondanza, Pompeii's main street. Lined with
shops, bars, and restaurants, it was a lively, pedestrian-only zone.

The three "beaver-teeth" stones are traffic barriers that kept chariots out. On the corner (just to the left), take a close look at the dark travertine column standing next to a white one. Notice that the marble drums of the white column are not chiseled entirely round—another construction project left unfinished when Vesuvius erupted.

• *Head toward Vesuvius, walking along the right side of the Forum. Immediately to the right of the Temple of Jupiter, a door leads into the market hall, where you'll find two glass cases.*

❻ Fish and Produce Market—Plaster Casts of Victims

As the frescoes on the wall (just inside on the left) indicate, this is where Pompeiians came to buy their food—fish, bread, chickens,

and so on. These fine examples of Roman art—with their glimpses of everyday life and mastery of depth and illusion—would not be matched until the Renaissance, a thousand years after the fall of Rome.

The glass cases hold casts of Pompeiians, eerily captured in their last moments. When Vesuvius erupted, 2,000 Pompeii citizens suffocated under the ash, their bodies buried in volcanic debris. While excavating, modern archaeologists detected hollow spaces underfoot, created when the victims' bodies decomposed. By gently filling the

holes with plaster, the archaeologists were able to create molds of the Pompeiians who were caught in the disaster. You're looking at modern plaster mixed with ancient bones.

• *Continue on, leaving the Forum through an arch behind the Temple of Jupiter. Here you'll find a pedestrians-only road sign (ahead on the right corner, above the REG VII INS IV sign) and more "beaver-teeth" traffic blocks. The modern cafeteria is the only eatery inside the archaeological site (with a coffee bar and WC). Twenty yards past the cafeteria, on the left-hand side at #24, is the entrance to the...*

❼ Baths of the Forum (Terme del Foro)

Pompeii had six public baths, each with a men's and a women's section. You're in the men's zone. The leafy courtyard at the entrance was the gymnasium. After working out, clients could relax with a hot bath *(caldarium),* warm bath *(tepidarium),* or cold plunge *(frigidarium).*

The first big, plain room you enter served as the **dressing room.** Holes on the walls were for pegs to hang clothing. The window (with Neptune underneath) was originally covered with a less-translucent Roman glass. Walk over the non-slip mosaics into the next room.

The *tepidarium* is ringed by mini-statues or *telamones* (male caryatids, figures used as supporting pillars), which divided the lockers. Clients would undress and warm up here, perhaps stretching out on one of the bronze benches near the bronze heater for a massage. Look at the ceiling—half crushed by the eruption and half intact, with its fine blue-and-white stucco work.

Next, admire the engineering in the steam-bath room, or *caldarium*. The double floor was heated from below—so nice with bare feet (look into the grate to see the brick support towers). The double walls with brown terra-cotta tiles held the heat. Romans soaked in the big tub, which was filled with hot water. Opposite the big tub is a fountain, which spouted water onto the hot floor, creating steam. The lettering on the fountain reminded those enjoying the room which two politicians paid for it...and how much it cost them (5,250 sestertii). To keep condensation from dripping annoyingly from the ceiling, fluting (ribbing) was added to carry water down the walls.

• *Today's visitors exit the baths through the original entry. If you're a bit hungry, immediately across the street is an ancient...*

❽ Fast-Food Joint

After a bath, it was only natural to want a little snack. So, just across the street is a fast-food joint, marked by a series of rectangular marble counters. Most ancient Romans didn't cook for themselves in their tiny apartments, so to-go places like this were commonplace. The holes in the counters held the pots for food. Each container was like a thermos, with a wooden lid to keep the soup hot, the wine cool, and so on. Notice the groove in the front doorstep and the holes out on the curb. The holes likely accommodated cords for stretching awnings over the sidewalk to shield the clientele from the hot sun, while the grooves were for the shop's folding accordion doors. Look at the wheel grooves in the pavement, worn down through centuries of use. There are also more stepping-stones for pedestrians to cross the flooded streets.

• *Just a few steps uphill from the fast-food joint is the...*

❾ House of the Tragic Poet (Casa de Poeta Tragico)

This house is typical Roman style. The entry is flanked by two family-owned shops (each with a track for a collapsing accordion door). The home is like a train running straight away from the street: atrium (with skylight and pool to catch the rain), den (where deals were made by the shopkeeper), and garden (with rooms facing it and a shrine to remember both the gods and family ancestors). In the entryway is the famous "Beware of Dog" *(Cave Canem)* mosaic.

Today's visitors enter the home by the back door (circle around to the left). The modern pipe exposed across the lane is the same as ones used in the ancient plumbing system, hidden beneath the raised sidewalk. Inside the house, the grooves on the marble well head were formed by generations of dragging the bucket up by rope. The richly frescoed dining room is off the garden. Diners lounged on their couches (the Roman custom) and enjoyed frescoes with fake "windows," giving the illusion of a bigger and airier room. Just to the right is a humble BBQ-style kitchen with a little closet for the toilet (the kitchen and bathroom shared the same plumbing).

• *Return to the fast-food place and continue about 10 yards downhill to the big intersection. From the center of the intersection, look left to see a giant arch, framing a nice view of Mount Vesuvius.*

❿ Aqueduct Arch—Running Water

Water was critical for this city of 20,000 people, and this arch was part of Pompeii's water-delivery system. A 100-mile-long aqueduct carried fresh water down from the hillsides to a big reservoir perched at the highest point of the city wall. Since overall water pressure was disappointing, Pompeiians built arches like the brick one you see here (originally covered in marble) with hidden water tanks at the top. Located just below the altitude of the main tank, these smaller tanks were filled by gravity, and provided each neighborhood with reliable pressure.

• *If you're thirsty, fill your water bottle from the modern fountain. Then continue straight downhill one block (50 yards) to #2 on the left.*

⓫ House of the Faun (Casa del Founo)

Stand across the street and marvel at the grand entry with *"HAVE"* (hail to you) as a welcome mat. Go in. Notice the two shrines above the entryway—one dedicated to the gods, the other to this wealthy family's ancestors.

You are standing in Pompeii's largest home, where you're greeted by the delightful small bronze statue of the *Dancing Faun,* famed for its realistic movement and fine proportion. (The original, described on page 400, is in Naples' Archaeological Museum.) With 40 rooms and 27,000 square feet, the House of the Faun covers an entire city block. The next floor mosaic, with an intricate diamond-like design, decorates the homeowner's office. Beyond that is the famous floor mosaic of the *Battle of Alexander*. (The original is also at the museum in Naples.) In 333 B.C., Alexander the Great beat Darius and the Persians. Romans had great respect for Alexander, the first great emperor before Rome. While most of Pompeii's nouveau riche had notoriously bad taste and stuffed their palaces with over-the-top, mismatched decor, this guy had class. Both the faun (an ancient copy of a famous Greek statue) and the Alexander mosaic show an appreciation for history.

The house's back courtyard leads to the exit in the far-right corner. It's lined with pillars rebuilt after the A.D. 62 earthquake. Take a close look at the brick, mortar, and fake marble stucco veneer.

• *Sneak out of the House of the Faun through its back door and turn right. (If this exit is closed, return to the entrance and make a U-turn left, around to the back of the house.) Thirty yards down, along the right-hand side of the street, are metal cages protecting...*

⓬ Original Lead Pipes

These 2,000-year-old pipes (made of lead imported from Britannia) were part of the city's elaborate water system. From the aqueduct-fed water tank at the high end of town, three independent pipe systems supplied water to the city: one for baths, one for private homes, and one for public water fountains. If there was a water shortage, democratic priorities prevailed: First the baths were cut off, then the private homes. The last water supply to go was the public fountains, where all citizens could get drinking and cooking water.

• *If the street's not closed off, take your first left (on Vicolo dei Vetti), walk about 20 yards, and find the entrance (on the left) to the...*

⓭ House of the Vetti (Casa dei Vetti)

Pompeii's best-preserved home has been completely blocked off for years; unfortunately, it's unlikely to reopen in time for your visit. The House of the Vetti was the bachelor pad of two wealthy mer-

chant brothers. If you can see the entry-way, you may spot the huge erection. This is not pornography. There's a meaning here: The penis and the sack of money balance each other on the goldsmith scale above a fine bowl of fruit. Translation: Only with a balance of fertility and money can you have abundance.

If it's open, step into the atrium with its ceiling open to the sky to collect light and rainwater. The pool, while decorative, was a functional water-supply tank. It's flanked by large money boxes anchored to the floor. The brothers were certainly successful merchants, and possibly moneylenders, too.

Exit on the right, passing the tight servant quarters, and go into the kitchen, with its bronze cooking pots (and an exposed lead pipe on the back wall). The passage dead-ends in the little Venus Room, which features erotic frescoes behind glass.

Return to the atrium and pass into the big colonnaded garden. It was replanted according to the plan indicated by traces of roots excavated in the volcanic ash. Richly frescoed entertainment rooms ring this courtyard. Circle counterclockwise. The dining room is finely decorated in black and "Pompeiian red" (from iron rust). Study the detail. Notice the lead humidity seal between the wall and the floor, designed to keep the moisture-sensitive frescoes dry. (Had Leonardo da Vinci taken this clever step, his *Last Supper* in Milan might be in better shape today.) Continuing around, you'll see more of the square white stones inlaid in the floor. Imagine them reflecting like cats' eyes as the brothers and their friends wandered around by oil lamp late at night. Frescoes in the Yellow Room (near the exit) show off the ancient mastery of perspective,

which would not be matched elsewhere in Europe for nearly 1,500 years.

• *Facing the entrance to the House of the Vetti, turn left and walk downhill one long block (along Vicolo dei Vetti) to a T-intersection (Via della Fortuna), marked by a stone fountain with a bull's head for a spout. Intersections like this were busy neighborhood centers, where the rent was highest and people gathered. With the fountain at your back, turn left, then immediately right, walking along a gently curving road (Vicolo Storto). On the left side of the street, at #22, find four big stone cylinders.*

⓮ Bakery and Mill (Forno e Mulini)

The brick oven looks like a modern-day pizza oven. The stubby stone towers are flour grinders. Grain was poured into the top, and donkeys or slaves pushed wooden bars that turned the stones. The powdered grain dropped out of the bottom as flour— flavored with tiny bits of rock. Each neighborhood had a bakery like this.

Continue to the next intersection (Via degli Augustali, where there's another fast-food joint) and turn left. As you walk, look at the destructive power of all the vines, and notice how deeply the chariot grooves have worn into the pavement. Deep grooves could break wagon wheels. The suddenly ungroovy stretch indicates that this road was in the process of being repaved when the big shake shut everything down.

• *Head about 50 yards down this (obviously one-way) street to #44 (on the left). Here you'll find the Taberna Hedones (with a small atrium, den, and garden). This bar still has its original floor and, deeper in, the mosaic arch of a grotto fountain. Just past the tavern, turn right and walk downhill to #18, on the right.*

⓲ Brothel (Lupanare)

You'll find the biggest crowds in Pompeii at a place that was likely popular 2,000 years ago, too—the brothel. Prostitutes were nicknamed *lupe* (she-wolves), alluding to the call they made when trying to attract business. The brothel was a simple place, with beds and pillows made of stone. The ancient graffiti includes tallies and exotic names of the women, indicating the prostitutes came from all corners of the Mediterranean (it also served as feedback from satisfied customers). The faded frescoes above the cells may have been a kind of menu for services offered. Note the idealized women (white, which was considered beautiful; one wears an early bra) and the rougher men (dark, considered horny). The bed legs came with little disk-like barriers to keep critters from crawling up.

• *Leaving the brothel, go right, then take the first left, and continue going downhill two blocks to the intersection with Pompeii's main drag, Via dell'Abbondanza. The Forum—and exit—are to the right, for those who may wish to opt out from here.*

The huge amphitheater—which is certainly skippable—is 10 minutes to your left. But for now, go left for 60 yards, then turn right just beyond the fountain, and walk down Via dei Teatri. Turn left before the columns (about 50 yards away), and head downhill another 60 yards to #28, which marks the...

⓳ Temple of Isis

This Egyptian temple served Pompeii's Egyptian community. The little white stucco shrine with the plastic roof housed holy water from the Nile. Isis, from Egyptian myth, was one of many foreign gods adopted by the eclectic Romans. Pompeii must have had a synagogue, too, but it has yet to be excavated.

• *Exit the temple where you entered, and go right. At the next intersection, turn right again, and head downhill to the adjacent theaters. Your goal is the large theater, but if it's closed for renovation, look at the smaller but similar theater (Piccolo Theater).*

⓱ Theater

Originally a Greek theater (Greeks built theirs with the help of a hillside), this was the birthplace of the Greek port here in 470

B.C. During Roman times, the theater sat 5,000 people in three sets of seats, all with different prices: the five marble terraces up close (filled with romantic wooden seats for two), the main section, and the cheap nosebleed section (surviving only on the right). The square stones above the cheap seats once supported a canvas rooftop. Take note of the high-profile boxes, flanking the stage, for guests of honor. From this perch, you can see the gladiator barracks—the colonnaded courtyard beyond the theater. They lived in tiny rooms, trained in the courtyard, and fought in the nearby amphitheater.

• *You've seen Pompeii's highlights. When you're ready to leave, backtrack to the main road and turn left, going uphill to the Forum, where you'll find the main entrance/exit.*

However, there's much more to see—three-quarters of Pompeii's 164 acres have been excavated, but this tour has covered only a third of the site. After the theater—if you still have energy to see more—go back to the main road, and take a right toward the eastern part of the site, where the crowds thin out. Go straight for about 10 minutes, then turn right down a dirt path (about 75 yards from the wall at the edge of the site), which leads to the...

⓲ Amphitheater

Climb to the upper level of the amphitheater (if the external stairs

are blocked, try the entrance to the left). With Vesuvius looming in the background, mentally replace the tourists below with gladiators and wild animals locked in combat. Walk along the top of the amphitheater and look down into the grassy rectangular area surrounded by columns. This is the **Palaestra,** an area once used for athletic training. Facing the other way, look for the bell tower that tops the roofline of the modern city of Pompei, where locals go about their daily lives in the shadow of the volcano, just as their ancestors did 2,000 years ago. *HAVE!*

ROMAN HISTORY

Three Millennia in Seven Pages

History in a Hurry

Ancient Rome lasted a thousand years (500 B.C.–A.D. 500), half as an expanding republic, half as a dominating empire. When Rome fell to invaders, all Europe suffered a thousand years of poverty and ignorance (A.D. 500–1500), though Rome's influence could still be felt in the Catholic Church. Popes rebuilt Rome for pilgrims—in Renaissance, then Baroque and Neoclassical styles (1500–1800). As capital of a newly united Italy, Rome followed fascist Mussolini into World War II (and lost), but rebounded in Italy's postwar economic boom.

Want more?

Legendary Birth (1200–500 B.C.)

Aeneas flees burning Troy (1200 B.C.), wanders like Odysseus, and finally finds a home along the Tiber. His descendants, Romulus

and Remus—orphaned at birth, suckled by a she-wolf, and raised by shepherds— grow up to steal wives and build a wall, thus founding Rome (753 B.C.).

Closer to fact, the local agrarian tribes were domi- nated by more sophisticated neighbors to the north (Etruscans) and south (Greek colonists). Their convenient location on the Tiber was perfect for a future power.

Sights
- Romulus' "huts" and wall (Palatine Hill)
- She-Wolf statue (Capitoline Museums)
- Frescoes of Aeneas and Romulus (National Museum of Rome)
- Bernini's Aeneas statue (Borghese Gallery)
- Etruscan wing (Vatican Museum)
- Etruscan Museum (in Villa Borghese Gardens)
- Etruscan legacy (the original Circus Maximus, the drained Forum)

The Republic (509–27 B.C.)

The city expands throughout the Italian peninsula (500–300 B.C.), then defeats Hannibal's North African Carthaginians (the Punic Wars, 264–146 B.C.) and Greece (168 B.C.). Rome is master of the Mediterranean, and booty and captured slaves pour in. Romans bicker among themselves over their slice of the pie, pitting the wealthy landowners (the ruling Senate) against the working class (plebs) and the rebellious slaves (Spartacus' revolt, 73 B.C.). In the chaos, charismatic generals like Julius Caesar, who can provide wealth and security, become dictators. Change is necessary...and coming.

Sights
- Forum's Curia, Temple of Saturn, Temple of Castor and Pollux, Rostrum, Basilica Aemilia, Temple of Julius Caesar, and Basilica Julia (all rebuilt later)
- Appian Way built, lined with tombs
- Aqueducts, which carry water to a growing city
- Portrait busts of citizens (National Museum of Rome)
- The republic's "S.P.Q.R." monogram and motto, seen today on statues, buildings, and even manhole covers: *Senatus Populusque Romanus,* or the "Senate and People of Rome." (Some northern Italians, who feel the South is dragging them down, translate S.P.Q.R. as *Sono Porci Questi Romani*—"These Romans Are Pigs.")

The Empire—The "Roman Peace," or Pax Romana (A.D. 1–200)

After Julius Caesar is killed by disgruntled republicans, his adopted son Augustus takes undisputed control, ends the civil wars, declares himself emperor, and adopts a family member to succeed him, setting the pattern of rule for the next 500 years.

Rome rules an empire of 54 million people, stretching from England to Africa, from Spain to Turkey. The city, with more than a million inhabitants, is decorated with Greek-style statues and monumental structures faced with marble...it is the marvel of the known world. The empire prospers on a (false) economy of booty, slaves, and trade, surviving the often turbulent and naughty behavior of emperors such as Caligula and Nero. You can see Roman history in the faces of the emperors by reading the ✪ National Museum of Rome Tour chapter.

Sights

- Colosseum
- Forum
- Palatine Hill palaces
- Ara Pacis ("Altar of Peace")
- Augustus' house (House of Livia and Augustus) on Palatine Hill
- Pantheon
- Trajan's Column and Forum
- Greek and Greek-style statues and emperors' busts (National Museum of Rome, Vatican Museum, Capitoline Museums)
- Piazza Navona (former stadium)
- Hadrian's Villa (Tivoli) and tomb (now Castel Sant'Angelo)

Rome Falls (200–476)

Corruption, disease, and the constant pressure of barbarians

pecking away at the borders slowly drain the unwieldy empire. Despite Diocletian's division of the empire and Constantine's legalization of Christianity (313), the city is sacked (410), and the last emperor checks out (476). Rome falls like a huge column, kicking up dust that will plunge Europe into a thousand years of darkness.

Church Architecture

History comes to life when you visit a centuries-old church. Even if you wouldn't know your apse from a hole in the ground, learning a few simple terms will enrich your experience. Note that not every church has every feature, and that a "cathedral" isn't a type of church architecture, but rather a designation for a church that's a governing center for a local bishop.

Aisles: The long, generally low-ceilinged arcades that flank the nave.

Altar: The raised area with a ceremonial table (often adorned with candles or a crucifix), where the priest prepares and serves the bread and wine for Communion.

Apse: The space beyond the altar, generally bordered with small chapels.

Choir: A cozy area, often screened off, located within the church nave and near the high altar, where services are sung in a more intimate setting.

Cloister: A square-shaped series of hallways surrounding an open-air courtyard, traditionally where monks and nuns got fresh air.

Facade: The outer wall of the church's main (west) entrance, viewable from outside and generally highly decorated.

Groin Vault: An arched ceiling formed where two equal barrel vaults meet at right angles. Less common usage: term for a medieval jock strap.

Narthex: The area (portico or foyer) between the main entry and the nave.

Nave: The long, central section of the church (running west to east, from the entrance to the altar) where the congregation stood through the service.

Transept: The north–south part of the church, which crosses (perpendicularly) the east–west nave. In a traditional Latin cross-shaped floor plan, the transept forms the "arms" of the cross.

West Portal: The main entry to the church (on the west end, opposite the main altar).

Sights
- Arch of Constantine
- The Forum's Basilica of Constantine
- Baths of Diocletian
- Old Roman Wall (gates at Via Veneto or Piramide)

Medieval Rome (500–1500)

The once-great city of a million people dwindles to a rough village of 50,000, with a corrupt pope, forgotten ruins, and malaria-carrying mosquitoes. Cows graze in the ruined Forum, and wolves prowl the Vatican at night. During the 1300s, even the popes leave Rome to live in France. What little glory Rome retains is in the pomp, knowledge, and wealth of the Catholic Church.

Sights
- The damage done to ancient Roman monuments, caused by disuse, barbarian looting, and pillaging for pre-cut stones
- Early Christian churches built before Rome fell (Santa Maria Maggiore, San Giovanni in Laterano, and San Clemente)
- Churches of Santa Maria sopra Minerva and Santa Maria in Trastevere
- Castel Sant'Angelo

Renaissance and Baroque Rome (1500–1800)

As Europe's economy recovers, energetic popes rebuild Rome to attract pilgrims. The best artists decorate palaces and churches,

carve statues, and build fountains. The city is not a great political force, but as the center of Catholicism during the struggle against Protestants (c. 1520–1648), it is an influential religious and cultural capital.

Renaissance Sights
- Michelangelo's Sistine Chapel (Vatican Museum), dome of St. Peter's, *Pietà* (St. Peter's), *Moses* (St. Peter-in-Chains Church), Christ statue (Santa Maria sopra Minerva), Capitol Hill Square, Santa Maria degli Angeli church (in former Baths of Diocletian)

- Raphael's *School of Athens* and *Transfiguration* (Vatican Museum)
- Paintings by Raphael, Titian, and others (Borghese Gallery)

Rome in World War II

By 1943, as bombs began falling just outside the walls of Rome, it was clear to all that Italy's alliance with Nazi Germany was a huge mistake, leading the country to ruin. The fascist Grand Council dismissed Mussolini, and the king ordered his arrest. The ex-dictator fled north, and fascism collapsed without violence. Rome was declared an "open city" (meaning a city with no military bases). Italy surrendered to the Allies.

The king fled to Allied-occupied southern Italy, abandoning Rome to Nazi forces, which occupied it for nine terrible months. The Romans and the Vatican joined forces to save some citizens from the Nazis.

The Gestapo demanded 50 kilos of gold from the Roman Jews, who, with great difficulty and help from non-Jews, succeeded in providing it. Regardless, more than 2,000 Jews were deported to Germany. After Italian partisans planted a bomb near the Trevi Fountain that killed 32 Germans, more than 300 people randomly chosen from Rome's prison were killed in retaliation. As the Allies marched closer, they bombed Rome and its surroundings, but avoided striking the center.

Thankfully, Hitler granted the occupying Nazi troops permission to leave the city, which he declared a "place of culture" that should not be "the scene of combat operations." Pope Pius XII agreed, declaring, "Whoever raises a hand against Rome will be guilty of matricide to the whole civilized world and in the eternal judgment of God." Finally, the Germans marched out, the Americans marched in (through the gate of San Giovanni) on June 4, 1944, and the exhausted city welcomed them with joy and relief.

Baroque Sights
- St. Peter's Square and interior (largely by Bernini)
- Bernini statues (at Borghese Gallery; also *St. Teresa in Ecstasy* at Santa Maria della Vittoria church) and fountains (Piazza Navona, Piazza Barberini)
- Ancient obelisks erected in squares (Piazza del Popolo, Piazza Navona)
- Trevi Fountain and Spanish Steps
- Gesù and San Ignazio churches
- Caravaggio's *Calling of St. Matthew* (San Luigi dei Francesi

Church) and other paintings (Borghese Gallery and Vatican Museum)
- Baroque paintings (Borghese Gallery)
- Borromini's facade of Santa Agnese Church (Piazza Navona)

Modern Rome (1800–present)

Rome becomes the capital of a newly reunited Italy (1870) under King Victor Emmanuel II, is modernized by fascist Mussolini, and survives the destruction of World War II to become a republic. Italy's postwar "economic miracle" makes Rome a world-class city of cinema, banking, and tourism.

Sights

- Victor Emmanuel II Monument, which honors modern Italy's first (democratic) king
- Mussolini: the balcony he spoke from (at Palazzo Venezia, on Piazza Venezia), his planned city (E.U.R.), grand boulevards (Via dei Fori Imperiali, Via della Conciliazione), his home (Villa Torlonia), and Olympic Stadium

- Cinecittà film studios and Via Veneto nightlife, which have faint echoes of Fellini's *La Dolce Vita*
- Subway system, broad boulevards, smog

Rome Today

After surviving the government-a-year turbulence and Mafia-tainted corruption of the postwar years, Rome is stabilizing. Today, the average Roman makes more money than the average Englishman. The city is less polluted and more organized. Several years ago, in celebration of the millennium, the Eternal City gave its monuments a facelift. The world turned its attention on Rome once again in 2005, as the Vatican mourned the death of a pope... and elected a new one. In 2010, Rome opened MAXXI, its new state-of-the-architecture museum of modern art. Today's Rome is ready for pilgrims, travelers, and you to come and make more history.

ROMAN HISTORY

APPENDIX

Contents

Tourist Information

The Italian national tourist offices **in the US** are a wealth of information. Before your trip, scan their website (www.italiantourism .com) or contact the nearest branch to briefly describe your trip and request information. They'll mail you a general-interest brochure and you can download many other brochures free of charge at their website. If you have a specific problem, they're a good source of sympathy.

In New York: Tel. 212/245-5618, brochure hotline tel. 212/245-4822, fax 212/586-9249, newyork@enit.it; 630 Fifth Ave. #1565, New York, NY 10111.

In Illinois: Tel. 312/644-0996, brochure hotline tel. 312/644-0990, fax 312/644-3019, chicago@enit.it; 500 N. Michigan Ave. #506, Chicago, IL 60611.

In California: Tel. 310/820-1898, brochure hotline tel. 310/820-0098, fax 310/820-6357, losangeles@enit.it; 12400 Wilshire Blvd. #550, Los Angeles, CA 90025.

In Rome, your best first stop is generally the tourist information office (abbreviated **TI** in this book). Many are scattered throughout Rome (listed on page 22; http://en.turismoroma.it). Useful websites are http://mv.vatican.va (the pope's website), along with www.inromenow.com, www.wantedinrome.com, and http://rome.angloinfo.com.

Communicating

Hurdling the Language Barrier

Many Italians—especially those in the tourist trade and in big cities such as Rome—speak English. Still, you'll get better treatment if you learn and use Italian pleasantries. In smaller, non-touristy towns, Italian is the norm. For a list of survival phrases, see page 469.

Note that Italian is pronounced much like English, with a few exceptions, such as: c followed by e or i is pronounced ch (to ask, *"Per centro?"*—To the center?—you say, pehr CHEHN-troh). In Italian, ch is pronounced like the hard c in Chianti (*chiesa*—church—is pronounced kee-AY-zah). Give it your best shot. Italians appreciate your efforts.

Telephones

Smart travelers use the telephone to reserve or reconfirm rooms, get tourist information, reserve restaurants, confirm tour times, or phone home. This section covers dialing instructions, phone cards, and types of phones (for more in-depth information, see www.ricksteves.com/phoning).

How to Dial

Calling from the US to Italy, or vice versa, is simple—once you break the code. The European calling chart later in this chapter will walk you through it.

Dialing Domestically Within Italy

Italy has a direct-dial phone system (no area codes). To call anywhere within Italy, just dial the number. For example, the number of one of my recommended Rome hotels is 06-482-4696. That's the number you dial whether you're calling it from Rome's main train station or from Milan.

Land lines start with 0; mobile lines start with 3; toll-free lines start with 80; and expensive toll lines begin with 8 and then any number other than 0. Keep in mind that Italian phone numbers vary in length; a hotel can have, say, an eight-digit phone number and a nine-digit fax number.

Dialing Internationally to or from Italy

If you want to make an international call, follow these steps:

1. Dial the international access code (00 if you're calling from Europe, 011 from the US or Canada).

2. Dial the country code of the country you're calling (39 for Italy, or 1 for the US or Canada).

3. Dial the local number. Note that in most European countries, you have to drop the zero at the beginning of the local number—but in Italy, you dial it. (The European calling chart lists specifics per country.)

Calling from the US to Italy: To call the recommended hotel in Rome from the US, dial 011 (the US international access code), 39 (Italy's country code), then 06-482-4696.

Calling from any European country to the US: To call my office in Edmonds, Washington, from anywhere in Europe, I dial 00 (Europe's international access code), 1 (the US country code), 425 (Edmonds' area code), and 771-8303.

Note: You might see a + in front of a European number. When dialing the number, replace the + with the international access code of the country you're calling from (00 from Europe, 011 from the US or Canada).

Public Phones and Hotel-Room Phones

To make calls from public phones, you'll need a prepaid phone card. There are two different kinds of phone cards: insertable and international. (Both types of phone card work only in Italy. If you have a live card at the end of your trip, give it to another traveler to use up.) Coin-op phones are virtually extinct.

Insertable Phone Cards: This type of card can only be used at a pay phone. These Telecom cards, considered "official" since they're sold by Italy's phone company, give you the best deal for calls within Italy and are reasonable for international calls. You can buy Telecom cards (in denominations of €5 or €10) at *tabacchi* shops, post offices, and machines near phone booths (many phone booths have signs indicating where the nearest phone-card sales outlet is located).

Rip off the perforated corner to "activate" the card, and then physically insert it into a slot in the pay phone. It displays how much money you have remaining on the card. Then just dial away. The price of the call is automatically deducted while you talk.

International Phone Cards: These are the cheapest way to make international calls from Europe—with the best cards it costs literally pennies a minute. They can also be used to make local calls, and work from any type of phone, including your hotel-room phone. To use the card, you'll dial a toll-free access number, then type in your scratch-to-reveal PIN number. If you're calling from

European Calling Chart

Just smile and dial, using this key:
AC = Area Code, LN = Local Number.

European Country	Calling long distance within ...	Calling from the US or Canada to ...	Calling from a European country to ...
Austria	AC + LN	011 + 43 + AC (without the initial zero) + LN	00 + 43 + AC (without the initial zero) + LN
Belgium	LN	011 + 32 + LN (without initial zero)	00 + 32 + LN (without initial zero)
Bosnia-Herzegovina	AC + LN	011 + 387 + AC (without initial zero) + LN	00 + 387 + AC (without initial zero) + LN
Britain	AC + LN	011 + 44 + AC (without initial zero) + LN	00 + 44 + AC (without initial zero) + LN
Croatia	AC + LN	011 + 385 + AC (without initial zero) + LN	00 + 385 + AC (without initial zero) + LN
Czech Republic	LN	011 + 420 + LN	00 + 420 + LN
Denmark	LN	011 + 45 + LN	00 + 45 + LN
Estonia	LN	011 + 372 + LN	00 + 372 + LN
Finland	AC + LN	011 + 358 + AC (without initial zero) + LN	999 (or other 900 number) + 358 + AC (without initial zero) + LN
France	LN	011 + 33 + LN (without initial zero)	00 + 33 + LN (without initial zero)
Germany	AC + LN	011 + 49 + AC (without initial zero) + LN	00 + 49 + AC (without initial zero) + LN
Gibraltar	LN	011 + 350 + LN	00 + 350 + LN
Greece	LN	011 + 30 + LN	00 + 30 + LN
Hungary	06 + AC + LN	011 + 36 + AC + LN	00 + 36 + AC + LN
Ireland	AC + LN	011 + 353 + AC (without initial zero) + LN	00 + 353 + AC (without initial zero) + LN

European Country	Calling long distance within ...	Calling from the US or Canada to ...	Calling from a European country to ...
Italy	LN	011 + 39 + LN	00 + 39 + LN
Montenegro	AC + LN	011 + 382 + AC (without initial zero) + LN	00 + 382 + AC (without initial zero) + LN
Morocco	LN	011 + 212 + LN (without initial zero)	00 + 212 + LN (without initial zero)
Netherlands	AC + LN	011 + 31 + AC (without initial zero) + LN	00 + 31 + AC (without initial zero) + LN
Norway	LN	011 + 47 + LN	00 + 47 + LN
Poland	LN	011 + 48 + LN (without initial zero)	00 + 48 + LN (without initial zero)
Portugal	LN	011 + 351 + LN	00 + 351 + LN
Slovakia	AC + LN	011 + 421 + AC (without initial zero) + LN	00 + 421 + AC (without initial zero) + LN
Slovenia	AC + LN	011 + 386 + AC (without initial zero) + LN	00 + 386 + AC (without initial zero) + LN
Spain	LN	011 + 34 + LN	00 + 34 + LN
Sweden	AC + LN	011 + 46 + AC (without initial zero) + LN	00 + 46 + AC (without initial zero) + LN
Switzerland	LN	011 + 41 + LN (without initial zero)	00 + 41 + LN (without initial zero)
Turkey	AC (if there's no initial zero, add one) + LN	011 + 90 + AC (without initial zero) + LN	00 + 90 + AC (without initial zero) + LN

- The instructions above apply whether you're calling a land line or mobile phone.
- The international access codes (the first numbers you dial when making an international call) are 011 if you're calling from the US or Canada, or 00 if you're calling from virtually anywhere in Europe (except Finland, where it's 999 or another 900 number, depending on the phone service you're using).
- To call the US or Canada from Europe, dial 00, then 1 (the country code for the US and Canada), then the area code and number. In short, 00 + 1 + AC + LN = Hi, Mom!

a hotel, be sure to dial the *freephone* number (starts with "80") provided on your card rather than the "local access" number (which would incur a charge).

You can buy the cards at small newsstand kiosks, *tabacchi* (tobacco) shops, Internet cafés, hostels, and hole-in-the-wall long-distance phone shops. Because there are so many brand names, simply ask for an international phone card (*carta telefonica prepagata internazionale,* KAR-tah teh-leh-FOHN-ee-kah pray-pah-GAH-tah in-ter-naht-zee-oh-NAH-lay). Tell the vendor where you'll be making most calls (*"per Stati Uniti"*—to America), and he'll select the brand with the best deal.

Buy a lower denomination in case the card is a dud. I've had good luck with the Europa card, which offers up to 350 minutes from Italy to the US for €5.

Hotel-Room Phones: Calling from your hotel room can be cheap for local calls (ask for the rates at the front desk first), but is often a rip-off for long-distance calls (unless you use an international phone card, explained above). Incoming calls are free, making this a cheap way for friends and family to stay in touch (provided they have a good long-distance plan for calls to Europe—and a list of your hotels' phone numbers).

US Calling Cards: These cards, such as the ones offered by AT&T, Verizon, or Sprint, are the worst option. You'll nearly always save a lot of money by using a locally purchased phone card instead.

Metered Phones: In Italy, some call shops have phones with meters. You can talk all you want, then pay the bill when you leave—but be sure you know the rates before you have a lengthy conversation. Note that charges can be "per unit" rather than per minute; find out the length of a unit.

Mobile Phones

Many travelers enjoy the convenience of traveling with a mobile phone.

Using Your US Mobile Phone: Your US mobile phone works in Europe if it's GSM-enabled, tri-band or quad-band, and on a calling plan that includes international calls. Phones from T-Mobile and AT&T, which use the same GSM technology that Europe does, are more likely to work overseas than Verizon or Sprint phones (if you're not sure, ask your service provider). Most US providers charge $1.29 per minute while roaming internationally to make or receive calls, and 20–50 cents to send or receive text messages.

You'll pay cheaper rates if your phone is electronically "unlocked" (ask your provider about this); then in Europe, you can simply buy a tiny **SIM card,** which gives you a European phone number. SIM cards are sold at mobile-phone stores and some newsstand kiosks for about $5–10, and generally include several minutes' worth of prepaid domestic calling time. When you buy a SIM card, you may need to show ID, such as your passport. Insert the SIM card in your phone (usually in a slot behind the battery), and it'll work like a European mobile phone. When buying a SIM card, always ask about fees for domestic and international calls, roaming charges, and how to check your credit balance and buy more time.

Many **smartphones,** such as the iPhone or BlackBerry, work in Europe—but beware of sky-high fees, especially for data downloading (checking email, browsing the Internet, watching videos, and so on). Ask your provider in advance how to avoid unwittingly "roaming" your way to a huge bill. Some applications allow for cheap or free smartphone calls over a Wi-Fi connection.

Using a European Mobile Phone: Mobile-phone shops all over Europe sell basic phones. Phones that are "locked" to work with a single provider start around $20; "unlocked" phones (which allow you to switch out SIM cards to use your choice of provider) start around $60. You'll also need to buy a SIM card and prepaid credit for making calls. (My Italian friends tell me that TIM is a reliable Italian mobile-phone company.) When you're in the phone's home country, domestic calls are reasonable, and incoming calls are free. You'll pay more if you're "roaming" in another country.

Calling over the Internet

Some things that seem too good to be true...actually are true. If you're traveling with a laptop, you can make calls using VoIP (Voice over Internet Protocol). With VoIP, two computers act as the phones, and the Internet-based calls are free (or you can pay a few cents to call from your computer to a telephone). If both computers have webcams, you can even see each other while you chat. The major provider is Skype (www.skype.com), followed by Google Talk (www.google.com/talk).

Useful Phone Numbers

Italy's toll-free numbers start with 80. These 80 numbers—called *freephone* or *numero verde* (green number)—can be dialed free from any phone without using a phone card. Note that you can't call Italy's toll-free numbers from America, nor can you count on reaching America's toll-free numbers from Italy.

Any Italian phone number that starts with 8 but isn't followed by a 0 is a toll call, generally costing €0.10–0.50 per minute.

Emergencies
English-Speaking Police Help: 113
Ambulance: 118
Road Service: 116

Embassies
US Embassy: 24-hour emergency line—tel. 06-46741, non-emergency—tel. 06-4674-2406 (Mon–Fri 8:30-12:30, closed Sat–Sun, Via Vittorio Veneto 121, www.usembassy.it)
Canadian Embassy: tel. 06-854-441 (Mon-Fri 9:00-12:00, closed Sat- Sun, Via Zara 30, www.Italy.gc.ca)

Travel Advisories
US Department of State: tel. 202/647-5225, www.travel.state.gov
Canadian Department of Foreign Affairs: Canadian tel. 800-267-6788, www.dfait-maeci.gc.ca
US Centers for Disease Control and Prevention: tel. 800-CDC-INFO (800-232-4636), www.cdc.gov/travel

Directory Assistance
Telephone Help (in English; free directory assistance): 170
Directory Assistance (for €0.50, an Italian-speaking robot gives the number twice, very clearly): 12

Internet Access
It's useful to get online periodically as you travel—to confirm trip plans, check train or bus schedules, get weather forecasts, catch up on email, blog or post photos from your trip, or call folks back home (explained earlier, under "Calling over the Internet").

Many hotels offer a computer in the lobby with Internet access for guests. Smaller places may sometimes let you sit at their desk for a few minutes just to check your email, if you ask politely. If your hotel doesn't have access, ask your hotelier to direct you to the nearest place to get online. Internet cafés and little hole-in-the-wall Internet-access shops (offering a few computers, no food, and cheap prices) are common in most cities.

Because of an anti-terrorism law in Italy, you may be asked to show your passport (carry it in your money belt) when using a public Internet terminal at an Internet café or in a hotel lobby. The proprietor will likely make a copy of your passport.

Traveling with a Laptop: With a laptop or netbook, it's easy to get online if your hotel has Wi-Fi (wireless Internet access) or a port in your room for plugging in a cable. Most hotels offer Wi-Fi for free; others charge by the minute or hour. A cellular modem—which lets your laptop access the Internet over a mobile phone network—provides more extensive coverage, but is much

APPENDIX

more expensive than Wi-Fi (in Italy, www.wind.it and www.tim.it offer pay-as-you-go mobile broadband).

Mail

While you can arrange for mail delivery to your hotel (allow 10 days for a letter to arrive), phoning and emailing are so easy that I've dispensed with mail stops altogether. Mail service in Italy has improved over the last few years, but even so, mail nothing precious from an Italian post office. Federal Express makes pricey two-day deliveries.

Transportation

By Car or Train?

If your trip will cover more of Italy than just Rome, you'll need to decide whether to rent a car or take trains. Cars are best for three or more traveling together (especially families with small kids), those packing heavy, and those scouring the countryside. Trains and buses are best for solo travelers, blitz tourists, and city-to-city travelers. While a car gives you the ultimate in mobility and freedom, enables you to search for hotels more easily, and carries your bags for you, the train zips you effortlessly from city to city, usually dropping you in the center and near the tourist office.

Trains

To travel by train cheaply in Italy, you can simply buy tickets as you go. Though train station lines can be long, ticket machines work well and are easy to use (see "Buying Tickets," later). Pay all ticket costs in the station before you board, or you'll pay a penalty on the train.

Types of Trains: You'll encounter several types of trains in Italy: pokey *regionali*, slow *diretto* and IR *(interregionali)*, medium-

speed *espresso*, fast IC (Intercity) and EC (Eurocity), and super-fast ES (Eurostar Italia, including Alta Velocità and Frecciarossa). If you're traveling with a railpass, note that reservations are optional for IC trains, but required for EC and international trains (€5) and ES trains (€10). Regional trains, such as most Rome-Civitavecchia connections, don't require reservations.

A new high-speed service in Italy—*Nuovo Transporto Viaggiatori* (NTV)—is expected to launch sometime in 2011 (for details, see www.ntvspa.it).

Italy's Public Transportation

APPENDIX

— RAIL   ⊥ PRIVATE RAIL   ···· SHIP   --- BUS

⊞ AIRPORT (NOT ALL SHOWN)

For point-to-point tickets, you'll pay more the faster you go, but even the fastest trains are affordable (for example, a second-class ticket on a Rome–Venice express train costs about €70).

Schedules: At the train station, the easiest way to check schedules is at a handy automated ticket machine (described later, under "Buying Tickets"). Enter the desired date, time, and destination to view all your options. Printed schedules are also posted at the station (departure posters are always yellow).

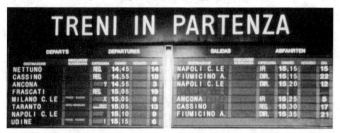

Newsstands sell up-to-date regional and all-Italy time-tables (€5, ask for the *orario ferroviario*). On the Web, check http://bahn.hafas.de/bin/query.exe/en (Germany's excellent all-Europe schedule website) or www.trenitalia.it. There is also a single all-Italy telephone number for train information (24 hours daily, toll tel. 892-021, Italian only, consider having your hotelier call for you).

Railpasses

It's usually better to buy point-to-point train tickets than a railpass for traveling in Italy. But if you're taking a multi-country trip, the Eurail Select Pass is worth considering (and mentioned below).

The **Italy Pass** for Italian State Railways saves neither time nor hassle. Use the price map on page 449 to add up your ticket costs. Although the pass covers the full cost of getting you from A to B on many trains in Italy, it doesn't include the price of seat reservations or overnight berths. Reservations are optional for many trains, but are required for the fastest trains between major Italian cities. While the pass does save you from having to buy each train ticket as you go, if you'll be taking a few fast trains, you'll still have to spend time in line or at ticket machines—essentially eliminating the point of buying this pass.

A 21-country **Eurail Global Pass** can work well for an all-Europe trip, but is a bad value for travel exclusively in Italy. A cheaper version, the **Eurail Select Pass,** allows you to tailor a pass to your trip, provided you're traveling in three, four, or five adjacent countries directly connected by rail or ferry. For instance, with a three-country pass allowing 10 days of train travel within a two-month period (about $700 for a single adult in 2010), you

Railpasses

Prices listed are for 2010 and are subject to change. For the latest prices, details, and train schedules (and easy online ordering), see my comprehensive *Guide to Eurail Passes* at www.ricksteves.com/rail.

"Saver" prices are per person for two or more people traveling together. "Youth" means under age 26. The fare for children 4–11 is half the adult individual fare or Saver fare. Kids under age 4 travel free.

ITALY PASS

	Individual 1st Class	Individual 2nd Class	Saver 1st Class	Saver 2nd Class	Youth 2nd Class
3 days in 2 months	$230	$188	$196	$160	$152
Extra rail days (max 7)	$27-30	$21-24	$22-26	$18-21	$18-20

ITALY RAIL & DRIVE PASS

Any 3 rail days and 2 car days in 2 months.

Car Category	1st Class	2nd Class	Extra Car Day
Economy	$360	$306	$68
Compact	390	336	98
Intermediate	419	365	126
Extra rail days (max 7)	35	26	

Prices are per person, two traveling together. Solo travelers pay about 20 percent more. To order a Rail & Drive pass, call your travel agent or Rail Europe at 800-438-7245. *This pass is not sold by Europe Through the Back Door.*

FRANCE–ITALY PASS

	Individual 1st Class	Individual 2nd Class	Saver 1st Class	Saver 2nd Class	Youth 2nd Class
4 days in 2 months	$338	$288	$288	$245	$220
Extra rail days (max 6)	39-41	33-35	33-35	28-30	25-27

Be aware of your route. Many daytime connections from Paris to Italy pass through Switzerland (an additional $60 2nd class or $90 1st class if not covered by your pass). Routes via Nice, Torino, or Modane will bypass Switzerland. Direct Paris–Italy day or night trains are covered by the pass, regardless of their route.

GREECE–ITALY PASS

	Individual 1st Class	Individual 2nd Class	Saver 1st Class	Saver 2nd Class	Youth 2nd Class
4 days in 2 months	$322	$257	$273	$219	$210
Extra rail days (max 6)	33	27	29	23	21

Covers deck passage on overnight Superfast Ferries between Patras, Greece and Bari or Ancona, Italy (starts use of one travel day). Or 30-50% discount on Hellenic Mediterranean Line ferry with basic cabin Patras-Corfu-Brindisi (does not use a travel day). Does not cover travel to or on Greek islands, except a 30% discount on Blue Star Ferries.

SELECTPASS

This pass covers travel in three adjacent countries. Please visit **www.ricksteves.com/rail** for four- and five-country options.

	Individual 1st Class	Saver 1st Class	Youth 2nd Class
5 days in 2 months	$411	$349	$268
6 days in 2 months	454	387	297
8 days in 2 months	538	460	349
10 days in 2 months	624	528	404

could choose France–Italy–Greece or Germany–Austria–Italy. A **France and Italy Pass** combines just those two countries and covers night trains to and from Paris via Switzerland (but if your route crosses Switzerland by day, you'll pay extra—so the Select Pass is a better choice if you want to see the Alps). Before you buy a Select Pass or France and Italy Pass, think carefully how many travel days you'll really need. Use the pass only for travel days that involve long hauls or several trips. Pay out of pocket for tickets on days you're taking only short, cheap rides.

For a summary of railpass deals and the latest prices, check my Guide to Eurail Passes at www.ricksteves.com/rail. If you decide to get a railpass, this guide will help you know you're getting the right one for your trip.

Point-to-Point Tickets

Train tickets are a good value in Italy. Fares are shown on the map on page 449, though fares can vary for the same journey, depending on the time of day, the speed of the train, and more. **First-class** tickets cost 50 percent more than **second-class.** While second-class cars go as fast as their first-class neighbors, Italy is one country where I would consider the splurge of first class. The easiest way to "upgrade" a second-class ticket once on board a crowded train is to nurse a drink in the snack car.

Discounts: Families with young children can get price breaks—kids ages 4 and under travel free; ages 4-11 at half-price. Sometimes the parents get a 20 percent price break. Ask for the "Offerta Familia" deal when buying tickets at a counter (or, at a ticket machine, choose "Yes" at the "Do you want ticket issue?" prompt, then choose "Familia"). The deal doesn't apply to all trains at all times, but it's worth checking out.

Discounts for youths and seniors require purchase of a separate card (Carta Verde for ages 12–26 costs €40; Carta Argento for ages 60 and over is €30), but the discount on tickets is so minor (10–15 percent respectively for domestic travel), it's not worth it for most.

Buying Tickets: Avoid train station ticket lines whenever possible by using automated ticket machines (in train stations) or going to local travel agencies. You'll be able to easily purchase tickets, make seat reservations, and even book a *cuccetta* (koo-CHEHT-tah; overnight berth).

Automated ticket machines (marked *Biglietto Veloce/Fast Ticket*) are user-friendly and found in all but the tiniest stations in Italy. You can pay by cash (they give change) or by debit or credit card. Select English, then wade through a menu of destinations. If you don't see the city you're traveling to, keep keying in the spelling until it's listed. You can choose from first- and second-class

Anatomy of an Italian Train Ticket

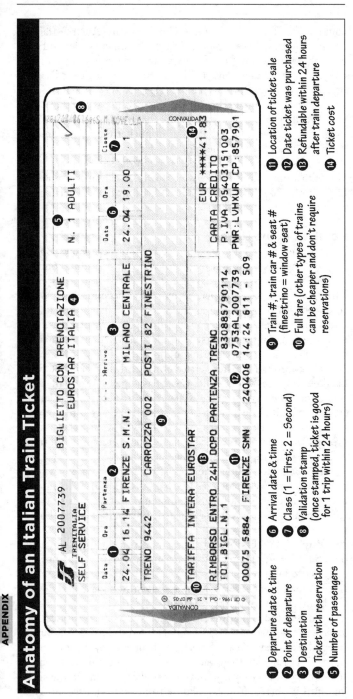

1. Departure date & time
2. Point of departure
3. Destination
4. Ticket with reservation
5. Number of passengers
6. Arrival date & time
7. Class (1 = First; 2 = Second)
8. Validation stamp (once stamped, ticket is good for 1 trip within 24 hours)
9. Train #, train car # & seat # (finestrino = window seat)
10. Full fare (other types of trains can be cheaper and don't require reservations)
11. Location of ticket sale
12. Date ticket was purchased
13. Refundable within 24 hours after train departure
14. Ticket cost

Train Costs in Italy

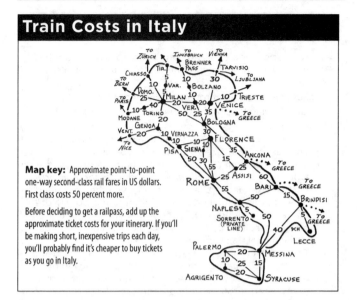

Map key: Approximate point-to-point one-way second-class rail fares in US dollars. First class costs 50 percent more.

Before deciding to get a railpass, add up the approximate ticket costs for your itinerary. If you'll be making short, inexpensive trips each day, you'll probably find it's cheaper to buy tickets as you go in Italy.

seats, request tickets for more than one traveler, and (on the high-speed Eurostar Italia trains) choose an aisle or window seat. When the machine prompts you—"Fidelity Card?"—choose no. Don't select a discount rate without being sure that you meet the criteria (for example, Americans are not eligible for certain EU or resident discounts). Railpass-holders can use the machines to make seat reservations. And you can even validate your ticket in the same machine if you're boarding your train right away.

You can also buy tickets and make reservations at **travel agencies** around town, such as the American Express office near the Spanish Steps (Mon–Fri 9:00–17:30, Sat 9:00–12:30, closed Sun, Piazza di Spagna 38, tel. 06-67641). The cost is the same, it can be more convenient (if you find yourself near a travel agency while you're sightseeing), and the language barrier can be smaller than at the station's ticket windows. But many travelers find it's easiest just to buy them at the ticket machines at the station.

You can't buy tickets online on the Italian train website (www.trenitalia.it) because it does not accept US credit cards.

Validating Tickets: Before boarding the train, you must validate (stamp) your train documents in the yellow box near the platform. This includes whatever you need to take a particular trip, which can be as simple as a single ticket, but can also involve a supplement, seat reservation, or *cuccetta* reservation on an overnight train. If you forget to stamp your ticket, go right away to the train conductor—before he comes to you—or you'll pay a fine. Note that you don't need to stamp a railpass or e-ticket.

Deciphering Italian Train Schedules

At the station, look for the big yellow posters labeled *Partenze*—Departures (ignore the white posters, which show arrivals).

Schedules are listed chronologically, hour by hour, showing the trains leaving the station throughout the day. Each schedule has columns:

- The first column *(Ora)* lists the time of departure.
- The next column *(Treno)* shows the type of train.
- The third column *(Classi Servizi)* lists the services available (first- and second-class cars, dining car, *cuccetta* berths, etc.) and, more importantly, whether you need reservations (usually denoted by an R in a box). Note that all Eurostar Italia (ES) and Alta Velocita (AV) trains, many InterCity (IC) and EuroCity (EC) trains, and most international trains require reservations.
- The next column lists the destination of the train *(Principali Fermate Destinazioni)*, often showing intermediate stops, followed by the final destination, with arrival times listed throughout in parentheses. Note that your final destination may be listed in fine print as an intermediate destination. For example, if you're going from Rome to Orvieto, scan the schedule and you'll notice that regional trains that go to Florence usually stop in Orvieto en route. Travelers who read the fine print end up with a far greater choice of trains.
- The next column *(Servizi Diretti e Annotazioni)* has pertinent notes about the train, such as "also stops in..." *(ferma anche a...)*, "doesn't stop in..." *(non ferma a...)*, "stops in every station" *(ferma in tutte le stazioni)*, "delayed..." *(ritardo...)*, and so on.
- The last column lists the track *(Binario)* the train departs from. Confirm the *binario* with an additional source: a ticket-seller, the electronic board that lists immediate departures, TV monitors on the platform, or the railway officials who are usually standing by the train unless you really need them.

For any odd symbols on the poster, look at the key at the end. Some of the phrasing can be deciphered easily, such as *servizio periodico* (periodic service—doesn't always run). For the trickier ones, ask a local or railway official, try your *Rick Steves' Italian Phrase Book & Dictionary*, or simply take a different train.

You can also check schedules—for trains anywhere in Italy, not just from the station you're currently in—at the handy ticket machines. Enter the date and time of your departure (to or from any Italian station), and you can view all your options.

Train Tips

This section contains information on making seat reservations, storing baggage, avoiding theft, and dealing with strikes.

Seat Reservations: Trains can fill up, even in first class. If you're on a tight schedule, you'll want to reserve a few days ahead for fast trains (see "Types of Trains," earlier). Purchasing required seat reservations onboard a train comes with a nasty penalty. Buying them at the station can be a time-waster unless you use the automatic ticket machines.

If you don't need a reservation, and if your train originates at your departure point (e.g., you're catching the Rome-Florence train in Rome), arriving at least 15 minutes before the departure time will help you snare a seat.

Some major stations have train composition posters on the platforms showing where first- and second-class cars are located when the trains arrive (letters on the poster are supposed to correspond to letters posted over the platform—but they don't always). Since most trains now allow you to make reservations up to the time of departure, conductors are no longer marking reserved seats with a card—instead, they simply post a list of the reservable and non-reservable seat rows (sometimes in English) in each train car's vestibule. This means that if you board a crowded train and get one of the last seats, you may be ousted when the reservation-holder comes along.

Baggage Storage: Many stations have *deposito bagagli* where you can safely leave your bag for about €8 per 12-hour period (payable when you pick up the bag, double-check closing hours). Due to security concerns, no Italian stations have lockers.

Theft Concerns: Italian trains are famous for their thieves. Never leave a bag unattended. I've noticed that police now ride the trains, and things seem more controlled. Still, for an overnight trip, I'd feel safe only in a *cuccetta* (a bunk in a special sleeping car with an attendant who keeps track of who comes and goes while you sleep—approximately €20 in a six-bed compartment, €25 in a less-cramped four-bed compartment).

Strikes: Strikes, which are common, generally last a day. Train employees will simply explain, *"Sciopero"* (strike). But in actuality, sporadic trains, following no particular schedule, lumber down the tracks during most strikes. When a strike is pending, travel agencies (and Web-savvy hoteliers) can check the Internet for you to see when the strike goes into effect and which trains will continue to run. If I need to get somewhere and know a strike is imminent, I leave early (heading off the strike, which often begins at 9:00), or I just go to the station with extra patience in tow and hop on anything rolling in the direction I want to go.

Renting a Car

If you're renting a car in Italy, bring your driver's license. You're also technically required to have an International Driving Permit—a translation of your driver's license (sold at your local AAA office for $15 plus the cost of two passport-type photos; see www.aaa .com). While that's the letter of the law, I've often rented cars in Italy without having—or being asked to show—this permit.

Rental companies require you to be at least 18 years old and have held your license for one year. Drivers under the age of 25 may incur a young-driver surcharge, and some rental companies do not rent to anyone 75 and over. If you're considered too young or old, look into leasing, which has less-stringent age restrictions.

Research car rentals before you go. It's cheaper to arrange most car rentals from the US. Call several companies and look online to compare rates, or arrange a rental through your home-town travel agent.

Most of the major US rental agencies (such as Alamo/ National, Avis, Budget, Dollar, Hertz, and Thrifty) have offices in Italy. It can be cheaper to use a consolidator, such as Auto Europe (www.autoeurope.com) or Europe by Car (www.ebctravel.com), but by using a middleman, you risk trading customer service for lower prices; if you have a problem with the rental company, you can't count on a consolidator to intervene on your behalf.

For the best rental deal, rent by the week with unlimited mileage. I normally rent the smallest, least-expensive model with a stick shift (cheaper than an automatic). Roads and parking spaces are narrow in Italy, so you'll do yourself a favor by renting the smallest car that meets your needs. For a three-week rental, allow $900 per person (based on two people sharing a car), including insurance, tolls, gas, and parking. For trips of this length, consider leasing (see below); you'll save money on insurance and taxes. Compare pick-up costs (downtown can be cheaper than the airport) and explore drop-off options.

You can sometimes get a GPS unit with your rental car or leased vehicle for an additional fee (around $15/day; be sure it's set to English and has all the maps you need before you drive off). Or, if you have a portable GPS device at home, consider taking it with you to Europe (buy and upload European maps before your trip).

When you pick up the rental car, check it thoroughly and make sure any damage is noted on your rental agreement. Find out how your car's lights, turn signals, wipers, and gas cap function, and know what kind of gas the car takes.

Returning a car at a big-city train station can be tricky; get precise details on the car drop-off location and hours. Note that rental offices usually close from midday Saturday until Monday morning. When you return the car, make sure the agent verifies its condition with you.

If you want a car for only a couple of days, a rail-and-drive pass (such as a EurailDrive, Selectpass Drive, or Italy Rail and Drive) can be put to thoughtful use. The basic Italy Rail and Drive Pass, which includes theft insurance and CDW (described below), comes with two days of car rental and three days of rail in two months. While rail-and-drive passes are convenient, they're also pricey, particularly for solo travelers.

Car Insurance Options

Accidents can happen anywhere, but when you're on vacation, the last thing you need is stress over car insurance. When you rent a car, you're liable for a very high deductible, sometimes equal to the entire value of the car. Limit your financial risk in case of an accident by choosing one of these two options: Buy Collision Damage Waiver (CDW) coverage from the car-rental company, or get coverage through your credit card (free, but more complicated).

In Italy, most car-rental companies' rates automatically include CDW coverage (which you sometimes can't decline). It's not unusual to decline CDW when you reserve your Italian car, only to find when you show up at the counter that you must buy it after all.

While each rental company has its own variation, the basic **CDW** costs $15–35 a day (figure roughly 25 percent extra) and reduces your liability, but does not eliminate it. When you pick up the car, you'll be offered the chance to "buy down" the basic deductible to zero (for an additional $10–30/day; sometimes called "super CDW").

If you opt for **credit card coverage,** there's a catch. You'll technically have to decline all coverage offered by the car-rental company, which means they can place a hold on your card (which can be up to the full value of the car). In case of damage, it can be time-consuming to resolve the charges with your credit card company. Before you decide on this option, quiz your credit card company about how it works.

Note that **theft insurance** (separate from CDW insurance) is mandatory in Italy. The insurance usually costs about $15–20 a day, payable when you pick up the car.

For more fine print about car-rental insurance, see www.rick steves.com/cdw.

Leasing

For trips of three weeks or more, leasing (which automatically includes zero-deductible collision and theft insurance) is the best way to go. By technically buying and then selling back the car, you save lots of money on tax and insurance. Leasing provides you a

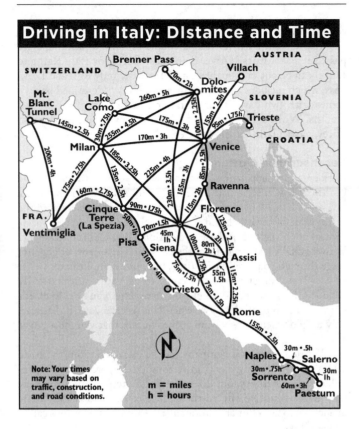

Driving in Italy: Distance and Time

new car with unlimited mileage and a 24-hour emergency assistance program. You can lease for as little as 17 days to as long as six months. Car leases must be arranged from the US. One of many companies offering affordable lease packages is Europe by Car (US tel. 800-223-1516, www.ebctravel.com).

Driving

Driving in Italy can be scary—a video game for keeps, and you only get one quarter. Italian drivers can be aggressive. They drive fast and tailgate as if it were required. They pass where Americans are taught not to—on blind corners and just before tunnels. Roads have narrow shoulders or none at all. Driving in the countryside is less stressful than driving through urban areas, but stay alert. On one-lane roads, larger vehicles have the right-of-way. If you're on a truckers' route, stifle your Good Samaritan impulse when you see provocatively dressed women standing by camper-vans at the side of the road; they're not having car trouble.

Road Rules: Stay out of restricted traffic zones or you'll risk huge fines. Car traffic is restricted in many city centers, including Rome. Don't drive or park anywhere with signs reading *Zona Traffico Limitato* (*ZTL*, often shown above a red circle, see image). If you do, your license plate will likely be photographed and a hefty (€100-plus) ticket mailed to your home without your ever having met a cop. Bumbling in and out of these zones can net you multiple fines. If your hotel is within a restricted area, it's best to ask your hotelier to direct you to parking outside the zone. (Although your hotelier can register your car as an authorized vehicle permitted to enter the zone, this usually isn't worth the hassle.)

As for other road rules, seatbelts are mandatory, and you should keep headlights on at all times outside of urban areas. Ask your car-rental company about additional rules, or check the US State Department website (www.travel.state.gov, click on "International Travel," then specify your country of choice and click "Traffic Safety and Road Conditions").

Tolls: Italy's freeway system, the autostrada, is as good as our interstate system, but you'll pay about a dollar for every 10 minutes of use. While I favor the freeways because I feel they're safer, cheaper (saving time and gas), and less nerve-racking than smaller roads, savvy local drivers know which toll-free *superstradas* are actually faster and more direct than the autostrada. For more information, visit www.autostrade.it.

Fuel: Gas is expensive—often about $6 per gallon. Diesel cars are more common in Europe than back home, so be sure you know what type of gas your car takes before you fill up. Gas pumps are color-coded for unleaded *(senza piombo)* or diesel *(gasolio)*. Autostrada rest stops are self-service stations open daily without a siesta break. Many 24-hour-a-day stations are entirely automated. Small-town stations are usually cheaper and offer full service but shorter hours.

Maps and Signage: A good map is essential. Learn the universal road signs (explained in charts in most road atlases and at service stations). Although roads are numbered on maps, actual road signs don't list route numbers. Instead, roads are indicated by blue signs with a city name on them (for example, if you want to take a road heading east out of Rome—marked route S-5 on your map—you'd follow signs to Tivoli, the next town along this road). The signs are inconsistent: They may direct you to the nearest big city or simply the next town along the route.

Theft: Cars are routinely vandalized and stolen. Thieves easily recognize rental cars and assume they are filled with a tourist's gear. Try to make your car look locally owned by hiding the "tourist-owned" rental-company decals and putting an Italian newspaper in your back window. Be sure all of your valuables are out of sight and locked in the trunk, or even better, with you or in your room.

Parking: White lines generally mean parking is free. Blue lines mean you'll have to pay—usually €1 per hour (use machine, leave time-stamped receipt on dashboard). If there's no meter, there's probably a roving attendant who will take your money. Study the signs. Often the free zones have a 30- or 60-minute time limit. Signs showing a street cleaner and a day of the week indicate which day the street is cleaned; there's a €100 tow-fee incentive to learn the days of the week in Italian.

Zona disco has nothing to do with dancing. Italian cars come equipped with a time disk (a cardboard clock), which you set at your arrival time and lay on the dashboard so the attendant knows how long you've been parked. This is a fine system that all drivers should take advantage of. (If your rental car doesn't come with a *zona disco,* pick one up at a tobacco shop or just write your arrival time on a piece of paper and place it on the dashboard.)

Garages are safe, save time, and help you avoid the stress of parking tickets. Take the parking voucher with you to pay the cashier before you leave.

Cheap Flights

If you're traveling beyond Rome, you might want to look into flying one of the affordable intra-European airlines. While trains are still the best way to connect places that are close together, a flight can save both time and money on long journeys.

One of the best websites for comparing inexpensive flights is www.skyscanner.com. Other comparison search engines include www.wegolo.com and www.whichbudget.com. Most budget airlines—such as easyJet, Ryanair, and Air Berlin—serve Rome.

Be aware of the potential drawbacks of flying on the cheap: nonrefundable and nonchangeable tickets, minimal or nonexistent customer service, treks to airports far outside of town, and pricey baggage fees. Especially if you're traveling with lots of luggage, a cheap flight can quickly become a bad deal. To avoid unpleasant surprises, read the small print before you book.

Resources

Resources from Rick Steves

Books: *Rick Steves' Rome 2011* is one of many books in my series on European travel, which includes country guidebooks, city guidebooks (Venice, Florence, Paris, London, etc.), Snapshot guides (excerpted chapters from my country guides), Pocket guides (full-color little books on big cities, including Rome), and my budget-travel skills handbook, *Rick Steves' Europe Through the Back Door*. My phrase books—for Italian, French, German, Spanish, and Portuguese—are practical and budget-oriented. My other books include *Europe 101* (a crash course on art and history) and *Travel as a Political Act* (a travelogue sprinkled with tips for bringing home a global perspective). For a list of my books, see the inside of the last page of this book.

Video: My public television **series,** *Rick Steves' Europe,* covers European destinations in 100 shows, with 14 episodes on Italy, including two on Rome. To watch episodes, visit www.hulu.com/rick-steves-europe; for scripts and other details, see www.ricksteves.com/tv.

Audio: My weekly public radio show, *Travel with Rick Steves,* features interviews with travel experts from around the world. I've also produced free self-guided audio tours of the top sights and neighborhoods in Rome, Florence, Venice, and more. I've combined all of my audio content into *Rick Steves Audio Europe,* an extensive online library organized by destination. Choose whatever interests you, and download it for free to your iPod, smartphone, or computer at www.ricksteves.com or iTunes.

Begin Your Trip at www.ricksteves.com

At our travel website, you'll find a wealth of free information on European destinations, including fresh monthly news and helpful tips from thousands of fellow travelers. You'll also find my latest guidebook updates (www.ricksteves.com/update) and my travel blog.

Our **online Travel Store** offers travel bags and accessories specially designed by me and my staff to help you travel smarter and lighter. These include my popular carry-on bags (roll-aboard and rucksack versions), money belts, totes, toiletries kits, adapters, other accessories, and a wide selection of guidebooks, planning maps, and DVDs.

Choosing the right **railpass** for your trip—amidst hundreds of options—can drive you nutty. We'll help you choose the best pass for your needs, plus give you a bunch of free extras.

Rick Steves' Europe Through the Back Door travel company offers **tours** with more than three dozen itineraries and about 400 departures reaching the best destinations in this book...and beyond. Our Italy tours include "the best of" in 17 days, Village Italy in 14 days, South Italy in 13 days, Venice–Florence–Rome in 10 days, the Heart of Italy in 9 days, Sicily in 9 days, and a week-long Rome tour. You'll enjoy great guides, a fun bunch of travel partners (with small groups of generally around 28), and plenty of room to spread out in a big, comfy bus. You'll find European adventures to fit every vacation length. For all the details, and to get our Tour Catalog and a free Rick Steves Tour Experience DVD (filmed on location during an actual tour), visit www.ricksteves.com or call us at 425/608-4217.

APPENDIX

Maps

The black-and-white maps in this book, designed by my well-traveled staff, are concise and simple. The maps are intended to help you locate recommended places and get to local TIs, where you can pick up more in-depth maps of towns or regions (usually free). Better maps are sold at newsstands and bookstores. Before you buy a map, look at it to be sure it has the level of detail you want. Drivers will want to pick up a good, detailed map in Europe (I'd recommend a 1:200,000- or 1:300,000-scale map).

Other Guidebooks

For most travelers, this book has more than enough information. But if you're heading beyond my recommended neighborhoods and destinations, $40 for extra maps and books can be money well-spent.

The following books are worthwhile, though are not updated annually; check the publication date before you buy. The tall, green Michelin guide to Rome has solid, encyclopedic coverage of sights, customs, and culture, though very little on hotels and restaurants (also sold in English in Italy). The Access guide to Rome is well-researched, organized by neighborhood, and color-coded for sights, hotels, and restaurants. Focusing mainly on sights, the colorful Eyewitness guide to Rome is fun for its great graphics and photos, but it's relatively skimpy on content and weighs a ton. You can buy it in Rome (no more expensive than in the US) or simply borrow it for a minute from other travelers at certain sights to make sure that you're aware of that place's highlights. *Let's Go Rome* is youth-oriented, with good coverage of hostels and nightlife.

For a book of city walking tours, try *City Secrets: Rome* (Kahn) or *City of the Soul: A Walk in Rome* (Murray). For a list of book-stores in Rome, see page 23.

If you'll be traveling elsewhere in Italy, consider *Rick Steves' Italy*, *Rick Steves' Venice*, or *Rick Steves' Florence & Tuscany*.

Recommended Books and Movies

To learn more about Rome past and present, check out a few of these books or films.

Non-Fiction

Written in the 18th century, Edward Gibbon's *Decline and Fall of the Roman Empire* is considered *the* classic history of ancient Rome.

Originally published as a series of *New Yorker* articles in the 1950s, *Rome and a Villa* reads as if it's Eleanor Clark's journal. Of Paul Hofmann's multiple books about Italy, *The Seasons of Rome* is the favorite among readers. Another good Americans-in-the-Eternal-City memoir is *As the Romans Do* (Epstein). A third of

Elizabeth Gilbert's spiritual memoir/travelogue *Eat, Pray, Love* takes place in Rome.

The holy center of Christendom has plenty of worthwhile books documenting its history. *Saints & Sinners* (Duffy) is a warts-and-all illustrated guide to the popes. In *When in Rome,* Robert Hutchinson writes as a lapsed (sometimes irreverent) Catholic discovering the roots of Christianity in Vatican City. *Michelangelo and the Pope's Ceiling* (King) describes the drama behind the masterpiece. *The Pope's Elephant* (Bedini), written by a historian from the Smithsonian, tells the story of Pope Leo X's favorite pet.

A Literary Companion to Rome (Varriano) also includes 10 self-guided walking tours. Kids (and adults who like cool pictures) enjoy David Macaulay's two books about Rome: *Rome Antics* and *City: A Story of Roman Planning and Construction* (both for ages nine and up).

Fiction

No modern crime drama or soap opera can top the world of ancient Roman politics. Colleen McCullough—who also wrote *The Thorn Birds*—describes the early days of the Roman Republic in her work of historical fiction, *The First Man in Rome.* Robert Graves wanders from Caesar Augustus to Caligula and beyond in *I, Claudius.*

Ancient Rome makes a great backdrop for mysteries, as shown in *Roman Blood* (Saylor) and *The Silver Pigs* (Davis), both the first in a series. *Cabal,* by Michael Dibdin, takes place in modern Rome. In the blockbuster book *Angels and Demons,* written by *The Da Vinci Code* author Dan Brown, murders are linked by Rome's Bernini statues.

For a literary take on Rome, try *Open City: Seven Writers in Postwar Rome* (edited by William Weaver).

Films

Two masterpieces of Italian Neorealism—set in the bleak, post-WWII years—take place in Rome: Roberto Rossellini's *Open City* (1945) and Vittorio De Sica's touching, heartbreaking film, *Bicycle Thieves* (1949).

A feel-good love story, *Roman Holiday* (1953) made a star out of Audrey Hepburn. *Three Coins in the Fountain* (1954) is another romantic crowd-pleaser.

During the era of epics, Hollywood couldn't get enough of ancient Rome. *Quo Vadis* (1951) contains three hours of religious-historic drama. *Ben-Hur* (1959) is a campy mash-up of Christianity, Charlton Heston, and chariot races. *Spartacus* (1960) cast Kirk Douglas as a rebel fighting Rome.

La Dolce Vita (1961) is Federico Fellini's seductive masterpiece. (His 1972 film *Roma* seems tacky in comparison.)

The warm-hearted Italian epic *Best of Youth* (2003) takes place in several Italian locations, including Rome; this story of two brothers gives you a good sense of the last several decades of Italian history.

Originally a BBC miniseries, *I, Claudius* (1976) puts Derek Jacobi and John Hurt at the center of a pulpy classic. The HBO miniseries *Rome* (2005–07) gives an *Upstairs-Downstairs* look at the lives and loves of Julius Caesar and Augustus. *Gladiator* returned to ancient Rome in 2000, and won five Academy Awards for its portrayal of life in the bloody arena.

The 2009 film *Angels and Demons,* based on the book by *The Da Vinci Code* author Dan Brown, is set in Rome. Banned from filming in Vatican City, cameramen disguised themselves as tourists to gather some of the shots. The 2010 film version of *Eat, Pray, Love,* starring Julia Roberts, was filmed partly in Rome and Naples.

Holidays and Festivals

Italy celebrates many holidays, which close sights and bring crowds. Note that the following list isn't complete. In Italy, holidays seem to strike without warning. For instance, every town has a festival honoring its patron saint. Your best source for information on holidays and festivals in Rome is the Rome TI office (http://en.turismoroma.it). You could also check with Italy's national tourist offices (www.italiantourism.com). The Vatican Museum closes for a multitude of Catholic holidays; check its schedule at http://mv.vatican.va.

Jan 1	New Year's Day
Jan 6	Epiphany
March 20	Rome Marathon (www.adventure -marathon.com)
April 21	City Birthday
April 24	Easter Sunday
April 25	Easter Monday
April 25	Italian Liberation Day
May 1	Labor Day
June 2	Anniversary of the Republic
June 23	Feast Day of Corpus Christi
June 24	St. John the Baptist's Day
June 29	Saints Peter and Paul's Day
July	Trastevere's Noantri Festival
Aug 10	St. Lawrence's Day
Aug 15	Assumption of Mary (Ferragosto)
Nov 1	All Saints' Day

2011

JANUARY

S	M	T	W	T	F	S
						1
2	3	4	5	6	7	8
9	10	11	12	13	14	15
16	17	18	19	20	21	22
23/30	24/31	25	26	27	28	29

FEBRUARY

S	M	T	W	T	F	S
		1	2	3	4	5
6	7	8	9	10	11	12
13	14	15	16	17	18	19
20	21	22	23	24	25	26
27	28					

MARCH

S	M	T	W	T	F	S
		1	2	3	4	5
6	7	8	9	10	11	12
13	14	15	16	17	18	19
20	21	22	23	24	25	26
27	28	29	30	31		

APRIL

S	M	T	W	T	F	S
					1	2
3	4	5	6	7	8	9
10	11	12	13	14	15	16
17	18	19	20	21	22	23
24	25	26	27	28	29	30

MAY

S	M	T	W	T	F	S
1	2	3	4	5	6	7
8	9	10	11	12	13	14
15	16	17	18	19	20	21
22	23	24	25	26	27	28
29	30	31				

JUNE

S	M	T	W	T	F	S
			1	2	3	4
5	6	7	8	9	10	11
12	13	14	15	16	17	18
19	20	21	22	23	24	25
26	27	28	29	30		

JULY

S	M	T	W	T	F	S
					1	2
3	4	5	6	7	8	9
10	11	12	13	14	15	16
17	18	19	20	21	22	23
24/31	25	26	27	28	29	30

AUGUST

S	M	T	W	T	F	S
	1	2	3	4	5	6
7	8	9	10	11	12	13
14	15	16	17	18	19	20
21	22	23	24	25	26	27
28	29	30	31			

SEPTEMBER

S	M	T	W	T	F	S
				1	2	3
4	5	6	7	8	9	10
11	12	13	14	15	16	17
18	19	20	21	22	23	24
25	26	27	28	29	30	

OCTOBER

S	M	T	W	T	F	S
						1
2	3	4	5	6	7	8
9	10	11	12	13	14	15
16	17	18	19	20	21	22
23/30	24/31	25	26	27	28	29

NOVEMBER

S	M	T	W	T	F	S
		1	2	3	4	5
6	7	8	9	10	11	12
13	14	15	16	17	18	19
20	21	22	23	24	25	26
27	28	29	30			

DECEMBER

S	M	T	W	T	F	S
				1	2	3
4	5	6	7	8	9	10
11	12	13	14	15	16	17
18	19	20	21	22	23	24
25	26	27	28	29	30	31

Dec 8   Feast of the Immaculate Conception
Dec 25   Christmas
Dec 26   St. Stephen's Day

Conversions and Climate

Numbers and Stumblers

- Europeans write a few of their numbers differently than we do. 1 = 1, 4 = 4, 7 = 7.
- In Europe, dates appear as day/month/year, so Christmas is 25/12/11.
- Commas are decimal points and decimals commas. A dollar and a half is 1,50, and there are 5.280 feet in a mile.
- When pointing, use your whole hand, palm down.
- When counting with fingers, start with your thumb. If you hold up your first finger to request one item, you'll probably get two.

- What Americans call the second floor of a building is the first floor in Europe.
- On escalators and moving sidewalks, Europeans keep the left "lane" open for passing. Keep to the right.

Roman Numerals

In the US, you'll see Roman numerals—which originated in ancient Rome—used for copyright dates, clocks, and the Super Bowl. In Italy, you're likely to observe these numbers chiseled on statues and buildings. If you want to do some numeric detective work, here's how: In Roman numerals, as in ours, the highest numbers (thousands, hundreds) come first, followed by smaller numbers. Many numbers are made by combining numerals into sets: V = 5, so VIII = 8 (5 plus 3). Roman numerals follow a subtraction principle for multiples of fours (4, 40, 400, etc.) and nines (9, 90, 900, etc.); the number four, for example, is written as IV (1 subtracted from 5), rather than IIII. The number nine is IX (1 subtracted from 10).

Rick Steves' Rome 2011—written in Roman numerals—would translate as *Rick Steves' Rome MMXI*. Big numbers such as dates can look daunting at first. The easiest way to handle them is to read the numbers in discrete chunks. For example, Michelangelo was born in MCDLXXV. Break it down: M (1,000) + CD (100 subtracted from 500, or 400) + LXX (50 + 10 + 10, or 70) + V (5) = 1475. It was a very good year.

M = 1000	XL = 40
CM = 900	X = 10
D = 500	IX = 9
CD = 400	V = 5
C = 100	IV = 4
XC = 90	I = duh
L = 50	

Metric Conversions (approximate)

A kilogram is 2.2 pounds, and one liter is about a quart, or almost four to a gallon. A kilometer is six-tenths of a mile. I figure kilometers to miles by cutting them in half and adding back 10 percent of the original (120 km: 60 + 12 = 72 miles, 300 km: 150 + 30 = 180 miles).

1 foot = 0.3 meter	1 square yard = 0.8 square meter
1 yard = 0.9 meter	1 square mile = 2.6 square kilometers
1 mile = 1.6 kilometers	1 ounce = 28 grams
1 centimeter = 0.4 inch	1 quart = 0.95 liter
1 meter = 39.4 inches	1 kilogram = 2.2 pounds
1 kilometer = 0.62 mile	32°F = 0°C

Clothing Sizes

When shopping for clothing, use these US-to-European comparisons as general guidelines (but note that no conversion is perfect).

- Women's dresses and blouses: Add 30 (US size 10 = European size 40)
- Men's suits and jackets: Add 10 (US size 40 regular = European size 50)
- Men's shirts: Multiply by 2 and add about 8 (US size 15 collar = European size 38)
- Women's shoes: Add about 30 (US size 8 = European size 38½)
- Men's shoes: Add 32–34 (US size 9 = European size 41; US size 11 = European size 45)

Rome's Climate

First line—average daily high; second line—average daily low; third line—average days without rain. For more detailed statistics for Rome (as well as the rest of the world), check www.world climate.com.

J	F	M	A	M	J	J	A	S	O	N	D
52°	55°	59°	66°	74°	82°	87°	86°	79°	71°	61°	55°
40°	42°	45°	50°	56°	63°	67°	67°	62°	55°	49°	44°
13	19	23	24	26	26	30	29	25	23	19	21

Temperature Conversion:
Fahrenheit and Celsius

For Weather   For Health

Europe takes its temperature using the Celsius scale, while we opt for Fahrenheit. For a rough conversion from Celsius to Fahrenheit, double the number and add 30. For weather, remember that 28°C is 82°F—perfect. For health, 37°C is just right.

Essential Packing Checklist

Whether you're traveling for five days or five weeks, here's what you'll need to bring. Remember to pack light to enjoy the sweet freedom of true mobility. Happy travels!

- ❏ 5 shirts
- ❏ 1 sweater or lightweight fleece jacket
- ❏ 2 pairs pants
- ❏ 1 pair shorts
- ❏ 1 swimsuit (women only—men can use shorts)
- ❏ 5 pairs underwear and socks
- ❏ 1 pair shoes
- ❏ 1 rain-proof jacket
- ❏ Tie or scarf
- ❏ Money belt
- ❏ Money—your mix of:
  - ❏ Debit card for ATM withdrawals
  - ❏ Credit card
  - ❏ Hard cash in US dollars ($20 bills)
- ❏ Documents (and back-up photocopies):
  - ❏ Passport
  - ❏ Printout of airline e-ticket
  - ❏ Driver's license
  - ❏ Student ID and hostel card
  - ❏ Railpass/car rental voucher
  - ❏ Insurance details
- ❏ Daypack
- ❏ Sealable plastic baggies
- ❏ Camera and related gear
- ❏ Empty water bottle
- ❏ Wristwatch and alarm clock
- ❏ Earplugs
- ❏ First-aid kit
- ❏ Medicine (labeled)
- ❏ Extra glasses/contacts and prescriptions
- ❏ Sunscreen and sunglasses
- ❏ Toiletries kit
- ❏ Soap
- ❏ Laundry soap
- ❏ Clothesline
- ❏ Small towel
- ❏ Sewing kit
- ❏ Travel information
- ❏ Necessary map(s)
- ❏ Address list (email and mailing addresses)
- ❏ Postcards and photos from home
- ❏ Notepad and pen
- ❏ Journal

If you plan to carry on your luggage, note that all liquids must be in three-ounce or smaller containers and fit within a single quart-size baggie. For details, see www.tsa.gov/travelers.

Hotel Reservation

To: _____   _____
          hotel   *email or fax*

From: _____   _____
              name   *email or fax*

Today's date: _____ /_____ /_____
                       day   *month*   *year*

Dear Hotel _____ ,
Please make this reservation for me:

Name: _____

Total # of people: _____   # of rooms: _____   # of nights: _____

Arriving: _____ /_____ /_____   My time of arrival (24-hr clock): _____
                 day *month* *year*   (I will telephone if I will be late)

Departing: _____ /_____ /_____
                   day *month* *year*

Room(s): Single___   Double ___   Twin ___   Triple ___   Quad___

With: Toilet ____   Shower ____   Bath ____   Sink only ____

Special needs: View___   Quiet___   Cheapest ___   Ground Floor___

Please email or fax confirmation of my reservation, along with the type of
room reserved and the price. Please also inform me of your cancellation
policy. After I hear from you, I will quickly send my credit-card information
as a deposit to hold the room. Thank you.

_____
Name

_____
Address

_____
City   *State*   *Zip Code*   *Country*

Before hoteliers can make your reservation, they want to know the information listed above. You can use this form as the basis for your email, or you can photocopy this page, fill in the information, and send it as a fax (also available online at www.ricksteves.com/reservation).

Italian Survival Phrases

Good day.	**Buon giorno.**	bwohn JOR-noh
Do you speak English?	**Parla inglese?**	PAR-lah een-GLAY-zay
Yes. / No.	**Sì. / No.**	see / noh
I (don't) understand.	**(Non) capisco.**	(nohn) kah-PEES-koh
Please.	**Per favore.**	pehr fah-VOH-ray
Thank you.	**Grazie.**	GRAHT-seeay
You're welcome.	**Prego.**	PRAY-go
I'm sorry.	**Mi dispiace.**	mee dee-speeAH-chay
Excuse me.	**Mi scusi.**	mee SKOO-zee
(No) problem.	**(Non) c'è un problema.**	(nohn) cheh oon proh-BLAY-mah
Good.	**Va bene.**	vah BEHN-ay
Goodbye.	**Arrivederci.**	ah-ree-vay-DEHR-chee
one / two	**uno / due**	OO-noh / DOO-ay
three / four	**tre / quattro**	tray / KWAH-troh
five / six	**cinque / sei**	CHEENG-kway / SEHee
seven / eight	**sette / otto**	SEHT-tay / OT-toh
nine / ten	**nove / dieci**	NOV-ay / deeAY-chee
How much is it?	**Quanto costa?**	KWAHN-toh KOS-tah
Write it?	**Me lo scrive?**	may loh SKREE-vay
Is it free?	**È gratis?**	eh GRAH-tees
Is it included?	**È incluso?**	eh een-KLOO-zoh
Where can I buy / find...?	**Dove posso comprare / trovare...?**	DOH-vay POS-soh kohm-PRAH-ray / troh-VAH-ray
I'd like / We'd like...	**Vorrei / Vorremmo...**	vor-REHee / vor-RAY-moh
...a room.	**...una camera.**	OO-nah KAH-meh-rah
...a ticket to ___.	**...un biglietto per ___.**	oon beel-YEHT-toh pehr
Is it possible?	**È possibile?**	eh poh-SEE-bee-lay
Where is...?	**Dov'è...?**	DOH-veh
...the train station	**...la stazione**	lah staht-seeOH-nay
...the bus station	**...la stazione degli autobus**	lah staht-seeOH-nay DAYL-yee OW-toh-boos
...tourist information	**...informazioni per turisti**	een-for-maht-seeOH-nee pehr too-REE-stee
...the toilet	**...la toilette**	lah twah-LEHT-tay
men	**uomini, signori**	WOH-mee-nee, seen-YOH-ree
women	**donne, signore**	DON-nay, seen-YOH-ray
left / right	**sinistra / destra**	see-NEE-strah / DEHS-trah
straight	**sempre diritto**	SEHM-pray dee-REE-toh
When do you open / close?	**A che ora aprite / chiudete?**	ah kay OH-rah ah-PREE-tay / keeoo-DAY-tay
At what time?	**A che ora?**	ah kay OH-rah
Just a moment.	**Un momento.**	oon moh-MAYN-toh
now / soon / later	**adesso / presto / tardi**	ah-DEHS-soh / PREHS-toh / TAR-dee
today / tomorrow	**oggi / domani**	OH-jee / doh-MAH-nee

In the Restaurant

I'd like...	**Vorrei...**	vor-REHee
We'd like...	**Vorremmo...**	vor-RAY-moh
...to reserve...	**...prenotare...**	pray-noh-TAH-ray
...a table for one / two.	**...un tavolo per uno / due.**	oon TAH-voh-loh pehr OO-noh / DOO-ay
Non-smoking.	**Non fumare.**	nohn foo-MAH-ray
Is this seat free?	**È libero questo posto?**	eh LEE-bay-roh KWEHS-toh POH-stoh
The menu (in English), please.	**Il menù (in inglese), per favore.**	eel may-NOO (een een-GLAY-zay) pehr fah-VOH-ray
service (not) included	**servizio (non) incluso**	sehr-VEET-seeoh (nohn) een-KLOO-zoh
cover charge	**pane e coperto**	PAH-nay ay koh-PEHR-toh
to go	**da portar via**	dah POR-tar VEE-ah
with / without	**con / senza**	kohn / SEHN-sah
and / or	**e / o**	ay / oh
menu (of the day)	**menù (del giorno)**	may-NOO (dayl JOR-noh)
specialty of the house	**specialità della casa**	spay-chah-lee-TAH DEHL-lah KAH-zah
first course (pasta, soup)	**primo piatto**	PREE-moh peeAH-toh
main course (meat, fish)	**secondo piatto**	say-KOHN-doh peeAH-toh
side dishes	**contorni**	kohn-TOR-nee
bread	**pane**	PAH-nay
cheese	**formaggio**	for-MAH-joh
sandwich	**panino**	pah-NEE-noh
soup	**minestra, zuppa**	mee-NEHS-trah, TSOO-pah
salad	**insalata**	een-sah-LAH-tah
meat	**carne**	KAR-nay
chicken	**pollo**	POH-loh
fish	**pesce**	PEH-shay
seafood	**frutti di mare**	FROO-tee dee MAH-ray
fruit / vegetables	**frutta / legumi**	FROO-tah / lay-GOO-mee
dessert	**dolci**	DOHL-chee
tap water	**acqua del rubinetto**	AH-kwah dayl roo-bee-NAY-toh
mineral water	**acqua minerale**	AH-kwah mee-nay-RAH-lay
milk	**latte**	LAH-tay
(orange) juice	**succo (d'arancia)**	SOO-koh (dah-RAHN-chah)
coffee / tea	**caffè / tè**	kah-FEH / teh
wine	**vino**	VEE-noh
red / white	**rosso / bianco**	ROH-soh / beeAHN-koh
glass / bottle	**bicchiere / bottiglia**	bee-keeAY-ray / boh-TEEL-yah
beer	**birra**	BEE-rah
Cheers!	**Cin cin!**	cheen cheen
More. / Another.	**Ancora un po.' / Un altro.**	ahn-KOH-rah oon poh / oon AHL-troh
The same.	**Lo stesso.**	loh STEHS-soh
The bill, please.	**Il conto, per favore.**	eel KOHN-toh pehr fah-VOH-ray
tip	**mancia**	MAHN-chah
Delicious!	**Delizioso!**	day-leet-seeOH-zoh

For more user-friendly Italian phrases, check out *Rick Steves' Italian Phrase Book & Dictionary* or *Rick Steves' French, Italian, and German Phrase Book*.

INDEX

INDEX

INDEX

MAP INDEX

Audio Europe

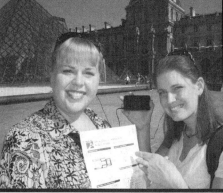

▶ Plan Your Trip

Browse thousands of articles and a wealth of money-saving tips for planning your dream trip. You'll find up-to-date information on Europe's best destinations, packing smart, getting around, finding rooms, staying healthy, avoiding scams and more.

▶ Eurail Passes

Find out, step-by-step, if a railpass makes sense for your trip—and how to avoid buying more than you need. Get a bunch of free extras!

▶ Graffiti Wall & Travelers' Helpline

Learn, ask, share—our online community of savvy travelers is a great resource for first-time travelers to Europe, as well as seasoned pros.

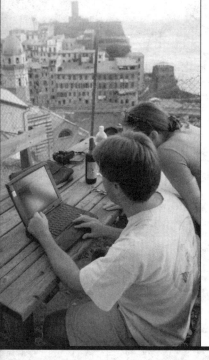

Rick Steves' Europe Through the Back Door, Inc.

NOW AVAILABLE: eBOOKS, APPS, DVDS, & BLU-RAY

eBOOKS

Most guides available as eBooks from Amazon, Barnes & Noble, Borders, Apple iBook and Sony eReader, beginning January 2011

RICK STEVES' EUROPE DVDs

Austria & the Alps
Eastern Europe, Israel & Egypt
England & Wales
European Travel Skills & Specials
France
Germany, Benelux & More
Greece & Turkey
Iran
Ireland & Scotland
Italy's Cities
Italy's Countryside
Rick Steves' European Christmas
Scandinavia
Spain & Portugal

BLU-RAY

Celtic Charms
Eastern Europe Favorites
European Christmas
Italy Through the Back Door
Surprising Cities of Europe

PHRASE BOOKS & DICTIONARIES

French
French, Italian & German
German
Italian
Portuguese
Spanish

JOURNALS

Rick Steves' Pocket Travel Journal
Rick Steves' Travel Journal

APPS

Rick Steves' Ancient Rome Tour
Rick Steves' Historic Paris Walk
Rick Steves' Louvre Tour
Rick Steves' Orsay Museum Tour
Rick Steves' St. Peter's Basilica Tour
Rick Steves' Versailles

PLANNING MAPS

Britain, Ireland & London
Europe
France & Paris
Germany, Austria & Switzerland
Ireland
Italy
Spain & Portugal

Credits

Researcher

To update this book, Rick relied on the help of...

Ben Cameron

 Ben experienced his first taste of European travel when he was three, exploring medieval castles with his parents. Returning after graduation, he was hooked and has spent much of his time since exploring Europe independently and leading tours for Rick Steves. When not living out of his backpack, Ben splits his time between Rome and Seattle.

Rick Steves' Guidebook Series

Country Guides

Rick Steves' Best of Europe

Rick Steves' Croatia &
   Slovenia

Rick Steves' Eastern Europe

Rick Steves' England

Rick Steves' France

Rick Steves' Germany

Rick Steves' Great Britain

Rick Steves' Ireland

Rick Steves' Italy

Rick Steves' Portugal

Rick Steves' Scandinavia

Rick Steves' Spain

Rick Steves' Switzerland

City and Regional Guides

Rick Steves' Amsterdam,
   Bruges & Brussels

Rick Steves' Athens &
   the Peloponnese

Rick Steves' Budapest

Rick Steves' Florence &
   Tuscany

Rick Steves' Istanbul

Rick Steves' London

Rick Steves' Paris

Rick Steves' Prague &
   the Czech Republic

Rick Steves' Provence &
   the French Riviera

Rick Steves' Rome

Rick Steves' Venice

Rick Steves' Vienna,
   Salzburg & Tirol

Rick Steves' Phrase Books

French

French/Italian/German

German

Italian

Portuguese

Spanish

Snapshot Guides

Excerpted chapters from country guides, such as *Rick Steves'
Snapshot Barcelona, Rick Steves' Snapshot Scotland,* and
Rick Steves' Snapshot Hill Towns of Central Italy.

Pocket Guides (new in 2011)

Condensed, pocket-size, full-color guides to Europe's top
cities: Paris, London, and Rome.

Other Books

Rick Steves' Europe 101: History and Art for the Traveler

Rick Steves' Europe Through the Back Door

Rick Steves' European Christmas

Rick Steves' Postcards from Europe

Rick Steves' Travel as a Political Act

Avalon Travel
a member of the Perseus Books Group
1700 Fourth Street
Berkeley, CA 94710, U.S.A.

Printed in the U.S.A. by Worzalla
First printing August 2010

Portions of this book were originally published in *Rick Steves' Mona Winks* © 2001, 1998,
1996, 1993, 1988 by Rick Steves and Gene Openshaw, and in *Rick Steves' Italy* © 2010,
2009, 2008, 2007, 2006, 2005, 2004, 2003, 2002, 2001, 2000, 1999 by Rick Steves.

ISBN 978-1-59880-657-1
ISSN 1527-4780

For the latest on Rick's lectures, guidebooks, tours, public radio show, and public television
series, contact Rick Steves' Europe Through the Back Door, Box 2009, Edmonds, WA
98020, tel. 425/771-8303, fax 425/771-0833, www.ricksteves.com, rick@ricksteves.com.

Europe Through the Back Door Reviewing Editor: Cameron Hewitt
ETBD Editors: Tom Griffin, Gretchen Strauch, Cathy McDonald, Cathy Lu, Jennifer
Madison Davis, Sarah McCormic
ETBD Managing Editor: Risa Laib
Avalon Travel Senior Editor and Series Manager: Madhu Prasher
Avalon Travel Project Editor: Kelly Lydick
Research Assistance: Ben Cameron
Copy Editor: Nikki Ioakimedes
Proofreader: Becca Freed
Indexer: Julie Kawabata
Production & Typesetting: McGuire Barber Design
Cover Design: Kimberly Glyder Design
Graphic Content Director: Laura VanDeventer
Maps & Graphics: David C. Hoerlein, Lauren Mills, Laura VanDeventer, Mike
Morgenfeld, Brice Ticen, Barb Geisler
Photography: Rick Steves, Gene Openshaw, Dominic Bonuccelli, David C. Hoerlein,
Laura VanDeventer, Cameron Hewitt, Bruce VanDeventer, Michael Potter, Anne Jenkins
Steves, Robyn Cronin, Amanda Scotese, Risa Laib
Sistine Chapel photo, page 227, © Erich Lessing / Art Resource, NY
Front Matter Color Photos: p. i, Victor Emmanuel Monument © Michael Potter
Front Cover Photo: Ponte Sant'Angelo, Hadrian's Tomb © Simeone Huber / Getty Images